Histo.
Paris C

# of 1871

By Prosper Olivier Lissagaray
Translated from the French by Eleanor Marx

Red and Black Publishers, St Petersburg, Florida 2007

First Published: in French, 1876;
Translated into English by Eleanor Marx, 1886

Publishers Cataloging in Publication Data –

Lissagaray, Prosper Olivier
    History of the Paris Commune of 1871/by Prosper Olivier Lissagaray,
translated from the French by Eleanor Marx
    p. cm.
    Illustrated
    ISBN: 978-0-9791813-4-4
    1. Paris (France) – History – Commune, 1871
    I. Title
    DC316 .L97 2007
    944.08   LCCN: 2007929493

Red and Black Publishers, PO Box 7542, St Petersburg, Florida, 33734
Contact us at: info@RedandBlackPublishers.com

Printed and manufactured in the United States of America

Contents

Introduction to the Red and Black Edition   5
Timeline of the Paris Commune   11
Introduction to the 1886 Edition   15
Preface   19
Prologue   21
Chapter 1: The Prussians enter Paris   57
Chapter 2: The coalition opens fire on Paris   65
Chapter 3: The eighteenth of March   71
Chapter 4: The Central Committee calls for elections   79
Chapter 5: Reorganization of the Public Services   89
Chapter 6: The mayors and the Assembly combine against Paris   95
Chapter 7: The Central Committee forces the mayors to capitulate   101
Chapter 8: Proclamation of the Commune   109
Chapter 9: The Commune at Lyons, St. Etienne and Creuzot   113
Chapter 10: The Commune at Marseilles, Toulouse and Narbonne   121
Chapter 11: The Council of the Commune wavers   129
Chapter 12: The Versaillese beat back the Commune patrols and massacre prisoners   135
Chapter 13: The commune is defeated at Marseilles and Narbonne   141
Chapter 14: The weaknesses of the Council   149
Chapter 15: The Commune's first combats   155
Chapter 16: The Manifesto and the germs of defeat   161
Chapter 17: Women of the Commune and the opposing armies   167
Chapter 18: The work of the Commune   175
Chapter 19: Formation of the Committee of Public Safety   195
Chapter 20: Rossel replaces Cluseret   203
Chapter 21: Paris bombarded: Rossel flees   209
Chapter 22: Conspiracies against the Commune   217
Chapter 23: The "Lefts" betray Paris   223
Chapter 24: The new Committee at work   231

Chapter 25: Paris on the eve of death   239
Chapter 26: The enemy enters Paris   247
Chapter 27: The invasion continues   253
Chapter 28: The street battles continue   263
Chapter 29: On the barricades   273
Chapter 30: The Left bank falls   283
Chapter 31: The Commune's last stand   291
Chapter 32: The Versaillese fury   303
Chapter 33: The fate of the prisoners   311
Chapter 34: The trials of the Communards   319
Chapter 35: The executions   331
Chapter 36: The balance-sheet of bourgeois vengeance   347
Glossary   361

Introduction to the Red and Black Edition

The Paris Commune was a crucial event for Marx and Engels, and a huge influence on the development of their political thought.

Until 1871, Marx had assumed that the working class would be able to seize the existing institutions of the bourgeois republic and use them as the basis for a socialist government after the revolution.

The Commune, however, completely changed Marx's thinking on this point, and made such a profound impact on him that he added an amendment to the *Communist Manifesto* on the matter. The Commune was, he wrote, the "political form at last discovered under which to work out the economic emancipation of labor."

It is worthwhile, therefore, to study the history and program of the Commune, in order to compare the Leninist states to a true revolutionary society, one that existed not merely in words and phrases, but within definite historical circumstances.

The first order of business for the Commune was the complete destruction of the old bourgeois state apparatus. Marx writes;

> From the outset, the Commune was compelled to recognize that the working class, once come to power, could not manage with the old state machine; that in order not to lose again its only just conquered supremacy, the working class must, on the one hand, do away with all the old repressive machinery, previously used against itself, and on

the other hand, safeguard itself against its own deputies and officials by declaring them all, without exception, subject to recall at any moment.

Engels hailed this action by the Commune as a "shattering of the former state power and its replacement by a new and real democratic state."

Lenin, in his pre-October days, writes of the similarity of the structure of the Paris Commune with the fledgling Russian "soviets", or councils. Indeed, in his remarkable booklet *State and Revolution*, Lenin envisions the "soviet" as serving at the center of a Russian socialist system in terms very similar to those pictured by the council communists and embodied in the Commune. During his discussion of the "soviets", Lenin pointed out that the Parisian revolutionary government was fundamentally different from the bourgeois state which it attempted to replace;

> The Commune substitutes for the venal and rotten parliamentarianism of bourgeois society institutions in which freedom of opinion and of discussion does not degenerate into deception, for the parliamentarians themselves have to work, have to execute their own laws, have themselves to test their results in real life, and to render account directly to their constituents. Representative institutions remain, but there is no parliamentarianism here as a special system, as the division of labor between the legislative and the executive as a privileged position for the representatives. We cannot imagine democracy, even proletarian democracy, without representative institutions, but we can and must imagine democracy without parliamentarianism.

The Commune, Marx points out, operated on the principle of direct democracy:

> The Commune was formed of the municipal councilors, chosen by universal suffrage in the various wards of the town, responsible and revocable at short terms. The majority of its members were naturally working men, or acknowledged representatives of the working class. The Commune was to be a working, not a parliamentary body, executive and legislative at the same time. Instead of continuing to be the agents of the central government, the police were at once stripped of their political attributes, and turned into the responsible and at all times revocable agents

of the Commune. So were officials of all other branches of the administration. From the members of the Commune downwards, the public service had to be done at workmen's wages. The vested interests and the representation allowances of the high dignitaries of state disappeared along with the high dignitaries themselves. . . The whole of the educational institutions were opened up to the public gratuitously, and at the same time cleared of all interference of church and state. . . Like the rest of public servants, magistrates and judges were to be elected, responsible and revocable.

The Commune was composed largely of Blanquists and Proudhonists, but, as usual, practical necessities forced the Communards to abandon ideology in favor of practical measures. The resulting Commune was claimed by both Marxists and Bakuninists, but clearly it owed a great deal to both.

Marx noted that the state built by the Commune was no longer a "state" — that is, it was no longer the political instrument of a ruling class. The Commune was not a state that stood outside of society or over it; it was, rather, a government formed directly from the ordinary people and directly responsible to them.

Not all governmental functions disappeared under the Commune. There was still a need for such things as record-keeping and the enforcement of criminal laws. These functions were, however, stripped of their political and class functions. Marx writes:

> While the merely repressive organs of the old governmental power were to be amputated, its legitimate functions were to be wrested from an authority usurping pre-eminence over society itself, and restored to the responsible agents of society.

Thus, the necessary governmental functions were returned as fully as possible to freely elected officials under the direct control of their electors. In this way, the features of Leninist repression — the political police, the entrenched party bureaucrats, the farcical elections, the state apparatus of censorship and judicial repression, the lopsided distribution of wealth — were avoided.

The Commune recognized that even its meager state apparatus had the potential to become an entrenched elite, and introduced several measures to combat any tendency towards a self-perpetuating bureaucracy. Marx writes;

Against the transformation of the state and the agents of the state from the servants of society into the masters of society — an inevitable transformation in all previous states — the Commune made use of two infallible expedients. In the first place, it filled all posts -- administrative, judicial and educational — by election on the basis of universal suffrage of all concerned, with the right of these same electors to recall their delegates at any time. And in the second place, all, officials, high or low, were paid only the wages received by other workers.

The Commune also recognized that a standing army that was responsible only to the government was merely a repressive tool. "The first decree of the Commune, therefore," writes Marx, "was the suppression of the standing army and the substitution for it of the armed people." The citizens of Paris were given basic military training and were organized into local militias to defend themselves from outside threats and internal counter-revolution. The best guarantee to keep a government responsible to the population, the Communards concluded, was to arm that population.

The Commune also recognized that the revolutionary government in Paris would not last if it could not encompass all of the country. While it lacked the means to carry out a national revolution, and thus fell to the guns of Versailles and Prussia, the Commune did lay a plan for a national revolutionary government under which to continue the social revolution. As Marx reports, "The cry of 'social republic' with which the Revolution of February was ushered in by the Paris proletariat, did but express a vague aspiration after a republic that was not only to supersede the monarchical form of class rule, but class rule itself. The Commune was the positive form of that republic":

In a rough sketch of national organization which the Commune had no time to develop, it states clearly that the Commune was to be the political form of even the smallest country hamlet, and that in the rural districts the standing army was to be replaced with a national militia with an extremely short term of service. The rural communes of every district were to administer their common affairs by an assembly of delegates to the central town, and these district assemblies were again to send delegates to the National Delegation in Paris, each delegate bound by the *mandat imperatif* of his constituents.

The local Communes were to be autonomous and elected, but they were not intended to be independent political entities. "The Communal Constitution," Marx wrote, "has been mistaken for an attempt to break up the nation into a federation of small states. The antagonism of the Commune against the state power has been mistaken for an exaggerated form of the ancient struggle against over-centralization." Instead, the Commune was to provide a national organization with the greatest possible local autonomy, while still maintaining a national framework.

Some tasks, such as the coordination of the national economy and the mobilization for national defense, had to be coordinated by a central government at the national level. The Commune's plans, however, recognized that this body had to be monitored and regulated. "The few but important tasks which still would remain for a central government were not to be suppressed," Marx writes, "but were to be discharged by Communal and therefore, strictly responsible agents."

In short, Marx concluded, the Commune proved that the old bourgeois form of government would "have to give way to the self-government of the producers."

It is this idea of "self-government of the producers" that separates the program of Marx and the council communists from the Leninists. Leninism in all its forms flatly rejects the notion of worker self-government. The Leninists fight, not for a government made up of the organized proletariat, but for an authoritarian party bureaucracy that acts "in the interests of the proletariat".

The Commune's program, by contrast, would have produced a national revolutionary government made up of autonomous decentralized self-governing bodies, a free association of producers such as that envisioned by Marx. Such a system can only be brought about by a broad mass-based movement which organizes the working class as a whole into a self-governing body.

The Paris Commune, we can see, was the first tentative step towards communist democracy. It was in essence a classless society; a government with no oppressed class to hold in check and no interests of its own to safeguard. It was not a government *over* the workers, but a government *of* the workers, whose sole task was to administrate and coordinate the activity of the self-governing producers.

The Commune stands in sharp contrast to the repressive states of the Leninist tradition. The Leninist state, with its massive parasitic bureaucracy, falls far short of the Commune's popularly-elected, revocable and responsible agents. Rather than "withering away", the Leninist states grew ever larger and more parasitic until they finally could be tolerated no longer. The Leninist monstrosities have nothing in common with the communist democracy foreseen by Marx and the council communists, and practiced at the Commune.

Timeline of the Paris Commune

1789
June 17 – Anti-royalist forces opposed to King Louis XVI of France meet in Paris and establish the National Assembly.

July 14 – Bastille Day. A crowd of Parisians storms the Bastille Prison and releases everyone held by the King of France.

October 5 – King Louis is taken from his palace at Versailles and is held in Paris as a virtual prisoner.

1793
January 21 – King Louis is executed by guillotine.

September 21 – the First Republic is declared.

1799
November 9 – Military leader Napoleon Bonaparte is declared First Consul and assumes near dictatorial powers.

1804
December 2 – Bonaparte crowns himself Emperor of France.

1815
June 18 – Napoleon Bonaparte is defeated at Waterloo. France returns to rule by a constitutional monarch.

1848
February 20 – King Louis Phillipe of France is overthrown, and the Second Republic is established.

December 10 – Louis Bonaparte, the nephew of the former Emperor Napoleon Bonaparte, wins election as President of the Second Republic.

1852
December 2 -- Bonaparte stages a coup and seizes total power from the Republic, declaring himself as Emperor Napoleon III.

1870
January 10 -- After journalist Victor Noir, a pro-democracy Republican, is killed by Bonaparte's cousin, massive demonstrations occur in Paris against the Second Empire.

July 19 – Bonaparte, in an attempt to rally support to his regime, declares war on Prussia, which is under the rule of Otto von Bismarck. The Franco-Prussian War begins.

September 2 – 83,000 French troops led by Bonaparte and Marshal MacMahon are defeated at Sedan and surrender.

September 4 – Upon hearing of Bonaparte's capture by the Prussians, a crowd of French people take over the Legislative Assembly in Paris, and proclaim the Third Republic. A Government of National Defense is established, which blames the war on Bonaparte but refuses to end the war until Prussia agrees to withdraw from the Alsace-Lorraine region.

September 19 – The Prussian Army reaches Paris and lays siege to the city.

October 27-30 – The French army is defeated in a series of battles and surrenders, leaving only the National Guard citizen militia to defend Paris.

October 31 -- Militant French workers led by Louis Auguste Blanqui seize City Hall (Hotel de Ville) and establish a Committee of Public Safety to serve as a shadow government.

November 1 – After promising to hold elections, the Government of National Defense seizes the Hotel de Ville and arrests Blanqui for treason.

1871

January 22 – Blanquists and other demonstrators gather outside the Hotel de Ville, and are fired upon by French troops.

January 28 – Paris is officially surrendered to the Prussians. The National Guard citizen militia, however, is allowed to retain its weapons, and they restrict the Prussian troops to a small section of the city. Paris workers hold demonstrations demanding that power be passed from the Government of National Defense to an elected city government (a commune).

February 8 – Elections are held for a new National Assembly to replace the Government of National Defense. No elections are held for a local commune government in Paris.

February 16 – Adolphe Thiers is elected President of the new National Assembly.

February 26 – Peace treaty is signed between the Thiers government and von Bismarck, ceding the Alsace-Lorraine region to Prussia.

March 11 – Fearing more riots and demonstrations by Paris workers, the National Assembly moves from the city to nearby Versailles.

March 18 – Thiers sends French army troops to Paris to disarm the National Guard. Instead, the French troops kill their own generals, Claude Martin Lecomte and Jacques Leonard Clement Thomas, and join the insurrectionaries.

March 26 – Paris workers organize their own elections for a municipal government (Paris Commune), and elect 92 trade unionists, socialists, anarchists and other radicals to the new government. Blanqui is elected as President of the Commune, despite the fact that he is still being held in prison by the National Assembly. The Commune declares revolutionary aims, noting that "the flag of the Commune is the flag of the World Republic". In a series of proclamations over the next few weeks, the Commune abolishes the draft, establishes the National Guard (consisting of all citizens capable of bearing arms) as the sole armed body, allows women the right to vote, freezes all payment of rents for two years, limits the salary of all government officials, decrees the separation of church and state, postpones all debts for three years, closes all pawnshops and returns all items to their owners, and abolishes interest on those debts, and proclaimed that workplaces that had been abandoned by their owners were now to be run by councils elected by the workers.

April 2 – Thiers asks Bismarck to release French prisoners of war to help take Paris and crush the Commune. French troops begin a siege of Paris. Communards move cannons to the heights of Montmartre.

April 7 – Theirs' forces capture the bridge at Neuilly, giving them an entryway into Paris.

April 11 – French army troops enter southern Paris, but are driven back with heavy losses by the National Guard.

May 16 – Paris workers pull down the Vendome Column, which celebrated the victories of Napoleon Bonaparte and was made out of bronze from captured guns.

May 21 – Prussian troops surrounding Paris allow National Assembly forces under Marshal MacMahon to enter Paris. They defeat the National Guard militia and the Commune is crushed.

May 21-28 --- *La Semaine Sanglante* ("Bloody Week"). MacMahon orders the summary execution of over 30,000 Communards, while another 38,000 are jailed and 7,000 are deported.

Introduction to the 1886 Edition

The following translation of Lissagaray's *Histoire de la Commune* was made many years ago, at the express wish of the author, who, besides making many emendations in his work, wrote nearly a hundred pages especially for this English version. The translation, in fact, was made from the *Histoire de la Commune* as prepared for a second edition — an edition which the French Government would not allow to be published. This explanation is necessary in view of the differences between the translation and the first edition of Lissagaray's book.

Written in 1876, there are necessarily passages in this history out of date today; as, for example, the references to the prisoners in New Caledonia, the exiles, and the amnesty. But for two reasons I prefer leaving this translation as it was originally. To have it "written up to date" would only be making patchwork of it. Secondly, I am loath to alter the work in any way. It had been entirely revised and corrected by my father. I want it to remain as he knew it.

Lissagaray's *Histoire de la Commune* is the only authentic and reliable history as yet written of the most memorable movement of modem times. It is true Lissagaray was a soldier of the Commune, but he has had the courage and honesty to speak the truth. He has not attempted to hide the errors of his party, or to gloss over the fatal weaknesses of the Revolution; and if he has erred, it has been on the side of moderation, in his anxiety not to make a single statement that could not be corroborated by overwhelming proofs of its truth. Wherever it was possible, the statements of the Versaillese in their

Parliamentary Inquiries, in their press, and in their books are used in preference to the statements of friends and partisans; and whenever the evidence of Communards is given, it is invariably sifted with scrupulous care. And it is this impartiality, this careful avoidance of any assertion that could be considered doubtful, which should recommend this work to English readers.

In England especially most persons are still quite ignorant of the events which led up to and forced the people of Paris into making that revolution which was to save France from the shame and disgrace of a fourth Empire. To most English people the Commune still spells "rapine, fear and lust", and when they speak of its "atrocities" they have some vague idea of hostages ruthlessly massacred by brutal revolutionises, of houses burnt down by furious petroleuses. Is it not time that English people at last learnt the truth? Is it not time they were reminded that for the sixty-five hostages shot, not by the Commune, but by a few people made mad by the massacre of prisoners by the Versaillese, the troops of law and order shot down thirty thousand men, women, and children, for the most part long after all fighting had ceased? If any Englishman, after reading Lissagaray's *History of the Commune*, still has any doubt as to what the "atrocities" of the Commune really were, he should turn to the Parisian correspondence for May and June, 1871, of the *Times, Daily News, and Standard.*

There he can learn what kind of "order reigned in Paris" after the glorious victory of Versailles.

Nor is it enough that we should be clear as to the "atrocities" of the Commune. It is time people understood the true meaning of this Revolution; and this can be summed up in a few words. It meant the government of the people by the people. It was the first attempt of the proletariat to govern itself. The workers of Paris expressed this when in their first manifesto they declared they "understood it was their imperious duty and their absolute right to render themselves masters of their own destinies by seizing upon governmental power". The establishment of the Commune meant not the replacing of one form of class rule by another, but the abolishing of all class rule. It meant the substitution of true co-operative, i.e., communist, for capitalistic production, and the participation in this Revolution of workers of all countries meant the internationalizing, not only the nationalising, of the, land and of private property.

And the same men who now cry out against the use of force used force — and what force! — to vanquish the people of Paris. Those who denounce Socialists as mere firebrands and dynamitards used fire and sword to crush the people into submission.

And what has been the result of these massacres, of this slaying of thousands of men, women, and children? Is Socialism dead? Was it drowned in the blood of the people of Paris? Socialism today is a greater power than it has ever been. The bourgeois Republic of France may join hands with the

Autocrat of Russia to blot it out; Bismarck may pass repressive laws, and democratic America may follow in his wake — and still it moves! And because Socialism is today a power, because in England even it is "in the air", the time has come for doing justice to the Commune of Paris. The time has come when even the opponents of Socialism will read, at least with patience if not with sympathy, an honest and truthful account of the greatest Socialist movement — thus far — of the century.

Eleanor Marx Aveling
June 1886

Preface

The history of the Third Estate was to have been the prologue to this history. But time presses; the victims are gliding into their graves; the perfidies of the Radicals threaten to surpass the worn-out calumnies of the Monarchists. I limit myself for the present to the strictly necessary introduction.

Who made the Revolution of the 18th March? What part was taken by the Central Committee? What was the Commune? How comes it that 100,000 Frenchmen are lost to their country? Who is responsible? Legions of witnesses will answer.

No doubt it is an exile who speaks, but an exile who has been neither member, nor officer, nor functionary of the Commune; who for five years has sifted the evidence; who has not ventured upon a single assertion without accumulated proofs; who sees the victor on the look-out for the slightest inaccuracy to deny all the rest; who knows no better plea for the vanquished than the simple and sincere recital of their history.

This history, besides, is due to their children, to all the workingmen of the earth. The child has the right to know the reason of the paternal defeats, the Socialist party the campaign of its flag in all countries. He who tells the people revolutionary legends, he who amuses them with sensational stories, is as criminal as the geographer who would draw up false charts for navigators.

Prosper Olivier Lissagaray
London, November 1877

Prologue

How the Prussians got Paris and the Rurals France

Daring — this word sums up all the politics of the day. (St. Just's Report to the Convention)

August 9, 1870 — In six days the Empire has lost three battles. Douai, Frossart, MacMahon have allowed themselves to be isolated, surprised, crushed. Alsace is lost, the Moselle laid bare. The dumb-founded Ministry has convoked the Chamber. Ollivier, in dread of a demonstration, denounces it beforehand as "Prussian". But since eleven in the morning an immense agitated crowd occupies the Place de la Concorde, the quays, and surrounds the Corps Législatif.

Paris is waiting for the word from the deputies of the Left. Since the announcement of the defeat they have become the only moral authority. Bourgeoisie, workingmen, all rally round them. The workshops have turned their army into the streets, and at the head of the different groups one sees men of tried energy.

The Empire totters — it has now only to fall. The troops drawn up before the Corps Législatif are greatly excited, ready to turn tail in spite of the decorated and grumbling Marshal y d'Hilliers. The people cry, "To the frontier". Officers answer aloud, "Ours is not here".

In the Salle des Pas Perdus well-known Republicans, the men of the clubs, who have forced their way in, roughly challenge the Imperial deputies, speak loudly of proclaiming the Republic. The pale-faced Mamelukes [originally a militia of Egyptian slave-soldiers, here used to mean the Right] steal behind the groups. M. Thiers arrives and exclaims: "Well, then, make your republic!" When the President, Schneider, passes to the chair, he is received with cries of "Resign!"

The deputies of the Left are surrounded by delegates from without. "What are you waiting for? We are ready. Only show yourselves under the colonnades at the gates." The honourable gentlemen seem confounded, stupefied. "Are there enough of you? Is it not better to put it off till tomorrow?" There are indeed only 100,000 men ready. Someone arrives and tells Gambetta, "There are several thousand of us at the Place Bourbon." Another, the writer of this history, says, "Make sure of the situation today, when it may still be saved. Tomorrow, having become desperate it will be forced upon you." But these brains seem paralysed; no word escapes these gaping mouths.

The sitting opens. Jules Favre proposes to this base Chamber, the abettor of our disasters, the humus of the Empire, to seize upon the government. The Mamelukes rise up in dudgeon, and Jules Simon, hair on end, returns to us in the Salle des Pas Perdus. "They threaten to shoot us," he shrieks: "I descended into the midst of the hall and said, 'Well, shoot us'." We exclaim, "Put an end to this." "Yes," says he, "we must make an end of it," — and he returns to the Chamber.

And thus ended their threatening looks. The Mamelukes, who know their Left, recover their self-assurance, throw Ollivier overboard and form a *coup d'état* Ministry. Schneider precipitately breaks up the sitting in order to get rid of the crowd. The people, feebly repulsed by the soldiers, repair in masses to the bridges, follow those who leave the Chamber, expecting every moment to hear the Republic proclaimed. M. Jules Simon, out of reach of the bayonets, makes a heroic discourse, and convokes the people to meet the next day at the Place de la Concorde. The next day the police occupy all the approaches.

Thus the Left abandoned to Napoleon III our two last armies. One effort would have sufficed to overthrow this pasteboard Empire. The people instinctively offered their help to render the nation unto herself. The Left repulsed them, refused to save the country by a riot, and, confining their efforts to a ridiculous motion, left to the Mamelukes the care of saving France. The Turks in 1876 showed more intelligence and elasticity.

During three weeks it was the story of Byzantium all over again — the fettered nation sinking into the abyss in the face of its motionless governing classes. All Europe cried, "Beware!" They alone heard not. The masses, deceived by a braggart and corrupt press, might ignore the danger, lull themselves with vain hopes; but the deputies have, must have, their hands full of crushing truths. They conceal them. The Left exhausts itself in exclamations. On the 12th M. Gambetta cries, "We must wage Republican war" — and sits down again. On the 13th Jules Favre demands the creation of a Committee of Defence. It is refused. He utters no syllable. On the 20th the Ministry announces that Bazaine has forced three army corps into the quarries of Jaumont; the next day the whole European press related, on the contrary, that Bazaine, three times beaten, had been thrown back upon Metz by 200,000 Germans. And no deputy rises to challenge the liars! Since the 26th they have known MacMahon's insane march upon Metz, exposing the last army of France, a mob of 80,000 conscripts, and vanquished, to 200,000 victorious Germans. M. Thiers, again restored to favour since the disasters, demonstrates in the committees and in the lobbies that this march is the way to utter ruin. The extreme Left says and puts it about that all is lost and of all these responsible persons seeing the state ship tempest-tossed, not one raises his hand to seize the helm.

Since 1813 France had seen no such collapse of the governing classes. The ineffable dastardliness of the *Cent jours* [the Hundred Days of 1815 between Napoleon I's return from exile on the island of Elba until his defeat at Waterloo] pales before this superior cowardice; for here Tartuffe [symbol of hypocrisy, from a play by Molière] is grafted upon Trimalcion. [Nero-like character in a play by Petronius] Thirteen months later, at Versailles, I hear, amidst enthusiastic applause, the Empire apostrophized, "Varus [Roman general, he committed suicide after his legions had been destroyed], give us back our legions." Who speaks, who applauds thus? The same great bourgeoisie, which, for eighteen years mute and bowed to the dust, offered their legions to Varus. The bourgeoisie accepted the Second Empire from fear of Socialism, even as their fathers had submitted to the first to make an end of the Revolution. Napoleon I rendered the bourgeoisie two services not overpaid by his apotheosis. He gave them an iron centralization and sent to their graves 15,000 wretches still kindled by the flame of the Revolution, who at any moment might have claimed the public lands granted to them. But he left the same bourgeoisie saddled for all masters. When they possessed themselves of the parliamentary government, to which Mirabeau wished to raise them at one bound, they were incapable of governing. Their mutiny of 1830, turned into a revolution by the people, made the belly master. The great bourgeois of 1830, like him of 1790, had but one thought — to gorge himself with privileges, to arm the bulwarks in defence of his domains, to perpetuate the proletariat. The fortune of his country is nothing to him, so that he fatten. To lead, to compromise France, the parliamentary king has as free license as Bonaparte. When by a new outburst of the people the bourgeoisie are compelled to seize the helm, after three years, in spite of massacre and proscription, it slips out of their palsied hands into those of the first comer.

From 1851 to 1869 they relapse into the same state as after the 18th Brumaire. Their privileges safe, they allow Napoleon III to plunder France, make her the vassal of Rome, dishonour her in Mexico, ruin her finances, vulgarize debauchery. All-powerful by their retainers and their wealth, they do not risk a "man, a dollar, for the sake of protesting. In 1869 the pressure from without raises them to the verge of power; a little strength of will and the government is theirs. They have but the desires of the eunuch. At the first sign of the impotent master they kiss the rod that smote them on 2nd December, making room for the plebiscite which rebaptizes the Empire.

Bismarck prepared the war, Napoleon III wanted it, the great bourgeoisie looked on. They might have stopped it by an earnest gesture. M. Thiers contented himself with a grimace. He saw in this war our certain ruin; he knew our terrible inferiority in everything; he could have united the Left, the *tiers-parti*, the journalists, have made palpable to them the folly of the attack, and, supported by this strength of opinion, have said to the Tuileries, to Paris if needs be, "War is impossible; we shall combat it as treason." He, anxious only to clear himself, simply demanded the despatches instead of speaking the true word, "You have no chance of success." And these great bourgeois, who would not have risked the least part of their fortunes without the most serious guarantees, staked 100,000 lives and the milliards of France on the word of a Leboeuf and the equivocations of a Grammont.

And what then is the lower middle class doing meanwhile? This lean class, which penetrates everything — industry, commerce, the administration — mighty by encompassing the people, so vigorous, so ready in the first days of our Hegira, [or hijrrah, a Muslim term meaning "emigration", but used for the start of a new era] will it not, as in 1792, rise for the common weal? Alas! it has been spoilt under the hot corruption of the Empire. For many years it has lived at random, isolating itself from the proletariat, whence it issued but yesterday, and whither the great barons of Capital will hurl it back again tomorrow. No more of that fraternity with the people, of that zeal for reform, which manifested themselves from 1830 to 1848. With its bold initiative, its revolutionary instinct, it loses also the consciousness of its force. Instead of representing itself, as it might so well do, it goes about in quest of representatives among the Liberals.

The friend of the people who will write the history of Liberalism in France wig save us many a convulsion. Sincere Liberalism would be folly in a country where the governing classes, refusing to concede anything, constrain every honest man to become a revolutionise. But it was never anything else than the Jesuitism of liberty, a trick of the bourgeoisie to isolate the workmen. From Bailly to Jules Favre, the moderates have masked the manoeuvres of despotism, buried our revolutions, conducted the great massacres of proletarians. The old clear-sighted Parisian sections hated them more than the down-right reactionists. Twice Imperial despotism rehabilitated them, and the lower middle class, soon forgetting their true part, accepted as defenders those who pretended to be vanquished like themselves. The men who had made abortive the movement of 1848 and paved the way for the 2nd December thus became during the darkness which followed it the acclaimed vindicators of ravished liberty. At the first dawn they appeared what they had ever been — the enemies of the working class. Under the Empire the Left never condescended to concern itself with the interests of the workmen. These Liberals never found for them a word, a protestation, even such as the Chambers of 1830-1848 sometimes witnessed. The young lawyers whom they had affiliated to themselves soon revealed their designs, rallying to the Liberal Empire, some openly, like Ollivier and Darimon, others with prudence, like Picard. For the timid or ambitious they founded the "open Left", a bench of candidates for public office; and in 1870 a number of Liberals indeed solicited official functions. For the "intransigants" there was the "closed Left", where the irreconcilable dragons Gambetta, Crémieux, Arago, Pelletan guarded the pure principles. These two groups of augurs thus held every fraction of bourgeois opposition — the timorous and the intrepid. After the plebiscite they became the holy synod, the uncontested chiefs of the lower middle class, more and more incapable of governing itself, and alarmed at the Socialist movement, behind which they showed it the hand of the Emperor. It gave them full powers, shut its eyes, and allowed itself to drift gradually towards the parliamentary Empire, big with portfolios for its patrons. The thunderbolt galvanized it into life, but only for a moment. At the bidding of the deputies to keep quiet, the lower middle class, the mother of the 10th August, docilely bent its head and let the foreigner plunge into the very bosom of France.

Poor France! Who will save thee? the humble, the poor, those who for six years contended for thee with the Empire.

While the upper classes sell the nation for a few hours of rest, and the Liberals seek to feather their nests under the Empire, a handful of men, without arms, unprotected, rise up against the still all-powerful despot. On the one hand, young men who are part of the bourgeoisie have gone over to the people, faithful children of 1789, resolved to continue the work of the Revolution; on the other hand, working men unite for the study and the conquest of the rights of labour. In vain the Empire attempts to split their forces, to seduce the working men. These see the snare, hiss the professors of Caesarian socialism, and from 1863, without journals, without a tribune, affirm themselves as a class, to the great scandal of the Liberal sycophants, maintaining that 1789 has equalized all classes. In 1867 they descend into the streets, make a demonstration at the tomb of Manin [Daniel Manin (1804-1857), an Italian nationalist leader who died an exile in France], and, despite the bludgeons of the sbirri, protest against Mentana [village where Garibaldi's troops were defeated by the French in 1867]. At this appearance of a revolutionary socialist party the Left gnashes its teeth. When some working men, ignorant of their own history, ask Jules Favre if the Liberal bourgeoisie will support them on the day of their rising for the Republic, the leader of the Left impudently answers, "Gentlemen, workmen, you have made the Empire; it is your business to unmake it." And Picard says, "socialism does not exist, or at any rate we will not treat with it."

Thus set right for the future, the working men continue the struggle single-handed. Since the re-opening of the public meetings they fill the halls, and, in spite of persecution and imprisonment, harass, undermine the Empire, taking advantage of every accident to inflict a blow. On the 26th October 1869 they threaten to march on the Corps Législatif; in November they insult the Tuileries by the election of Rochefort; in December they goad the Government by the *Marseillaise*; in January, 1870, they go 200,000 strong to the funeral of Victor Noir, and, well directed, would have swept away the throne.

The Left, terrified at this multitude, which threatens to overwhelm them, brands their leaders as desperados or as police agents. They, however, keep to the fore, unmasking the Left, defying them to discussion, keeping up at the same time a running fire on the Empire, They form the vanguard against the plebiscite. At the war rumours they are the first to make a stand. The old dregs of chauvinism, stirred by the Bonapartists, discharge their muddy waters. The Liberals remain impassible or applaud; the working men stop the way. On the 15th July, at the very same hour when Ollivier from the tribune invokes war with a light heart, the revolutionary socialists crowd the boulevards crying, *Vive la paix!* and singing the pacific refrain –

> The people are our brothers
> And the tyrants our enemies.

From the Château d'Eau to the Boulevard St. Denis they are applauded, but are hissed in the Boulevards Bonne Nouvelle and Montmartre, and come to blows with certain bands shouting for war.

The next day they meet again at the Bastille, and parade the streets, Ranvier, a painter on porcelain, well known in Belleville, marching at their head with a banner. In the Faubourg Montmartre the *sergents-de-ville* charge them with drawn swords.

Unable to influence the bourgeoisie, they turn to the working men of Germany, as they had done in 1869: "Brothers, we protest against the war, we who wish for peace, labour, and liberty. Brothers, do not listen to the hirelings who seek to deceive you as to the real wishes of France." Their noble appeal received its reward. In 1869 the students of Berlin had answered the pacific address of the French students with insults. The working men of Berlin in 1870 spoke thus to the working men of France: "We too wish for peace, labour, and liberty. We know that on both sides of the Rhine there are brothers with whom we are ready to die for the Universal Republic." Great prophetic words! Let them be inscribed on the first page of the Golden Book just opened by the workmen.

Thus towards the end of the Empire there was no life, no activity, save in the ranks of the proletariat and the young men of the middle class who had joined them. They alone showed some political courage, and in the midst of the general paralysis of the month of July 1870, they alone found the energy to attempt at least the salvation of France.

They lacked authority; they failed to carry with them the lower middle class, for which they also combat, because of their utter want of political experience. How could they have acquired it during eighty years, when the ruling class not only withheld fight from them, but even the right to enlighten themselves? By an internal Machiavellianism they forced them to grope their way in the dark, so that they might hand them over the more easily to dreamers and sectarians. Under the Empire, when the public meetings and journals reappeared, the political education of the workmen had still to be effected. Many, abused by morbid minds, in the belief that their affranchisement depended on a *coup-de-main* gave themselves up to whoever spoke of overthrowing the Empire. Others, convinced that even the most thorough-going bourgeois were hostile to Socialism, and only courted the people in furtherance of their ambitious plans, wanted the workmen to constitute themselves into groups independent of all tutelage. These different currents crossed each other. The chaotic state of the party of action was laid bare in its journal, the *Marseillaise,* a hot mish-mash of doctrinaires and desperate writers united by hatred of the Empire, but without definite views and above all, without discipline. Much time was wanted to cool down the first effervescence and get rid of the romantic rubbish which twenty years of oppression and want of study had made fashionable. However, the influence of the Socialists began to prevail, and no doubt with time they would have classified their ideas, drawn up their programme, eliminated the mere spouters, entered upon serious action. Already, in 1869, workingmen's societies, founded for mutual credit, resistance and study, had united in a Federation, whose headquarters were the Place de la Corderie du Temple. The International setting forth the most adequate idea of the revolutionary movement of our century, under the guidance of Varlin, a bookbinder of rare intelligence, of Duval, Theisz, Frankel, and a few devoted men, was beginning to gain Power in France. It also met at the Corderie, and urged on the more slow and reserved workmen's societies. The public meetings of 1870 no longer resembled the earlier ones; the people wanted useful discussions. Men like Millière, Lefrançais, Vermorel, Longuet, etc. seriously competed with the mere declaimers. But many years would have been required for the development of the party of labour, hampered by young bourgeois adventurers in search of a reputation, Encumbered with conspiracy-mongers and romantic visionaries, still Ignorant of the administrative and political mechanism of the bourgeois regime which they attacked.

Just before the war some discipline was attempted. Some tried to move the deputies of the left and met them at Crémieux's. They found them stupefied, more afraid of a *coup-d'état* than of the Prussian victories. Crémieux, pressed to act, answered naively, "Let us wait for a new disaster, as, for instance, the fall of Strasburg."

It was indeed necessary to wait, for without these shadows nothing could be done. The Parisian lower middle class believed in the extreme Left, as it had believed in our armies. Those who wished to do without them failed. On the 14th the friends of Blanqui attempted to raise the outlying districts, attacked the quarters of the firemen of La Villette, and put the sergents-de-ville to flight. Masters of the field, they traversed the boulevard up to Belleville, crying, *Vive la République! Death to the Prussians!* No one joined them. The crowd looked on from afar, astonished, motionless, rendered suspicious by the police agents, who thus drew them off from the real enemy — the Empire. The Left pretended to believe in the Prussian agent, to reassure the bourgeoisie, and Gambetta demanded the immediate trial of the prisoners of La Villette. The Minister Palikao had to remind him that certain forms must be observed, even by military justice. The court-martial condemned ten to death, although almost all the accused had had nothing to do with the affray. Some true-hearted men, wishing to prevent these executions, went to Michelet, who wrote a touching letter on their behalf. The Empire had no time to carry out the sentences.

Since the 25th MacMahon was leading his army into the snares laid by Moltke. On the 29th, surprised, and beaten at Beaumont l'Argonne, he knew himself over-reached, and yet pushed forward. Palikao had written to him on the 27th: "If you abandon Bazaine we shall have the Revolution in Paris." And to ward off the Revolution he exposed France. On the 30th he threw his troops into the pit of Sedan; on the 1st September the army was surrounded by 200,000 enemies, and 700 cannons crowned the heights. The next day Napoleon III delivered up his sword to the King of Prussia. The telegraph announced it; all Europe knew it that same night. The deputies, however, were silent; they remained so on the 3rd. On the 4th only, at midnight, after Paris had passed through a day of feverish excitement, they made up their minds to speak. Jules Favre demanded the abolition of the Empire and a Commission charged with the defence, but took care not to touch the Chamber. During the day some men of tried energy had attempted to raise the boulevards, and in the evening an anxious crowd pressed against the railings of the Corps Législatif, crying: *Vive la République*. Gambetta met them and said, "You are wrong; we must remain united; make no revolution." Jules Favre surrounded on his leaving the Chamber, strove to calm the people.

If Paris had been guided by the Left, France would have capitulated that very hour more shamefully than Napoleon III. But on the morning of the 4th of September the people assemble, and amongst them National Guards armed with their muskets. The astonished gendarmes give way to them. Little by little the Corps Législatif is invaded. At ten o'clock notwithstanding the desperate efforts of the Left, the crowd fills the galleries. It is time. The Chamber, on the point of forming a Ministry, try to seize the government. The Left support this combination with all its might, waxing indignant at the mere mention of a Republic. When that cry bursts forth from the galleries, Gambetta makes unheard-of efforts and conjures the people to await the result of the deliberations of the Chamber — a result known before hand. It is the project of M. Thiers: a Government Commission named by the Assembly; peace demanded and accepted at any price; after that disgrace, the parliamentary monarchy. Happily a new crowd of invaders bursts its way through the doors, while the occupants of the galleries glide into the hall. The people expel the deputies. Gambetta, forced to the tribune, is obliged to announce the abolition of the Empire. The crowd, wanting more than this, asks for the Republic, and carries off the deputies to proclaim it at the Hôtel-de-Ville.

This was already in the hands of the people. In the Salle du Trône were some of those who for a month had attempted to rouse public opinion. First on the ground, they might, with a little discipline, have influenced the constitution of the government. The Left surprised them haranguing, and, incited by an acclaiming multitude, Jules Favre took the chair, which Millière gave up to him, saying, "At the present moment there is but one matter at stake — the expulsion of the Prussians." Jules Favre, Jules Simon, Jules Ferry, Gambetta, Crémieux, Emmanuel Arago, Glais-Bizoin, Pelletan, Gamier-Pages, Picard, uniting, proclaimed themselves the Government, and read their own names to the crowd, which answered by adding those of men like Delescluze, Ledru-Rollin, Blanqui. They, however, declared they would accept no colleagues but the deputies of Paris. The crowd applauded. This frenzy of just-emancipated serfs made the Left masters. They were clever enough to admit Rochefort.

They next applied to General Trochu, named governor of Paris by Napoleon. This general had become the idol of the Liberals because he had sulked a little with the Empire. His whole military glory consisted in a few pamphlets. The Left had seen much of him during the last crisis. Having attained to power, it begged him to direct the defence. He asked, firstly, a place for God in the new regime; secondly, for himself the presidency of the council. He obtained everything. The future will show what secret bond so quickly united the men of the Left to the loyal Breton who had promised "to die on the steps of the Tuileries in defence of the dynasty".

Twelve individuals thus took possession of France. They invoked no other title than their mandate as representatives of Paris, and declared themselves legitimate by popular acclamation.

In the evening the International and syndicates of the workmen sent delegates to the Hôtel-de-Ville. They had on the same day sent a new address to the German working men. Their fraternal duty fulfilled, the French workmen gave themselves up the defence. Let the Government organize it and they would stay by it. The most suspicious were taken in. On the 7th, in the first number of his paper *La Patrie en Danger*, Blanqui and his friends offered the Government their most energetic, their absolute co-operation.

All Paris abandoned itself to the men of the Hôtel-de-Ville, forgetting their late defections, investing them with the grandeur of the danger. To seize, to monopolize the government at such a moment, seemed a stroke of audacity of which genius alone is capable. Paris, deprived for eighty years of her municipal liberties, accepted as mayor the lachrymose Etienne Arago. In the twenty arrondissements he named the mayors he liked, and they again named the adjuncts agreeable to themselves. But Arago announced early elections and spoke of reviving the great days of 1792. At this moment Jules Favre, proud as Danton, cried to Prussia, to Europe: "We will cede neither an inch of our territories nor a stone of our fortresses," and Paris rapturously applauded this dictatorship announcing itself with words so heroic. On the 14th when Trochu held the review of the National Guard, 250,000 men stationed in the boulevards, the Place de la Concorde, and the Champs-Elysées cheered enthusiastically, and renewed a vow like that of their fathers on the morning of Valmy.

Yes, Paris gave herself up without reserve — incurable confidence — to that same Left to which she had been forced to do violence in order to make her revolution. Her outburst of will lasted but for an hour. The Empire once overthrown, she re-abdicated. In vain did far-seeing patriots try to keep her on the alert; in vain did Blanqui write, "Paris is no more impregnable than we were invincible. Paris, mystified by a braggart press, ignores the greatness of the peril; Paris abuses confidence." Paris abandoned herself to her new masters, obstinately shutting her eyes. And yet each day brought with it new ill omens. The shadow of the siege approached, and the Government of Defence, far from evacuating the superfluous mouths, crowded the 200,000 inhabitants of the suburbs into the town. The exterior works did not advance. Instead of throwing all Paris into the work, and taking these descendants of the levellers of the Camp-de-Mars out of the *enceinte* in troops of 100,000 drums beating, banners flying, Trochu abandoned the earthworks to the ordinary contractors. The heights of Chatillon, the key to our forts of the south, had hardly been surveyed, when on the 19th the enemy presented himself, sweeping from the plateau an affrighted troop of zouaves and soldiers who did not wish to fight. The following day, that Paris which the press had declared could not be invested, was surrounded and cut off from France.

This gross ignorance very soon alarmed the Revolutionists. They had promised their support, but not blind faith. Since the 4th of September, wishing to centralize the forces of the party of action for the defence and the maintenance of the Republic, they had invited the public meetings in each arrondissement to name a Committee of Vigilance charged to control the mayors and to delegate four members to a Central Committee of the twenty arrondissements. This tumultuous mode of election had resulted in a committee composed of working men, employees and authors, known in the revolutionary movements of the last years. This committee had established itself in the hall of the Rue de la Corderie, lent by the International and the Federation of trade unions.

These had almost suspended their work, the service of the National Guard absorbing all their activity. Some of their members again met in the Committee of Vigilance and in the Central Committee, which caused the latter to be erroneously attributed to the International. On the 4th it demanded by a manifesto the election of the municipalities, the police to be placed in their hands, the election and control of all the magistrates, absolute freedom of the press, public meeting and association, the expropriation of all articles of primary necessity, their distribution by allowance, the arming of all citizens, the sending of commissioners to rouse the provinces. But Paris was then infected with a fit of confidence. The bourgeois journals denounced the committee as Prussian. The names of some of the signers were, however, well known in the meetings and to the press: Ranvier, Millière, Longuet, Vallès, Lafrançais, Mallon, etc. Their posters were torn down.

On the 20th, after Jules Favre's application to Bismarck, the Committee held a large meeting in the Alcazar and sent a deputation to the Hôtel-de-Ville to demand war "to the end' and the early election of the Commune of Paris. Jules Ferry gave his word of honour that the government would not treat at any price, and announced the municipal elections for the end of the month. Two days later a decree postponed them indefinitely.

Thus this Government, which in seventeen days had prepared nothing, which had allowed itself to be blocked up without even a struggle refused the advice of Paris, and more than ever arrogated to itself the right of directing the defence. Did it then possess the secret of victory? Trochu had just said, "All resistance is a heroic madness;" Picard, "We shall defend ourselves for honour's sake, but all hope is chimerical;" the elegant Crémieux, "The Prussians will enter Paris like a knife goes into butter;" the chief of Trochu's staff, "We cannot defend ourselves; we have decided not to defend ourselves"; and, instead of honestly warning Paris, saying, "Capitulate at once or, conduct the combat yourselves," these men, who declared defence impossible, claimed its undivided direction.

What then is their aim? To negotiate. Since the first defeats they have no other. The reverses which exalted our fathers only made the Left more cowardly than the Imperialist deputies. On the 7th of August Jules Favre, Jules Simon, and Pelletan had said to Schneider, "We cannot hold out; we must come to terms as soon as possible." All the following days the Left had only one policy — to urge the Chamber to possess itself of the government in order to negotiate, hoping to get into office afterwards. Hardly established, these defenders sent M. Thiers all over Europe to beg for peace, and Jules Favre to run after Bismarck to ask his conditions — a step that revealed to the Prussian with what tremblers he had to deal.

When all Paris cried to them, "Defend us; drive back the enemy," they applauded, accepted, but said to themselves, "You shall capitulate." There is no more crying treason in history. The asinine confidence of the immense majority no more diminishes the crime than the foolishness of the dupe excuses the cheater. Did the men of the 4th September, yes or no, betray the mandate they received? "Yes," will be the verdict of the future.

A tacit mandate, it is true, but so clear, so formal, that all Paris started at the news of the proceedings at Ferrières. If the Defenders had gone a step farther, they would have been swept away. They were obliged to adjourn, to give way to what they termed the "madness of the siege," to simulate a defence. In point of fact, they did not abandon their idea for an hour, esteeming themselves the only men in Paris who had not lost their heads.

"There shall be fighting since those Parisians will have it so, but only with the view to soften Bismarck." On his return from the review, this scene of hopeful enthusiasm manifested by 250,000 armed men is said to have affected Trochu, who announced that it would perhaps be possible to hold the ramparts. Such was the maximum of his enthusiasm: to hold out — not to open the gates. As to these 250,000 men, uniting them with the 240,000 mobiles, soldiers and marines gathered together in Paris, and with all these forces forming a powerful scourge to drive the enemy back to the Rhine, of this he never dreamt. His colleagues thought of it as little, and only discussed with him the more or less cavilling they might venture upon with the Prussian invader.

He was all for mild proceedings. His devoutness forbade him to useless blood. Since, according to all military manuals, the great town was to fall, he would make that fall as little sanguinary as possible. Besides, the return of M. Thiers, who might at any moment bring back the treaty, was waited for. Leaving the enemy to establish himself tranquilly round Paris, Trochu organized a few skirmishes for the lookers-on. One single serious engagement took place on the 30th at Chevilly, when, after a success, we retreated, abandoning a battery for want of reinforcements and teams. Public opinion, still hoaxed by the same men that had cried, "To Berlin!" believed in a success. The revolutionists only were not taken in. The capitulation of Toul and of Strasbourg was to them a solemn warning. Flourens, chief of the 63rd battalion, but who was the real commander of Bellevine, could no longer restrain himself. With the head and heart of a child, an ardent imagination, guided only by his own impulse, Flourens conducted his battalions to the Hôtel-de-Ville, demanded the mass mobilization, sorties, municipal elections, and putting the town on short rations. Trochu, who, to amuse him, had given him the title of major of the rampart, made an elaborate discourse;

the twelve apostles argued with him, and wound up by showing him out. As delegates came from all sides to demand that Paris should have a voice in her own defence, should name a council, her Commune, the Government declared on the 7th that their dignity forbade them to concede these behests. This insolence caused the movement of the 8th October. The committee of the twenty arrondissements protested in an energetic placard. Seven or eight hundred persons cried "*Vive la Commune!*" under the windows of the Hôtel-de-Ville. But the multitude had not yet lost faith. A great number of battalions hastened to the rescue; the Government passed them in review. Jules Favre opened the flood-gates of his rhetoric and declared the election impossible because — unanswerable reason! — everybody ought to be at the ramparts.

The majority greedily swallowed the bait. On the 16th, Trochu having written to his crony Etienne Arago, "I shall pursue the plan I have traced for myself to the end," the loungers announced a victory, and took up the burden of their August song on Bazaine, "Let him alone; he has his plan." The agitators looked like Prussians, for Trochu, as a good Jesuit, had not failed to speak of "a small number of men whose culpable views serve the projects of the enemy." Then Paris allowed herself during the whole month of October to be rocked asleep to the sound of expeditions commencing with success and always terminated by retreats. On the 13th we took Bagneux, and a spirited attack would have repossessed us of Chatillon: Trochu had no reserves. On the 21st a march on the Malmaison revealed the weakness of the investment and spread panic even to Versailles. Instead of pressing forward, General Ducrot engaged only six thousand men, and the enemy repulsed him, taking two cannons. The Government transformed these repulses into successful reconnoitres, and coined money out of the despatches of Gambetta, who, sent to the provinces on the 8th, announced imaginary armies, and intoxicated Paris with the account of the brilliant defence of Châteaudun.

The mayors encouraged this pleasant confidence. They sat at the Hôtel-de-Ville with their adjuncts, and this Assembly of sixty-four members could have seen clearly what the Defence was if they had had the least courage. But it was composed of those Liberals and Republicans of whom the Left is the last expression. They knocked at the door of the Government now and then, timidly interrogated it, and received only vague assurances, in which they did not believe, but made every effort to make Paris believe.

But at the Corderie, in the clubs, in the paper of Blanqui, in the *Reveil* of Delescluze, in the *Combat* of Félix Pyat, the plan of the men of the Hôtel-de-Ville is exposed. What is the meaning of these partial sorties which are never sustained? Why is the National Guard hardly armed, unorganized, withheld from every military action? Why is the casting of cannon not proceeded with? Six weeks of idle talk and inactivity cannot leave the least doubt as to the incapacity or ill-will of the Government. This same thought occupies all minds. Let the make room for those that believe in the Defence; let Paris win of herself; let the Commune of 1792 be revived to save the city and France. Every day this resolution sinks more deeply into virile minds. On the 27th the *Combat,* which preached in high-flown phraseology whose musical rhythm struck the muses more than the nervous dialectics of Blanqui, hurls a terrific thunderbolt. "Bazaine is about to surrender Metz, to treat for peace in the name of Napoleon III; his aide-de-camp is at Versailles." The Hôtel-de-Ville immediately contradicted this news, "as infamous as it is false. The glorious soldier Bazaine has not ceased harassing the besieging army with brilliant sorties." The Government called down upon the journalist "the chastisement of public opinion." At this appeal the drones of Paris buzzed, burnt the journal, and would have torn the journalist to pieces if he had not decamped. The next day the *Combat* declared that they had the statement from Rochefort, to whom Flourens had communicated it. Other complications followed. On, the 20th a surprise made us masters of Bourget, a village in the north-east of Paris, and on the 29th the general staff announced this success as a triumph. The whole day it left our soldiers without food, without reinforcements, under the fire of the Prussians, who, returning on the 30th 15,000 strong, recovered the village from its 1,600 defenders. On the 31st of October, Paris on awaking received the news of three disasters: the loss of Bourget, the capitulation of Metz, together with the whole army of the "glorious Bazaine", and the arrival of M. Thiers for the purpose of negotiating an armistice.

The men of the 4th September believed they were saved, that their goal was reached. They had posted up the armistice side by side with capitulation, "good and bad news," convinced that Paris, despairing of victory, would accept peace with open arms. Paris started up as with an electric shock, at the same time rousing Marseilles, Toulouse, and Saint-Etienne. There was such spontaneity of indignation, that from eleven o'clock, in pouring rain, the masses came to the Hôtel-de-Ville crying "No armistice". Notwithstanding the resistance of the mobiles who defended the entrance, they invaded the vestibule. Arago and his adjuncts hastened thither, swore that the Government was exhausting itself in efforts to save us. The first crowd retired; a second followed hard upon. At twelve o'clock Trochu appeared at the foot of the staircase, thinking to extricate himself by a harangue; cries of "Down with Trochu" answered him. Jules Simon relieved him, and, confident in his rhetoric, even went to the square in front of the Hôtel-de-Ville and expatiated upon the comforts of the armistice. The people cried "No armistice." He only succeeded in backing out by asking the crowd to name six delegates to accompany him to the Hôtel-de-Ville. Trochu, Jules Favre, Jules Ferry, and Picard received them. Trochu in Ciceronic periods demonstrated the uselessness of Bourget, and pretended that he had only just learnt the capitulation of Metz. A voice cried, "You are a liar." A deputation from the Committee of the twenty arrondissements and of the

Committees of Vigilance had entered the hall a little while before. Others, wishing to pump Trochu, invited him to continue his speech. He recommenced, when a shot was fired in the square, putting an end to the monologue and scaring away the orator. Calm being re-established, Jules Favre supplied the place of the general, and took up the thread of his discourse.

While these scenes were going on in the Salle du Trône, the mayors, so long the accomplices of Trochu, were deliberating in the hall of the municipal council. To quell the riot, they proposed the election of municipalities, the formation of battalions of the National Guard, and their joining them to the army. The scapegoat Etienne Aragot was sent to offer this salve to the Government. At two o'clock an immense crowd inundated the Place de l'Hôtel-de-Ville, crying, "Down with Trochu! *Vive la Commune!*" and carrying banners with the inscription "No armistice." They had several times come into collision with the militia. The delegates who entered the Hôtel-de-Ville brought no answer. About three o'clock, the crowd, growing impatient, rushed forward, breaking through the militia, and forcing Félix Pyat, come to the Hôtel-de-Ville as a sight-seer, into the Salle des Maires. He exclaimed, struggled, protested that this was against all rules. The mayors supported him as well as they could, and announced that they had demanded the election of the municipalities, and that the decree in that sense was about to be signed. The multitude, still pushing forward, goes up to the Salle du Trône, cutting short the oration of Jules Favre, who had rejoined his colleagues in the Government-room.

While the people were thundering at the door, the defenders voted the proposition of the mayors — but in principle, not fixing the date for the elections: another jesuitical trick. Towards four o'clock the mass penetrated into the room. Rochefort in vain promised the municipal elections. They asked for the Commune! One of the delegates of the Committee of the twenty arrondissements, getting upon the tables proclaimed the abolition of the Government. A Commission was charged to proceed with the elections within forty-eight hours. The names of Dorian, the only Minister who had taken the defence to heart, of Louis Blanc, Ledru-Rollin, Victor Hugo, Raspail, Delescluse, Félix Pyat, Blanqui and Millière were received with acclamation.

Had this Commission seized on authority, cleared the Hôtel-de-Ville, posted up a proclamation convoking the electors with the briefest delays the day's work would have been beneficially concluded. But Dorian refused. Louis Blanc, Victor Hugo, Ledru-Rollin, Raspail, Félix Pyat, and Mottu. Interminable discussions followed, the disorder became terrible. The men of the 4th September felt they were saved, and smiled as they looked at the conquerors who allowed victory to slip through their fingers.

Thenceforth all became involved in an inextricable imbroglio. Every room had its government, its orators. The confusion was such that about eight o'clock reactionary National Guards could, under Flourens' nose, pick up Trochu and Jules Ferry, while others carried off Blanqui when some *franc-tireurs* tried to rescue him. In the office of the mayor, Etienne Arago and his adjuncts convoked the electors for the next day under the presidency of Dorian and Schoelcher. Towards ten o'clock their announcement was posted up in Paris.

The whole day Paris had looked on. "On the morning of the 31st October," says Jules Ferry, "the Parisian population, from highest to lowest, was absolutely hostile to us. Everybody thought we deserved to be dismissed." Not only did Trochu's battalions not stir, but one of the best, led to the succour of the Government by General Tamisier, commander-in-chief of the National Guard, raised the butt end of their guns on arriving at the Place de l'Hôtel-de-Ville. In the evening everything changed when it became known that the members of the Government were prisoners, and above all who were their substitutes. The measure seemed too strong. Such a one, who might have accepted Ledru-Rollin or Victor Hugo, could not make up his mind to Flourens and Blanqui. In vain the whole day drums had been beating to arms; in the evening they proved effective. Battalions refractory in the morning arrived at the Place Vendôme, most of them believing, it is true, that the elections had been granted; an assemblage of officers at the Bourse only consented to wait for the regular vote on the strength of Dorian and Schoelcher's placard. Trochu and the deserters from the Hôtel-de-Ville again found their faithful flock. The Hôtel-de-Ville, on the other hand, was getting empty.

Most of the battalions of the Commune, believing their cause victorious, had returned to their quarters. In the edifice there remained hardly a thousand unarmed men, the only troops being Flourens' unmanageable *tirailleurs*, while he wandered up and down amidst this mob. Blanqui signed and again signed. Delescluze tried to save some remnants from this great movement. He saw Dorian, received the formal assurance that the elections of the Commune would take place the next day, those of the Provisional Government the day after; put these assurances upon record in a note where the insurrectional committee declared itself willing to wait for the elections, and had it signed by Millière, Flourens and Blanqui. Millière and Dorian went to communicate this document to the members of the Defence. Millière proposed to them to leave the Hôtel-de-Ville together, while charging Dorian and Schoelcher to proceed with the elections, but on the express condition that no prosecutions were to take place. The members of the Defence accepted, and Millière was just saying to them, "Gentlemen, you are free," when the National Guards asked for written engagements. The prisoners became indignant that their word should be doubted, while Millière and Flourens could not make the Guards understand that signatures are illusory. During this mortal anarchy the battalions of order grew larger, and Jules Ferry attacked the door opening on the Place Lobau. Delescluze and Dorian informed him of the arrangement which they believed concluded, and induced him to wait. At three o'clock in the morning chaos still reigned supreme. Trochu's drums were beating on the Place de l'Hôtel-de-Ville. A battalion of Breton *mobiles* debauched in the midst of the Hôtel-de-Ville through subterranean passage of the Napoleon Barracks, surprised and disarmed many of the *tirailleurs*. Jules Ferry invaded the Government room. The indisciplinable mass offered no resistance. Jules Favre and his colleagues were set free. As the Bretons became menacing, General Tamisier reminded them of the convention entered upon during the evening, and, as a pledge of mutual oblivion, left the Hôtel-de-Ville between Blanqui and Flourens. Trochu paraded the streets amidst the pompous pageantry of his battalions.

Thus this day, which might have buoyed up the Defence, ended in smoke. The desultoriness, the indiscipline of the patriots restored to the Government its immaculate character of September. It took advantage of it that very night to tear down the placards of Dorian and Schoelcher; it accorded the municipal elections for the 5th, but in exchange demanded a plebiscite, putting the question in style, "Those who wish to maintain the Government will vote *aye.*" In vain the Committee of the twenty arrondissements issued a manifesto; in vain the *Réveil*, the *Patrie en Danger*, the *Combat*, enumerated the hundred reasons which made it necessary to answer *No.* Six months after the plebiscite which had made the war, the immense majority of Paris voted the plebiscite that made the capitulation. Let Paris remember and accuse herself. For fear of two or three men she opened fresh credit to this Government which added incapacity to insolence, and said to it, "I want you" 322,000 times. The army, the mobiles, gave 237,000 ayes. There were but 54,000 civilians and 9,000 soldiers to say boldly, no.

How did it happen that those 60,000 men, so clear-sighted, prompt and energetic, could not manage to direct public opinion? Simply because they were wanting in *cadres*, in method, in organizers. The feel of the siege had been unable to discipline the revolutionary Sporty, in such dire confusion a few weeks before, nor had the patriarchs of 1848 tried to do so. The Jacobins like Delescluze and Blanqui, instead of leading the people, lived in an exclusive circle of friends. Félix Pyat, vibrating between just ideas and literary epilepsy, only became practical when he had to save his own skin. The others, Ledru-Rollin, Louis Blanc, Schoelcher, the hope of the Republicans under the Empire, returned from exile shallow, pursy, rotten to the core with vanity and selfishness, without courage or patriotism, disdaining the Socialists. The dandies of Jacobinism, who called themselves Radicals, Floquet, Clémenceau, Brinon, and other democratic politicians, carefully kept aloof from the working men. The old Montagnards themselves formed a group of their own, and never came to the Committee of the twenty arrondissements, which only wanted method and political experience to become a power. So it was only a centre of emotions, not of direction — the

Gravilliers section of 1870-71, daring, eloquent, but, like its predecessor, treating of everything by manifestos.

There at least was life, a lamp, not always bright, but always burning. What is the lower middle class contributing now? Where are their Jacobins, even their Cordeliers? At the Corderie I see the workers of the lower middle class, men of the pen and orators, but where is the bulk of the army?

All is silent. Save the faubourgs, Paris was a vast sick chamber, where no one dared to speak above his breath. This moral abdication is the true psychological phenomenon of the siege, all the more extraordinary in that it coexisted with an admirable ardour for resistance. Men who speak of going to seek death with their wives and children, who say, "We will burn our houses rather than surrender them to the enemy," get angry at any controversy as to the power entrusted to the men of the Hôtel-de-Ville. If they dread the giddy-headed, the fanatics, or compromising collaborators, why do they not take the direction of the movement into their own hands? But they confine themselves to crying, "No insurrection before the enemy! No fanatics!" as though capitulation were better than an insurrection; as though the 10th of August 1792 and 31st May 1793 had not been insurrections before the enemy; as though there were no medium between abdication and delirium. And you, citizens of the old sections of 1792-93, who furnished ideas to the Convention and the Commune, who dictated to them the means of safety, who directed the clubs and fraternal societies, entertained in Paris a hundred luminous centres, do you recognise your offspring in these gulls, weaklings, jealous of the people, prostrate before the Left like devotees before the host?

On the 5th and 7th they renewed their plebiscitory vote, naming twelve of the twenty mayors named by Arago. Four amongst them, Dubail, Vautrain, Tirard, and Desmarets, belong to the pure reaction. The greater part of the adjuncts were of the Liberal type. The faubourgs, always at their post, elected Delescluze in the nineteenth arrondissement and Ranvier, Millière, Lefrançais, and Flourens in the twentieth. These latter could not take their seats. The Government, violating the convention of Dorian and Tamisier, had issued warrants for their arrest, and for that of about twenty other revolutionaries. Thus, out of seventy-five effective members, mayors and adjuncts, there were not ten revolutionaries.

These shadows of municipal councillors looked upon themselves as the stewards of the Defence, forbade themselves any indiscreet question, were on their best behaviour, feeding and administering Trochu's patient. They allowed the insolent and incapable Ferry to be appointed to the central *mairie*, and Clément-Thomas, the executioner of June 1848, to be made commander-in-chief of the National Guard. For seventy days, feeling the pulse of Paris growing from hour to hour more weak, they never had the honesty, the courage to say to the Government, "Where are you leading us?"

Nothing was lost in the beginning of November. The army, the mobiles, the marines numbered, according to the plebiscite, 246,000 men and 7,000 officers: 125,000 National Guards capable of serving a campaign might easily have been picked out in Paris, and 129,000 left for the defence of the interior. The necessary armaments might have been furnished in a few weeks, the cannon especially, every one depriving himself of bread in order to endow his battalion with five pieces, the traditional pride of the Parisians. "Where find 9,000 artillerymen?" said Trochu. Why, in every Parisian mechanic there is the stuff of a gunner, as the Commune has sufficiently proved. In everything else there was the same superabundance. Paris swarmed with engineers, overseers, foremen, who might have been drilled into officers. There lying wasted were all the materials for a victorious army.

The gouty martinets of the regular army saw here nothing but barbarism. This Paris, for which Hoche, Marcea, Kleber [generals of the French Revolution] would have been neither too young, nor too faithful, nor too pure, had for generals the residue of the Empire and Orleanism, Vinoy of December, Ducrot, Luzanne, Leflô, and a fossil like Chaboud-Latour. In their pleasant intimacy they made much fun of the defence. Finding, however, that the joke was lasting a little too long, the 31st October enraged them. They conceived an implacable, rabid hatred to the National Guard, and up to the last hour refused to utilize it.

Instead of amalgamating the forces of Paris, of giving to all the same *cadres*, the same uniforms, the same flag, the proud name of National Guard, Trochu had maintained the three divisions: the army, mobiles, and civilians. This was the natural consequence of his opinion of the Defence. The army, incited by the staff, shared its hatred of Paris, who imposed on it, it was said, useless fatigues. The mobiles of the provinces, prompted by their officers, the cream of the country squires, became also embittered. All, seeing the National Guard despised, despised it, calling them, "*Les à outrance! Les trente sous!*" (Since the siege the Parisians received thirty sous — 1s. 2 1/2d. — as indemnity.) Collisions were to be feared every day.

The 31st October changed nothing in the real state of affairs. The Government broke off the negotiations, which, notwithstanding their victory, they could not have pursued without foundering, decreed the creation of marching companies in the National Guard, and accelerated the cannon-founding, but did not believe a whit the more in defence, still steered towards peace. Riots formed the chief subject of their preoccupation. It was not only from the "folly of the siege" that they wished to save Paris, but above all from the revolutionaries. In this direction they were pushed on by the big bourgeoisie. Before the 4th September the latter had declared they "would not fight if the working class were armed, and if it had any chance of prevailing"; and on the evening of the 4th September Jules Favre and Jules Simon had gone to the Corps Législatif to reassure them, to explain to them that the new tenants would not damage the house. But the irresistible force of events had provided the proletariat with arms, and to make them inefficient in their hands became now the supreme aim of the bourgeoisie. For two months they had been biding their time, and the plebiscite told them it had come. Trochu held Paris, and by the clergy they held Trochu, all the closer in that he believed himself to be amenable only to his conscience. Strange conscience, full of trapdoors, with more complications than those of a theatre. Since the 4th of September the General had made it his duty to deceive Paris, saying, "I shall surrender thee, but it is for thy good." After the 31st October he believed his mission twofold — saw in himself the archangel, the St. Michael of threatened society. This marks the second period of the defence. It may perhaps be traced to a cabinet in the Rue des Postes, for the chiefs of the clergy saw more clearly than any one else the danger of inuring the working men to war. Their intrigues were full of cunning. Violent reactionists would have spoilt all, precipitated Paris into a revolution. They applied subtle tricks in their subterranean work, watching Trochu's every movement, whetting his antipathy to the National Guard, penetrating everywhere into the general staff, the ambulances, even the *mairies*. Like the fisherman struggling with too big a prey, they bewildered Pads, now apparently allowing her to swim in her own element, then suddenly weakening her by the harpoon. On the 28th November Trochu gave a first performance to a full-band accompaniment. General Ducrot, who commanded, presented himself like a leonidas: "I take the oath before you, before the whole nation. I shall return to Paris dead or victorious. You may see me fall; you will never see me retreat." This action exalted Paris. She fancied herself on the eve of Jemmapes, when the Parisian volunteers scaled the artillery-defended heights; for this time the National Guard was to take part in the proceedings.

We were to force an opening by the Marne in order to join the mythical armies of the provinces, and cross the river at Nogent. Ducrot's engineer had taken his measures badly; the bridges were not in a fit state. It was necessary to wait till the next day. The enemy, instead of being surprised, was able to put himself on the defensive. On the 30th a spirited assault made us masters of Champigny. The next day Ducrot remained inactive, while the enemy, emptying out of Versailles, accumulated its forces upon Champigny. On the 2nd they recovered part of the village. The whole day we fought severely. The former deputies of the Left were represented on the field of battle by a letter to their "very dear president." That evening we camped in our positions, but half frozen, the "dear president" having ordered the blankets to be left in Paris, and we had set out — a proof that the whole dons had been done in mockery — without tents or ambulances. The following day Ducrot declared we must retreat, and, "before Paris, before the whole nation," this dishonoured braggart sounded the retreat. We had 8,000 dead or wounded out of the 100,000 men who had been sent out, and of the 50,000 engaged.

For twenty days Trochu rested on his laurels. Clément-Thomas took advantage of this leisure time to disband and stigmatize the tirailluers of Belleville, who had, however, had many dead and wounded in their ranks. On the mere report of the commanding general at Vincennes, he also stigmatized the 200th battalion. Flourens was arrested. On the 20th of December these rabid purgers of our own ranks consented to take a little notice of the Prussians. The mobiles of the Seine were launched without cannons against the walls of Stains and to the attack of Bourget. The enemy received them with a crushing artillery. An advantage obtained on the right of the Ville-Evrard was not followed up. The soldiers returned in the greatest consternation, some of them crying, *Vive la paix!* Each new enterprise betrayed Trochu's plan, enervated the troops, but had no effect on the courage of the National Guards engaged. During two days on the plateau D'Ouron they sustained the fire of sixty pieces. When there was a goodly number of dead, Trochu discovered that the position was of no importance, and evacuated.

These repeated foils began to wear out the credulity of Paris. From hour to hour the sting of hunger was increasing, and horse-flesh had become a delicacy. Dogs, cats, and rats were eagerly devoured. The women waited for hours in the cold and mud for a starvation allowance. For bread they got black grout, that tortured the stomach. Children died on their mothers' empty breasts. Wood was worth its weight in gold, and the poor had only to warm them the despatches of Gambetta, always announcing fantastic successes. At the end of December their privations began to open the eyes of the people. Were they to give in, their arms intact?

The mayors did not stir. Jules Favre gave them little weekly receptions, where they gossiped about the cuisine of the siege. Only one did his duty — Delescluze. He had acquired great authority by his articles in the *Réveil*, as free of partiality as they were severe. On the 30th December he challenged Jules Favre, said to his colleagues, "You are responsible," demanded that the municipal council should be joined to the Defence. His colleagues protested, more especially Dubail and Vacherot. He returned to the charge on the 4th of January, laid down a radical motion — the dismissal of Trochu and of Clément-Thomas, the mobilization of the National Guard, the institution of a council of defence, the renewal of the Committee of War. No more attention was paid him than before.

The Committee of the twenty arrondissements supported Delescluze in issuing a red poster on the 6th: "Has the Government which charged itself with the national defence fulfilled its mission? No. By their procrastination, their indecision, their inertia, those who govern us have led us to the brink of the abyss. They have known neither how to administer nor how to fight. We die of cold, almost of hunger. Sorties without object, deadly struggles without results, repeated failures. The Government has given the measure of its capacity; it is killing us. The perpetuation of this regime means capitulation. The politics, the strategies, the administration of the Empire continued by the men of the 4th of September have been judged. Make way for the people! Make way for the Commune!" This was outspoken and true. However incapable of action the Committee may have been, its ideas were just and precise, and to the end of the siege it remained thee indefatigable, sagacious monitor of Paris.

The multitude who wanted illustrious names, paid no attention to these posters. Some of those who had signed it were arrested. Trochu, however, felt under attack, and the very same evening had posted on the walls, "The governor of Paris will never capitulate." And Paris again applauded, four months after the 4th September. It was even wondered at that, in spite of Trochu's declaration, Delescluze and his adjuncts should tender their resignations.

Nevertheless, without obstinately shutting one's eyes it was impossible not to see the precipice to which the Government was hurrying us on. The Prussians bombarded our houses from the forts of Issy and of Vanves, and on the 30th December, Trochu, having declared all further action impossible, invoked the opinion of all his generals, and wound up by proposing that he should be replaced. On the 2nd, 3rd, and 4th January the Defenders discussed the election of an Assembly which was to follow the catastrophe. But for the irritation of the patriots, Paris would have capitulated before the 15th.

The faubourgs no longer called the men of the Government other than "the band of Judas." The great democratic lamas, who had withdrawn after the 31st October, returned to the Commune, thus their own helplessness and the common sense of the people. Republican Alliance, where Ledru-Rollin officiated before half-a-dozen incense bearers, the Republican Union, and other bourgeois chapels, went so far as to very energetically demand a Parisian Assembly to organize the defence. The Government felt it had no time to lose. If the bourgeoisie joined the people, it would become impossible to capitulate without a formidable uprising. The population which cheered under the shells would not allow itself to be given up like a flock of sheep. It was necessary to mortify it first, to cure it of its "infatuation", as Jules Ferry said, to purge it of its fever. "The National Guard will only be satisfied when 10,000 National Guards have fallen," they said at the Government table. Urged on by Jules Favre and Picard on the one hand, and on the other by the simple-minded Emmanuel Arago, Garnier-Pages, and Pelletan, the quack Trochu consented to give a last performance.

It was got up as a farce at the same time as the capitulation. On the 19th the Council of Defence stated that a new defeat would be the signal of the catastrophe. Trochu was willing to accept the mayors as coadjutors on the question of capitulation and revictualling. Jules Simon and Garnier-Pages were willing to surrender Paris, and only make some reserve with regard to

France. Garnier-Pages proposed to name by special elections mandatories charged to capitulate. Such was their vigil before the battle.

On the 18th the din of trumpets and drums called Paris to arms and put the Prussians on the alert. For this supreme effort Trochu had been able to muster only 84,000 men, of whom nineteen regiments belonged to the National Guard. He made them pass the night, which was cold and rainy, in the mud of the fields of Mont-Valdrien.

The attack was directed against the defences that covered Versailles from the side of La Bergerie. At ten o'clock, with the impulse of old troops, the National Guards and the mobiles, who formed the majority of the left wing and centre, had stormed the redoubt of Montretout, the part of Buzenval, a part of St. Cloud, pushing forward as far as Garches, occupying, in one word, all the posts designated. General Ducrot, commanding the left wing, had arrived two hours behind time, and though his army consisted chiefly of troops of the line, he did not advance.

We had conquered several commanding heights which the generals did not arm. The Prussians were allowed to sweep these crests at their ease, and at four o'clock sent forth assault columns. Ours gave way at first, then, steadying themselves, checked the onward movement of the enemy. Towards six o'clock, when the hostile fire diminished, Trochu ordered a retreat. Yet there 40,000 reserves between Mont-Valdérien and Buzenval. Out of 150 artillery pieces, thirty only had been employed. But the generals, who during the whole day had hardly deigned to communicate with the National Guard, declared they could not hold out a second night, and Trochu had Montretout and all the conquered positions evacuated. Battalions returned weeping with rage. All understood that the whole affair was a cruel mockery.

Paris, which had gone to sleep victorious, awoke to the sound of Trochu's alarm-bell. The General asked for an armistice of two days to carry off the wounded and bury the dead. He said, "We want time, carts, and many litters." The dead and wounded did not exceed 3,000 men.

This time Paris at last saw the abyss. Besides, the Defenders, disdaining all further disguise, suddenly dropped the mask. Jules Favre and Trochu summoned the mayors. Trochu declared that all was lost and any further struggle impossible. The sinister news immediately spread over the town.

During four months' siege, patriotic Paris had foreseen, accepted all; pestilence, assault, pillage, everything save capitulation. On this the 20th of January found Paris, notwithstanding her credulity, her weakness, the same Paris as on the 20th September. Thus, when the fatal word was uttered, the city seemed at first wonder-struck, as at the sight of some monstrous, unnatural crime. The wounds of four months opened again, crying for vengeance. Cold, starvation, bombardment, the long nights in the trenches, the little children dying by thousands, death scattered abroad in the sorties, and all to end in shame, to form an escort for Bazaine, to become a second

Metz. One fancied one could hear the Prussian sneering. With some, stupor turned into rage. Those who were longing for the surrender threw themselves into attitudes. The white-livered mayors even affected to fly into a passion. On the evening of the 21st they were again received by Trochu. That same morning all the generals had unanimously decided that another sortie was impossible. Trochu very philosophically demonstrated to the mayors the absolute necessity of making advances to the enemy, but declared he would have nothing to do with it, insinuating that they should capitulate in his stead. They cut wry faces, protested, still imagining they were not responsible for this issue.

After their departure the Defenders deliberated. Jules Favre asked to tender his resignation. But he, the apostle, insisted upon being by them, fancying thus to cheat history into the belief that he had to the last resisted capitulation. The discussion was growing heated when, at three o'clock in the morning, they were informed of the rescue of Flourens and other political prisoners confined at Mazas. A body of National Guards headed by an adjunct from the eighteenth arrondissement had presented themselves an hour before in front of the prison. The bewildered governor had let them have their way. The Defenders, fearing a repetition of the 31st October, hurried on their resolution replacing Trochu by Vinoy.

He wanted to be implored. Jules Favre and Leflô had to show him the people in arms, an insurrection imminent. At that very moment, the morning of the 22nd, the prefect of police, declaring himself powerless, had sent in his resignation. The men of the 4th September had fallen so low as to bend their knees before those of the 2nd December. Vinoy condescended to yield.

His first act was to arm against Paris, to dismantle her lines before the Prussians, to recall the troops of Suresne, Gentilly, Les Lilas, to call out the cavalry and gendarmerie. A battalion of mobiles commanded by Vabre, a colonel of the National Guard, fortified itself in the Hôtel-de-Ville. Clément-Thomas issued a furious proclamation: "The factions are joining the enemy." He adjured the "entire National Guard to rise in order to smite them." He had not called upon it to rise against the Prussians.

There were signs of anger afloat, but no symptoms of a serious collision. Many revolutionaries, well aware that all was at an end, would not support a movement which, if successful, would have saved the men of the Defence and forced the victors to capitulate in their stead. Others, whose patriotism was not enlightened by reason, still warm from the ardour of Buzenval, believed in a *sortie en masse*. We must at least, said they, save our honour. The evening before, some meetings had voted that an armed opposition should be offered to any attempt at capitulation, and had given themselves a rendezvous before the Hôtel-de-Ville.

At twelve o'clock the drums beat to arms at the Batignolles. At one o'clock several armed groups appeared in the square of the Hôtel-de-Ville; the crowd was gathering. A deputation, led by a member of the Alliance, was received by G. Chaudey, adjunct to the mayor, for the Government was seated at the Louvre since the 31st October. The orator said the wrongs of Paris necessitated the nomination of the Commune. Chaudey answered that the Commune was nonsense; that he always had, and always would oppose it. Another, more eager deputation arrived. Chaudey received it with insults. Meanwhile the excitement was spreading to the crowd that filled the square. The 101st battalion arrived from the left bank crying "Death to the traitors!" when the 207th of the Batignolles, who had marched down the boulevards, debauched on the square through the Rue du Temple and drew up before the Hôtel-de-Ville, whose doors and windows were closed. Others joined them. Some shots were fired, the windows of the Hôtel-de-Ville were clouded with smoke, and the crowd dispersed with a cry of terror. Sheltered by lamp-posts and some heaps of sand, some National Guards sustained the fire of the mobiles. Others fired from the houses in the Avenue Victoria. The fusillade had been going on for half an hour when the gendarmes appeared at the corner of the Avenue. The insurgents, almost surrounded, made a retreat. About a dozen were arrested and taken to the Hôtel-de-Ville, where Vinoy wanted to despatch them at once. Jules Ferry recoiled, and had them sent before the regular court-martials. Those who had got up the demonstration and the inoffensive crowd of spectators had thirty killed or wounded, among others a man of great energy, Commandant Sapia. The Hôtel-de-Ville had only one killed and two wounded.

The same evening the government closed all the clubs and issued numerous warrants. Eighty-three persons, most of them innocent, were melted. This occasion was also taken advantage of to send Delescluze, notwithstanding his sixty-five years, and an acute bronchitis which was undermining his health, to rejoin the prisoners of the 31st October, thrown pell-mell into a damp dungeon at Vincennes. The *Réveil* and the *Combat* were suppressed.

An indignant proclamation denounced the insurgents as "the partisans of the foreigners," the only resource left the men of the 4th September in this shameful crisis. In this only they were Jacobins. Who served the enemy? The Government ever ready to negotiate, or the men ever offering a desperate resistance? History will tell how at Metz an immense army, with cadres, well-trained soldiers, allowed itself to be given over without a single marshal, *chef-de-corps,* or a regiment rising to save it from Bazaine; whereas the revolutionaries of Paris, without leaders, without organization, before 240,000 soldiers and mobiles gained over to peace, delayed the capitulation for months and revenged it with their blood.

The simulated indignation of traitors raised only a feeling of disgust. Their very name, "Government of Defence," cried out against them. On the very day of the affray they played their last farce. Jules Simon having assembled the mayors and a dozen superior officers, offered the supreme command to the military men who could propose a plan. This Paris, which they had received exuberant with life, the men of the 4th September, now that they had exhausted and bled her, proposed to abandon to others. Not one of those present resented the infamous irony. They confined themselves to refusing this hopeless legacy. This was exactly the thing Jules Simon waited for. Someone muttered, "We must capitulate." It was General Lecomte. The mayors understood why they had been convoked, and a few of them squeezed out a tear.

From this time forth Paris existed like the patient who is expecting amputation. The forts still thundered, the dead and the wounded were still brought in, but Jules Favre was known to be at Versailles. On the 27th at midnight the cannon were silenced. Bismarck and Jules Favre had come to an *honourable* understanding. Paris had surrendered.

The next day the Government of the Defence published the basis of the negotiations — a fortnight's armistice, the immediate convocation of an Assembly, the occupation of the forts, the disarmaments of all the soldiers and mobiles with the exception of one division. The town remained gloomy. These days of anguish had stunned Paris. Only a few demonstrations were made. A battalion of the National Guard came before the Hôtel-de-Ville crying "Down with the traitors!" In the evening, 400 officers signed a pact of resistance, naming as their chief Brunel, an ex-officer expelled from the army under the Empire for his republican opinions, and resolved to march on the forts of the east, commanded by Admiral Saisset, whom the press credited with the reputation of a Beaurepaire. At midnight the call to arms and the alarm bell summoned the tenth, thirteenth, and twentieth arrondissements. But the night was icy cold, the National Guard too enervated for an act of despair. Two or three battalions only came to the rendezvous. Brunel was arrested two days after.

On the 29th January the German flag was hoisted on our forts. All had been signed the evening before. 400,000 men armed with muskets and cannons capitulated before 200,000. The forts, the enceinte were disarmed. Paris was to pay 200,000,000 francs in a fortnight. The Government boasted of having preserved the arms of the National Guard, but every one knew that to take these it would have been necessary to storm Paris. In the end, not content with surrendering Paris, the Government of the National Defence surrendered all France. The armistice applied to all the armies of the provinces save Bourbaki's, the only one that would have profited by it.

On the following days there arrived some news from the provinces. It was known that Bourbaki, pressed by the Prussians, had, after a comedy of suicide, thrown his whole army into Switzerland. The aspect and the weakness of the Delegation of the Defence in the provinces had just began to reveal themselves, when the *Mot d'Ordre* founded by Rochefort, who had abandoned the Government after the 31st October, published a proclamation by Gambetta, stigmatizing a shameful peace, and a whole litany of Radical decrees: ineligibility of all the great functionaries and official deputies of the

Empire; dissolution of the *conseils-généraux,* revocation of some of the judges who had formed part of the mixed commission of the 2nd December. It was ignored that during the whole war the Delegation had acted in contradiction to its last decrees, which, coming from a fallen power, were a mere electoral trick, and Gambetta's name was placed on most of the electoral lists.

Some bourgeois papers supported Jules-Favre and Picard, who had been clever enough to make themselves looked upon as the out-and-outers of the Government; none dared to go so far as to support Trochu, Simon and Ferry. The variety of electoral lists set forth by the republican party explained its impotence during the siege. The men of 1848 refused to accept Blanqui, but admitted several members of the International in order to usurp its name, and their list, a medley of Neo-Jacobins and Socialists, entitled itself "the fist of the Four Committees." The clubs and working men's groups drew up lists of a more outspoken character; one bore the name of the German Socialist deputy, Liebknecht. The most decided one was that of the Corderie.

The International and the Federal Chamber of the working-men's societies, mute and disorganized during the siege, again taking up their programme, said, "We must also have working men amongst those in power." They came to an arrangement with the Committee of the twenty arrondissements, and the three groups issued the same manifesto. "This," said they, "is the list of the candidates presented in the name of a new world by the party of the disinherited. France is about to reconstitute herself; working men have the right to find and take their place in the new order of things. The socialist revolutionary candidatures signify the denial of the right to discuss the existence of the Republic; affirmation of the necessity for the accession of working men to political power; overthrow of the oligarchical Government and of industrial feudalism." Besides a few names familiar to the public, Blanqui, Gambon, Garibaldi, Felix Pyat, Ranvier, Tridon, Longuet, Lefrançais, Vallès, these Socialist candidates were known only in the working men's centres — mechanics, shoemakers, ironfounders, tailors, carpenters, cooks, cabinetmakers, carvers. Their proclamations were but few in number. These disinherited could not compete with bourgeois enterprise. Their day was to come a few weeks later, when two-thirds of them were to be elected to the Commune. Now those only received a mandate who were accepted by the middle-class papers, five in all: Garibaldi, Gambon, Félix Pyat, Tolain, and Malon.

The list of representatives of the 8th February was a harlequinade, including every republican shade and every political crotchet. Louis Blanc, who had played the part of a goody during the siege, and who was supported by all the committees except that of the Corderie, headed the procession with 216,000 votes, followed by Victor Hugo, Gambetta, and Garibaldi; Delescluze obtained 154,000 votes. Then came a motley crowd of Jacobin fossils, radicals, officers, mayors, journalists, and inventors. One single member of the Government slipped in, Jules Favre, although his private life had been exposed by Millière, who was also elected. By a cruel injustice, the vigilant sentinel, the only journalist who during the siege had always shown sagacity, Blanqui, found only 52,000 votes, about the number of those who opposed the plebiscite, while Félix Pyat received 145,000 for his piping in the *Combat.*

This confused incongruous ballot affirmed at least the republican idea. Paris, trampled upon by the Empire and the Liberals, clung to the Republic, who gave her promise for the future. But even before her vote had been proclaimed she heard coming forth from the provincial ballot boxes a savage cry of reaction. Before a single one of her representatives had left the town, she saw on the way to Bordeaux a troop of rustics, of *Pourceaugnacs,* of sombre clericals, spectres of 1815, 1830, 1848, high and low reactionaries, who, mumbling and furious, came by the grace of universal suffrage to take possession of France. What signified this sinister masquerade? How had this subterranean vegetation contrived to pierce and overgrow the summit of the country?

It was that Paris and the provinces should be crushed, that the Prussian Shylock should drain our milliards and cut his pound of flesh, that the state of slew should for four years weigh down upon forty-two departments, that 100,000 Frenchmen should be cut off from life or banished from their native soil, that the black brotherhood should conduct their processions over France, to bring about this great conservative machination, which from the first hour to the last explosion, the revolutionaries of Paris and of the provinces had not ceased to denounce to our treacherous or sluggish governors.

In the provinces the field and the tactics were not the same. The conspiracy, instead of being carried on within the Government, circumvented it. During the whole month of September the reactionaries hid in their lairs. The Government of National Defence had only forgotten one element of defence — the provinces, seventy-six departments. Yet they were agitating, showed life; they alone held in check the reaction. Lyons had even understood her duty earlier than Paris; in the morning of the 4th September she proclaimed the Republic, hoisted the red flag and named a Committee of Public Safety. Marseilles and Toulouse organized regional commissions. The Defenders understood nothing of this patriotic zeal, thought France disjointed, and delegated to put it right again two very tainted relics, Crémieux and Glais-Bizoin, together with a former governor of Cayenne, the Bonapartist Admiral Fourichon.

They reached Tours on the 18th. The patriots hastened thither to meet them. In the west and south, they had already organized Leagues to marshal the departments against the enemy and supply the want of a central impulse. They surrounded the delegates of Paris, asking them for orders, vigorous measures, the sending of commissioners, and promised their absolute co-operation. The scoundrels answered, "We are face to face, let us speak frankly. Well, then, we have no longer any army; all resistance is impossible. We only hold out for the sake of making better conditions." We ourselves witnessed the scene. There was but one cry of indignation: "What! is this your answer when thousands of Frenchmen come to offer you their lives and fortunes?"

On the 28th, the Lyonese broke out. Hardly four departments separated them from the enemy, who might at any moment come to levy a contribution on their city, and since the 4th September they had in vain demanded arms. The municipality, elected on the 16th in place of the Committee of Public Safety, passed its time in squabbling with the Prefect, Challemel-Lacour, an arrogant Neo-Jacobin. On the 27th, instead of any serious measures of defence, the council had reduced by five-pence the pay of the working men employed in the fortifications, and appointed Cluseret general without troops of an army to be created.

The Republican committees of Les Brotteaux, of La Guillotière, of La Croix-Rousse, and the Central Committee of the National Guard decided to urge on the Hôtel-de-Ville, and laid before it on the 28th an energetic programme of defence. The working men of the fortifications, led by Saigne, supported this step by a demonstration. They filled the Place des Terreaux, and what with the speeches, what with the excitement, invaded the Hôtel-de-Ville. Saigne proposed the nomination of a revolutionary commission, and perceiving Cluseret, named him commander of the National Guard. Cluseret, much concerned for his future, only appeared on the balcony to propound his Plan and recommend calm. However, the commission being constituted, he no longer dared to resist, but set out in search of his troops. At the door, the mayor, Hénon, and the prefect arrested him. They had penetrated into the Hôtel-de-Ville by the Place de la Comédie. Saigne, springing upon the balcony, announced the news to the crowd, which, throwing itself upon the Hôtel-de-Ville, delivered the prospective general and in turn arrested the mayor and the prefect.

The bourgeois battalions soon arrived at the Place des Terreaux; shortly after those of La Croix-Rousse and of La Guillotière emerged. Great misfortune might have resulted from the first shot. They parleyed. The commission disappeared and the general swooned.

This was a warning. Other symptoms manifested themselves in several towns. The prefects even presided over Leagues and met each other. At the commencement of October, the Admiral of Cayenne had only been able to set on foot 30,000 men, and nothing came from Tours but a decree convoking the election for the 16th.

On the 9th, when Gambetta alighted from his balloon, all the patriots started. The Conservatives, who had begun to creep out of their recesses, quickly drew back again. The ardour and the energy of his first proclamation carried people away. Gambetta held France absolutely; he was all-powerful.

He disposed of the immense resources of France, of innumerable men; of Bourges, Brest, L'Orient, Rochefort, Toulon for arsenals; workshops like Lille, Nantes, Bordeaux, Toulouse, Marseilles, Lyons; the seas free; incomparably greater strength than that of 1793, which had to fight at the same time the foreigner and internal rebellions. The centres were kindling. The municipal councils made themselves felt, the rural districts as yet showing no signs of resistance; the national reserve intact. The burning metal needed only moulding.

The debut of the delegate was a serious blunder. He executed the decree of Paris for the adjournment of the elections, which promised to be republican and bellicose. Bismarck himself had told Jules Favre that he did not want an Assembly, because this Assembly would be for war. Energetic circulars, some measures against the intriguers, formal instructions to the prefects, would have brightened and victoriously brought out this patriotic fervour. An Assembly fortified by all the republican aspirations, vigorously led, sitting in a populous town, would have increased the national energy a hundred-fold, brought to light unhoped-for talents, and might have exacted everything from the country, blood and gold. It would have proclaimed the Republic, and in case of being obliged by reverses to negotiate, would have saved her from foundering, prevented reaction. But Gambetta's instructions were formal. "Elections at Paris would bring back days like June," said he. "We must do without Paris," was our answer. All was useless. Besides, several prefects, incapable of influencing their surroundings, predicted pacific election. Lacking the energy to grapple with the real difficulties of the situation, Gambetta fancied he might shift them by the expedient clap-trap of his dictatorship.

Did he bring a great political revolution? No. His whole programme was. "To maintain order and liberty and push on the war." Crémieux had called the Bonapartists "republicans going astray." Gambetta believed, or pretended to believe, in the patriotism of the reactionaries. A few pontifical zouaves who offered themselves, the abject submission of the Bonapartist generals, the wheedling of a few bishops, sufficed to delude him. He continued the tactics of his predecessors, to conciliate everybody; he spared even the functionaries. In the department of Finance and Public Instruction, he and his colleagues forbade the dismissal of any official. The War Office for a long time remained under the supreme direction of a Bonapartist, and always carried on an underhand war against the defence. Gambetta maintained in some prefectures the same employees who had drawn up the proscription lists of the 2nd December, 1851. With the exception of a few justices of the peace and a small number of magistrates, nothing was changed in the political personnel, the whole subordinate administration remaining intact.

Was he wanting in authority? His colleagues of the council did not even dare to raise their voices; the prefects knew only him; the generals put on the manner of school boys in his presence. Was a personnel wanting? The Leagues contained solid elements; the petty bourgeoisie and proletariat might have given the cadres.

Gambetta saw here only obstacles, chaos, federalism, and roughly dismissed their delegates. Each department possessed groups of known, tried republicans, to whom the administration and the part of spurring the Defence under the direction of commissioners might have been entrusted. Gambetta refused almost everywhere to refer to them; the few whom he appointed he knew how to fetter closely. He vested all power in the prefects, most of them ruins of 1848, or his colleagues of the Conférence Molé, nerveless, loquacious, timorous, anxious to have themselves well spoken of, and many anxious to feather themselves a nest in their department.

The Defence in the provinces set out on these two crutches — the War Office and the prefects. On this absurd plan of conciliation the Government was conducted.

Did the new delegate at least bring a powerful military conception? "No one in the Government, neither General Trochu nor General Leflô, no one had suggested a military operation of any kind." Did he at least possess that quick penetration which makes up for want of experience? After twenty days in the provinces he comprehended the military situation no better than he had done at Paris. The capitulation of Metz drew from him indignant proclamations, but he understood no more than his colleagues of the Hôtel-de-Ville that this was the very moment to make a supreme effort.

With the exception of three divisions (30,000) men and the greater part of their cavalry, the Germans had been obliged to employ for the investment of Paris all their troops, and they had no reserve left them. The three divisions at Orléans and Châteaudun were kept in check by our forces of the Loire. The cavalry, while infesting a large extent of territory in the west, north and east, could not hold out against infantry. At the end of October, the army before Paris, strongly fortified against the town, was not at all covered from the side of the provinces. The appearance of 50,000 men, even of young troops, would have forced the Prussians to raise the blockade.

Moltke was far from disregarding the danger. He had decided in case of need to raise the blockade, to sacrifice the park of artillery then being formed at Villecoublay, to concentrate his army for action in the open country, and only to re-establish the blockade after the victory, that is to say, after the arrival of the army of Metz. "Everything was ready for our decampment; we only had to team the horses," reported an eye-witness, the Swiss Colonel D'Erlach. The official papers of Berlin had already prepared public opinion for this event.

The blockade of Paris raised, even momentarily, might have led, under the pressure of Europe, to an honourable peace; this was almost certain. Paris and France recovering their salutary buoyancy, the revictualling of the great town, and the consequent prolongation of her resistance, would have given the time necessary for the organization of the provincial armies.

At the end of October our army of the Loire was in progress of formation, the 15th corps at Salbris, the 16th at Blois, already numbering 80,000 men. If it had driven through between the Bavarians at Orléans and the Prussians at Châteaudun; if — and this was an easy matter with its numerical superiority — it would have beaten the enemy one after another, the route to Paris would have been thrown open, and the deliverance of Paris almost sure.

The Delegation of Tours did not see so far. It confined its efforts to recovering Orléans, in order to establish there an entrenched camp; so on the 26th General D'Aurelles de Paladines, named by Gambetta commander-in-chief of the two corps, received the order to rescue the town from the Bavarians. He was a senator, a bigoted, rabid reactionary, at best fit only to be an officer of zouaves, fuming in his heart at the defence. It was resolved to make the attack from Blois instead of conducting the 15th corps on foot, which by Romorantin would have taken forty-eight hours, the Delegation sent it by the Vierzon railway to Tours, a journey which took five days and could not be hidden from the enemy. Still, on the 28th, D'Aurelles encamped before Blois, with at least 40,000 men, and the next day he was to have left for Orléans.

On the 28th, at nine o'clock in the evening, the commander of the German troops had him informed of the capitulation of Metz. D'Aurelles, jumping at this pretext, telegraphed to Tours that he should call off his movement.

A general of some ability, of some good faith, would, on the contrary, have precipitated everything. Since the army before Metz, now disengage, would swoop down upon the centre of France, there was not a day to lose to get ahead of it. Every hour told. This was the critical juncture of the war.

The delegation of Tours was as foolish as D'Aurelles. Instead of dismissing him, it contented itself with moans, ordering him to concentrate his forces. This concentration was terminated on the 3rd November. D'Aurelles then had 70,000 men established from Mer to Marchenoir. He might have aired before events overtook him. That very day a whole brigade of Prussian cavalry had been obliged to abandon Mantes and to retreat before bands of franc-tieurs; French forces were observed to be marching from Courville in the direction of Chartres. D'Aurelles did not stir, and the Delegation remained as paralysed as he. "M. le Ministre", wrote on the 4th November the Delegate at War, M. de Freycinet, "for some days the army and myself do not know if the Government wants peace or war. At this Moment, when we are just disposing ourselves to accomplish projects laboriously Prepared, rumours of an armistice disturb the minds of our generals, and I myself, I seek to revive their spirits and push them on, I know not whether the next day I shall not be disavowed by the Government."

Gambetta the same day answered: "I agree with you as to the detestable influence of the political hesitations of the Government. From today we must decide on our march forward;" and on the 7th D'Aurelles still remained motionless. At last, on the 8th, he set out, and went about fifteen kilometres, and in the evening again spoke of making a halt. All his forces togethered 100,000 men. On the 9th he made up his mind to attack at Coulmiers. The Bavarians immediately evacuated Orléans. Far from pursuing them, D'Aurelles announced that he was going to fortify himself before the town. The Delegation let him do as he liked, and gave him no orders to pursue the enemy. Three days after the battle Gambetta came to the headquarters and approved of D'Aurelle's plan. The Bavarians during this respite had fallen back upon Toury, and two divisions hurried from Metz by the railway arrived before Paris. Moltke could at his ease direct the 17th Prussian division towards Toury, where it arrived on the 12th. Three other corps of the army of Metz approached the Seine by forced marches. The ignorance of the Delegation, the obstruction of Trochu, the ill-will and blunders of D'Aurelles, frustrated the only chances of raising the blockade of Paris.

On the 19th, the army of Metz protected the blockade in the north and in the south. Henceforth the Delegation had but one part to play — to prepare sound, manoeuvrable armies for France, and find the necessary time for this, as in ancient times the Romans did, and in our days the Americans. It preferred bolstering up vain appearances, amusing public opinion with the din of arms, imagining that they could thus puzzle the Prussians also. It threw upon them men raised but a few days before, without instruction, without discipline, without instruments of war, fatally destined to defeat. The prefects charged with the organization of the mobiles, and those on the point of being mobilized, were in continual strife with the generals, and lost themselves in the details of the equipments. The generals, unable to make anything of those ill-supplied contingents, only advanced on compulsion. Gambetta on his arrival had said in his proclamation "We will make young leaders," and the important commands were given to the men of the Empire, worn out, ignorant, knowing nothing of patriotic wars. To these young recruits, who should have been electrified by stirring appeals, D'Aurelles preached the word of the Lord and the interest of the service. The accomplice of Bazaine, Bourbaki, on his return from England, received the command of the army of the East. The weakness of the new Delegate encouraged the resistance of all malcontents. Gambetta asked the officers whether they would accept service under Garibaldi; he not only allowed them to refuse, but even released a curé who in the pulpit had set a price on the General's head. He humbly explained to the royalist officers that the question at issue was not to defend the Republic but the territory. He gave leave to the pontifical zouaves to hoist the banner of the Sacred Heart. He suffered Admiral Fourichon to contend for the disposal of the navy with the Delegation. He indignantly rejected every project for an enforced loan, and refused to sanction those voted in some departments. He left the railway companies masters of the transport, in the hands of reactionaries, always ready to raise difficulties. From the end of November, these boisterous and contradictory orders, these accumulations of impracticable decrees, these powers given and taken back, clearly proved that only a sham resistance was meant.

The country obeyed, giving everything with passive blindness. The contingents were raised without difficulty; there were no refractory recruits in rural districts, although the gendarmerie were absent with the army; the Leagues had given way on the first remonstrance. There .was only a movement on the 31st October. The Marseilles revolutionaries, indignant at the weakness of their Municipal Council, proclaimed the Commune. Cluseret, who from Geneva had asked the "Prussian" Gambetta for the command of an army corps, appeared at Marseilles, got himself named general, again backed out and retired to Switzerland, his dignity forbidding him to serve as a simple soldier. At Toulouse, the population expelled the general. At Saint-Etienne the Commune existed for an hour. But everywhere a word sufficed to replace the authority in the hands of the Delegation; such was the apprehension of everybody of creating the slightest embarrassment. . This abnegation only served the reactionaries. The Jesuits, who resumed their intrigues, had been reinstated by Gambetta at Marseilles, whence the indignation of the people had expelled them. The delegate cancelled the suspension of papers that published letters from Chambord and D'Aumale. He protected the judges who had formed part of the mixed commission" released the one who had decimated the department of the Var, and dismissed the prefect of Toulouse for having suspended the functions of another in the Haute-Garonne. The Bonapartists mustered again. When the prefect of Bordeaux, an ultra-moderate Liberal, asked for the authorization to arrest some of their ringleaders, Gambetta severely answered him, "These are practices of the Empire, not of the Republic." Crémieux, too, said, "The Republic is the reign of law."

Then the Conservative Vendée arose. Monarchists, clericals, capitalists, waited for their time; cowering in their castles, all their strongholds remained intact; seminaries, tribunals, general councils, which for a long time the Delegation refused to dissolve *en masse.* They were clever enough to figure here and there in the field of battle, in order to preserve the appearance of patriotism. In a few weeks they had seen through Gambetta and found out the Liberal behind the Tribune.

Their campaign was laid and conducted by the only serious political tacticians France possesses — by the Jesuits, masters of the clergy. The arrival of M. Thiers provided the apparent leader.

The men of the 4th September had made him their ambassador. France, almost without diplomatists since Talleyrand, has never possessed one more easily gulled than this little man. He had gone naively to London, to

Petersburg, to Italy, whose inveterate enemy he had always been, begging for vanquished France alliances which had been refused her when yet intact. He was trifled with everywhere. He obtained but one interview with Bismarck, and negotiated the armistice rejected by the 31st October. When he arrived at Tours in the first days of November, he knew that peace was impossible, and that henceforth it must be war to the knife. Instead of courageously making the best of it, of placing his existence at the service of the Delegation, he had but one object, to baffle the defence.

It could not have had a more redoubtable enemy. The success of this man, without ideas, without principles of government, without comprehension of progress, without courage, would have been impossible everywhere, save with the French bourgeoisie. But he has always been at hand when a Liberal was wanted to shoot down the people, and he is a wonderful artist in Parliamentary intrigue. No one has known like him how to attack, to isolate a Government, to group prejudices hatred, and interests, to hide his intrigues behind a mask of patriotism and common sense. The campaign of 1870-71 will certainly be his masterpiece. He had made up his mind as to the lion's share due to the Prussians, and took no more notice of them than they had crossed the Moselle. For him the enemy was the defender. When our poor mobiles, without cadres, without military training, succumbed to a temperature as fatal as that of 1812, M. Thiers exulted at our disasters. His house had become headquarters for the Conservative notabilities. At Bordeaux especially it seemed to be the true seat of Government.

Before the investment the reactionary press of Paris had no provincial service, and from the outset cooled down the Delegation. After the arrival of M. Thiers it carried on a regular war. It never ceased harassing, accusing, pointing out the slightest shortcomings, with a view not to instruct, but to slander, and to wind up by the foregone conclusion: Fighting is madness, disobedience legitimate. From the middle of December this watchword, faithfully followed by all the papers of the party, spread over the rural districts.

For the first time country squires found their way to the ear of the peasant. This war was about to draw off all the men who were not in the army or in the Garde Mobile, and camps were being prepared to receive them. The prisons of Germany held 260,000 men; Paris, the Loire, the army of the East, more than 350,000. Thirty thousand were dead, and thousands filled the hospitals. Since the month of August France had given at least 700,000 men. Where are they to stop? This cry was echoed in every cottage: "It is the Republic that wants war! Paris is in the hands of the *levellers*." What does the French peasant know of his fatherland, and how many could say where Alsace lies? It is he above all whom the bourgeoisie have in view when they resist compulsory education. For eighty years all their efforts tended to transform into coolies the descendants of the volunteers of 1792.

Before long a spirit of revolt infected the mobiles, almost everywhere commanded by noted reactionaries. Here an equerry of the Emperor, there rabid royalists led battalions. In the army of the Loire they muttered, "We will not fight for M. Gambetta." Officers of the mobilized troops boasted of never having exposed the lives of their men.

In the beginning of 1871 the provinces were undermined from end to end. Some general councils that had been dissolved met publicly, declaring that they considered themselves elected. The Delegation followed the progress of this enemy, cursed M. Thiers in private, but took good care not to arrest him. The revolutionaries who came to tell it the lengths things were going to were curtly shown out. Gambetta, worn out, not believing in the defence, thought only of conciliating the men of influence and rendering himself acceptable for the future.

At the signal of the elections, the scenery, laboriously prepared, appeared all of a piece, showing the Conservatives grouped, supercilious, their lists ready. We were far now from the month of October, when, in many departments, they had not dared to put forward their candidates. The decrees on the ineligibility of the high Bonapartist functionaries only affected shadows. The coalition, disdaining the broken-down men of the Empire, had carefully formed a personnel of pig-tailed nobles, well-to-do farmers, captains of industry, men likely to do the work bluntly. The clergy had skilfully united on their lists the Legitimists and Orleanists, perhaps laid down the basis for a fusion. The vote was carried like a plebiscite. lie republicans tried to speak of an honourable peace; the peasants would only hear of peace at any price. The towns knew hardly how to make a stand; at the utmost elected Liberals. Out of 750 members, the Assembly counted 450 born monarchists. The apparent chief of the campaign, the king of Liberals, M. Thiers, was returned in twenty-three departments.

The conciliator *à outrance* could rival Trochu. The one had worried out Paris, the other the Republic.

Chapter 1
The Prussians enter Paris

Neither the head of the executive power, nor the National Assembly, supporting and strengthening one another, did anything to provoke the Paris insurrection. (Dufaure's speech against amnesty, session of 18th May, 1876.)

The invasion brought back the *Chambre introuvable* of 1816 [ultra-right wing parliament under the Bourbon restoration in 1816]. After having dreamt of a regenerated France soaring towards the light, to feel oneself hurled back half a century, under the yoke of the Jesuits of the Congregation, of the brutal rurals! There were men who lost heart. Many spoke of expatriating themselves. The thoughtless said, "The Chamber will only last a day, since it has no mandate but to decide on peace and war." Those, however, who had watched the progress of the conspiracy and the leading part taken in it by the clergy, knew beforehand that these men would not allow France to escape their clutches before they crushed her.

Men just escaped from famine-stricken but ardent Paris found in the Bordeaux Assembly the Coblentz of the first emigration, but this time invested with the power to glut rancours that had been accumulating for forty years. Clericals and Conservatives were for the first time allowed, without the interference of either emperor or king, to trample to their hearts' content on atheistic, revolutionary Paris, which had so often shaken off their yoke and baffled their schemes. At the first sitting their choler burst out. At the farther end of the hall, sitting alone on his bench, shunned by all, an old man rose and asked to address the Assembly. Under his cloak glared a red shirt. It was Garibaldi. At the call of his name, he wished to answer, to say in a few words that he resigned the mandate with which Paris had honoured him. His voice drowned in howls. He remained standing, raising his hand, but the insults redoubled. The chastisement, however, was at hand. "Rural majority! disgrace of France!" cried from the gallery, a young vibrating voice, that of Gaston Crémieux, of Marseilles. The deputies rose threatening. Hundreds of "Bravos" answered from the galleries, overwhelming the rurals. After the sitting the crowd cheered Garibaldi and hooted his insulters. The National Guard presented arms, despite the rage of M. Thiers, who under the peristyle railed at the commanding officer. The next day the people returned, forming lines in front of the theatre, and forced the reactionary deputies to undergo their republican cheers. But they knew their strength, and from the beginning of the sittings opened their attack. One of the rurals, pointing to the representatives of Paris, cried, "They are stained with the blood of civil war!" And when one of these representatives cried, *Vive la République!* the majority hooted him, saying, "You are only a fraction of the country." On the next day the Chamber was surrounded by troops, who kept off the republicans.

At the same time the Conservative papers united in their hissings against Paris, denying even her sufferings. The National Guard, they said, had fled before the Prussians; its only exploits had been the 31st October and 22nd January. These calumnies fructified in the provinces, long since prepared to receive them. Such was their ignorance of the siege, that they had named some of them several times — Trochu, Ducrot, Ferry, Pelletan, Garnier-Pages, Emmanuel Arago — to whom Paris had refused a single vote.

It was the duty of the Parisian representatives to clear up this darkness, to recount the siege, to denounce the men responsible for the failure of the defence, to explain the significance of the Parisian vote, to unfurl the flag of republican France against the clerico-monarchical coalition. They remained silent, contenting themselves with puerile party meetings, from which Delescluze turned away as heartbroken as from the Assembly of the Paris mayors. Our Epimenides of 1848 answered with stereotyped humanitarian phrases the clashing of arms of the enemy, who all the while affirmed his programme: to patch up a peace, to bury the Republic, and for that purpose to checkmate Paris. Thiers was named chief of the executive power with general acclamation, and chose for his Ministers Jules Favre, Jules Simon, Picard and Leflô, who might still pass muster with the provincial republicans.

These elections, these menaces, these insults to Garibaldi, to the Paris representatives; Thiers, the incarnation of the Parliamentary monarchy, as first magistrate of the Republic — blow after blow was struck at Paris, a feverish, hardly revictualled Paris, hungering still more for liberty than bread. This then was the reward for five months of suffering and endurance. These provinces, which Paris had invoked in vain during the whole siege, dared now to brand her with cowardice, to throw her back from Bismark to Chambord. Well, then, Paris was resolved to defend herself even against France. The new, imminent danger, the hard experience of the siege, had exalted her energy and endowed the great town with one collective soul.

Already, towards the end of January, some republicans, and also some bourgeois intriguers in search of a mandate, had tried to group the National Guards with a view to the elections. A large meeting, presided over by Courty, a merchant of the third arrondissement, had been held in the Cirque. They had there drawn up a list, decided to meet again to deliberate in case of double electoral returns, and had named a committee charged to convoke all the companies regularly. This second meeting was held on the 15th in the Vauxhall, Douané Street. But who then thought of the elections? One single thought prevailed: the union of all Parisian forces against the triumphant rurals. The National Guard represented all the manhood of Paris. The clear, simple, essentially French idea of confederating the battalions had long been in every mind. It was received with acclamation and resolved that the confederate battalions should be grouped round a Central Committee.

A commission during the same sitting was charged to elaborate the statutes. Each arrondissement represented — eighteen out of twenty — named a commissar. Who were these men? The agitators, the revolutionaries of La Corderie, the Socialists? No; there was not a known name amongst them. All those elected were men of the middle classes, shopkeepers, employees, strangers to the coteries, till now for the most part strangers even to politics. Courty, the president, was known only since the meeting at the Cirque. From the first day the idea of the federation appeared what it was — universal, not sectarian, and therefore powerful. The next day, Clément-Thomas declared to the Government that he could no longer be answerable for the National Guard, and sent in his resignation. He was provisionally replaced by Vinoy.

On the 24th, in the Vauxhall, before 2,000 delegates and guards, the commission read the statutes it had drawn up, and pressed the delegates to proceed immediately to the election of the Central Committee. The Assembly was tempestuous, disquiet, little inclined for calm deliberations. Each of the last eight days had brought with it more insulting menaces from Bordeaux. They were going, it was said, to disarm the battalions, suppress the thirty sous, the only resource of the working men, and exact at once the arrears of rent and overdue commercial bills. Besides, the armistice, prolonged for a week, was to expire on the 26th, and the papers announced that the Prussians would enter Paris on the 27th. For a week this nightmare had weighed on all the patriots. The meeting, too, proceeded at once to consider these burning questions. Varlin proposed: The National Guard only recognizes the leaders elected by itself. Another: The National Guard protests through the Central Committee against any attempt at disarmament, and declares that in case of need it will offer armed resistance. Both propositions were voted unanimously. And now, was Paris to submit to the entry of the Prussians, to let them parade her boulevards? It could not even be discussed. The whole assembly, springing up over-excited, raised one cry of war. Some warnings of prudence are disdained. Yes, they would oppose their arms to the entry of the Prussians. The proposition would be submitted by the delegates to their respective companies. And adjourning to the 3rd March, the meeting broke up its sitting and marched *en masse* to the Bastille, carrying along with it a great number of soldiers and mobiles.

Since the morning, Paris, fearing the loss of her liberty, had gathered round her revolutionary column, as she had before crowded round the statue of Strasbourg when trembling for France. The battalions marched past, headed by drums and flags, covering the rails and pedestal with crowns of immortelles. From time to time a delegate ascended the plinth, and from this tribune of bronze harangued the people, who answered with cries of *Vive la République!* Suddenly a red flag was carried through the crowd into the monument, reappearing soon after at the balustrade. A formidable cry saluted it, followed by a long silence. A man, climbing the cupola, had the daring to go and fix it in the hand of the statue of Liberty surmounting the column. Thus, amidst the frantic cheering of the people, for the first time since 1848, the flag of equality overshadowed this spot, redder than its flag by the blood of a thousand martyrs.

The following day the pilgrimages were continued, not only by National Guards, but by the soldiers and mobiles. The army gave way to the inspiration of Paris. The mobiles arrived preceded by their quartermasters carrying large black crowns; the trumpeters, posted at each corner of the pedestal, saluted them, and the crowd cheered them to the echo. Women dressed in black suspended a tricolour flag bearing the inscription, "The republican women to the martyrs." When the pedestal was covered, the crowns and flowers soon wound themselves entirely round the bust, encircling it from top to bottom with yellow and black flowers, red and tricolour oriflammes, symbols of mourning for the past and hope in the future.

On the 26th the demonstrations became innumerable and irritated. A police agent, surprised taking down the names of the battalions, was seized and thrown into the Seine. Twenty-five battalions marched past, sombre, a prey to a terrible anguish. The armistice was about to expire and the *Journal Officiel* did not speak of a prorogation. The journals announced the entry of the German army by the Champs-Elysées for the next day. The Government was sending the troops to the left bank of the Seine and clearing out the Palace de l'Industrie. They forgot only the cannons of the National Guards accumulated at the Place Wagram and at Passy. Already the carelessness of the capitulationists had delivered 12,000 more muskets to the Prussians than were stipulated for. Who could tell if the latter would not stretch out their hands to these fine pieces, cast with the flesh and blood of the Parisians, marked with the numbers of the battalions? Spontaneously all Paris rose. The bourgeois battalions of Passy, in accord with the municipality, set the example, drawing the pieces of the Ranelagh to the Parc Monceaux. Other battalions came to fetch their cannon in the Park Wagram, wheeling them by the Rues St. Honoré and Rivoli to the Place des Vosges, under the protection of the Bastille.

During the day the troop sent by Vinoy to the Bastille had fraternized with the people. In the evening, the rappel, the tocsin, the trumpets had thrown thousands of armed men into the streets, who came to mass themselves at the Bastille, the Château d'Eau, and the Rue de Rivoli. The prison of St. Pélagie was forced and Brunel set free. At two o'clock in the morning, forty thousand men remounted the Champs-Elysées, and the Avenue de la Grande Armée, silent, in good order, to encounter the Prussians. They waited till daybreak. On their return, the battalions of Montmartre seized all the cannon they found on their way, and took them to the *mairie* of the eighteenth arrondissement and to the Boulevard Omano.

To this feverish but chivalrous outburst Vinoy could only oppose an order of the day stigmatizing it. And this Government that insulted Paris, asked her to immolate herself for France! A proclamation posted up on the morning of the 27th announced the prolongation of the armistice, and for the 1st of March the occupation of the Champs-Elysées by 30,000 Germans.

At two o'clock the commission charged to draw up the statutes for a Central Committee held a sitting at the *mairie* of the third arrondissement. Some of its members since the evening before, considering themselves invested with powers by the situation, had tried to organize a permanent sub-committee in this *mairie;* but not being numerous enough, they had adjourned until the next day and consulted the chiefs of the battalions. The sitting, presided over by Captain Bergeret, was stormy. The delegates of the battalion of Montmartre, who had established a committee of their own in the Rue des Rosiers, would speak only of fighting, showed their *mandats impératifs,* and recalled the resolution of the Vauxhall. It was almost unanimously resolved to take up arms against the Prussians. The mayor, Bonvalet, rather uneasy at having such guests, had the *mairie* surrounded, and, half by persuasion, half by force, succeeded in getting rid of them.

During the whole day the faubourgs had armed and seized the munitions; the rampart pieces were remounted on their carriages; the mobiles, forgetting that they were prisoners of war, went to retake their arms. In the evening one crowd inveigled the marines of La Pepinière Barracks and led them to the Bastille to fraternize with the people.

A catastrophe was inevitable but for the courage of a few men who dared to oppose this dangerous current. All the societies that met at the Place de la Corderie, the Central Committee of the twenty arrondissements, the International, and the Federation, looked with reserve upon this Central Committee, composed of unknown men, who had never taken part in the revolutionary campaigns. On leaving the *mairie* of the third arrondissement, some delegates of battalions who belonged to the sections of the International came to the Corderie to tell of the sitting and the desperate resolution come to. Every exertion was made to pacify them, and speakers were sent to the Vauxhall, where a large meeting was being held; they succeeded in making themselves heard. Many other citizens made great efforts to recall the people to reason. The next morning, the 28th. the three groups of the Corderie published a manifesto conjuring the working men to beware. "Every attack," said they, "would serve to expose the people to the blows of the enemies of the Revolution, who would drown all social demands in a sea of blood." Pressed on all sides, the Central Committee was obliged to yield, as it announced in a proclamation signed by twenty-nine names. "Every aggression would result in the immediate overthrow of the Republic. Barricades will be established all round the quarters to be occupied by the enemy, so he will parade in a camp shut out from our town." This was the first official appearance of the Central Committee. The twenty-nine unknown men capable of thus pacifying the National Guard were applauded even by the bourgeoisie, who did not seem to wonder at their power.

The Prussians entered Paris on the 1st March. This Paris which the people had taken possession of was no longer the Paris of the nobles and the great bourgeoisie of 1815. Black flags hung from the houses, but the deserted streets, the closed shops, the dried-up fountains, the veiled statues of the Place de la Concorde, the gas not lighted at night, still more pregnantly announced a town in its agony. Prostitutes who ventured into the quarters of the enemy were publicly whipped. A café in the Champs-Elysées which had opened its doors to the victors was ransacked. There was but one *grand seigneur* in the Faubourg St. Germain to offer his house to the Prussians.

Paris was still wincing under this affront, when a new avalanche of insults poured down upon her from Bordeaux. Not only had the Assembly not found a word or act to help her in this painful crisis, but its papers, the *Journal Officiel* at their head, were indignant that she should have thought of defending herself against the Prussians. A proposition was being signed in the bureaux to fix the seat of the Assembly outside of Paris. The projected law on overdue bills and house-rents opened the prospect of numberless failures. Peace had been accepted, hurriedly voted like an ordinary business. Alsace, the greater part of Lorraine, 1,600,000 Frenchmen torn from their fatherland, five milliards to pay, the forts to the east of Paris to be-occupied till the payment of the first 500,000,000 francs, and the departments of the East till the entire payment; this was what Trochu, Favre, and the coalition cost us, the price for which Bismarck permitted us the *Chambre introuvable*. And to console Paris for so much disgrace, M. Thiers appointed as General of the National Guard the incapable and brutal commander of the first army of the Loire, D'Aurelles de Paladines. Two senators, Vinoy and D'Aurelles, two

Bonapartists, at the head of Republican Paris — this was too much. All Paris had the presentiment of a *coup-d'éitat*.

That evening there were large groups gathered in the boulevards. The National Guards, refusing to acknowledge D'Aurelles as their commander, proposed the appointment of Garibaldi. On the 3rd two hundred battalions sent their delegates to Vauxhall. Matters began with the reading of the statutes. The preamble declared the Republic "the only Government by law and justice superior to universal suffrage, which is its offspring." "The delegates," said Article 6, "must prevent every attempt whose object would be the overthrow of the Republic." The Central Committee was composed of three delegates for each arrondissement, elected by the companies, battalions, legions and of the *chefs-de-légion*. While awaiting the regular election, the meeting there and then named a provisional executive committee. Varlin, Pindy, Jacques Durand, and some other Socialists of the Corderie formed part of it, an understanding having been come to between the Central Committee, or rather the commission which had drawn up the statutes, and the three groups of the Corderie. Varlin carried a unanimous vote on the immediate re-election of the officers of the National Guard. Another motion was put: "That the department of the Seine constitute itself an independent republic in case of the Assembly attempting to decapitalize Paris," — a motion unsound in its conception, faultily drawn up, which seemed to isolate Paris from the rest of France — an anti-revolutionist, anti-Parisian idea, cruelly exploited against the Commune. Who then was to feed Paris if not the provinces? Who was to save our peasants if not Paris? But Paris had been confined to solitary life for six months; she alone to the last moment had declared for the continuation of the struggle at any price, alone affirmed the Republic by a vote. Her abandonment, the vote of the provinces, the rural majority, made so many men ready to die for the universal republic, fancy that the Republic might be shut up within Paris.

Chapter 2
The coalition opens fire on Paris

The Republic was threatened by the Assembly, it was said. Gentlemen, when the insurrection broke out, the Assembly was noted politically by only two acts: nominating the head of the executive power and accepting a republican cabinet. (Speech against amnesty by Larcy of the Centre Left, session of 18th May, 1876.)

To the rural plebiscite the Parisian National Guard had answered by their federation; to the threats of the monarchists, to the projects of decapitalization, by the demonstration of the Bastille; to D'Aurelles' appointment, by the resolutions of the 3rd March. What the perils of the siege had not been able to effect the Assembly had brought about — the union of the middle class with the proletariat. The immense majority of Paris looked upon the growing army of the Republic without regret. On the 3rd the Minister of the Interior, Picard, having denounced "the anonymous Central Committee," and called upon "all good citizens to stifle these culpable demonstrations," no one stirred. Besides, the accusation was ridiculous. The Committee showed itself in the open day, sent its minutes to the papers, and had only held a demonstration to save Paris from a catastrophe. It answered the next day: "The Committee is not anonymous; it is the union of the representatives of free men aspiring to the solidarity of all the members of the National Guard. Its acts have always been signed. It repels with contempt the calumnies which accuse it of inciting to pillage and civil war." The signatures followed.

The leaders of the coalition saw clearly which way events were drifting. The republican army each day increased its arsenal of muskets, and especially of cannon. There were now pieces of ordnance at ten different places — at the Barrière d'Italie, at the Faubourg St. Antoine, at the Buttes Montmartre. Red posters informed Paris of the formation of the Central Committee of the federation of the National Guards, and invited citizens to organize in each arrondissement committees of battalions and councils of legions, and to appoint the delegates to the Central Committee. The ensemble, the ardour of the movement seemed to bear witness to the powerful organization of the Central Committee. A few days more and the answer of the people would be complete if a blow were not struck at once.

What they misunderstood was the stout heart of the enemy. The victory of the 22nd January blinded them. They believed in the stories of their journals, in the cowardice of the National Guards, in the bragging of Ducrot, who, in the bureaux of the Assembly swore eternal hatred to the demagogues, but for whom, he said, he would have conquered. The bullies of the reaction fancied they could swallow Paris at a mouthful.

The operation was conducted with clerical skill, method, and discipline. Legitimists and Orleanists, disagreeing as to the name of the monarch, had accepted the compromise of Thiers, an equal share in the Government, which was called "the pact of Bordeaux." Besides, against Paris there could be no division.

From the commencement of March the provincial papers held forth at the same time, speaking of incendiarism and pillage in Paris. On the 4th there was but one rumour in the bureaux of the Assembly — that an insurrection had broken out; that the telegraphic communications were cut off; that General Vinoy had retreated to the left bank of the Seine. The Government, which propagated these rumours despatched four deputies, who were also mayors, to Paris. They arrived on the 5th, and found Paris perfectly calm, even gay. The mayors and adjuncts, assembled by the Minister of the Interior, attested to the tranquillity of the town. But Picard, no doubt in the conspiracy, said, "This tranquillity is only apparent. We must act." And the ultra-Conservative Vautrain added, "We must take the bull by the horns and arrest the Central Committee."

The Right never ceased baiting the bull. Sneers, provocations, insults, were showered upon Paris and her representatives. Some among them, Rochefort, Tridon, Malon, and Ranc, when withdrawing after the vote mutilating the country, were followed by cries of "Pleasant journey to you." Victor Hugo defending Garibaldi was hooted. Delescluze demanding the impeachment of the members of the National Defence was no better listened to. Jules Simon declared that he would maintain the law against association. On the 10th the breach was opened. A resolution was passed that Paris should no longer be the capital, and that the Assembly should sit at Versailles.

This was calling forth the Commune, for Paris could not remain at the same time without a Government and without a municipality. The field of battle once found, despair was to supply it with an army. The Government had already decided to continue the pay of the National Guards to those only who should ask for it. The Assembly decreed that the bills due on the 13th November, 1870, should be made payable on the 13th March, that is, in three days. The Minister Dufaure obstinately refused any concession on this point. Notwithstanding the urgent appeals of Millière, the Assembly refused to pass any protective bill for the tenants whose house-rents had been due for six months. Two or three hundred thousand workmen, shopkeepers, model makers, small manufacturers working in their own lodgings, who had spent their little stock of money and could not yet earn any more, all business being at a standstill, were thus thrown upon the tender mercies of the landlord, of hunger and bankruptcy. From the 13th to the 17th of March 150,000 bills were dishonoured. Finally, the Right obliged M. Thiers to declare from the tribune "that the Assembly could proceed to its deliberations at Versailles without fearing the paving stones of rioters," thus constraining him to act at once, for the deputies were to meet again at Versailles on the 20th.

D'Aurelles commenced operations against the National Guard, declaring he would submit it to rigorous discipline and purge it of its bad elements. "My first duty," said his order of the day, "is to secure the respect due to law and property" — this eternal provocation on the part of the bourgeoisie when lifted to supreme power by revolutionary events.

The other senators also joined in. On the 7th Vinoy threw into the streets with a pittance of eight shillings a head the twenty-one thousand mobiles of the Seine. On the 11th, the day on which Paris learnt of her decapitation and the ruinous decrees, Vinoy suppressed six Republican journals, four of which, *Le Cri du Peuple, Le Mot d'Ordre, Le Père Duchêne,* and *Le Vengeur,* had a circulation of 200,000. The same day the court-martial which judged the accused of the 31st October condemned several to death, among others Flourens and Blanqui. Thus everybody was hit — bourgeois, republicans, revolutionaries. This Assembly of Bordeaux, the deadly foe of Paris, a stranger to her in sentiment, mind, and language, seemed a Government of foreigners. The commercial quarters as well as the faubourgs rang with a general outcry against it.

From this time the last hesitation disappeared. The mayor of Montmartre, Clémenceau, had been intriguing for several days to effect the surrender of the cannon, and he had even found officers disposed to capitulate; but the battalion protested, and on the 12th, when D'Aurelles sent his teams, the guards refused to deliver the pieces. Picard, making an attempt at firmness, sent for Courty, saying, "The members of the Central Committee are risking their heads," and obtained a quasi-promise. The Committee expelled Courty.

It had since the 6th met at the hall of the Corderie. Although keeping aloof from, and entirely independent of, the three other groups, the reputation of the place was useful to it. It gave evidence of good policy and baffled the intrigues of the commandant, Du Bisson, an officer who had served abroad and been employed in undertakings of an equivocal character, and who was trying to constitute a Central Committee from above with the battalion leaders. The Central Committee sent three delegates to this group, where they met with lively opposition. One chief of battalion, Barberet, showed himself particularly restive; but another, Faltot, carried away the Assembly, saying, "I am going over to the people." The fusion was concluded on the 10th, the day of the general meeting of the delegates. The Committee presented its weekly report. It recounted the events of the last days, the nomination of D'Aurelles, the menaces of Picard, remarking very justly, "That which we are, events have made us: the reiterated attacks of a press hostile to democracy have taught it, the menaces of the Government have confirmed it; we are the inexorable barrier raised against every attempt at the overthrow of the Republic." The delegates were invited to push forward the elections of the Central Committee. An appeal to the army was drawn up: "Soldiers, children of the people! Let us unite to serve the Republic. Kings and emperors have done us harm enough." The next day the soldiers lately arrived from the army of the Loire gathered in front of these red posters, which bore the names and addresses of all the members of the Committee.

The Revolution, bereft of its newspapers spoke now through posters, of the greatest variety of colour and opinion, plastered on all the walls. Flourens and Blanqui, condemned in contumacy, posted up their protestations. Sub-committees were being formed in all the popular arrondissements. That of the thirteenth arrondissement had for its leader a young iron founder, Duval, a man of cold and commanding energy. The sub-committee of the Rue des Rosiers surrounded their cannon by a ditch and had them guarded day and night. All these committees quashed the orders of D'Aurelles and were the true commanders of the National Guard.

No doubt Paris was roused, ready to redeem her abdication during the siege. This Paris, lean and oppressed by want, adjourned peace and business, thinking only of the Republic. The provisional Central Committee, without troubling itself about Vinoy, who had demanded the arrest of all its members, presented itself on the 15th at the general assembly of the Vauxhall. Two hundred and fifteen battalions were represented, and acclaimed Garibaldi as commander-in-chief of the National Guard. An orator, Lullier, led the Assembly astray. He was an ex-naval officer, completely crack-brained, with a semblance of military instruction, and when not heated by alcohol having intervals of lucidity which might deceive any one. He was named commanding colonel of the artillery. Then came the names of those elected members of the Central Committee, about thirty in all, for several arrondissements had not yet voted. This was the regular Central Committee which was to be installed at the Hôtel-de-Ville. Many of those elected had formed part of the preceding commission. The others were all equally obscure, belonging to the proletariat and small middle class, known only to their battalions.

What mattered their obscurity? The Central Committee was not a Government at the head of a party. It had no Utopia to initiate. A very simple idea, fear of the monarchy, could alone have grouped together so many battalions. The National Guard constituted itself an assurance company against a *coup-d'état;* for if Thiers and his agents repeated the word "Republic," their own party and the Assembly cried *Vive le Roi!* The Central Committee was a sentinel, that was all.

The storm was gathering; all was uncertain. The International convoked the Socialist deputies to ask them what to do. But no attack was planned, nor even suggested. The Central Committee formally declared that the first shot would not be fired by the people, and that they would only defend themselves in case of aggression.

The aggressor, M. Thiers, arrived on the 15th. For a long time he had foreseen that it would be necessary to engage in a terrible struggle with Paris; but he intended acting at his own good time, to retake the town when disposing of an army of forty thousand men, well picked, carefully kept aloof from the Parisians. This plan has been revealed by a general officer. At that moment Thiers had only the mere wreck of an army.

The 230,000 men disarmed by the capitulation, mostly mobiles or men having finished their term of service, had been sent home in hot haste, as they would only have swelled the Parisian army. Already some mobiles, marines, and soldiers had laid the basis of a republican association with the National Guards. There remained to Vinoy only the division allowed him by the Prussians and 3,000 sergeants-de-ville or gendarmes, in all 15,000 men, rather ill-conditioned. Lefô sent him a few thousand men picked up in the armies of the Loire and of the North, but they arrived slowly, almost without cadres, harassed, and disgusted at the service. At Vinoy's very first review they were on the point of mutinying. They left them straggling through Paris, abandoned, mixing with the Parisians, who succoured them, the women bringing them soup and blankets to their huts, where they were freezing. In fact, on the 19th the Government had only about 25,000 men, without cohesion and discipline, two-thirds of them gained over to the faubourgs.

How disarm 100,000 men with this mob? For, to carry off the cannon, it was necessary to disarm the National Guard. The Parisians were no longer novices in warfare. "Having taken our cannon," they said, "they will make our muskets useless." The coalition would listen to nothing. Hardly arrived, they urged M. Thiers to act, to lance the abscess at once. The financiers — no doubt the same who had precipitated the war to give fresh impulse to their jobbery — said to him, "You will never be able to carry out financial operations if you don"t make an end of these scoundrels." All these declared the taking of the cannon would be mere child's play.

They were indeed hardly watched, but because the National Guard knew them to be in a safe place. It would suffice to pull up a few paving stones to prevent their removal down the narrow steep streets of Montmartre. On the first alarm all Paris would hasten to the rescue. This had been seen on the 16th when gendarmes presented themselves to take from the Place des Vosges the cannon promised Vautrain. The National Guards arrived from all sides and unscrewed the pieces, and the shopkeepers of the Rue des Tournelles commenced unpaving the street.

An attack was nonsensical, and it was this that determined Paris remain on the defensive. But M. Thiers saw nothing, neither disaffection of the middle classes nor the deep irritation of faubourgs. The little man, a dupe all his life, even of a MacMahon prompted by the approach of the 20th March, spurred on by Jules Favre and Picard, who, since the failure of the 31st of October, believed the revolutionaries incapable of any serious action, and jealous to play the part of a Bonaparte, threw himself head foremost into the venture. On the 17th he held a council, and, without calculating his forces or those of the enemy, without forewarning the mayors — Picard had formally promised them not to attempt to use force without consulting them — without listening to the chiefs of the bourgeois battalions, this Government, too weak to arrest even the twenty-five members of the Central Committee, gave the order to carry off two hundred and fifty cannon guarded by all Paris.

Chapter 3
The Eighteenth of March

We then did what we had to do: nothing provoked the Paris insurrection. (Dufaure's speech against amnesty, session of 18th May, 1876.)

The execution was as foolish as the conception. On the 18th of March, at three o'clock in the morning, several columns dispersed in various directions to the Buttes Chaumont, Belleville, the Faubourg du Temple, the Bastille, the Hôtel-de-Ville, Place St. Michel, the Luxembourg, the thirteenth arrondissement and the Invalides. General Susbielle marched on Montmartre with two brigades about 6,000 men strong. All was silent and deserted. The Paturel brigade took possession of the Moulin de la Galette without striking a blow. The Lecomte brigade gained the Tower of Solferino only meeting with one sentinel, Turpin, who crossed bayonets with them and was hewn down by the gendarmes. They then rushed to the post of the Rue des Rosiers, stormed it, and threw the National Guards into the caves of the Tower of Solferino. At six o'clock the surprise was complete. M. Clémenceau hurried to the Buttes to congratulate General Lecomte. Everywhere else the cannon were surprised in the same way. The Government triumphed all along the line, and D'Aurelles sent the papers a proclamation written in the conqueror's vein.

There was only one thing wanting — teams to convey the spoil. Vinoy had almost forgotten them. At eight o'clock they began to put some horses to the pieces. Meanwhile the faubourgs were awaking and the early shops opening. Around the milkmaids and before the wineshops the people began talking in a low voice; they pointed to the soldiers, the machine-gun [a multiple-barrelled gun, forerunner of the modern machine-gun] levelled at the streets, the walls covered with the still wet poster signed by M. Thiers and his Ministers. They spoke of paralysed commerce, suspended orders, frightened capital:

"Inhabitants of Paris, in your interest the Government has resolved to act. Let the good citizens separate from the bad ones; let them aid public force; they will render a service to the Republic herself," said MM. Pouyer-Quertier, De Larcy, Dufaure and other Republicans. The conclusion is borrowed from the phraseology of December: "The culpable shall be surrendered to justice. Order, complete, immediate and unalterable, must be re-established." They spoke of order — blood was to be shed.

As in our great days, the women were the first to act. Those of the 18th March, hardened by the siege — they had had a double ration of misery — did not wait for the men. They surrounded the machineguns, apostrophized the sergeant in command of the gun, saying, "This is shameful; what are you doing there?" The soldiers did not answer. Occasionally a non-commissioned officer spoke to them: "Come, my good women, get out of the way." At the same time a handful of National Guards, proceeding to the post of the Rue Doudeauville, there found two drums that had not been smashed, and beat the rappel. At eight o'clock they numbered 300 officers and guards, who ascended the Boulevard Ornano. They met a platoon of soldiers of the 88th, and, crying, *Vive la République!* enlisted them. The post of the Rue Dejean also joined them, and the butt-end of their muskets raised, soldiers and guards together marched up to the Rue Muller that leads to the Buttes Montmartre, defended on this side by the men of the 88th. These, seeing their comrades intermingling with the guards, signed to them to advance, that they would let them pass. General Lecomte, catching sight of the signs, had the men replaced by *sergents-de-ville,* and confined them in the Tower of Solferino, adding, "You will get your deserts." The *sergents-de-ville* discharged a few shots, to which the guards replied. Suddenly a large number of National Guards, the butt-end of their muskets up, women and children, appeared on the other flank from the Rue des Rosiers. Lecomte, surrounded, three times gave the order to fire. His men stood still, their arms ordered. The crowd, advancing, fraternized with them, and Lecomte and his officers were arrested.

The soldiers whom he had just shut up in the tower wanted to shoot him, but some National Guards having succeeded in disengaging him with great difficulty — for the crowd took him for Vinoy — conducted him with his officers to the Château-Rouge, where the staff of the battalions of the National Guard was seated. There they asked him for an order to evacuate the Buttes. He signed it without hesitation. The order was immediately communicated to the officers and soldiers of the Rue des Rosiers. The gendarmes surrendered their chassepots, and even cried, *Vive la République!* Three discharges from the cannon announced the recapture of the Buttes.

General Paturel, who wanted to carry away the cannon, surprised at the Moulin de la Galette, came into collision with a living barricade in the Rue Lepic. The people stopped the horses, cut the traces, dispersed the artillerymen, and took back the cannon to their post. In the Place Pigalle, General Susbielle gave the order to charge the crowd collected in the Rue Houdon, but the chasseurs, intimidated, spurred back their horses and were laughed at. A captain, dashing forward, sabre in hand, wounded a guard, and fell, pierced with balls. The General fled. The gendarmes, who commenced firing from behind the huts, were soon dislodged, and the bulk of the soldiers went over to the people.

At Belleville, the Buttes Chaumont, the Luxembourg, the troops fraternized everywhere with the crowds that had collected at the first alarm.

By eleven o'clock the people had vanquished the aggressors at all points, preserved almost all their cannon, of which only ten had been carried off, and seized thousands of chassepots. All their battalions were now on foot, and the men of the faubourgs commenced unpaving the streets.

Since six o'clock in the morning D'Aurelles had had the rappel beaten in the central quarters, but in vain. Battalions formerly noted for their devotion to Trochu sent only twenty men to the rendezvous. All Paris, on reading the posters, said "This is the *coup-d'état*. At twelve o'clock D'Aurelles and Picard sounded the alarm: "The Government calls on you to defend your homes, your families, your property. Some misguided men, under the lead of some secret leaders, turn against Paris the cannon kept back from the Prussians." These reminiscences of June, 1848, this accusation of indelicacy toward the Prussians, failing to rouse any one, the whole Ministry came to the rescue: "An absurd rumour is being spread that the Government is preparing a *coup-d'état*. It has wished and wishes to make an end of an insurrectional Committee, whose members only represent Communist doctrines." These alarms, repeatedly sounded, raised in all 500 men.

The Government were at the Foreign Office, and, after the first reverses, M. Thiers had given the order to fall back with all the troops on the Champs-de-Mars. When he saw the desertion of the National Guards of the Centre, he declared that it was necessary to evacuate Paris. Several Ministers objected, wanted a few points to be guarded — the Hôtel-de-Ville, its barracks occupied by the brigade Derroja, the Ecole Militaire — and that they should take a position on the Trocadero. The little man, quite distracted, would only hear of extreme measures. Lefô, who had almost been made a prisoner at the Bastille, vigorously supported him. It was decided that the whole town should be evacuated, even the forts on the south, restored by the Prussians a fortnight before. Towards three o'clock the popular battalions of the Gros Caillou marched past the Hôtel-de-Ville, headed by drums and trumpets. The Council believed itself surrounded. M. Thiers escaped by a back stair, and left for Versailles so out of his senses that at the bridge of Sèvres he gave the written order to evacuate Mont-Valérien.

At the self-same hour when M. Thiers ran away, the revolutionary battalions had not yet attempted any attack or occupied any official posts. The aggression of the morning had surprised the Central Committee, as it had all Paris. The evening before they had separated as usual, giving themselves a rendezvous for the 18th, at eleven o'clock at night, behind the Bastille, at the school in the Rue Basfroi; the Place de la Corderie, actively watched by the police, no longer being safe. Since the 15th new elections had added to their numbers, and they had appointed a Committee of Defence. On the news of the attack, some ran to the Rue Basfroi, others applied themselves to raising the battalions of their quarters: Varlin at the Batignolles, Bergeret, recently named *chef-de-légion,* at Montmartre, Duval at the Panthéon, Pindy in the third arrondissement, Faltot in the Rue de Sèvres. Ranvier and Brunel, without belonging to the Committee, were agitating Belleville and the tenth arrondissement. At ten o'clock a dozen members met together, overwhelmed with messages from all sides, and receiving from time to time some prisoners. Positive intelligence only came in towards two o'clock. They then drew up a kind of plan by which all the federalist battalions were to converge upon the Hôtel-de-Ville, and then dispersed in all directions to transmit orders.

The battalions were indeed on the alert, but did not march. The revolutionary quarters, fearing a resumption of the attack, and ignoring the plenitude of their victory, were strongly barricading themselves, and remained where they were. Even Montmartre was only swarming with guards in search of news, and disbanded soldiers for whom collections were being made, as they had had nothing to eat since the morning. Towards half-past three o'clock the Committee of Vigilance of the eighteenth arrondissement, established in the Rue de Clignancourt, was informed that General Lecomte was in great danger. A crowd, consisting chiefly of soldiers, surrounded the Château-Rouge and demanded the General. The members of the Committee of Vigilance, Ferré, Jaclard, and Bergeret, immediately sent an order to the commander of the Château-Rouge to guard the prisoner, who was to be put on trial. When the order arrived Lecomte had just left.

He had long been asking to be taken before the Central Committee. The chiefs of the post, much perturbed by the cries of the crowd, anxious to get rid of their responsibility, and believing this Committee was sitting in the Rue des Rosiers, decided to conduct the General and his officers there. They arrived at about four o'clock, passing through a terribly irritated crowd, yet no one raised a hand against them. The General was closely guarded in a small front room on the ground floor. There the scenes of the Château-Rouge recommenced. The exasperated soldiers asked for his death. The officers of the National Guard made desperate efforts to quiet them, crying, "Wait for the Committee." They succeeded in posting sentinels and appeasing the commotion for a time.

No member of the Committee had arrived when, at half-past four, formidable cries filled the street, and hunted by a fierce multitude, a man with a white beard was thrust against the wall of the house. It was Clément-Thomas, the man of June, 1848, the insulter of the revolutionary battalions. He had been recognized and arrested at the Chaussée des Martyrs, where he was examining the barricades. Some officers of the National Guard, a Garibaldian captain, Herpin-Lacroix, and some franc-tireurs had tried to stop the deadly mass, repeating a thousand times, "Wait for the Committee! Constitute a court-martial!" They were jostled, and Clément-Thomas was again seized and hurled into the little garden of the house. Twenty muskets levelled at him battered him down. During this execution the soldiers broke the windows of the room where General Lecomte was confined, threw themselves upon him, dragging him towards the garden. This man, who in the morning had three times given the order to fire upon the people, wept, begged for pity, and spoke of his family. He was forced against the wall and fell under the bullets.

These reprisals over, the wrath of the mass subsided. They allowed the officers of Lecomte's suite to be taken back to the Château-Rouge, and at nightfall they were set at liberty.

While these executions took place, the people, so long standing on the defensive, had begun to move. Brunel surrounded the Prince Eugène Barracks, held by the 120th of the line. The colonel, accompanied by about a hundred officers, assuming lofty airs, Brunel had them all locked up. Two thousand chassepots fell into the hands of the people. Brunel continued his march by the Rue du Temple towards the Hôtel-de-Ville. The Imprimerie Nationale was occupied at five o'clock. At six the crowd attacked the doors of the Napoléon Barracks with hatchets. A discharge was made, fired from the opening, and three persons fell; but the soldiers made signs from the windows of the Rue de Rivoli, crying, "It is the gendarmes who have fired. *Vive la République!*" Soon after they opened the doors and allowed their arms to be carried off.

At half-past seven the Hôtel-de-Ville was almost surrounded. The gendarmes who occupied it fled by the subterranean passage of the Lobau Barracks. About half-past eight Jules Ferry and Vabre, entirely abandoned by their men, left without any order by the Government, also stole away. Shortly after Brunel's column arrived at the place and took possession of the Hôtel-de-Ville, where Ranvier arrived at the same time by the quays.

The number of the battalions augmented incessantly. Brunel had given order to raise barricades in the Rue de Rivoli, on the quays, manned all the approaches, distributed the posts, and sent out strong patrols. One of these, surrounding the *mairie* of the Louvre, where the mayors were deliberating, almost succeeded in catching Ferry, who saved himself by jumping out of a window. The mayors returned to the *mairie* of the Place de la Bourse.

They had already met there during the day together with many adjuncts, much offended at the senseless governmental attack, waiting for information and for ideas. Towards four o'clock they sent delegates to the Government. M. Thiers had already made off. Picard politely showed them out. D'Aurelles washed his hands of the whole affair, saying the lawyers had done it. At night, however, it became necessary to take a resolution. The federal battalions already surrounded the Hôtel-de-Ville and occupied the Place Vendôme, whither Varlin, Bergeret, and Arnold had conducted the battalions of Montmartre and the Batignolles. Vacherot, Vautrain, and a few reactionaries spoke of resisting at any price, as though they had had an army to back them. Others, more sensible, sought for some expedient. They thought they could calm down everything by naming as prefect of police Eduard Adam, who had distinguished himself against the insurgents of June, 1848, and as General of the National Guards the giddy Proudhonist Langlois, a former Internationalist, who had been for the movement of the 31st of October in the morning, against it in the evening, and was named deputy, thanks to a scratch received while gesticulating at Buzenval. The delegates went to propose this brilliant solution to Jules Favre. He refused outright, saying, "We cannot treat with assassins." This comedy was only played to justify the evacuation of Paris, which he concealed from the mayors. During the conference it was announced that Jules Ferry had abandoned the Hôtel-de-Ville. The other Jules feigned surprise, and engaged the mayors to call out the battalions of order for the purpose of replacing the vanished army.

They returned overwhelmed by this raillery, humbled at having been altogether left in the dark about the intention of the Government. If possessed of some political courage, they would have gone straight to the Hôtel-de-Ville, instead of commencing to deliberate again in their *mairie*. At last, at ten o'clock in the morning, Picard informed them that they might bring out their Lafayette. They immediately sent Langlois to the Hôtel-de-Ville.

Some members of the Central Committee had been there since ten o'clock, generally very anxious and very hesitant. Not one of them had dreamt that power would fall so heavily upon their shoulders. Many did not want to sit at the Hôtel-de-Ville. They deliberated. At last it was decided that they would only stay during the two or three days wanted for the elections. Meanwhile it was necessary to ward off any attempt at resistance. Luilier was present, buzzing around the Committee, in one of his intervals of grave lucidity, promising to ward off all danger and appealing to the vote of Vauxhall. He had played no part during the whole day. The Committee committed the blunder of appointing him commander-in-chief of the

National Guard, while Brunel, who had rendered such service since the morning, was already installed in the Hôtel-de-Ville.

At three o'clock, Langlois, the competitor of Luilier, announced himself. He was full of confidence in himself, and had already sent his proclamation to the *Journal Officiel.* "Who are you?" the sentinels asked him. "General of the National Guard," answered Langlois. Some deputies of Paris, Lockroy, Cournet, etc. accompanied him. The Committee consented to receive them. "Who has named you?" said they to Langlois. "M. Thiers." They smiled at this madman's aplomb. As he pleaded the rights of the Assembly they put him to the test; "Do you recognize the Central Committee?" "No." He decamped and ran away after his proclamation.

The night was calm, fatally calm for liberty. By the gates of the south Vinoy marched off his regiments, his artillery, and his baggage to Versailles. The disbanded troops jogged along peevishly, insulting the gendarmes. The staff, true to its traditions, had lost its head, and left in Paris three regiments, six batteries, and all the gunboats, which it would have sufficed to leave to the current of the river. The slightest demonstration by the federals would have stopped this exodus. Far from thinking of closing the gates, the new commander of the National Guard — he boasted of it before the council of war — left open all issues to the army.

Chapter 4
The Central Committee calls for elections

Our broken hearts appeal to yours. (Mayors and adjuncts of Paris and deputies of the Seine to the National Guard. and all Citizens.)

Paris only became aware of her victory on the morning of the 19th of March. What a change in the scene, even after all the scene-shifting in the drama enacted during these last seven months! The red flag floated above the Hôtel-de-Ville. With the early morning mists the army, the Government, the Administration had evaporated. From the depths of the Bastille, from the obscure Rue Basfroi, the Central Committee was lifted to the summits of Paris in the sight of all the world. Thus on the 4th September the Empire had vanished; thus the deputies of the Left had picked up a derelict power.

The Committee, to its great honour, had only one thought, to restore its power to Paris. Had it been sectarian, hatching decrees, the movement would have ended like that of the 31st October. Happily it was composed of newcomers, without a past, and without political pretensions; men of the small middle-class, as well as workmen, shopkeepers, commercial clerks, mechanics, sculptors, architects, caring little for systems, anxious above all to save the Republic. At this giddy height they had but one idea to sustain them, that of securing to Paris her municipality.

Under the Empire this was one of the favourite schemes of the Left, by which it had mainly won over the Parisian petty bourgeoisie, much humiliated at the sight of Governmental nominees enthroned at the Hôtel-de-Ville for full eighty years. Even the most pacific amongst them were shocked, scandalized by the incessant increase of the budget, the multiplied loans, and the financial swindling of Haussmann. And how they applauded Picard, revindicating for the largest and most enlightened city of France at least the rights enjoyed by the smallest village, or when he defied the Pasha of the Seine to produce regular accounts! — Towards the end of the Empire, the idea of an elective municipal council had taken root; it had to a certain extent been put into practice during the siege, and now its total realization could alone console Paris for her decentralization.

On the other hand, the popular masses, insensible to the bourgeois ideal of a municipal council, were bent on the Commune. They had called for it during the siege as an arm against the foreign enemy; they still called for it as a lever for uprooting despotism and misery. What did they care for a council, even elective, but without real liberties and fettered to the state — without authority over the administration of schools and hospitals, justice and police, and altogether unfit for grappling with the social slavery of its fellow-citizens? What the people strove for was a political form allowing them to work for the amelioration of their condition. They had seen all the constitutions and all the representative governments run counter to the will of the so-called represented elector, and the state power, grown more and more despotic, deprive the workman even of the right to defend his labour, and this power, which has ordained even the very air to be breathed, always refusing to interfere in capitalist brigandage. After so many failures, they were fully convinced that the actual governmental and legislative regime was from its very nature unable to emancipate the working man. This emancipation they expected from the autonomous Commune, sovereign within the limits compatible with the maintenance of the national unity. The communal constitution was to substitute for the representative lording it over his elector the strictly responsible mandatory. The old state power grafted upon the country, feeding upon its substance, usurping supremacy on the foundation of divided and antagonistic interests, organizing for the benefit of the few, justice, finance, army, and police, was to be superseded by a delegation of all the autonomous communes.

Thus the municipal question, appealing to the legitimate susceptibilities of the one, to the bold aspirations of the other, gathered all classes round the Central Committee.

At half-past eight they held their first sitting in the same room where Trochu had been enthroned. The president was a young man of about thirty-two; Eduard Moreau, a small commission agent. "He was not in favour," he said, "of sitting at the Hôtel-de-Ville , but since they were there, it was necessary at once to regularize their situation, tell Paris what they wanted, proceed to the elections within the briefest term possible, provide for the public services, and protect the town from a surprise."

Two of his colleagues immediately said, "We must first march on Versailles, disperse the Assembly, and appeal to France, to pronounce."

Another, the author of the Vauxhall motion, said, "No. We have only the mandate to secure the rights of Paris. If the provinces share our views, let them imitate our example."

Some wanted to consummate the revolution before referring to the electors. Others opposed this vague suggestion. The Committee decided to proceed at once to the elections, and charged Moreau to draw up an appeal. While it was being signed, a member of the Committee arrived, saying, "Citizens, we have just been told that most of the members of the Government are still in Paris; an attempt at resistance is being organized in the first and second arrondissements; the soldiers are leaving for Versailles. We must take prompt measures to lay hands on the Ministers, disperse the hostile battalions, and prevent the enemy from leaving the town."

In fact, Jules Favre and Picard had hardly left Paris. The clearing of the Ministries was publicly going on; columns of soldiers were still marching off through the gates of the left bank. But the Committee continued signing, neglecting this traditional precaution — the shutting of the gates — and lost itself in the elections. It saw not — very few saw as yet — that this was a death struggle with the Assembly of Versailles.

The Committee, distributing the work to be done, appointed the delegates who were to take possession of the Ministries and direct the various services. Some of these delegates were chosen outside the Committee, from amongst those who were reputed men of action, or the revolutionaries. Some one having spoken of an increase of pay, his colleagues indignantly answered, "We are not here to imitate the Government of the Defence. We have lived till now on our pay; it will still suffice." Arrangements were made for the permanent presence of some members at the Hôtel-de-Ville, and then they adjourned at one o'clock.

Outside the joyous clamour of the people enlivened the streets. A spring sun smiled on the Parisians. This was their first day of consolation and of hope for eight months. Before the barricades of the Hôtel-de-Ville, at the Buttes Montmartre, in all the boulevards, onlookers were thronging. Who then spoke of civil war? Only the *Journal Officiel*. It recounted the events in its own way. "The Government had exhausted every means of conciliation," and in a despairing appeal to the National Guard it said, "A committee taking the name of Central Committee has assassinated in cold blood the Generals Clément-Thomas and Lecomte. Who are the members of this Committee? Communists, Bonapartists, or Prussians? Will you take upon yourselves the responsibility of these assassinations?" These lamentations of runaways moved only a few companies of the centre. Yet — a grave symptom this — the young bourgeois of the Polytechnic School came to the *mairie* of the second arrondissement, where the mayors had flocked, and the university students, till now the advanced guard of all our revolutions, pronounced against the Committee.

For this revolution was made by proletarians. Who were they? What did they want? At two o'clock every one hurried to see the wall-posters of the Committee just issued from the Imprimerie Nationale. "Citizens, the people of Paris, calm and impassible in their strength, have awaited without fear, as without provocation, the shameless fools who want to touch our Republic. Let Paris and France together lay the foundation of a true Republic, the only Government which will for ever close the era of revolutions. The people of Paris is convoked to make its elections." And turning to the National Guard: "You have charged us to organize the defence of Paris and of your rights. Our mandate has now expired. Prepare, and at once make your communal elections. Meanwhile we shall, in the name of the people, hold the Hôtel-de-Ville." Twenty names followed, which, save three or four, Assi, Lullier, and Varlin, were only known through the posters of the last few days. Since the morning of the 10th August, 1792, Paris has not seen in her Hôtel-de-Ville such an advent of obscure men.

And yet their posters were respected, their battalions circulated freely. They took possession of the posts; at one o'clock the Ministries of Finance and of the Interior; at two o'clock the Naval and War Offices, the telegraph, the *Journal Officiel,* and Duval was installed at the Prefecture de Police. And they had hit the mark. What indeed could be said against this new-born power whose first word was its own abdication?

Everything around them bore a warlike aspect. Let us cross the half-open barricades of the Rue de Rivoli. Twenty thousand men camped in the square of the Hôtel-de-Ville, bread stuck on the end of their muskets. Fifty ordnance pieces, cannon, and machine-guns drawn up along the façade served as the statuary around the town hall. The court and staircases were encumbered with guards taking their meals, the large Salle du Trône swarming with officers, guards, and civilians. In the hall on the left, which was used by the staff, the noise subsided. The room by the river-side, at the corner of the edifice, was the ante-chamber of the Committee. About fifty men were writing there, bending over a long table. There discipline and silence reigned. We were far from the anarchists of the 31st October. From time to time the door, guarded by two sentinels, opened to a member of the Committee who carried orders or made inquiries.

The sitting had recommenced. A member asked the Committee to protest against the executions of Clement-Thomas and Lecomte, to which it was entirely foreign. "Take care not to disavow the people," answered another, "for fear they in turn should disavow you." A third said, the *Journal Officiel* declares the execution took place under our eyes. We must stop these calumnies. The people and the bourgeoisie have joined hands in this revolution. This union must be maintained. You want everybody to take part in the elections. "Well, then," he was apostrophized, "abandon the people in order to gain the bourgeoisie; the people will withdraw, and you will see if it is with the bourgeois that revolutions are made."

The Committee decided that a note should be inserted in the *Journal Officiel* to re-establish the truth. Eduard Moreau proposed and read the draft of a manifesto, which was adopted.

The Committee were discussing the date and mode of the elections when it was informed that a large meeting of the chiefs of battalions, the mayors and deputies of the Seine was being held at the *mairie* of the third arrondissement. M. Thiers during the morning, had given over to the union of the mayors the provisional administration of Paris, and they were trying their authority on the National Guard. The Committee was assured that they intended to convoke the electors.

"If it is so," said several members, "we must come to an agreement with them to make the situation regular." Others, remembering the siege, simply wanted to have them arrested. One member said, "If we wish to have France with us, we must not frighten her. Think what an effect the arrest of the deputies and mayors would produce, and what, on the other hand, the effect of their adhesion would be." Another, "It is important to collect an imposing number of voters. All Paris will go to the ballot-boxes if the representatives and mayors join us." "Say rather," cried an impetuous colleague, "that you are not equal to your position; that your only preoccupation is to disengage yourselves." They finally decided to send Arnold to the *mairie* as delegate.

He was badly enough received. The most radical adjuncts and deputies, Socialists like Millière and Malon, flatly declared against the Hôtel-de-Ville, appalled at the dangerous initiative of the people. Many too said, "Who are these unknown men?" Even at the Corderie, Internationalists and former members of the Committee of the twenty arrondissements maintained a diffident attitude. However, the meeting decided to send commissioners to the Hôtel-de-Ville, for, whether they liked it or not, there was the power.

The Central Committee had, in the meantime, fixed the elections for the Wednesday, decreed the raising of the state of siege, the abolition of the court-martials, and amnesty for all political crimes and offences. It held a third sitting at eight o'clock to receive the commissioners. These were the deputies Clémenceau, Millière, Tolain, Cournet, Malon, and Lockroy, the mayors Bonvalet and Mottu, the adjuncts Murat, Jaclard, and Léo Meillet.

Clémenceau, half accomplice, half dupe of M. Thiers' *coup-d'état*, in his quality of mayor and deputy, was the spokesman. He was prolix and pedantic. "The insurrection has been undertaken upon an illegitimate motive; the cannon belong to the State. The Central Committee is without a mandate and in no wise holds Paris. Numerous battalions were gathering round the deputies and mayors. Soon the Committee will become ridiculous and its decrees will be despised. Besides, Paris has no right to revolt against France, and must absolutely acknowledge the authority of the Assembly. The Committee has but one other way of getting out of the difficulty — to submit to the union of the deputies and mayors, who are resolved to obtain from the Assembly the satisfaction claimed by Paris."

He was frequently interrupted during this speech. What! They dared speak of an insurrection! Who had begun the civil war, attacked first? What had the National Guards done but answer a nocturnal aggression, taken back cannon paid for by themselves? What had the Central Committee done but follow the people and occupy the deserted Hôtel-de-Ville?

A member of the Committee said, "The Central Committee has received a regular, imperative mandate. This mandate forbids them to allow the Government or the Assembly to touch their liberties or the Republic. Now the Assembly has never ceased putting the existence of the Republic in question. It has placed a dishonoured general at our head, decapitalized Paris, tried to ruin her commerce. It has sneered at our sufferings, denied the devotion, the courage, the abnegation Paris has shown during the siege, hooted her best-loved representatives, Garibaldi and Victor Hugo. The plot against the Republic is evident. The attempt was commenced by gagging the press; they hoped to terminate it by the disarming of our battalions. Yes, our case was one of legitimate defence. If we have bowed our heads under this new affront, there was an end of the Republic. You have just spoken of the Assembly of France. The mandate of the Assembly has expired. As to France, we had not the pretension of dictating her laws — we have too often suffered under hers — but we will not submit to her rural plebiscites. You see it; the question is no longer to know which of our mandate is the most regular. We say to you the revolution is made; but we are not usurpers. We wish to call upon Paris to name her representatives. Will you aid us, and proceed with us to consult the elections? We eagerly accept your cooperation." As he spoke of autonomous communes and their federation, "Have a care," said Millière, "if you unfurl this flag they will launch all France upon Paris, and I foresee days fatal as those of June [1848]. The hour of the social revolution has not yet struck. Progress is obtained by slower marches. Descend from the heights where you have placed yourselves. Victorious today, your insurrection may be vanquished tomorrow. Make as much of it as you can, but do not hesitate to content yourselves with little. I adjure you to leave the field open to the union of the mayors and deputies; your confidence will be well placed."

One of the Committee: "Since the social revolution has been spoken of, I declare our mandate does not go so far." (Others of the Committee, "Yes! Yes! Yes!" "No! No!") "You have spoken of a federation, of Paris as a free town. Our duty is more simple. It is to proceed to the elections. The people will afterwards decide on their action. As to yielding to the deputies and mayors, this is impossible. They are unpopular and have no authority in the Assembly. The elections will take place with or without their concurrence. Will they help us? We will receive them with open arms. If not, we shall do without them, and, if they attempt to obstruct our way, we shall know how to reduce them to impotency."

The delegates resisted. The discussion grew hot. "But, in fine," said Clémenceau, "what are your claims? Do you confine your mandate to asking the Assembly for a municipal council?"

Many of the Committee: "No! No!" "We want," said Varlin, "not only the election of the municipal council, but real municipal liberties, the suppression of the prefecture of police, the right of the National Guard to name its own leaders and to reorganize itself, the proclamation of the Republic as the legal Government, the pure and simple remittance of the rents due, an equitable law on overdue bills, and the Parisian territory banned the army."

Malon: "I share your aspirations, but the situation is perilous. It is clear that the Assembly will listen to nothing as long as the Committee occupies the Hôtel-de-Ville. If, on the contrary, Paris entrusts herself again to her legal representatives, I believe they could do more than you."

The discussion was protracted until half-past ten; the Committee defending its right to proceed to the elections, the delegates their pretension of superseding the Committee. They at last agreed that the Committee should send four of its members to the second arrondissement. Varlin, Moreau, Arnold, and Jourde were appointed.

There they found the whole staff of Liberalism: deputies, mayors, and adjuncts; Louis Blanc, Schoelcher, Carnot, Peyrat, Tirard, Floquet, Desmarets, Vautrain, and Dubail, about sixty altogether. The cause of the people there had a few partisans, sincere, but terribly dismayed by the uncertain future. The mayor of the second arrondissement, Tirard, presided, a Liberal, nervous, haughty, one of those who had helped to paralyse Paris in the hands of Trochu. In his evidence before the Rural Committee of Inquiry, he has mutilated, travestied this sitting, where the Radico-Liberal bourgeoisie laid bare all its baseness. We shall now, for the instruction of and in justice to the people, give the plain truth.

The delegates: "The Central Committee does not wish anything better than to come to an agreement with the municipalities, if they will proceed with the elections."

Schoelcher, Tirard, Peyrat, Louis Blanc, all the Radicals and Liberals in chorus: "The municipalities will not treat with the Central Committee. There is only one authority — the union of the mayors invested with the delegation by the Government."

The delegates: "Let us not discuss the point. The Central Committee exists. We have been named by the National Guard and we hold the Hôtel-de-Ville. Will you proceed to make the elections?"

"But what is your programme?"

Varlin set it forth. He was attacked from all sides. The four delegates had to face twenty assailants. The great argument of the Liberals was that Paris could not convoke herself, but ought to wait for the permission of the

Assembly. A reminiscence this of the times of the siege, when they fell prone before the Government of the Defence.

The delegates affirmed, on the contrary: "The people has the right to convoke itself. It is an undeniable right, which it has more than once made use of in our history in moments of great peril, and at present we are passing through such a crisis, since the Assembly of Versailles is making for monarchy."

Then recriminations followed: "You are now face to face with force," said the delegates. "Beware of letting loose a civil war by your resistance." "It is you who want a civil war," replied the Liberals. At midnight Moreau and Arnold, quite disheartened, withdrew. Their colleagues were about to follow, when some adjuncts entreated them to stay. "We promise," said the mayors and deputies, "to make every effort to obtain the municipal elections with the shortest delay." "Very well," answered the delegates, "but we maintain our position; we want guarantees." The deputies and mayors, growing obstinate, pretended that Paris must surrender unconditionally. Jourde was about to retire, when some of the adjuncts again detained him. For a moment they seemed to be coming to an understanding. The Committee was to give up all the administrative services to the mayors, and let them occupy one part of the Hôtel-de-Ville; itself, however, was to continue sitting there, to retain the exclusive direction of the National Guard, and to watch over the security of the town. This agreement only required to be confirmed by the issue of a common proclamation, but when the heading of the latter came to be discussed, the contest grew more violent than before. The delegates proposed, "The deputies, mayors, and adjuncts, in accord with the Central Committee." These gentlemen, on the contrary, desired to hide themselves behind a mask. For an hour Louis Blanc, Tirard, and Schoelcher overwhelmed the delegates with indignities. Louis Blanc cried to them, "You are insurgents against a most freely elected Assembly. We, the regular mandatories, we cannot avow a transaction with insurgents. We should be willing to prevent a civil war, but not to appear as your auxiliaries in the eyes of France." Jourde answered the manikin that this transaction, in order to be accepted by the people of Paris, must be publicly consented to, and, despairing of making anything out of this meeting, withdrew.

And amongst this elite of the liberal bourgeoisie, former exiles, publicists, historians of our revolutions, not one indignant voice protested, "Let us cease these cruel disputes, this barking at a revolution. Woe to us if we do not recognize the force manifesting itself through unknown men! The Jacobins of 1794 denied it, and they perished; the Montagnards of 1848 abandoned it, and they perished; the Left under the Empire, the Government of the National Defence, disdained it, and our integrity as a nation has perished. Let us open our eyes, our hearts; let us break out of the beaten track. No; we will not widen the gulf that the days of June, 1848, and the Empire have placed between us and the workmen. No; with the disasters of

France in view, we shall not allow her living forces still in reserve to be touched. The more abnormal, monstrous our situation is, the more we are bound to find the solution, even under the eye of the Prussian. You, the Central Committee, who are the spokesmen of Paris, we, who are listened to by Republican France, we will mark out a field for common action. You supply the force, the broad aspirations, we the knowledge of realities and their inexorable behests. We shall present to the Assembly this charter free from all Utopian views, equally regardful of the rights of the nation and of those of the capital. If the Assembly rejects it, we shall be the first to make the elections, to ask for your suffrage. And when France sees Paris raising her force counterpoised by prudence at her Hôtel-de-Ville, vigorous newcomers allied with men of old repute, the only possible bulwark against royalists and clericals, she will rise as in the days of the Federation, and at her voice Versailles will have to yield."

But what was to be expected of men who had not even been able to pluck up sufficient courage to wrench Paris from Trochu? Varlin single-handed had to stand their combined attack. Exhausted, worn out — this contest had lasted five hours — he at last gave way, but under protest. On returning to the Hôtel-de-Ville, he recovered all his wonted energy, his calm intelligence, and told the Committee he now saw the snare, and advised it to reject the pretensions of the mayors and deputies.

Chapter 5
Reorganization of the Public Services

I thought the Paris insurgents would be unable to steer their own ship. (Jules Favre, Inquiry into the 18th of March.*)*

Thus no agreement had been come to, only one of the four delegates having, from sheer weariness, given way to a certain extent. So on the morning of the 20th, when the mayor Bonvalet and two adjuncts sent by the mayors came to take possession of the Hôtel-de-Ville, the members of the Committee unanimously exclaimed, "We have not treated." But Bonvalet, feigning to believe in a regular agreement, continued, "The deputies are today going to ask for the municipal franchises. Their negotiations cannot succeed if the administration of Paris is not given up to the mayors. On pain of frustrating the efforts which will save you, you must fulfil the engagements of your delegates."

One of the Committee: "Our delegates received no mandate to enter into such engagements for us. We do not ask to be saved."

Another: "The weakness of the deputies and of the mayors is one of the causes of the revolution. If the Committee abandons its position and disarms, the Assembly will grant nothing."

Another: "I have just come from the Corderie. The Committee of the second arrondissement is holding a sitting, and it adjures the Central Committee to remain at its post till the elections."

Others were about to speak, when Bonvalet declared that he had come to take possession of the Hôtel-de-Ville, not to discuss, and walked off. His superciliousness confirmed the worst suspicions. Those who the evening before had been favourable to making terms said, "These men want to betray us." Behind the mayors the Committee beheld the implacable reaction. In any case, to ask them for the Hôtel-de-Ville was to ask their fives, for the National Guards would have believed them traitors, and punished them on the spot. In one word, compromise had become impossible. The *Journal Officiel*, for the first time in the hands of the people, and the news posters had spoken.

"The election of the municipal council will take place on Wednesday next, 22nd March," decreed the Central Committee. And in a manifesto it said, "The offspring of a Republic whose device bears the great word Fraternity, the Central Committee pardons its traducers, but it would convince the honest people who have believed their calumnies through ignorance. It has not been secret, for its members have signed their names to all its proclamations. It has not been unknown, for it was a free expression of the suffrage of 215 battalions. It has not been the fomenter of disorder, for the National Guard has committed no excess. And yet provocations have not been wanting. The Government calumniated Paris and set on the provinces against her, wished to impose on us a general, attempted to disarm us, and said to Paris, "Thou hast shown thyself heroic, we are afraid of thee, hence we will tear from thee the crown of the capital of France." What has the Central Committee done in answer to these attacks? It has founded the Federation, preached moderation, generosity. One of the greatest causes of anger against us is the obscurity of our names. Alas! many names were known, well known, and this notoriety has been fatal to us. Notoriety is cheaply gained; often hollow phrases or a little cowardice suffice; recent events have proved this. Now that our object is attained, we say to the people, who esteemed us enough to listen to the advice that has often clashed with their impatience, "Here is the mandate you entrusted to us." There, where our personal interest commences, our duty ends. Do your will. You have freed yourselves. Obscure a few days ago, obscure we shall return to your ranks, and show our governors that it is possible to descend the steps of your Hôtel-de-Ville, head erect, with the certainty of receiving at the bottom the pressure of your loyal and hardy hands." By the side of the proclamation of an eloquence so vivid and so novel the deputies and the mayors posted up a few dry and colourless lines, where they promised to demand of the Assembly that same day the election of all the chiefs of the National Guard and the establishment of a municipal council.

At Versailles they found a wildly excited crowd. The terrified functionaries who arrived from Paris spread terror about them, and five or six insurrections were announced from the provinces. The coalition was dismayed. Paris victorious, the Government in flight this was not what had

---

been promised. These conspirators, blown up by the mine which they had themselves sprung, raised the cry of conspiracy, spoke of taking refuge at Bourges. Picard had certainly telegraphed to all the provinces, "The, army, to the number of 40,000 men, is concentrated at Versailles;" but the only army to be seen was straggling bands of soldiers wandering about the streets. All Vinoy had been able to do was to place a few posts along the routes of Châtillon and Sèvres, and protect the approaches to the Assembly with a few machine-guns.

The President, Grévy, who during the whole war had cowered in the provinces, sullenly hostile to the defence, opened the sitting by stigmatizing this criminal insurrection "which no pretext could extenuate." Then the deputies of the Seine commenced a procession towards the tribune. Instead of a collective manifesto, they laid before the Assembly a series of fragmentary propositions, without connection; without general views, and without a preamble to explain them. First a bill convoking with the least delay the elections of Paris, then another granting to the National Guard the election of its chiefs. Millière alone thought of the overdue commercial bills, and proposed to prolong them for six months.

Till then exclamations only and half-muttered insults had been levelled at Paris, but no formal act of accusation. In the evening sitting a deputy applied this requisite. Trochu made a sortie. In this monstrous scene, which a Shakespeare only could depict, the gloomy man who had softly slipped the great town into the hands of William, threw his own treason upon the revolutionaries, accusing them of having almost a dozen times brought the Prussians into Paris. And the Assembly, grateful for his services, his hatred, giving him the crown he merited, covered him with applause. Another came to fan this rage. The evening before the National Guards had arrested two generals in uniform in a train arriving from Orléans. One of them was Chanzy, unknown to the crowd, who took him for D'Aurelles. They could not have been released without endangering their lives, but a deputy, Turquet, who accompanied them, was immediately set free. He rushed off to the Chamber, told them a fairy tale, and affected to be much moved in speaking of his companions. "I hope," said the hypocrite, "that they will not be assassinated." This story was accompanied by the furious yelling of the Assembly.

From the first sitting one could see what the struggle between Versailles and Paris was to be. The monarchical conspirators, abandoning their dream for a moment, hastened to do the most urgent work first: to save themselves from the Revolution. They surrounded M. Thiers and promised him their absolute support to crush Paris. Thus this Ministry, that a truly National Assembly would have impeached, became, even through its crime, all-powerful. Scarcely recovered from the fright of their stampede, M. Thiers and his Ministers dared to play the swaggerers. And indeed, would not the provinces hasten to their rescue, as in June, 1848? And proletarians without political education, without administration, without money, how could they be able "to steer their barque"?

In 1831 the proletarians, masters of Lyons, had failed in their attempt at self-government, and how much greater was the difficulty for those of Paris! All new powers had until then found the administrative machine in working order, in readiness for the victor. On the 20th March the Central Committee found it taken to pieces. At the signal from Versailles the majority of functionaries had abandoned their posts. Taxes, street inspection, lighting, markets, public charity, telegraphs, all the respiratory and digestive apparatus of the town of 1,600,000 souls, everything had to be extemporized. Certain mayors had carried off the seals, the registers, and the cash of their *mairies*. The military intendance left without a farthing six thousand sick in the hospitals and ambulances. M. Thiers had tried to disorganize even the management of the cemeteries.

Poor man! who never knew anything of our Paris, of her inexhaustible strength, her marvellous elasticity. The Central Committee received support from all sides. The committees of arrondissements furnished a personnel to the *mairies*; some of the lower middle class lent their experience, and the most important services were set to rights in no time by men of common sense and energy, which soon proved superior to routine. The employees who had remained at their posts in order to hand over the funds to Versailles were soon discovered and obliged to flee.

The Central Committee overcame a more menacing difficulty. Three hundred thousand persons without work, without resources of any kind, were waiting for the thirty sous upon which they had lived for the last seven months. On the 19th, Varlin and Jourde, delegates to the finance department, took possession of that Ministry. The coffers, according to the statement of accounts handed over to them, contained 4,600,000 francs; but the keys were at Versailles, and, in view of the movement for conciliation then being carried on, the delegates did not dare to force the locks. The next day they went to ask Rothschild to open them a credit at the bank, and he sent word that the funds would be advanced. The same day the Central Committee broached the question more forcibly, and sent three delegates to the bank to request the necessary advances. They were answered that a million was placed at the disposition of Varlin and Jourde, who at six o'clock in the evening were received by the governor, M. Rouland. "I expected your visit," he said. "On the morning following a change of Government, the bank has always to find the money for the newcomers. It is not my business to judge events; the Bank of France has nothing to do with politics. You are a *de facto* Government, and the bank gives you for today a million. Only be so kind as to mention in your receipt that this sum has been requisitioned on account of the town of Paris. The delegates took away a million francs in bank notes. All the employees of the Ministry of Finance had disappeared since the morning, but with the help of a few friends the sum was rapidly divided among the paying officers. At ten o'clock the delegates were able to tell the Central Committee that the pay was being distributed in all the arrondissements.

The bank acted prudently: the Central Committee firmly held Paris. The mayors and deputies had not been able to unite more than three or four hundred men, although they had charged Admiral Saisset with the organization of the resistance. The Committee was so sure of its strength that it had the barricades demolished. Everybody came to it, the garrison of Vincennes spontaneously surrendering themselves with the fort. Its victory was too complete, for it was perilous, obliging it to disperse its troops in order to take possession of the abandoned forts on the south. Lullier, entrusted with this mission, had the forts of Ivry, Bicêtre, Montrouge, Vanves, and Issy occupied on the 19th and 20th. The last to which he sent the National Guard, Mont-Valérien, was the key of Paris, and, at that time, of Versailles.

For thirty-six hours the impregnable fortress had remained empty. On the evening of the 18th, after the order of evacuation, it had to defend it only twenty muskets and some chasseurs of Vincennes, interned there for mutiny. The same evening they burst open the locks of the fortress and returned to Paris.

When the evacuation of Mont-Valérien became known at Versailles, generals and deputies begged M. Thiers to have it reoccupied. He obstinately refused, declaring this fort had no strategical value. During the whole day of the 19th they still failed. At last Vinoy, in his turn, urged by them, succeeded on the 20th, at one o'clock in the morning, in wresting an order from M. Thiers. A column was immediately despatched, and at mid-day a thousand soldiers occupied the fortress. Not until evening, at eight o'clock, did the battalions of Ternes present themselves; the governor easily got rid of their officers. Lullier, on making his report to the Central Committee, said he had occupied all the forts, and even named the battalion which, according to him, was then in possession of Mont-Valérien.

Chapter 6
The mayors and the Assembly combine against Paris

The thought of witnessing a massacre filled me with anguish.
(Jules Favre, Inquiry into the 4th of September.)

On the 21st the situation stood out in bold relief.

At Paris — the Central Committee, with it all the workmen and all the generous and enlightened men of the lower middle-class. The Committee said, "We have but one object — the elections. Everybody is welcome to cooperate with us, but we shall not leave the Hôtel-de-Ville before they have been made."

At Versailles — the Assembly: all the monarchists, all the great bourgeoisie, all the slaveholders. They yelled, "Paris is only a rebel, the Central Committee a band of brigands."

Between Versailles and Paris — a few Radical deputies, all the mayors, many adjuncts. They comprised the Liberal bourgeois, that sacred herd that makes all revolutions and allows all the empires to be made. Despised by the Assembly, disdained by the people, they cried to the Central Committee, "Usurpers!" and to the Assembly, "You will spoil all."

The day of the 21st is memorable, for on it all these voices made themselves heard.

The Central Committee: "Paris has in nowise the intention of separating from France; far from it. For France she has borne with the Empire and the

Government of the National Defence, with all their treachery and defections, certainly not to abandon her now, but only to say to her as an elder sister: Sustain thyself as I have sustained myself; oppose thyself to oppression as I have done."

And the *Journal Officiel*, in the first of those articles where Moreau, Longuet, and Rogeard commented upon the new revolution, said:

"The proletarians of the capital, amidst the failures and treasons of the ruling classes, have understood that the hour has struck for them to save the situation by taking into their own hands the direction of public affairs. Hardly possessed of the government, they have hastened to convoke the people of Paris to the ballot-boxes. There is no example in history of a provisional government so anxious to divest itself of its mandate. In the presence of conduct so disinterested, one may well ask how a press can be found unjust enough to pour out upon these citizens slander, contumely, and insult? The working men, those who produce everything and enjoy nothing, are they then for ever to be exposed to outrage? The bourgeoisie, which has accomplished its emancipation, does it not understand that now the time for the emancipation of the proletariat is come? Why, then, does it persist in refusing the proletariat its legitimate share?"

It was the first socialist note struck in the movement. Parisian revolutions never remain purely political. The approach of the foreigner, the abnegation of the workmen, had, on the 4th September, silenced all social demands. Peace once concluded, the workmen in power, their voice would naturally make itself heard. How just was this complaint of the Central Committee! What an act of accusation the French proletariat could draw up against its masters! And on the 18th March, 1871, could not the people, making greater their great words of 1848, say, "We had placed eighty years of patience at the service of our country"?

The same day the Central Committee suspended the sale of objects pledged in the pawnshops, prolonged the overdue bills for a month, and forbade landlords to dismiss their tenants till further notice. In three lines it did justice, beat Versailles, and gained Paris.

On the other hand, the representatives and mayors told the people, "No election; everything is for the best. We wanted the maintenance of the National Guard; we shall have it. We wanted Paris to recover her municipal liberty; we shall have it. Your requests have been brought before the Assembly. The Assembly *has satisfied them* by a unanimous vote, which guarantees the municipal elections. Awaiting these, the only legal elections, we declare that we shall abstain from the elections announced for to-morrow, and we protest against their illegality."

Thrice-lying address! The Assembly had not said a word of the National Guard; it had promised no municipal liberty, and several of the signatures were suppositious.

The bourgeois press followed suit. Since the 19th the Figarist papers, supported by the police, the altar, and the alcove, the Liberal gazettes, by which Trochu had prepared the capitulation of Paris, had not ceased to fall foul of the federal battalions. They spoke of the public coffers and private property being pillaged, of Prussian gold streaming into the faubourgs, of documentary evidence hurtful to the members of the Central Committee destroyed by them. The Republican journals also discovered gold in the movement, but Bonapartist gold; and the best of them, naïvely convinced that the Republic belonged to their patrons, inveigled against the accession of the proletariat, saying, "These people dishonour us." Emboldened by the mayors and deputies, they all agreed to revolt; and on the 21st, in a collective declaration, asked the electors to consider as null and void the illegal convocation of the Hôtel-de-Ville.

Illegality! Thus the question was put by the Legitimists, twice imposed on us by foreign bayonets; by the Orléanists, raised to power through barricades; by the brigands of December; even by the exiles returned home, thanks to an insurrection. What! When the bourgeois, who make all laws, always act illegally, how are the workmen to proceed, against whom all the laws are made?

These attacks of the mayors and deputies and of the press screwed up the courage of the Hectors of the reaction. For two days this rabble of runaways, who during the siege had infested the cafés of Brussels and the Haymarket of London, gesticulated on the fashionable boulevards, asking for order and work. On the 21st, at about ten o'clock, at the Place de la Bourse, about a hundred of these strange working men marched round the Stock Exchange, banners flying, and advancing along the boulevards to the cries of *"Vive l'Assemblée!"* came to the Place Vendôme, shouting before the general staff, "Down with the Committee!" The commander of the Place, Bergeret, told them to send delegates. "No, no!" cried they; "no delegates! You would assassinate them!" The federals, losing patience, had the Place cleared. The riotous fops gave themselves a rendezvous for the next day before the new Opera-House.

At the same hour the Assembly made its demonstration. The draft of an address to the people and the army, a tissue of lies and insults to Paris, having just been read, and Millière having pointed out that it contained some unfortunate expressions, was hooted. The demand of the Left to at least conclude the address with the words *"Vive la République!"* was frantically refused by an immense majority. Louis Blanc and his group, entreating the Assembly to immediately examine their project of municipal law and oppose a vote to the elections that the Committee announced for the next day, M. Thiers answered, "Give us time to study the question." "Time!" exclaimed M. Clémenceau, "We have none to lose." Then M. Thiers gave those drones a lesson they richly deserved: "What would be the use of concessions?" said he. "What authority have you at Paris? Who would listen to you at the Hôtel-de-Ville? Do you think that the adoption of a bill would disarm the party of brigands, the party of assassins?" Then he charged Jules Favre to expatiate on this theme for the special benefit of the provinces. For an hour and a half that bitter follower of Guadet, spinning round Paris his elaborate periods, limed her with his venom. No doubt he again saw himself on the 31st October, when the people held him in their power and pardoned him, a cruel remembrance for his rankling spirit. He commenced by reading the declaration of the press, "courageously written," said he, "under the knife of the assassins." He spoke of Paris as in the power of "a handful of scoundrels, putting above the right of the Assembly I know now what bloody and rapacious ideal." Then, humbly supplicating monarchists and Catholics: "What they want," cried he, "what they have realized, is an attempt at that baleful doctrine which in philosophy may be called individualism and materialism, and which in politics means the Republic placed above universal suffrage." At this idiotic quibbling the Assembly burst into roars of applause. "These new doctors," continued he, "have the pretension of separating Paris from France. But let the insurgents know this: if we left Paris, it was with the intention of returning in order to combat them resolutely." (Bravo! bravo!) Then stirring the panic of those rurals who every moment expected to see the federal battalions coming down upon them: "If some of you fall into the hands of these men, who have only usurped power for the sake of violence, assassination and theft, the fate of the unfortunate victims of their ferocity would be yours." And finally, garbling, improving with ferocious skill the maladroitness of an article in the *Journal Officiel* on the execution of the generals: "No more temporizing. For three days I combated the exigencies of the victor who wanted to disarm the National Guard. I ask pardon for it of God and of man." Each new insult, each banderillo thrust into the flesh of Paris, drew from the Assembly mad hurrahs. Admiral Saisset stamped, emphasising certain phrases of the speaker with his hoarse interjections. Goaded by these wild cheers, Jules Favre doubled his invective. Since the Gironde, since Isnard's curse, Paris had not undergone such an imprecation. Even Langlois, unable to stand it any longer, exclaimed, "Oh, it is outrageous, atrocious to speak thus!" And when Jules Favre concluded, implacable, impassible, only foaming a little at the mouth: "France will not be lowered to the bloody level of the wretches who oppress the capital," the whole Assembly rose raving. "Let us appeal to the provinces," shrieked the rurals. And Saisset: "Yes, let us appeal to the provinces and march on Paris." In vain one of the deputies of the Seine adjured the Assembly not to let them return to Paris empty-handed. This great bourgeoisie, which had just surrendered the honour, the fortune, and the territory of France to the Prussians, trembled with rage at the mere thought of conceding anything to Paris.

After this horrible scene, the Radical deputies found nothing better to do than to issue a lachrymose address inviting Paris to be patient. The Central

Committee was obliged to adjourn the elections till the 23rd, for several *mairies* belonged to the enemy; but on the 22nd it warned the papers that provocation to revolt would be severely repressed.

The matadors of reaction, reanimated by Jules Favre's speech, took this warning for an idle boast. On the 22nd at mid-day they assembled at the Place du Nouvel Opera. At one o'clock they numbered a thousand dandies, petty squires, journalists, notorious familiars of the Empire, who marched down the Rue de la Paix to the cry of *"Vive l'ordre!"* Their plan was, under the cloak of a pacific demonstration, to force the Place Vendôme and to expel the Federals from it; then, masters of the *mairie* of the first arrondissement, of half of the second and of Passy, they would have cut Paris in two and menaced the Hôtel-de-Ville. Admiral Saisset followed them.

Before the Rue Neuve St. Augustin these pacific demonstrationmen disarmed and ill-treated two detached sentries of the National Guard. Seeing this, the Federals of the Place Vendôme seized their muskets and hurried in marching order to the top of the Rue Neuve des Petits-Champs. They were but 200, the whole garrison of the place; the two cannon levelled at the Rue de la Paix had no cartridges. The reactionists soon encountered the first line with the cry, "Down with the Committee! Down with the assassins!" waving a banner and their handkerchiefs, while some of them stretched out their hands to seize the muskets. Bergeret and Maljournal, members of the Committee, in the first ranks, summoned the rioters to retire. Furious cries of "Cowards! brigands!" drowned their voices, and sword-canes were pointed at them. Bergeret made a sign to the drummers. A dozen times the *sommations* were made and repeated. For several minutes only the roll of the drums was heard, and between these savage cries. The ranks in the rear of the demonstration pushed on those in front and tried to break through the lines of the Federals. At last, despairing no doubt of succeeding by mere bravado, the insurgents fired their revolvers; two guards were killed and seven wounded; Maljournal was struck in the thigh.

The muskets of the guards went off, so to say, spontaneously. A volley and a terrible cry, followed by silence more dismal. In a few seconds the crowded Rue de la Paix was emptied. In the deserted road, strewn with revolvers, sword-canes, and hats, lay about a dozen corpses. If the Federals had only aimed at foes' hearts, there would have been 200 killed, for in this compact mass no shot would have missed. The insurgents had killed one of their own, the Vicomte de Molinat, fallen in the front ranks, his face towards the square, a ball in the back of his head. On his body was found a dagger fixed by a small chain. An adroit ball struck in the rear the chief editor of the *Paris Journal*, the Bonapartist De Pène, one of the basest revilers of the movement.

The runaways traversed Paris shouting, "Murder!" The shops of the boulevards were closed and the Place de la Bourse filled with rabid groups. At four o'clock some of the reactionary companies appeared, resolute, in good order, their muskets on their shoulders, and took possession of the quarters of the Bourse.

At three o'clock the event became known at Versailles. The Assembly had just rejected Louis Blanc's bill on the municipal council, and Picard was reading another one refusing all justice to Paris, when the news arrived. The Assembly precipitately raised the sitting; the Ministers looked dumbfounded.

All their swaggering of the evening before had only been meant to frighten Paris, to encourage the men of order, and provoke a *coup-de-main.* The incident had occurred, but the Central Committee triumphed. For the first time M. Thiers began to believe that this Committee, able to repress a riot, might after all be a Government.

The news in the evening was more reassuring. The fusillade seemed to have roused the *men of order.* They were flocking to the Place de la Bourse. A great many officers just returned from Germany came to offer their help. The reactionary companies were establishing themselves solidly in the *mairie* of the ninth arrondissement and reoccupying that of the sixth, dislodging the Federals of the St. Lazare station, guarding all the approaches of the occupied quarters, and forcibly arresting the passers-by. They formed a town within the town. The mayors were constituting a permanent committee in the *mairie* of the second arrondissement. Their resistance was now provided with an army.

Chapter 7
The Central Committee forces the mayors to capitulate

The Central Committee was equal to the occasion. Its proclamations, its Socialist articles in the *Officiel*, the truculence of the mayors and deputies, had at last rallied round it all the revolutionary groups. It had also added to its members some men better known to the masses. By its order the Place Vendôme was provided with barricades; the battalions of the Hôtel-de-Ville were reinforced; strong patrols remounted the boulevards before the reactionary posts of the Rues Vivienne and Drouot. Thanks to it, the night passed tranquilly.

As the elections on the next day had become impossible, the Committee declared they could only take place on the 26th, and said to Paris: "The reaction, excited by your mayors and your deputies, has declared war on us. We must accept the struggle and break this resistance." It announced that it would summon before it all the journalists libelling the people. It sent a battalion of Belleville to reoccupy the *mairie* of the sixth, and replaced by its delegates the mayors and adjuncts of the third, tenth, eleventh, twelfth, and eighteenth arrondissements, in spite of their protestations. M. Clémenceau wrote that he yielded to force, but would not himself resort to force. This was all the more magnanimous that his whole force consisted of himself and his adjunct. The Federals installed themselves at the Battignolles on the railway lines, and stopped the trains, thus preventing the occupation of the St. Lazare station. Lastly, the Committee proceeded energetically against the Bourse.

The reaction counted upon famine to make the Committee capitulate. The million of the Monday was gone; a second one had been promised. On the Thursday morning, Varlin and Jourde, going to fetch an instalment, received only threats. They wrote to the governor: "To starve out the people, such is the aim of a party that styles itself honest. Famine disarms no one; it will only encourage devastation. We take up the gauntlet that has been flung down to us." And, without deigning to take any notice of the swash-bucklers of the Bourse, the Committee sent two battalions to the bank, which had to give in.

At the same time the Committee neglected nothing in order to reassure Paris. Numerous ticket-of-leave men had been let loose upon the town. The Committee denounced them to the vigilance of the National Guard, and posted upon the doors of the Hôtel-de-Ville, "Every individual taken in the act of stealing will be shot." Picard's police had failed to put an end to the gamblers who every night since the siege had encumbered the streets; a single order of the Committee sufficed. The great scarecrow of the reactionaries was the Prussians, and Jules Favre had announced their early intervention. The Committee published the despatches that had passed between it and the commander of Compiegne, to this effect: "The German troops will remain passive so long as Paris does not take a hostile attitude." The Committee had answered with great dignity: "The Revolution accomplished at Paris is of an essentially municipal character. We are not qualified to discuss the preliminaries of peace voted by the Assembly." Paris was therefore without anxiety on that head.

The only disturbance proceeded from the mayors. Authorized by M. Thiers, they appointed as chief of the National Guards Saisset, the madman of the sitting of the 21st, giving him Langlois and Schoelcher as coadjutors, and made every effort to attract National Guards to the Place de la Bourse, where they distributed the pay due to the guards of the invaded *mairies*. Many came only to get the pay, not to fight. Even the chiefs began to be divided amongst themselves. The most rabid certainly spoke of sweeping away everything before them. Those were Vautrain, Dubail, Denormandie, Degouve-Denuncques, and Heligon, an ex-working man, an idle fellow, admitted into the bourgeois servants' hall, and bumptious like other lackeys. But many others flagged and thought of conciliation, especially since some of the deputies and adjuncts — Millière, Malon, Dereure, and Jaclard had withdrawn from the union of the mayors, thus still further setting forth its frankly reactionary character. Finally, some soft-headed mayors, still believing that the Assembly needed only enlightenment, extemporized a melodramatic scene.

They arrived at Versailles on the 23rd, at the moment when the rurals, again plucking up their courage, made an appeal to the provinces to march on Paris. In most solemn attitude these mayors put in their appearance before the tribune of the president, girdled with their official scarfs. The Left applauded, crying *"Vive la République!"* The Larnourettes returned the compliment. But the Right and the Centre cried *"Vive la France!* Order! Order!" and with clenched hands they challenged the deputies of the Left, who naively answered, "You insult Paris!" to which the others replied, "You insult France!" and they left the House. In the evening a deputy, who was also a mayor, Arnaud De l'Ariege, read from the tribune the declaration that they had brought, and wound up by saying, "We are on the eve of an awful civil war. There is but one way to prevent it — that the election of the commander-in-chief of the National Guard be fixed for the 28th, and that of the municipal council for the 3rd of April." These propositions were referred to the Committee.

The mayors returned home indignant. A despatch of the evening before had already disquieted Paris. M. Thiers announced to the provinces that the Bonapartist Ministers, Rouher, Chevreau, and Boitelle, arrested by the people of Boulogne, had been protected, and that Marshal Canrobert, one of the accomplices of Bazaine, had offered his services to the Government. The insult inflicted upon the mayors irritated the whole middle-class, and called forth a sudden change in their Republican journals. The attacks against the Central Committee relaxed. Even the Moderates began to expect the worst from Versailles.

The Central Committee took advantage of this change of opinion. Having just been informed of the proclamation of the Commune at Lyons, it spoke out all the more clearly in its manifesto of the 24th. "Some battalions, misled by their reactionary chiefs, have thought it their duty to block our movements. Some mayors and deputies, forgetting their mandates, have encouraged this resistance. We rely upon your courage for the accomplishment of our mission. It is objected that the Assembly promises us at some indefinite period the election of the municipal council and that of our chiefs, and that consequently our resistance ought not to be prolonged. We have been deceived too often to be entrapped again; the left hand would take back what the right hand gives. See what the Government has already done. In the Chamber, through the voice of Jules Favre, it has challenged us to a terrible civil war, called on the provinces to destroy Paris, and covered us with the most odious calumnies."

Having spoken, the Committee now acted, and named three generals — Brunei, Duval, and Eudes. It had to confine the drunkard Lullier, who, assisted by a staff of traitors, had the evening before allowed a whole regiment of the army encamped at the Luxembourg to leave Paris with arms and baggage. Now, too, it was known that Mont-Valerien was lost by his fault.

The generals made a profession not to be misunderstood: "This is no longer a time for parliamentarism. We must act. Paris wishes to be free. The great city will not permit public order to be disturbed with impunity."

A direct caution this, addressed to the camp of the Bourse, which, moreover, was visibly growing less. The desertions from it multiplied at every sitting of the rurals. Women came to fetch their husbands. The Bonapartist officers, overshooting the mark, irritated moderate Republicans. The programme of the mayors — submission to Versailles — discouraged the middle class. The general staff of this helter-skelter army had been foolishly established at the Grand Hôtel. There sat the crazy trio — Saisset, Langlois, and Schoelcher — who, from extreme confidence, had fallen into a state of utter dejection. The most crack-brained of them, Saisset, took upon himself to announce by placards that the Assembly had granted the complete recognition of the municipal franchise, the election of all the officers of the National Guard, including the general-in-chief, modifications of the law on the overdue commercial bills, and a bill on rents favourable to the tenants. This gigantic hoax only mystified Versailles.

The Committee, pushing forward, ordered Brunei to seize the *mairies* of the first and second arrondissements. Brunei, with 600 men of Belleville, two pieces of artillery, and accompanied by two delegates of the Committee, Lisbonne and Protot, presented himself at three o'clock at the *mairie of* the Louvre. The bourgeois companies assumed an air of resistance. Brunei had his cannon advanced, when the passage was at once opened to him. He declared to the adjuncts, Meline and Adam, that the Committee would proceed with the elections as soon as possible. The adjuncts, intimidated, sent to the *mairie of* the second arrondissement to ask for the authorization to treat. Dubail answered that they might promise the elections for the 3rd April. Brunei insisted on appointing the 30th March. The adjuncts acquiesced. The National Guards of the two camps saluted this agreement with enthusiastic acclamations, and mingling their ranks, marched to the *mairie of* the second arrondissement. In the Rue Montmartre a few companies of the Bourse army, trying to stop the way, were told, "Peace is made," and they let them pass. At the *mairie* of the second arrondissement, Schoelcher, who presided at the meeting of the mayors, Dubail, and Vautrain resisted, refusing to ratify the convention, insisting on the date of the 3rd April. But the great majority of their colleagues accepted that of the 30th, and the election of the commander-in-chief of the National Guard for the 3rd April. Immense cheers hailed the good news, and the popular battalions, saluted by the bourgeois battalions, marched through the Rue Vivienne and the boulevards, dragging along their cannon, mounted by lads with green branches in their hands.

The Central Committee could not accept this transaction. Twice it had postponed the elections. A new adjournment would have given certain mayors five days for plotting and playing into the hands of Versailles. Besides, the Federal battalions, on foot since the 18th, were really tired out. Ranvier and Arnold the same evening went to the *mairie* of the second arrondissement to say that the Hôtel-de-Ville adhered to the date of the 26th for the elections. The mayors and adjuncts, many of whom had only the one purpose, as they have avowed since, of gaining time, inveighed against a breach of faith. The delegates protested, for Brunel had had no mandate but that of occupying the *mairies*. For several hours everything was tried to talk over the delegates, but they held their ground, and went away at two o'clock in the morning without any conclusion being arrived at. After their departure the more intractable discussed the chance of resistance. The irrepressible Dubail wrote a call to arms, sent it to the printing-office, and spent the whole night with his faithful Heligon in transmitting orders to the chiefs of battalions and providing the *mairie* with machine-guns.

While they were thus bent upon resistance the rurals thought themselves betrayed. Every day they became more nervous, being deprived of their creature-comforts, obliged to camp in the lobbies of the castle of Versailles, exposed to all winds and to all panics. They felt weary of the incessant interference of the mayors, and were thunderstruck by the proclamation of Saisset. They fancied that M. Thiers was coquetting with the mob, that the *petit bourgeois*, as he hypocritically called himself, wanted to cozen the monarchists, and, using Paris as his lever, overthrow them. They spoke of removing him, and appointing as commander-in-chief one of the D'Orleans, Joinville or D'Aumale. Their plot might have come to a head at the evening sitting, when the proposition of the mayors was to be read. M. Thiers was beforehand with them, implored the Assembly to adjourn the discussion, adding that an ill-considered word might cost torrents of blood. Grevy shuffled through the sitting in ten minutes. But the rumour of a plot got abroad.

Saturday was the last day of the crisis. Either the Central Committee or the mayors had to disappear. The Committee on that very morning placarded: "The transport of machine-guns to the *mairie* of the second arrondissement compels us to maintain our resolution. The election will take place on the 26th March". Paris, which had believed peace concluded, and for the first time in five days had passed a quiet night, was very angry at seeing the mayors recommence the wrangle. The idea of the election had made its way in all ranks, and many papers declared for it, even among those that had signed the protestation of the 21st. No one could understand this quarrel about a date. One irresistible current of fraternization swayed the whole town. The ranks of the two or three hundred soldiers of order who had remained faithful to Dubail dwindled away from hour to hour, leaving Admiral Saisset alone to make his proclamation in the desert of the Grand Hôtel. The mayors had no longer an army when, at ten o'clock, Ranvier came to ask for their final decision. Their dispute grew hot when some deputies of Paris on their return from Versailles announced the news that the Duc d'Aumale was proclaimed lieutenant-general. Several mayors and adjuncts then at last understood that the Republic was at stake, and, convinced of their impotence, capitulated. The draft of a poster was drawn up to be signed by the mayors, deputies, and for the Central Committee by the two delegates Ranvier and Arnold. The Committee wanted to sign *en masse,* and slightly modified the text, saying, "The Central Committee, round which the deputies of Paris, the mayors, and adjuncts have rallied, convokes. . ." Thereupon some of the mayors, on the look-out for a pretext, rose, crying, "This is not our convention; we said the deputies, the mayors, the adjuncts, and the members of the Committee ... ;" and, at the risk of rekindling the embers, posted up the protest. Yet the Committee might well say, "Which have rallied?" since it had yielded no point. However, Paris overruled the mischief-mongers. Admiral Saisset had to disband the four men who remained to him. Tirard in a poster advised the electors to vote; for M. Thiers that same morning had given him the hint, "Do not continue a useless resistance. I am reorganizing the army. I hope that in a fortnight or three weeks we shall have a sufficient force to relieve Paris."

Five deputies only signed the address for the election, MM. Lockroy, Floquet, Clémenceau, Tolain, and Greppo; the rest of Louis Blanc's group had kept aloof from Paris for several days. These weaklings, having all their life sung the glories of the Revolution, when it rose up before them ran away appalled, like the Arab fisherman at the apparition of the genie.

With these mandarins of the tribune of history and of journalism, mute and lifeless, contrast strangely the sons of the multitude, obscure, but rich in will, faith, and eloquence. Their farewell address was worthy of their advent: "Do not forget that the men who will serve you best are those whom you will choose from amongst yourselves, living your life, suffering the same ills. Beware of the ambitious as much as the upstarts. Beware also of mere talkers. Shun those whom fortune has favoured, for only too rarely is he who possesses fortune prone to look upon the working man as a brother. Give your preference to those who do not solicit your suffrages. True merit is modest, and it is for the workingmen to know those who are worthy, not for these to present themselves."

They could indeed "come down the steps of the Hôtel-de-Ville head erect," these obscure men who had safely anchored the revolution of the 18th March. Named only to organize the National Guard, thrown up at the head of a revolution without precedent and without guides, they had been able to resist the impatient, quell the riot, re-establish the public services, victual Paris, baffle intrigues, take advantage of all the blunders of Versailles and of the mayors, and, harassed on all sides, every moment in danger of civil war, known how to negotiate, to act at the right time and in the right place. They had embodied the tendency of the movement, limited their programme to communal revindications, and conducted the entire population to the ballot-box. They had inaugurated a precise, vigorous, and fraternal language unknown to all bourgeois powers.

And yet they were obscure men, all with an incomplete education, some of them fanatics. But the people thought with them. Paris was the brazier, the

Hôtel-de-Ville the flame. In the Hôtel-de-Ville, where illustrious bourgeois have only accumulated folly upon defeat, these new-comers found victory because they listened to Paris.

May their services absolve them from two grave faults — allowing the escape of the army and of the functionaries, and the retaking of the Mont-Valérien by Versailles. It has been said that on the 19th or 20th they ought to have marched on Versailles. But on the first alarm these would have fled to Fontainebleau, with the Administration and the Left, everything that was wanted to govern and deceive the provinces. The occupation of Versailles would only have displaced the enemy, and it would not have been for long, as the popular battalions were too badly provided, too badly commanded, to hold at the same time this open town and Paris.

At all events, the Central Committee left its successor all the means necessary to disarm the enemy.

Chapter 8
Proclamation of the Commune

A considerable part of the population and the National Guard of Paris calls on the support of the departments for the re-establishment of order. (Circular from Thiers to the Prefects, 27th March.)

This week ended with the triumph of Paris. Paris-Commune again resumed her part as the capital of France, again became the national initiator. For the tenth time since 1789 the workmen put France upon the right track.

The bayonets of Prussia had laid bare our country, such as eighty years of bourgeois domination had left it — a Goliath at the mercy of his driver.

Paris broke the thousand fetters which bound France down to the ground, like Gulliver a prey to ants; restored the circulation to her paralysed limbs; said, "The life of the whole nation exists in each of her smallest organisms; the unity of the hive, and not that of the barracks. The organic cell of the French Republic is the municipality, the commune."

The Lazarus of the Empire and of the siege resuscitated, having torn the napkin from his brow and shaken off the grave-clothes, was about to begin a new existence with the regenerated Communes of France in his train. This new life gave to all Paris a youthful aspect. Those who had despaired a month before were now full of enthusiasm. Strangers addressed each other and shook hands. For indeed we were not strangers, but bound together by the same faith and the same aspirations.

Sunday the 26th was a day of joy and sunshine. Paris breathed again, happy like one just escaped from death or great peril. At Versailles the streets looked gloomy, gendarmes occupied the station, brutally demanded passports, confiscated all the journals of Paris, and at the slightest expression of sympathy for the town arrested you. At Paris everybody could enter freely. The streets swarmed with people, the cafés were noisy; the same lad cried out the *Paris Journal* and the *Commune;* the attacks against the Hôtel-de-Ville, the protestation of a few malcontents, were posted on the walls by the side of the posters of the Central Committee. The people were without anger because without fear. The voting paper had replaced the chassepot.

Picard's bill only gave Paris sixty municipal councillors, three for each arrondissement, whatever might be its population. Thus the 150,000 inhabitants of the eleventh arrondissement had the same number of representatives as the 45,000 of the sixteenth. The Central Committee had decreed that there was to be a councillor for every 20,000 inhabitants, and for each fraction of 10,000; ninety in all. The elections were to be conducted with the lists of February and in the usual manner; only the Committee had expressed the wish that for the future open voting should be considered the only mode worthy of democratic principles. All the faubourgs obeyed, and gave an open vote. The electors of the St. Antoine quarter formed in long columns, and, headed by a red flag, their voting papers stuck in their hats, filed before the column of the Bastille, and in the same order marched to their sections.

The adhesion and convocation of the mayors dissipating all scruple, also made the bourgeois quarters vote. The elections became legal since plenipotentiaries of the Government had given their consent. Two hundred and eighty-seven thousand men voted, relatively a far greater number than in the elections of February; for since the opening of the gates after the siege, a great part of the leisured classes had rushed to the provinces, there to recover their health.

The elections were conducted in a way becoming a free people. At the approach to the halls, no police, no intrigues. And yet M. Thiers dared telegraph to the provinces: "The elections will take place to-day without liberty and without moral authority." The liberty was so absolute that in all Paris not one single protestation occurred.

The moderate papers even commended the articles of the *Officiel,* in which the delegate Longuet set forth the role of the future Communal Assembly: "Above all, it must define its mandate, fix the boundaries of its attributes. Its first work must be the discussion and the drawing up of its charter. This done, it must consider the means of having that statute of the municipal autonomy recognized and guaranteed by the central power." The plainness, the prudence, the moderation which marked all official acts was beginning to move the most obdurate. Only the hatred of the Versaillese did not abate. That same day M. Thiers cried from the tribune, "No, France will not let those wretches triumph who would drown her in blood."

The next day 200,000 "wretches" came to the Hôtel-de-Ville there to install their chosen representatives, the battalion drums beating, the banners surmounted by the Phrygian cap and with red fringe round the muskets; their ranks, swelled by soldiers of the line, artillerymen, and marines faithful to Paris, came down from all the streets to the Place de Greve like the thousand streams of a great river. In the middle of the Hôtel-de-Ville, against the central door, a large platform was raised. Above it towered the bust of the Republic, a red scarf slung round it. Immense red streamers beat against the frontal and the belfry, like tongues of fire announcing the good news to France. A hundred battalions thronged the square, and piled their bayonets, lit up by the sun, in front of the Hôtel-de-Ville. The other battalions that could not get into the place lined the streets up to the Boulevard de Sebastopol and to the quays. The banners were grouped in front of the platform, some tricolour, all with red tassels, symbolizing the advent of the people. While the square was filling, songs burst forth, the bands played the *Marseillaise* and the *Chant du Départ,* trumpets sounded the charge, and the cannon of the old Commune thundered on the quay.

Suddenly the noise subsided. The members of the Central Committee and of the Commune, their red scarfs over their shoulders, appeared on the platform. Ranvier said, "Citizens, my heart is too full of joy to make a speech. Permit me only to thank the people of Paris for the great example they have given the world." A member of the Committee announced the names of those elected. The drums beat a salute, the bands and two hundred thousand voices chimed in with the *Marseillaise.* Ranvier, in an interval of silence, cried out, "In the name of the People the Commune is proclaimed."

A thousandfold echo answered, "*Vive la Commune!*" Caps were flung up on the ends of bayonets, flags fluttered in the air. From the windows, on the roofs, thousands of hands waved handkerchiefs.. The quick reports of the cannon, the bands, the drums, blended in one formidable vibration. All hearts leaped with joy, all eyes filled with tears. Never since the great Federation had Paris been thus moved.

The filing off was very cleverly managed by Brunel, who, while having the square evacuated on the one hand, brought in those battalions that were outside, all equally anxious to acclaim the Commune. Before the bust of the Republic the flags were lowered, the officers saluted with their sabres, the men raised their muskets. Not until seven o'clock did the last procession pass by.

The agents of M. Thiers returned in dismay to tell him, "It was really the whole of Paris that took part in the demonstration." And the Central Committee might well exclaim in its enthusiasm, "To-day Paris opened a fresh page in the book of history, and there inscribed her powerful name. Let the spies of Versailles, who are prowling around us, go and tell their masters what the common movement of an entire population means. Let these spies carry back to them the image of the magnificent spectacle of a people recovering their sovereignty."

This lightning would have made the blind see. 187,000 voters. 200,000 men with the same watchword. This was not a secret committee, a handful of factious rioters and bandits, as had been said for ten days. Here was an immense force at the service of a definite idea communal independence, the intellectual life of France — an invaluable force in this time of universal anaemia. a godsend as precious as the compass saved from the wreck and saving the survivors. This was one of those great historical turning-points when a people may be remoulded.

Liberals, if it was in good faith that you called for decentralization under the Empire; Republicans, if you have understood June, 1848, and December, 1851; Radicals, if you really want the self-government of the people — listen to this new voice, avail yourselves of this marvellous opportunity.

But the Prussian! What does it matter? Why not forge arms under the eye of the enemy? Bourgeois, was it not in sight of the foreigner that your ancestor Etienne Marcel tried to remake France? And your Convention, did not it fast act in the very midst of the hurricane?

What did they answer? Death to Paris!

The red sun of civil discord melts veneer and all masks. There they are side by side as in 1791, 1794, and 1848, Monarchists, Clericals, Liberals, Radicals, all of them, their hands raised against the people — one army in different uniforms. Their decentralization is rural and capitalist federalism; their self-government, the exploitation of the budget by themselves, just as the whole political science of their statesmen consists only in massacre and the state of siege.

What bourgeoisie in the world after such immense disasters would not with careful heed have tended such a reservoir of living force?

They, seeing this Paris capable of engendering a new world, her heart swelled with the best blood of France, had but one thought — to bleed Paris.

Chapter 9
The Commune at Lyons, St. Etienne and Creuzot

All parts of France have united and rallied around the Assembly and the government. (Circular from Thiers to the Provinces, evening of the 23rd.)

What was the state of the provinces?

For some days, without any of the Parisian journals, they lived upon lying despatches of M. Thiers, 103 then looked at the signatures to the proclamations of the Central Committee, and finding there neither the Left nor the democratic paragons, said, "Who are these unknown men?" The Republican bourgeois, misinformed on the events occurring during the siege of Paris — very cleverly hoodwinked, too, by the Conservative press — cried, like their fathers who in their time had said, "Pitt and Coburg", when unable to comprehend popular movements, "These unknown men can be nothing but Bonapartists." The people alone showed true instinct.

The Paris Commune found its first echo at Lyons. This was a necessary reverberation. Since the advent of the Assembly the workmen found themselves watched. The municipal councillors, weak men, some of them, almost to reaction, had lowered the red flag under the pretext that "the proud flag of resistance a *outrance* should not survive the humiliation of France". The clumsy trick had not deceived the people, who, at the

Guillotière, mounted guard round their flag. The new prefect, Valentin, an ex-officer as brutal as vulgar, a kind of Clément-Thomas, sufficiently forewarned the people what sort of Republic was in store for them.

On the 19th, at the first news, Republicans were on the alert, nor did they hide their sympathy for Paris. The next day Valentin issued a provocative proclamation, seized the Parisian journals, and refused to communicate any despatches. On the 21st, in the municipal council, some of the members grew indignant, and one said, "Let us at least have the courage to be the Commune of Lyons." On the 22nd, at mid-day, eight hundred delegates of the National Guard assembled at the Palais de St. Pierre. A motion was put proposing to choose between Paris and Versailles. A citizen just arrived from Paris explained the movement there, and many wanted the meeting to declare itself immediately for Paris. The Assembly finally sent delegates to the Hôtel-de-Ville to ask for the extension of the municipal liberties, the appointment of the mayor as chief of the National Guard, and his investiture with the functions of prefect.

The municipal council was just sitting. The mayor, Hénon, a wooden-headed relic of 1848, opposed all resistance to Versailles. The mayor of the Guillotière, Crestin, a known Republican, demanded that they should at least protest. Others wanted the council to extend its prerogatives. Hénon threatened to tender his resignation if they went on like that, and proposed they should repair to the prefect, who was then convoking the reactionary battalions.

The delegates of the Palais de St. Pierre arrived, and were roughly received by Hénon. One deputation succeeded another, always meeting with the same rebuffs. However, during this time the battalions of Brotteaux and La Guillotière were preparing, and at eight o'clock a dense mass filled the Place des Terreaux in front of the Hôtel-de-Ville, crying, "*Vive la Commune! Down with Versailles!*" The reactionary battalions did not respond to the prefect's appeal.

Part of the council had met again at nine o'clock, while the others, together with Hénon, were still wrangling with the delegates. After an answer from the mayor, which left them no hope of coming to an understanding, the delegates invaded the council-chamber, and the crowd, apprised of this, rushed into the Hôtel-de-Ville. The delegates, sitting down round the council table, named Crestin mayor of Lyons. He refused, and, summoned to give his reasons, declared that the direction of the movement belonged to those who had initiated it. After a great uproar, the National Guards acclaimed a Communal Commission, at the head of which they placed five municipal councillors — Crestin, Durand, Bouvatier, Perret and Velay. The delegates sent for Valentin, and asked him if he were for Versailles. He answered that his proclamation could leave no doubt on that head whereupon he was put under arrest. Then they decided on the proclamation of the Commune, the dissolution of the municipal council, the dismissal of the prefect and of the general of the National Guard, who was to be replaced by Ricciotti Garibaldi, noted alike by — his name and his services in the army of the Vosges. These resolutions were announced to the people and hailed with cheers. The red flag was again unfurled from the balcony.

The next day, the 23rd March, early in the morning, the five councillors named the evening before backed out, thus obliging the insurgents to present themselves single-handed to Lyons and the neighbouring towns. "The Commune", they said, "must demand for Lyons the right to impose and administer her own taxes, to have her own police, and to dispose of her National Guard, which is to occupy all posts and forts." This rather meagre programme was a little further expanded by the committees of the National Guard and the Republican Alliance: "With the Commune, the taxes will be lightened, the public money will no longer be squandered, social institutions demanded by the working-class will be founded. Much misery and suffering will be alleviated pending the final disappearance of that hideous social evil, pauperism." Insufficient proclamations these, inconclusive, mute as to the danger of the Republic and the clerical conspiracy, the only levers by which the lower middle-class might have been roused.

So the Commission found itself isolated. It had taken the fort of Charpennes, accumulated cartridges, set the cannons and machine guns round the Hôtel-de-Ville; but the popular battalions, except two or three, had withdrawn without leaving a picket, and the resistance was being organized. General Crouzat at the station picked up all the soldiers, marines, and mobiles dispersed about Lyons. Hénon named Bouras a general of the National Guard. The officers of the battalions of order protested against the Commune, and placed themselves at the disposition of the municipal council, which sat in the, cabinet of the mayor, close to the Commission.

Forgetting it had dissolved the Council the evening before it invited the Council to hold their sitting in the ordinary council-room. They arrived at four o'clock. The Commission gave up the place to them, National Guards occupying that part of the room reserved to the public. Had there been some vigour in this middle class, some foreboding of the Conservative atrocities, the Republican councillors would have taken the lead of this popular movement; but they were still, some of them, the same mercantile aristocrats, chary of their gold and their persons during the war of national defence; the others, the same overweening Radicals who had always striven for the subordination instead of the emancipation of the working-class. While they were deliberating without coming to any resolution, the assistants, growing impatient, uttered a few exclamations shocking to their lordliness, and they brusquely raised the sitting in order to go and draw up an address with Hénon.

In the evening two delegates of the Central Committee of Paris arrived at the club of the Rue Duguesclin. They were taken to the Hôtel-de-Ville, where from the large balcony they harangue the mass, who answered with cries of "*Vive Paris! Vive la Commune!* and Ricciotti's name was again acclaimed.

But this was only a demonstration. The delegates were themselves too inexperienced to keep alive and direct this movement. On the 24th there remained on the Place de Terreaux but a few groups of idlers. The *rappel* sounded in vain. The four important journals of Lyons, Radical, Liberal and Clerical, "energetically repudiated all connivance with the Parisian, Lyonese, and other insurrections"; and General Crouzat spread the rumour that the Prussians, camping at Dijon, threatened to occupy Lyons within twenty-four hours if order were not re-established. The Commission, more and more deserted, again turned to the Council, which now held its sitting at the Bourse, proposing to hand over the administration to them. The Council refused to treat. "No," said the mayor, "We will never accept the Commune." And as the mobiles from Belfort were announced, the Council decided to give them a solemn reception. This was a declaration of war.

The parley had been going on the whole afternoon until late into the evening. Little by little the Hôtel-de-Ville grew empty, and the members of the Commission disappeared. At four o'clock in the morning the only two who remained cancelled their powers, dismissed the sentries who guarded the prefect, and left the Hotel-de-Ville. The next day Lyons found her Commune gone.

On the same evening, when dying out at Lyons, the revolutionary movement burst forth at St. Etienne. Since the 31st October, when they had almost succeeded in officially proclaiming the Commune, the Socialists had not ceased calling for it, despite the resistance, and even the threats, of the municipal council.

There were two Republican centres — the Committee of the National Guard, spurred on by the revolutionary club of the Rue de la Vierge, and the Republican Alliance at the head of the advanced Republicans. The municipal council was, with one or two exceptions, composed of those Radicals who knew not how to resist the people without being crushed by the reaction. The Committee and the Alliance agreed to ask for its renewal.

The 18th March was enthusiastically welcomed by the workmen. The Radical organ, *L'Eclaireur*, said, without drawing any conclusion: "If the Assembly prevails, the Republic is done for; if, on the other hand, the deputies of Paris separate from the Central Committee, they must have a good reason for it." The people went straight on. On the 23rd the Club de la Vierge sent delegates to the Hôtel-de-Ville to ask for the Commune. The mayor promised to submit the question to his colleagues. The Alliance also came to demand the adjunction to the council of a certain number of delegates.

The next day, the 24th, the delegations returned. The Council tendered their resignation, and declared they would only officiate till their replacement by the electors, to be convoked with the briefest delay. This was a defeat, for the same day the prefect ad *interim,* Morellet, urged the population not to proclaim the Commune. but to respect the authority of the Assembly. At seven o'clock in the evening a company of the National Guard took over sentry duty to the cries of *"Vive la Commune!"* The Central Committee invited the Alliance to join them in taking possession of the Hôtel-de-Ville. The Radicals refused, saying that the promise of the Council sufficed; that the movements of Paris and Lyons were of a vague character, and that it was necessary to affirm order and public tranquillity.

During these negotiations the people had assembled at the Club de la Vierge, accusing the first delegates of weakness, resolved to send others, and to accompany them, so that they could not give way. At ten o'clock two columns of 400 men each drew up before the railings at the Hôtel-de-Ville. These had been closed by order of the new prefect, M. De l'Espée, manager of an iron works, who had just then arrived, eager to subdue the disturbers. But the people began pulling down the railings, and it was necessary to let in their delegates. They found the mayor and Morellet, asked for the Commune, and provisionally the convening of a popular commission. The mayor refused, the former prefect obstinately tried to demonstrate that the Commune was a Prussian invention. Hopeless of convincing the delegates, he went to warn M. De l'Espée — the prefecture being contiguous to the *mairie* — and both then making off by the garden, succeeded in rejoining General Lavoye, the commander of the garrison.

At midnight the delegates, unable to obtain anything, declared that nobody would be allowed to leave the Hôtel-de-Ville, and proceeding to the rails, told the demonstrators to reflect. Some ran off in quest of arms, others penetrated into the Salles des Prudhommes, where they held a meeting. The night passed tumultuously. The delegates, who had just learned the miscarriage of the movement at Lyons wavered. The people threatened and were for beating the *rappel.* The mayor refused. At last, at seven o'clock, he found an expedient, and promised to propose a plebiscite on the establishment of the Commune. A delegate read this declaration to the people, who at once withdrew from the Hôtel-de-Ville.

At the same moment M. De l'Espée conceived the brilliant idea of beating the *rappel,* which the people had in vain asked for since midnight. He picked up some National Guards on the side of order, re-entered the now empty Hôtel-de-Ville, and promulgated his victory. The municipal council informing him of the morning's agreement, De l'Espée refused to fix the date of the elections. Besides, said he, the general had promised him the aid of the garrison.

At eleven o'clock the prefect's call to arms had reassembled all the popular battalions. Groups formed before the Hôtel-de-Ville, crying *"Vive la Commune!"* De l'Espée sent for his troops, consisting of 250 foot-soldiers and two squadrons of hussars, who came up sluggishly. The multitude surrounded them; the Council protested; and the prefect had to discharge his warriors, there remaining to face the crowd only a line of firemen, and in the Hôtel-de-Ville two companies, of which but one was favourable to the party of order.

Towards mid-day a delegation summoned the Council to keep their promise. The councillors present — only few in number — were not averse to accepting as coadjutors two delegates from each company, but De l'Espée formally declared against any concession. At four o'clock a very numerous delegation from the Committee presented itself. The prefect spoke of retrenching and of strengthening the gates for defence; but the firemen raised the butt end of their muskets, opened the passage, and De l'Espée had to receive some of the delegates.

The crowd outside waxed unruly, impatient at these useless parleys. At half-past four the workmen from the manufactory of arms arrived, when a shot was fired from one of the houses of the square, killing Lyonnet, a working man. A hundred shots answered; the drums beat, the trumpets sounded the charge, and the battalions rushed into the Hôtel-de-Ville, while others searched the house whence the attack was supposed to have come.

At the noise of the firing the prefect broke off the conference and tried to escape as on the night before, mistook his way, was recognised and seized, together with the deputy of the *procureur de la République,* brought back with the latter into the large hall, and shown from the balcony. The crowd hooted him, convinced that he had given the order to fire upon the people. One of the reactionary guards, M. De Ventavon, on his flight from the *mairie*, was taken for the murderer of Lyonnet, and carried about on the litter on which the corpse had just been transported to the hospital.

The prefect and the procureur's deputy were left in the large hall in the midst of exasperated men. Many accused De l'Espée of having provoked the shooting down of the miners of Aubin under the Empire. He protested, stating that he had been director of the mines of Archambault, not those of Aubin. Little by little, the crowd, tired out, dispersed, and at eight o'clock about forty guards only remained in the hall. The prisoners took some food, when the president of the Commune, which was constituting itself in a neighbouring room, seeing everything calm, also withdrew. At nine o'clock the crowd returned, crying *"La Commune! La Commune! Sign!"* De l'Espée offered to sign his resignation, but added that he did so under compulsion. The prisoners were in the charge of two men, Victoire and Fillon, the latter an old exile, quite distracted, who turned now at the crowd, now against the prisoners. At ten o'clock, being depressed by the throng of people, Fillon, as in a dream, faced about, fired two shots from his revolver, killing his friend Victoire and wounding a drummer. Instantaneously the muskets were levelled at him, and Fillon and De l'Espée fell dead. The deputy, covered by the corpse of Fillon, escaped the discharge. The next day he and M. De Ventavon were set free.

During the evening a Commission constituted itself, chosen from amongst the officers of the National Guards and the habitual orators of the Club de la Vierge. It had the station occupied, took possession of the telegraph, seized the cartridges of the powder-magazine, and convoked the electors for the 29th. "The Commune," it said, "does not mean incendiarism, nor theft, nor pillage, as so many are pleased to give out, but the conquest of the franchises and the independence ravished from us by imperial and monarchical legislation; it is the true basis of the Republic." This was the whole preamble. In this hive of industry, surrounded by the thousands of miners of la Ricamarie and Firminy, they found not a word to say on the social question. The Commission only knew how to beat the *rappel*, which as at Lyons, was not responded to.

The next day, Sunday, the town, calm and curious, read the proclamation of the Commune, posted up side by side with the appeals of the general and of the procureur. While this latter, as became a good Radical, spoke of a Bonapartist plot, the general invited the Council to withdraw its resignation. He went to the councillors, who had taken refuge in the barracks, and said to them, "My soldiers won"t fight, but I have a thousand chassepots. If you will make use of them, forward!" The councillors protested their unfitness for military exploits; but at the same time, as at Lyons, refused to communicate with the Hôtel-de-Ville, considering "that one can only treat with honest men".

On the 27th the Alliance and *L'Eclaireur* altogether withdrew, and the Commission gradually dwindled down. In the evening, the few faithful still holding out received two young men, whom the delegates from the Central Committee at Lyons had sent. They urged resistance; but the Hôtel-de-Ville was being deserted, and on the morning of the 28th there were only about a hundred left. At six o'clock General Lavoye presented himself with the francs-tireurs of the Vosges and some troops come from Montbrison. The National Guards, on his appeal to lay down their arms in order to avoid blood-shed, consented to evacuate the *mairie*.

Numerous arrests were made. The Conservatives overwhelmed the Commune with the customary insults, and recounted that cannibals had been seen amongst the murderers of the prefect. *L'Eclaireur* did not fail to demonstrate that the movement was purely Bonapartist. The working men felt themselves vanquished, and at the solemn funeral of M. De L'Espée not loud but deep curses were uttered.

At Creuzot, also the proletarians were defeated. Yet the Socialists administered the town from the 4th September, the mayor, Durnay, being a former workman at the iron works. On the 25th, at the news from Lyons, they spoke of proclaiming the Commune. At their review on the 26th the National Guards cried "*Vive la Commune!*" and the crowd accompanied them to the Place de la Mairie, held by the colonel of cuirassiers, Gerhardt. He ordered the foot-soldiers to fire. They refused. He then ordered the cavalry to charge; but the guards levelled their bayonets and invaded the *mairie*. Dumay pronounced the abolition of the Versailles Government, proclaimed the Commune, and the red flag was hoisted.

But there, as everywhere else, the people did not move. The commander of Creuzot came back the next day with a reinforcement, dispersed the crowd, which was standing curious and passive in the square, and took possession of the *mairie*.

In four days all the revolutionary centres of the east, Lyons, St. Etienne, and Creuzot, were lost to the Commune.

Chapter 10
The Commune at Marseilles, Toulouse and Narbonne

Since the elections of the 8th February, the advent of the reactionists, the nomination of M. Thiers, the patched-up and shameful peace, the monarchy in prospect, the defiances and the defeats were as bitterly resented by the valiant town of Marseilles as by Paris. There the news of the 18th March fell upon a powder-magazine. Nevertheless, further details were looked for, when the 22nd brought the famous despatch of Rouher-Canrobert.

The clubs, playing a great part in the ardent life of Marseilles, were at once thronged. The prudent and methodical Radicals went to the club of the National Guard; the popular elements met at the El Dorado. There they applauded Gaston Crémieux, an elegant and effeminate speaker, now and then happy at epigrammatic turns, as, for instance, at Bordeaux. Gambetta owed him his election at Marseilles under the Empire. Crémieux at once hurried to the club of the National Guard, denounced Versailles, told them they could not allow the Republic to perish, but ought to act. The club, though highly indignant at the despatch, cautioned him against over-hastiness. The proclamations of the Central Committee, they said, did not announce any clearly defined politics. Signed by unknown names, they might well proceed from Bonapartists.

This Jacobin argument was ridiculous at Marseilles, where the despatch of M. Thiers had given the signal for the commotion. Who smacked of

Bonapartism — these unknown men rising against Versailles, or M. Thiers patronizing Rouher and his Ministers, and boasting of Canrobert's offer?

After a speech of Bouchet, the deputy of the *procureur de la République,* Gaston Cremieux reconsidered his first impulsive step, and accompanied by the delegates of the club, repaired to the El Dorado. There he read and made comments upon the *Officiel* of Paris, which he had got from the prefect, and calmed the excitement. "The Government of Versailles have raised their crutch against what they call the insurrection of Paris; but it has broken in their hands, and their attempt has brought forth the Commune. Let us swear that we are united for the defence of the Government of Paris, the only one that we recognize". They separated, ready for resistance, but resolved to bide their time.

Thus the excited population still checked itself when the prefect goaded it by the most stupid of provocations. This Admiral Cosnier, a distinguished naval officer, but politically a mere cipher, quite out of his element in these surroundings, where he had only just arrived, was the passive tool of the reaction, which since the 4th September had already several times fallen out with the National Guard — the civiques — who had proclaimed the Commune and expelled the Jesuits. The Rev. Father Tissier, though absent, was still its leader. The moderation of the town he mistook for cowardice. Like M. Thiers on the 17th he believed himself strong enough to make a brilliant stroke.

In the evening the Admiral held council with the mayor, Bories, an old wreck of 1848, who had dabbled in all the clerico-liberal coalitions, the *procureur de la République,* Guibert, a timid trimmer, and General Espivent de la Villeboisnet, one of those cruel caricatures in which the civil wars of South America abound. An obtuse Legitimist, a besotted zealot, the Syllabus incarnate, a carpet knight and former member of the Mixed Commissions of 1851, [The 'syllabus of Modem Errors" was a papal document condemning all forms of liberalism. The Mixed Commissions were in fact set up in January 1852 after Louis Napoleon's coup d'etat of the previous December. They consisted of prefects, prosecutors and selected officers to try oppositionists in areas placed under a state of siege. The accused were not allowed witnesses or counsel. 20,000 people were sentenced, and about half of them transported to North Africa and Cayenne.] During the war he had been expelled from Lille by the people, indignant alike at his utter incapacity and his antecedents. He brought the council the mot d'ordre of the priests and reactionaries, and proposed convoking the National Guards to make an armed demonstration in favour of Versailles. He would have asked for more, no doubt, but the garrison was solely composed of remnants of the army of the East and of a few disbanded artillery men. Cosnier, quite led astray, approved of the demonstration, and gave orders to the mayor and to the colonel of the National Guards to prepare for it.

On the 23rd March, at seven o'clock in the morning, the call to arms sounded. The ingenious idea of the prefect had spread over the town, and the popular battalions made ready to do it honour. From ten o'clock they arrived at the Cours du Chapitre, and the artillery of the National Guard was drawn up along the Cours St. Louis. At twelve, francs-tireurs, National Guards, soldiers of all arms mingling, gathered in the Cours Belzunce. Soon all the battalions of the Belle-de Mai and of Endourre mustered in full strength, while the battalions of order remained invisible.

The municipal council, taking fright, disavowed the demonstration and posted up a Republican address. The club of the National Guard joined the council and demanded the return of the Assembly to Paris and the exclusion from public functions of all the accomplices of the Empire. The deputy of the procureur, Bouchet, tendered his resignation.

All this time the battalions were marching up and down crying "*Vive Paris!*" Popular orators harangued them, and the club, apprehensive of an imminent explosion, sent Gaston Crémieux, Bouchet, and Frayssinet, to ask the prefect to break up the ranks and communicate the despatches from Paris. The delegates were discussing with Cosnier, when a terrific clamour rose from without. The prefecture was besieged.

At four o'clock the battalions, on foot for six hours, had moved, headed by their drums. Twelve or thirteen thousand men having marched through the Canebière and the Rue St. Férreol drew up before the prefecture. The delegates of the club tried to parley, when a shot was fired, and the crowd, rushing into the prefecture, arrested the prefect, his two secretaries, and General Ollivier. Gaston Cremieux appeared on the balcony, spoke of the rights of Paris, and recommended the maintenance of order. The crowd cheered, but still continued to enter and ask for arms. G. Crémieux had two columns formed and sent them to the iron works of Menpenti, whose guns were surrendered.

During this tumult a Commission of six members was formed: G. Crémieux, Job, Etienne, a street-porter, Maviel, a shoemaker, Gaillard, a mechanic, and Allerini, who deliberated in the midst of the crowd. Crémieux proposed setting at liberty the prisoners just made, but from all sides they cried, "Keep them as sureties." The Admiral was conducted into a neighbouring room, closely watched, and strange mania of all these popular movements — asked for his resignation. Cosnier, quite out of his latitude, signed what he was asked for.

The Commission posted up a proclamation that all the powers were concentrated in its hands, and feeling the necessity of strengthening itself, invited the municipal council and the club of the National Guard to send three delegates each. The council named David Bosc, Desservy, and Sidore; the club, Bouchet, Cartoux, and Fulgéras. The next day they made a moderate proclamation: "Marseilles has wished to prevent the civil war provoked by the circulars of Versailles. Marseilles will support a regularly constituted Republican Government sitting in the capital. The Departmental Commission, formed with the agreement of all Republican groups, will watch over the Republic till a new authority emanating from a regular Government sitting at Paris relieves it."

The names of the municipal council and of the club reassured the middle-class. The reactionaries continued drawing in their horns, and the army had evacuated the town during the night. Leaving the prefect in the trap into which he had thrust him, the coward Espivent, on the investment of the prefecture, went to hide himself at the mistress's of a commander of the National Guard named Spir, on whom he afterwards conferred the knighthood of the Legion of Honour for this service to moral order. At midnight he sneaked off and rejoined the troops, who, without hindrance from the people, lulled into security by their victory, reached the village of Aubagne, about seventeen kilometres from Marseilles.

Thus Marseilles was entirely in the hands of the people. The victory was even too complete for heads prone to exultation. That "city of the sun" is not propitious to soft tints; its sky, its fields, its men all affect crude colours. On the 24th the civil guards hoisted the red flag and already deemed the Commission too lukewarm. Sidore, Desservy and Fulgéras, regardless of their duty, kept aloof from the prefecture; Cartoux had gone to Paris for information, and so the whole burden weighed upon Bosc and Bouchet, who with Gaston Crémieux, strove to regularise the movement. Having said that the red flag was inopportune, and the detention of the hostages useless, they soon became suspected and menaced. On the evening of the 24th, Bouchet, quite discouraged, gave in his resignation, but, on Crémieux's complaint to the club of the National Guard, consented to resume his post.

These disagreements were already bruited about the town, and on the 25th the Commission was obliged to announce that "the most perfect accord united it with the municipal council." But the latter on the same day declared itself the only existing power, and called upon the National Guard to rouse from apathy. Trimming between the reaction and the people, it began that miserable play that was to end in ignominy.

While the Liberals were imitating the Tirards and the deputies of the extreme Left, to whom Dufaure referred in his despatches, Espivent in every point copied General Thiers. He had rifled all the administrative departments of Marseilles. The treasury office of the garrison had been shuffled off to Aubagne. Fifteen hundred Garibaldians of the army of the Vosges and soldiers who were rejoining their depots in Africa were left without bread, without pay, without *feuilles-de-routes,* and would have remained without refuge if Gaston Crémieux and Bouchet had not caused a provisional quarter-master to be named by the council. Thanks to the Commission, those who had shed their blood for France received bread and shelter. Gaston Cremieux said to them in an address, "You will remember when the time comes, the fraternal hand that we have held out to you." He was a mild enthusiast, who beheld the revolution under rather a bucolic aspect.

On the 26th the isolation of the Commission became more obvious. No one armed against it, but no one joined it. Almost all the mayors of the department refused to post up its proclamations, and at Arles a demonstration in favour of the red flag miscarried. The fiery spirits at the prefecture did nothing to explain the import of the flag which they had unfurled, and, in the midst of this dull calm, in view of Marseilles looking on curiously, it hung from the campanile of the prefecture motionless and mute as an enigma.

The capital of the south-west also saw its insurrection die out. Toulouse had vibrated at the thunder-burst of the 18th March. In the Faubourg St. Cyprien there was an intelligent and valiant working men's population that formed the very sinews of the National Guard, and had since the 19th relieved the watch to the cries of *"Vive* Paris!" A few revolutionaries summoned the prefect, Duportal, to pronounce for or against Paris. For a month the *Emancipation,* which he directed, had made a campaign against the rurals, and he had even in a public meeting emphasized his Republican views. But he was not the man to take the initiative, and refused to break with Versailles. The clubs, however, beset him, obliging the officers of the National Guard to take an oath to defend the Republic, and asked for cartridges. M. Thiers, seeing that Duportal would after all follow their lead, named as prefect Kératry, the former prefect of police of the 4th September. He arrived on the night of the 21st-22nd at the house of the general of the division, Nansouty, and being told that the garrison consisted of only 600 disbanded men, and that the whole National Guard would declare for Duportal, he beat his retreat on Agen.

On the 23rd the National Guard prepared a demonstration in order to take possession of the arsenal, when Duportal and the mayor rushed off to the Capitol, the Hôtel-de-Ville of Toulouse. The mayor declared that the intended review was not to take place, and Duportal that he would tender his resignation rather than pronounce for the movement. But the generals, afraid of this outbreak of the faubourg, took refuge in the arsenal. The mayor and the municipal council, understanding it would no longer do to continue their Platonic role, fled in their turn, and hence Duportal, left alone in this prefecture, shone forth as a great revolutionary, and therefore all the more worthy of the sympathy of the National Guard. He exerted himself to reassure the generals, went to the arsenal, intimated there his firm resolution to maintain order in the name of the Government of Versailles, the only one he recognised as legitimate, and was so successful that they advised M. Thiers to keep him in his post. Kératry, availing himself of his declaration, requested his aid to take possession of the prefecture, and Duportal gave him a rendezvous before the officers of the mobiles and of the National Guard, convoked for the next day, the 24th. Kératry understood and remained at Agen.

The object of this meeting was to find the volunteers against Paris asked for by the Assembly. Four officers of mobiles out of sixty offered their services to Versailles. The officers of the National Guard did not come to the prefecture, but, on the contrary, prepared at that same moment a demonstration against Kératry. At one o'clock 2,000 men were assembled in the Place du Capitole, and, their banner flying, repaired to the prefecture, where Duportal received their officers. One of them declared that, far from supporting the Assembly, they were ready to march against it, and that if M. Thiers did not make peace with Paris they would proclaim the Commune. At this name cries burst forth from all corners of the room, "*Vive la Commune! Vive* Paris!*" The officers, growing hot, decreed the arrest of Kératry, proclaimed the Commune, and summoned Duportal to place himself at their head. He tried to back out, and proposed to act only as the officious prompter of the chiefs of the Commune; but the officers, inveighing against defection, induced him to come out to the square of the prefecture, where he was acclaimed by the National Guard, and they proceeded to the Capitol.

Hardly arrived in the large hall, the leaders seemed much embarrassed. They offered the presidency in turn to the mayor, to other municipal councillors, who slunk away, and to Duportal, who got off by drawing up a manifesto, which was read from the large balcony. "The Commune of Toulouse," it said, "declares for the Republic one and indivisible, urges the deputies of Paris to be the intermediaries between the Government and the great town, and summons M. Thiers to dissolve the Assembly." The mass cheered this milk-and-water Commune, which believed in the deputies of the Left and the oppression of M. Thiers by the rural majority.

In the evening some officers of the National Guard appointed an Executive Commission, composed, with two or three exceptions, of mere talkers; in this the principal leaders of the movement did not figure. It contented itself with posting up the manifesto, and neglected the smallest precautions, even that of occupying the railway station. The generals, nevertheless, did not dare to stir from their arsenal, where they were joined on the 26th by the first president of the court and the procureur-general, who launched an address calling upon the population to rally round them. The National Guard wanted to answer by storming the arsenal, and already the faubourg flocked to the Capitol. But the Commission preferred to negotiate, sent word to the arsenal that it would dissolve if the Government appointed a Republican prefect in the stead of Kératry and entirely abandoned Duportal, who, it is true, had done nothing. The negotiations lasted all the evening, and the National Guard, tired out, deceived by their chiefs, and fancying everything settled, returned to their homes.

Kératry, well informed of all these failures, arrived the next day at the railway station with three squadrons of cavalry, proceeded to the arsenal, broke off the negotiations, and gave the order to march. At one o'clock the Versaillese army, 200 cavalry and 600 ill-assorted soldiers strong, opened its campaign. One column occupied the St. Cyprien Bridge, in order to separate the town from the faubourg, another proceeded to the prefecture, and the third, with Nansouty, Kératry, and the magistrates, marched on the Capitol.

About 300 men filled the courts, the windows, and the terrace. The Versaillese deployed their troops and placed six guns in line at about sixty yards from the edifice, thus recklessly exposing their infantry and artillery men to the muskets of the insurgents. The first president of the court and the procureur-general advanced to parley, but obtained nothing. Kératry read the riot act, his voice being drowned by cries. A single blank-cartridge volley would have scared soldiers and artillery men, who might besides have been harassed on both flanks. But the leaders had fled from the Capitol. The courage of a few men might still have brought about a fight, when the Republican Association interposed, persuaded the guards to retreat, and saved Kératry. The prefecture was taken just as easily, and that same evening Kératry installed himself there. The members of the Executive Commission the next day published a manifesto of such platitude as to secure them impunity, and one of them got himself named mayor by Kératry.

Thus the generous working men of Toulouse, who had risen to the cry of "*Vive Paris!*" were left in the lurch by those who had raised the insurrection. A disastrous check this for Paris, for the whole south would have followed the example of Toulouse if victorious.

The man of thought and energy, wanting in all these movements, appeared in the insurrection of Narbonne. The old city, Gallic in its enthusiasm, Roman in its tenacity, is the true centre of democracy in the department of Aude. Nowhere during the war had a more vigorous protest been entered against the shortcomings of Gambetta. For this very reason the National Guards of Narbonne had not yet received their muskets, when those of Carcassonne had long since been armed. At the news of the 18th March, Narbonne did not hesitate, but declared for Paris. To proclaim the Commune, an exile of the Empire, a man of strong convictions and firm character, Digeon, was at once applied to. Digeon, as modest as he was resolute, offered the direction of the movement to his comrade in exile, Marcou, the recognized chief of the democracy in the Aude, one of the most ardent opponents of Gambetta during the war. Marcou, a crafty lawyer, afraid of compromising himself, and dreading the energy of Digeon in the chief town of the department, induced him to leave for Narbonne. Digeon arrived there on the 23rd, and first thought of converting the municipal council to the principles of the Commune. But on the refusal of the mayor, Raynal, to summon the council, the people, out of all patience, invaded the Hôtel-de-Ville on the evening of the 24th, and arming themselves with the muskets held by the municipality, installed Digeon and his friends. He appeared on the balcony, proclaimed the Commune of Narbonne united to that of Paris, and immediately proceeded to take measures of defence.

The following day Raynal tried to rally the garrison, and some companies formed before the Hôtel-de-Ville; but the people, especially the women, worthy of the Parisian sisters, disarmed the soldiers. A captain and a lieutenant were retained as hostages; the rest of the garrison went and shut itself up in the St. Bernard Barracks. As Raynal still continued stirring up resistance, the people arrested him on the 26th; and Digeon, with the three hostages, at the head of a detachment of Federals, went to take possession of the prefecture, placing pickets at the railway station and telegraph office. To get arms he forced the arsenal, where, despite their lieutenant, who commanded them to fire, the soldiers surrendered their guns. The same day the delegates from the neighbouring Communes arrived, and Digeon set to work to generalize the movement.

He had clearly understood that the departmental insurrections would soon founder if not well combined, and he wanted to hold out a helping hand to the rising of Toulouse and of Marseilles. Béziers and Cette had already promised him their support, and he was preparing to leave for Béziers, when, on the 28th, two companies of Turcos arrived, soon followed by other troops sent from Montpellier, Toulouse, and Perpignan. From this moment Digeon was obliged to stand on the defensive. He had barricades thrown up, reinforced the posts, and ordered the Federals always to await the attacks and to aim at the officers.

We shall return to this subject later on. Paris now recalls us. The other provincial movements were but momentary vibrations. On the 28th, when Paris was still elated with victory, all the Communes of France were already swept away save those of Marseilles and Narbonne.

Chapter 11
The Council of the Commune wavers

The Place de l'Hôtel-de-Ville was still astir when the newly elected members of the Commune assembled in the municipal council-hall.

The ballot had returned sixteen mayors, adjuncts, and Liberals of all shades, a few Radicals, and about sixty revolutionaries of all sorts.

How came these latter to be chosen? All must be told, and virile truth at last substituted for the stale flattery of the old romantic school styling itself "revolutionary". There might be something more terrible than the defeat: to misconstrue or to forget its causes.

Responsibility weighs heavily enough upon the elected, but we must not charge it all to one side — the electors also have their share of it.

The Central Committee had told the people on Sunday the 19th, "Prepare for your communal elections." They thus had a whole week in which to frame a mandate and select their mandatories. No doubt the resistance of the mayors and the occupation of the military posts kept away many of the revolutionary electors from their arrondissements, but there still remained enough citizens to conduct the work of selection.

Never had a mandate been more indispensable, for the question at issue was to give Paris a communal constitution acceptable to all France. Never did Paris stand in such need of enlightened and practical men, capable at once of negotiating and of combating.

Yet there was never less preparatory discussion. A few men only recalled to prudence a people habitually so over-scrupulous in electoral matters, and which had just made a revolution to get rid of their representatives. The

Committee of the twenty arrondissements issued a manifesto very pertinent in several points, and which might have served as an outline; the two delegates at the Home Office tried, through an article in the *Officiel*, to impress Paris with the importance of her vote. Not a single assembly framed the general programme of Paris; only two or three arrondissements gave some sort of mandate.

Instead of voting for a programme, they voted for names. Those who had demanded the Commune, made a mark at the Corderie or during the siege, were elected without being asked for further explanations, some even twice, like Flourens, in spite of the blunders of the 31st October. Only seven or eight, and those not the best, of the obscure men of the Central Committee were named, the latter, it is true, having decided not to present itself for election. The public meetings in many arrondissements sent up the most violent talkers, romanticists sprung up during the siege, and lacking all knowledge of practical life. Nowhere were the candidates put to any test. In the ardour of the struggle they took no thought for the morrow. One might have fancied that the object in view was a simple demonstration, not the founding of a new order of things.

Twenty-four workmen only were elected, and of these a third belonged rather to the public meetings than to the International or the working men's societies. The other delegates of the people were chosen from the middle-class and the so-called liberal professions, accountants, publicists — there were as many as twelve of these doctors and lawyers. These, save a few really studious men, whether veterans or new-comers, were as ignorant as the workmen of the political and administrative mechanism of the bourgeoisie, albeit full of their own personality. The safety of the Central Committee lay in this, that it was unadorned with great men, each one provided with a formula of his own. The Council of the Commune, on the contrary, abounded in chapels, groups, semi-celebrities, and hence endless competition and rivalry.

Thus the precipitation and heedlessness of the revolutionary electors sent up to the Hôtel-de-Ville a majority of men, most of them devoted, but chosen without discernment, and, into the bargain, abandoned them to their own inspirations, to their whims, without any determined mandate to restrain and guide them in the struggle entered upon.

Time and experience would no doubt have corrected this negligence, but time was wanting. The people never hold sway but for an hour, and woe to them if they are not then ready, armed from head to foot. The elections of the 26th March were irreparable.

Only about sixty of those elected were present at the first sitting. At its opening, the Central Committee came to congratulate the Council. The chairman by seniority, Beslay, a capitalist of a fraternizing turn of mind, made the opening speech. He very happily defined this young revolution: "The enfranchisement of the Commune of Paris is the enfranchisement of all the communes of the Republic. Your adversaries have said that you have struck the Republic. It is as with the pile, to be driven deeper into the earth. The Republic of 1793 was a soldier, who wanted to centralize all the forces of the nation; the Republic of 1871 is a workman, who above all wants liberty to construct peace. The Commune will occupy itself with all that is local, the Department with what is regional, the Government with what is national. Let us not overstep this limit, and the country and the Government will be happy and proud to applaud this revolution." This was the naive illusion of an old man, who, nevertheless, had had the experience of a long political life. This programme, so moderate in its form, was nothing less than the death-knell of the great bourgeoisie, as shown during this very sitting.

There were already some jarring notes. The violent and the giddy-headed launched out into random motions, and wanted the Commune to declare itself omnipotent. Tirard, elected by his arrondissement, took advantage of this occasion to withdraw, stating that his mandate was purely municipal, that he could not recognize the political character of the Commune; gave in his resignation, and ironically bade farewell to the Council: "I leave you my sincere good wishes; may you succeed in your task," etc.

The insolence of this dishonest man, who for eight days had been busy in fomenting civil war and now threw up the mandate solicited in his address to the electors, evoked general indignation. The more impatient wanted to have him arrested, others to declare his mandate forfeited. He escaped scot-free because he had said at the Versailles tribune, "When you enter the Hôtel-de-Ville, you are not sure to return from it."

This incident no doubt induced the Council to vote the secrecy of their sittings, their awkward pretext being that the Commune was not a parliament. This decision produced a very bad effect, violating the best traditions of the great Commune of 1792-93, as it gave the Council the appearance of a conspiracy, and it was found necessary to quash it two weeks after, when the newspapers abounded in fantastic reports, as a natural consequence of the secret sittings. But the publicity never consisted in anything but the insertion of curtailed reports in the *Officiel*. The Council never admitted the public, whose presence would have prevented many errors.

The next day the Council subdivided itself into commissions charged with the various services. A Military Commission, and others of Finance, Justice, Public Safety, Labour and Exchange, Provisions, Foreign Affairs, Public Services, and Education were named. The Executive Commission was composed of Lefrançais, Duval, Félix Pyat, Bergert, Tridon, Eudes, and Vaillant, of whom Duval, Bergeret, and Eudes also belonged to the Military Commission.

It had just been voted that all decrees should be signed *The Commune* — a vote too soon forgotten — when the delegates of the Central Committee were announced. After waiting half an hour they were introduced. "Citizens," said their spokesman, "the Central Committee comes to hand over to you its revolutionary powers. We resume the functions defined by our statutes."

This was the moment for the Council to affirm its authority. The only representative of the population, alone responsible, it should now have absorbed all powers, not tolerating the co-existence of a Committee which was sure always to remember the paramount position it had held and strive to recover it. In the previous sitting, the Council had done justice to the Central Committee in voting that they had deserved well of Paris and the Republic, and now taking them at their word, ought to have declared that the role of the Committee had come to an end. Instead of an authoritative decision in this sense, recriminations were resorted to.

A member of the Council recalled the promise of the Central Committee to dissolve after the elections. Unless they aimed at power, there was no necessity for the maintenance of their organization. Varlin and Beslay defended the existence of the Committee, which was combated by Jourde and Rigault. The delegates, who would have yielded to a peremptory word, held out against this weakness. "This is," they said, "the Federation that has saved the Republic. The last word is not yet said. To dissolve this organization is to break your strength. The Central Committee does not pretend to share in the government. It remains the bond of union between you and the National Guard, the right hand of the Revolution. We again become what we were, the great *conseil de famille* of the National Guard."

This simile made a marked impression. The debate was prolonged, and the delegates of the Committee withdrew, no conclusion having been arrived at.

Thereupon, without preamble, like a Jack-in-the-box, Félix Pyat jumped up and proposed the abolition of the conscription.

On the 3rd March he had stolen away from the National Assembly, as he had on the 31st October deserted the Hôtel-de-Ville, and, a few days after, sneaked out of prison. On the 18th March he did not stir, while Delescluze had joined the revolution from the first day. Félix Pyat waited for the triumph, and on the eve of the elections came to beat the drum before the Committee, "which teaches modesty to the proudest name and inspires men of genius with a feeling of inferiority." Elected by about 12,000 votes in the tenth arrondissement, he was now forward to take his seat at the Hôtel-de-Ville.

The hour awaited for twenty years had at last struck; he was about to tread the boards. Amidst the crowd of dramatists, miracle-workers, romanticists, visionaries, and Jacobin relics, trailing since 1830 at the heels of the social revolution, his business had been that of appeals to regicide and revolutionary insurgency, of epistles, allegories, toasts, invocations, evocations, pieces of rhetoric on the events of the day, tinkering with the old Montagnard wares, and doing them up with a little humanitarian varnish.

Under the Empire his rabid manifestoes had been the joy of the police and of the Bonapartist journals, excellent sops to throw to the people, who could not extract from them a practical idea or a grain of sense. This intoxication was more than half-feigned. The dishevelled madman of the stage behind the scenes turned crafty and wary to a degree. At bottom he was only a splenetic sceptic, sincere only in his self-idolatry. He came to the Commune his pockets crammed with decrees.

When he read his motion, it was lustily cheered by the romanticists and passed at once. Yet still in the morning the Council had intimated nothing of the sort, but only stated in the proclamation in which they presented themselves to Paris: "Today the decision on house-rents, tomorrow that on the overdue bills, the public services re-established and simplified, and the National Guards reorganized, these are our first acts." And now it abruptly encroached upon national affairs. Commune in the morning, Constituent Assembly in the evening.

If they wanted to change the revolution from a communal into a national one, they ought to have said so, boldly set forth their whole programme, and demonstrated to France the necessity of their attempt. But what signified this decree, improvised at random, without a preliminary declaration and without a sequel? This *quid pro quo* was not even taken up. Under pretext of avoiding parliamentarism, the matters at issue were hurried over.

Then the Council decreed the general exemption of rents due between October, 1870, and July, 1871. Versailles had offered only delays; this was contrary to equity. The Council exempted rents for the good reason that property ought to bear its share of the general sacrifices; but it did not exempt a lot of industrialists who had made scandalous profits during the siege. This was contrary to justice.

Finally, they neglected to announce themselves to the provinces, already so forsaken by the Central Committee. A commission had certainly been charged to draw up an address, but its work had not pleased, and another one had been named, so that what with one commission and another, the programme of the Commune was kept in suspense for twenty-two days, and the Council had allowed all the insurrections of the provinces to die out without giving them any advice or ideas.

These encroachments, this disorder, disturbed Paris with the thought that the new power had neither very clear ideas nor consciousness of the situation. The Liberal fraction of the Council took advantage of this pretext to withdraw. If their convention of the 20th had been sincere, if they had cared for the destinies of Paris, the mayor and adjuncts elected would have courageously stood by their mandates. Like those of the provinces, they deserted, but were still more culpable, since they had not protested against their elections. Many had never been seen at the Hôtel-de-Ville; others wrung their hands, lamenting, "Where are we going?" Some shammed mortal illness: "You see I am at my last gasp." Those who have been most abusive since, then sought for humble evasions. Not one broke boldly.

Their resignations, the double elections, left twenty-two seats vacant on the 30th, when the Council verified the credentials. Faithful to the best traditions of the French Republic, it admitted the Hungarian Frankel, one of the most intelligent members of the International, elected in the thirteenth arrondissement. Six candidates had not received the eighth part of the votes required by the law of 1849; the Council passed by this irregularity because the arrondissements of these candidates, composed of reactionary quarters, were emptying themselves from day to day.

The men of order, twice chastised, continued migrating to Versailles, which they stocked with a new store of rancour and rhodomontades. The town had assumed a warlike aspect; all announced that the struggle was near at hand. Already M. Thiers had cut off Paris from France. On the eve of the April term, the 31st March, the director of the general post-office, Rampont, belying the word of honour he had given the delegate of the Central Committee, Thiesz, made off after having disorganized the postal service, and M. Thiers suppressed all the goods trains and kept back all correspondence destined for Paris.

On the 1st April he officially announced war. "The Assembly," he telegraphed to the prefects, "is sitting at Versailles, where the organization of one of the finest armies that France has ever possessed is being completed. Good citizens may then take heart and hope for the end of a struggle which will be sad but short." A cynical boast of that same bourgeoisie which had refused to organize armies against the Prussians. "One of the finest armies," was as yet only the rabble of the 18th March, strengthened by five or six regiments; about 35,000 men, with 3,000 horses, and 5,000 gendarmes or sergents-de-ville, the only corps that had any solidity.

Paris would not believe in the existence even of this army. The popular papers demanded a sortie, speaking of the journey to Versailles as a promenade. The most impetuous was the *Vengeur,* in which Félix Pyat furiously shook his cap and bells. He exhorted the Commune "to press Versailles. Poor Versailles! it no longer remembers the 5th and 6th October, 1789, when the women of the Commune alone sufficed to catch its king." On the morning of Sunday the 2nd April the same member of the Executive Commission announced to Paris: "Yesterday at Versailles the soldiers, requested to vote by *aye* or *no* if they were to march on Paris, answered No!"

Chapter 12
The Versaillese beat back the Commune patrols and massacre prisoners

That very day, the 2nd April, at one o'clock, without warning, without summons, the Versaillese opened fire and launched their shells into Paris.

For several days their cavalry had exchanged shots with our advance posts at Chatillon and Putteaux. We occupied Courbevoie, that commands the route to Versailles, which made the rurals very anxious. On the 2nd, at ten o'clock in the morning, three brigades of the best Versailles troops, 10,000 strong, arrived at the cross-roads of Bergeres. Six or seven hundred cavalry of the brigade Gallifet supported this movement, while we had only three federal battalions at Courbevoie, in all five or six hundred men, defended by a halffinished barricade on the St. Germain road. Their watch, however, was well kept; their vedettes had killed the head-surgeon of the Versaillese army, whom they had mistaken for a colonel of gendarmerie.

At mid-day the Versaillese, having cannonaded the barracks of Courbevoie and the barricade, launched themselves to the assault. At the first shots from our men they scampered off, abandoning on the road cannon and officers. Vinoy was obliged to come himself and rally the renegades. Meanwhile the 113th of the line outflanked Courbevoie on the right, and the infantry of the marines turned left, marching through Putteaux. Too inferior in number and fearing to be cut off from Paris, the Federals evacuated Courbevoie, and, pursued by shells, fell back on the Avenue de Neuilly, leaving twelve dead and some prisoners. The gendarmes had taken five, one of whom was a child of fifteen, beating them unmercifully, and shot them at the foot of Mont-Valérien. This expedition concluded, the army regained its cantonment.

At the report of the cannon all Paris started. No one believed in an attack, so completely did all, since the 28th, live in an atmosphere of confidence. It was no doubt an anniversary, a misunderstanding at the utmost. When the news, the ambulance-carriages, arrived; when the word was spoken, "The siege is recommencing!" an explosion of horror shook all the quarters. An affrighted hive, such was Paris. The barricades were again thrown up, the call to arms beaten everywhere, and the cannon drawn to the ramparts of the Porte-Maillot and of the Ternes. At three o'clock 80,000 men were on foot crying, "To Versailles!" The women excited the battalions, and spoke of marching in the vanguard.

The Executive Commission met and posted up a proclamation: "The royalist conspirators have attacked; despite the moderation of our attitude, they have attacked. Our duty is to defend the great city against these culpable aggressions." In the Commission, the generals Duval, Bergeret, and Eudes declared for an attack. "The enthusiasm," they said, "is irresistible, unique. What can Versailles do against 100,000 men? We must sally out." Their colleagues resisted, especially Félix Pyat, confronted with his rant and vapourings of the morning. His buffoonery stood him in the stead of a life-preserver. "One does not start," said he, "at random, without cannon, with cadres, and without leaders;" and he demanded the return of the strength of the troops. Duval, who since the 19th March had been strongly bent upon a sortie, violently rebuked him: "Why, then, for three days have you shouted, 'To Versailles'?" The most energetic opponent of the sortie was Lefrançais. Finally, the four civil members — that is, the majority — decided that the generals should present a detailed statement as to their forces in men, artillery, munitions, and transports. The same evening the Commission named Cluseret delegate at War jointly with Eudes, who, being a member of the so-called party of action, owed this post only to the patronage of his old cronies.

In spite of the majority of the Commission, the generals set out. They had, anyway received no formal order to the contrary. Félix Pyat had even concluded by saying, "After all, if you think you are ready . . ." They saw Flourens always ready for a *coup-de-main,* other colleagues equally adventurous, and, on their own authority, certain of being followed by the National Guard. They sent the *chefs-de-légion* the order to form columns. The battalions of the right bank were to concentrate at the Place Vendôme and Place Wagram; those of the left bank, at the Place d'Italie and Champ-de-Mars.

These movements, without staff officers to guide them, were very badly executed. Many men marched hither and thither, grew tired. Yet at midnight there were still about 20,000 men on the right bank of the Seine and about 17,000 on the left.

From eight o'clock to midnight the Council was sitting. The inexorable Félix Pyat, always pertinent, demanded the abolition of the budget of public worship. The majority immediately satisfied him. He might just as well have decreed the abolition of the Versaillese army. Of the sortie, of the military preparations deafening Paris, no one breathed a word in the Council — no one disputed the field with the generals.

The plan of the latter, which they communicated to Cluseret, was to make a strong demonstration in the direction of Rueil, while two columns were to march on Versailles by Meudon and the plateau of Chatillon. Bergeret, assisted by Flourens, was to operate on the right; Eudes and Duval were to command the columns of the centre and the left. A simple idea, and easy of execution with experienced officers and solid heads of columns. But most of the battalions had been without leaders since the 18th March, the National Guards without cadres, and the generals who assumed the responsibility of leading 40,000 men had never conducted a single battalion into the field. They neglected even the most elementary precautions, knew not how to collect artillery, ammunition-wagons or ambulances, forgot to make an order of the day, and left the men for several hours without food in a penetrating fog. Every Federal chose the leader he liked best. Many had no cartridges, and believed the sortie to be a simple demonstration. The Executive Commission had just posted up a despatch from the Place Vendôme, headquarters of the National Guard: "Soldiers of the line are all coming to us, and declare that, save the superior officers, no one wants to fight."

At three o'clock in the morning Bergeret's column, about 10,000 men strong and with only eight ordnance pieces, arrived at the bridge of Neuilly. It was necessary to give the men, who had taken nothing since the evening before, time to recover themselves. At dawn they moved in the direction of Rued. The battalions marched by sections in line in the middle of the road, without scouts, and cheerfully climbed the Plateau des Bergeres, when suddenly a shell burst into their ranks, followed by a second. Mont-Valérien had opened fire.

A terrible panic broke up the battalions, amidst thousandfold cries of "Treason!" the whole National Guard believing that we occupied Mont-Valérien. Many members of the Commune, of the Central Committee, at the Place Vendôme, knew the contrary, and very foolishly concealed it, living in the hope that the fortress would not fire. It possessed, it is true, only two or three badly appointed guns, the range of which the Guards might have escaped by one quick movement; but, surprised when in a state of blind confidence, they fancied themselves betrayed, and fled on all sides. Bergeret exhausted every means to stay them. A shell cut in two the brother of his chief-of-staff, an officer of the regular army gone over to the Commune. The greater part of the Federals dispersed in the fields and regained Paris. The 91st only and a few others, 1,200 men in all, remained with Bergeret, and, dividing into small groups, reached Rueil. Shortly after, Flourens arrived by the road of Asnières, bringing hardly a thousand men. The rest had lagged behind in Paris or on the way. Flourens, pressing forward all the same, arrived at the Malmaison, put Gallifet's chasseurs to flight, and the Parisian vanguard pushed on as far as Bougival.

The Versaillese, surprised by this sortie, only drew up very late, towards ten o'clock. Ten thousand men were launched against Bougival, and the batteries placed on the hill of La Jonchere cannonaded Rueil. Two brigades of cavalry on the right and that of Gallifet on the left defended the wings. The Parisian vanguard — a mere handful of men — offered a determined resistance, in order to give Bergeret time to operate his retreat, which commenced towards one o'clock, on Neuilly, where they fortified the bridge-head. Some valiant men, who had obstinately held out in Rueil, with great difficulty gained the bridge of Asnières, whither they were pursued by the cavalry, who took some prisoners.

Flourens was surprised at Rueil, and the house which he occupied with some officers surrounded by gendarmes. As he prepared to defend himself, the officer of the detachment, Captain Desmarets, cleft his head with so furious a blow of the sabre that the brains gushed out. The body was thrown into a dust-cart and taken to Versailles, where the fine ladies gathered to enjoy the spectacle. Thus ended the large-hearted man, beloved of the Revolution.

At the extreme left Duval had passed the night with six or seven thousand men on the plateau of Chatillon. Towards seven o'clock he formed a column of picked men, advanced to Petit-Bicetre, dispersed the outpost of General du Barail, and sent an officer to reconnoitre Villecoublay, that commanded the route. The officer announced that the roads were free, and the Federals advanced without fear. When near the hamlet firing commenced. The men deployed as skirmishers, and Duval, uncovered in the middle of the road, set them the example. They held out for several hours. A few shells would have sufficed to dislodge the enemy; but Duval had no artillery. Even cartridges were already wanting, and he had to send to Chatillon for more.

The bulk of the Federals who occupied the redoubt, confounded in an inextricable disorder, already believed themselves surrounded on all sides. The messengers of Duval on their arrival begged, menaced, but could not obtain either reinforcements or munitions. An officer even ordered a retreat. The unfortunate Duval, totally abandoned, was assailed by the Derroja brigade and the whole Pellé division, 8,000 men. He retired with his troops to the plateau of Chatillon.

Our efforts in the centre were not more fortunate. Ten thousand men had left the Champ-de-Mars at three o'clock in the morning with Ranvier and

Avrial. General Eudes as his whole battle array had ordered the troops to move on. At six o'clock the 61st reached the Moulineaux, defended by gendarmes; these were soon forced to retreat to Meudon, strongly occupied by a Versaillese brigade entrenched in the villas and armed with machine-guns. The Federals had only eight pieces, while Paris possessed hundreds, and each of these had only eight rounds. At six o'clock, weary of shooting at walls, they retreated to Molineaux. Ranvier went in search of cannon, and mounted them in the fort of Issy, thus preventing the Versaillese from taking the offensive.

We were beaten at all points, and the Communalist papers shouted "Victory!" Led astray by staffs which did not even know the names of the generals, the Executive Commission announced the junction of Flourens and Duval at Courbevoie. Félix Pyat, again become bellicose, six times cried in his *Vengeur*, "To Versailles!" Despite the runaways of the morning, the popular enthusiasm did not flag. A battalion of 300 women marched up the Champs-Elysées, the red flag at their head, demanding to sally forth against the enemy. The evening papers announced the arrival of Flourens at Versailles.

At the ramparts the sad truth was discovered. Long files of guards re-entered by all the gates, and at six o'clock the only army outside Paris was the guards on the Chatillon plateau. A few shells falling in their midst completed the disorder. Some of the men threatened Duval, who was making desperate efforts to keep them together. He remained, surrounded only by a handful of men, but always equally resolute. The whole night he, usually so taciturn, did not cease repeating, "I will not retreat."

The next day at eight o'clock the plateau and the neighbouring villages were surrounded by the Derroja brigade and Pellé's division. "Surrender and your lives will be spared," General Pellé had told them. The Parisians surrendered. The Versaillese at once seized the soldiers fighting in the ranks of the Federals and shot them. The prisoners, between two lines of chasseurs, were sent on to Versailles, while their officers, bare-headed, their braid torn off, were put at the head of the convoy.

At Petit-Bicetre they met the general-in-Chief, Vinoy. He commanded that the officers be shot, but the leader of the escort reminding him of General Pellé's promise, Vinoy said, "Is there a commander?" "Myself," said Duval, darting from the ranks. Another advanced: "I am the chief of Duval's staff." Then the commander of the volunteers of Montrouge placed himself by their side. "You are awful scoundrels," said Vinoy; and, turning to his officers, 'shoot them." Duval and his comrades disdained to reply, cleared a ditch, leant against a wall on which were inscribed the words, "Duval, gardener." They disrobed, and, crying *"Vive la Commune!"* died for it. A horseman tore off Duval's boots and carried them about as a trophy, and an editor of the *Figaro* took possession of his bloodstained collar.

Thus the army of order inaugurated the civil war by the massacre of the prisoners. It had begun on the 2nd; on the 3rd, at Chatou, General Gallifet had three Federals shot who were surprised in an inn taking their meal, and then he published a ferocious proclamation: "War has been declared by the bandits of Paris. They have assassinated my soldiers. It is a merciless war which I declare against these assassins. I had to make an example."

The general who called the combatants of Paris "bandits" and these assassinations "an example" was a scamp of high life, first ruined, then kept by actresses. Famous for his brigandage in Mexico, he had in a few years obtained a generalship of brigade by the charms of his wife, prominent in the orgies of the Imperial court. Nothing is more edifying in this civil war than the standard-bearers of the "honest people."

Their band in full strength hastened to the Paris Avenue at Versailles to receive the prisoners of Chatillon. The whole Parisian emigration, functionaries, dandies, women of the world and of the streets, all came with the rage of hyenas to strike the Federals with their fists, with canes and parasols, pushing off their képis and cloaks, crying, "Down with the assassins! To the guillotine!" Amongst these "assassins" was the geographer Elisée Reclus, taken with Duval. In order to give them time to glut their fury, the escort made several halts before conducting their prisoners to the barracks of the gendarmes. They were thrown into the docks of Satory, and thence carried to Brest in cattle-trucks.

Picard wanted to associate all the honest people of the provinces in this baiting. "Never," telegraphed this pimply-looking Falstaff, "have baser countenances of a base demagogy met the afflicted gaze of honest men."

Already, the evening before, after the assassinations of Mont-Valérien and of Chatou, M. Thiers had written to his prefects, "The moral effect is excellent." Odious repetition of those words, "Order reigns in Warsaw," and "The chassepot has done wonders." And it is well known that it was not the French bourgeoisie, but a daughter of the people who spoke those great words, "I have never seen French blood shed without my hair standing on end."

Chapter 13
The Commune is defeated at Marseilles and Narbonne

The same sun that saw the scale turn against Paris looked also on the defeat of the people of Marseilles.

The paralytic Commission still continued to doze, when, on the 26th, Espivent beat the réveille, placed the department in a state of siege, and issued a proclamation *à la* Thiers. The municipal council began to tremble, and on the 27th withdrew their delegates from the prefecture. Gaston Crémieux and Bouchet were at once sent to the *mairie* to announce that the Commission was ready to withdraw before the council. The council asked for time to consider.

The evening was passing away, and the Commission searching for a loophole by which to escape from a position become untenable, when Bouchet proposed to telegraph to Versailles that they would resign their powers into the hands of a Republican prefect. Poor issue of a great movement! They knew what the Republican prefects of M. Thiers were. The Commission, jaded, discouraged, let Bouchet draw up the telegram, when Landeck, Amouroux, and May arrived, sent, they said, by Paris. They spoke in the name of the great town. Bouchet wanted to verify their powers and contested their validity, which were indeed more than contestable, whereat the members of the Commission grew indignant. The magic name of victorious Paris resuscitated the enthusiasm of the first hours, and Bouchet left the place. At midnight the municipal council decided to maintain its resolution, and communicated this to the club of the National Guard, who immediately followed their example. At half-past one in the morning the delegates of the club informed the Commission that their powers were at an end. The Liberal bourgeoisie, coward-like, stole away, the Radicals backed out, and the people remained alone to face the reaction.

This was the second phase of the movement. The most exalted of the three delegates, Landeck, became an authority paramount to the Commission. The cold-blooded Republicans who heard him and knew of his past dealings with the Imperialist police, suspected a Bonapartist under the grossly ignorant bully. He was indeed but a juggler, meant for the itinerant stage, of grotesque vanity, and shrinking from nothing, because ignorant of everything. The situation waxed tragic with this mountebank for a leader. Crémieux, unable to find another issue, was still for the solution of the evening before. On the 28th he wrote to the municipal council that the Commission was ready to retire, leaving them the responsibility of events, and urged his colleagues to release the hostages; this only rendered him the more suspect of moderatism. Closely watched, threatened, he lost heart at these disputes, and that same evening left the prefecture. His secession divested the Commission of all authority. It succeeded in discovering his retreat, made an appeal to his devotion to the cause, and led him back to the prefecture, there to resume his strange part of a chief at once captive and responsible.

The municipal council did not answer Crémieux's letter and on the 29th the Commission renewed its proposal. The council still remained silent. In the evening 400 delegates of the National Guard met at the museum, decided to federate the battalions, and appointed a commission charged to negotiate between the Hôtel-de-Ville and the prefecture. But these delegates represented only the revolutionary element of the battalions, and the Hôtel-de-Ville plunged more and more into a slough of despond.

A war of proclamations now ensued between the two powers. On the 30th the council answered the deliberations of the museum meeting with a proclamation from the leaders of the reactionary battalions. The Commission launched a manifesto demanding the autonomy of the Commune and the abolition of prefectures; immediately after, the council declared the general secretary of the prefect the legal representative of the Government, and invited him to retake his post. The secretary turned a deaf ear and took refuge aboard *La Couronne,* many councillors also betaking themselves to the frigate — gratuitous cowardice, since the most notorious reactionaries went to and fro without being in the least interfered with. The energy of the Commission was mere show; it arrested only two or three functionaries, the procureur Guibert, the deputy, and for a short time the director of the customhouse, and the son of the mayor. General Ollivier was set free as soon as it became known that he had refused to form part of the Mixed

Commissions of 1851. They were even so loose as to leave a post close to the prefecture in the hands of chasseurs forgotten by Espivent. The flight of the council, therefore, appeared only the more shameful. The town continued to be calm, gay, facetious. One day the patrol boat *Le Renard* coming to show its cannon at the Canebière, the crowd thronging on the quay hooted so much that it was obliged to slip its cable and rejoin the frigate in the new harbour.

The Commission inferred that no one would dare to attack them, and thus took no measures of defence. They might easily have armed the heights of Notre-Dame-de-la-Garde, which commanded the town, and enlisted a great number of Garibaldians, some officers of the last campaign having offered to organize everything. The Commission thanked them, said that the troops would not come, and that even if they did, they would fraternize with the people. They contented themselves with hoisting the black flag, addressing a proclamation to the soldiers, and accumulating at the prefecture arms and cannon without projectiles of corresponding calibre. Landeck, for his part, wanting to distinguish himself, declared Espivent's grade forfeited, and in his place nominated a former cavalry sergeant named Pelissier. "Until the assumption of his functions," said the decree, "the troops will remain under the orders of General Espivent." This gross farce dated from the 1st April. Before the court-martial which tried him, Pelissier hit the mark. When asked, "Of what armies were you general?" "I was general of the situation," was his reply; and indeed he never did lead any troops. On the morning of the 24th the workmen had returned to their work, for the National Guards, save the guardians of the prefecture, were not paid. Men to garrison the posts were found with difficulty, and at midnight the prefecture had but a hundred defenders.

A *coup-de-main* would have been easy, and some rich bourgeois wanted to try it. The men were there and the manoeuvres agreed upon. At midnight the Commission was to be carried off and the prefecture taken possession of, while Espivent was to march on the town so as to get there by daybreak. An officer was despatched to Aubagne. The general refused under the pretext of prudence, but his retinue revealed the true motive of the refusal. "We have stolen away from Marseilles like thieves," they told the messenger; "we want to re-enter it as conquerors."

Such a performance seemed rather difficult with the army of Aubagne, 600 or 700 men, without cadres and without discipline. One single regiment, the 6th Chasseurs, showed a more martial carriage. But Espivent relied upon the sailors of *La Couronne,* the National Guards of order, in continual relations with him, and above all, on the well-known supineness of the Commission.

The latter tried to strengthen itself by the adjunction of delegates from the National Guard. They voted the dissolution of the municipal council, and the Commission convoked the electors for the 3rd April. This measure, if taken on the 24th March, might perhaps have settled everything, but on the 2nd April it was only a stroke in the air.

On the 3rd, at the news from Versailles, Espivent sent an order to the leaders of the reactionary battalions to hold themselves in readiness. In the evening, at eleven o'clock, Garibaldian officers came to inform the prefecture that the troops at Aubagne were moving. The Commission recommenced its old refrain: "Let them come; we are ready to receive them." At half-past one they decided to beat the retreat, and towards four o'clock some men mustered at the prefecture. About a hundred franc-tireurs established themselves at the station, where the Commission had not even thought of placing a battery.

At five o'clock Marseilles was on the alert. Some reactionary companies appeared at the Place du Palais de justice and in the Cours Bonaparte; the sailors of *La Couronne* were drawn up before the Bourse; the first shots were fired at the station.

Espivent's troops presented themselves at three points — the station, the Place Castellane, and La Plaine. The franc-tireurs, notwithstanding a fine defence, were soon surrounded and obliged to retreat. The Versaillese shot the Federalist stationmaster under the eyes of his son, a child of sixteen, who threw himself at the feet of the officer, offering his life for his father's. The second stationmaster, Funel, was able to escape with only a broken arm. The columns of La Plaine and L'Esplanade pushed their advanced posts as far as 300 yards from the prefecture.

The Commission, still in the clouds, sent an embassy to Espivent. Crémieux and Pélissier set out, followed by an immense mass of men and children, crying "*Vive Paris!*" At the outposts of the Place Castellane, the seat of the staff, the commander of the 6th Chasseurs, Villeneuve, came forward towards the delegates. "What are your intentions?" asked Crémieux. "We want to re-establish order. "What! you would dare fire on the people?" cried Crémieux, and commenced haranguing, when the Versaillese threatened to order their infantry to march on. The delegates then had themselves conducted to Espivent. He first spoke of putting them under arrest, but then would allow them five minutes for the evacuation of the prefecture. Crémieux on his return found the infantry men struggling with the crowd, who sought to disarm them. A new current of people, preceded by a black flag, arrived, making a vigorous push against the soldiers. A German officer of Espivent's staff arrested Pelissier, but the Versaillese leaders, seeing their men waver, ordered a retreat.

The mass applauded, believing they would disband. Two infantry corps had already refused to march, and the Place de la Prefecture was filled with groups certain of success. Suddenly, towards ten o'clock, the infantry men emerged from the Rues de Rome and De l'Ar   . The people shouted and surrounded them, when many raised the butt-end of their muskets. One officer who, urging on his company, made them cross bayonets, fell, his head pierced by a bullet. His men charged the Federals, who took refuge and were taken prisoners in the prefecture, whither the infantry men followed. The volleys of the National Guards of order and the infantry men from the Cours Bonaparte and from the house of the Freres Ignorantins, keeping up a running fire were replied to by the Federals from the windows of the prefecture.

The shooting had lasted two hours, and no reinforcement arrived in support of the Federals. Untouchable in the prefecture, a solid square building, they were none the less vanquished, having neither provisions nor sufficient ammunition, and it would have sufficed to wait with arms shouldered till they had exhausted their cartridges. But the general of the Sacré Coeur would not put up with such a half-triumph. This was his first campaign; he wanted blood, and, above all, noise. Since eleven o'clock he had had the prefecture bombarded from the top of Notre-Dame-de-la-Garde, a distance of about 500 yards. The Fort St. Nicolas also opened its fire, but its shells, less far-seeing than those of Notre-Dame-de-la-Garde, dashed down upon the aristocratic houses of the Cours Bonaparte, killing one of those heroic guards of order who fired from behind the soldiers. At three o'clock the prefecture hoisted a flag of truce. Espivent continued to fire. An envoy was sent to him, but he insisted upon their unconditional surrender. At five o'clock more than 300 shells had traversed the edifice, wounding many Federals. Little by little, the defenders, seeing that they were not supported, left the place. The prefecture had long ceased firing when Espivent was still bombarding it. The fright of this brute was so great that he continued firing shells till night-fall. At half past seven the sailors of *La Couronne* and *Le Magnanime* courageously stormed the prefecture, void of all its defenders.

They found the hostages safe and sound, as were the chasseurs taken prisoner in the morning. Yet the Jesuitic repression was atrocious. The men of order arrested at random, and dragged their victims into the lamp-stores of the station. There an officer scrutinized the prisoners, made a sign to one or the other of them to step out, and blew out his brains. The following days there were rumours of summary executions in the barracks, the forts and the prisons. The number of dead the people lost is unknown, but it exceeded 150, besides many wounded who concealed themselves. The Versaillese had thirty killed and fifty wounded. More than 900 persons were thrown into the casemates of the Château d'If and of the Fort St. Nicolas. Crémieux was arrested at the porter's of the Israelite Cemetery. He voluntarily gave himself up to those who sought him, strong in his good faith, and still believing in the judges. The brave Etienne was also taken. Landeck, of course, had made his exit in good time.

On the 5th Espivent entered triumphantly, acclaimed with savage frenzy by the reactionaries. But from the further ranks of the crowd cries and hisses rose against the murderers. At the Place St. Ferréol a captain was fired at, and the people stoned the windows of a house from which the sailors had been cheered.

Two days after the struggle, on its return from *La Couronne,* the municipal council recovered its voice to strike the vanquished.

The National Guard was disarmed, a fierce reaction raged, the Jesuits again lorded it, and Espivent paraded about, receiving ovations to the cries of *"Vive Jésus! Vive le Sacré Coeur!"* The club of the National Guard was closed, Bouchet arrested, and the Radicals, insulted, persecuted, once more saw what it costs to desert the people.

Narbonne, too, was subdued. On the 30th March the prefect and the procureur-general issued a proclamation in which they spoke of "the handful of factious men", presented themselves as upholders of the true Republic, and telegraphed everywhere the failure of the provincial movements. "Is this a reason," Digeon answered in a poster, "to lower before force this red flag dyed in the blood of our martyrs? Let others consent to live eternally oppressed." Whereupon he prepared for battle, and barricaded the streets leading to the Hotel-de-Ville. The women, always to the fore, pulled up pavements and piled up furniture. The authorities, afraid of serious resistance, sent M. Marcou to his friend Digeon. The Brutus of Carcassonne strode through the Hôtel-de-Ville, accompanied by two Republicans of Limoux, to offer in the name of the procureur-general a full and complete amnesty to those who would evacuate the edifice. They offered Digeon twenty-four hours to gain the frontier. Digeon assembled his council, and all refused to fly. M. Marcou hastened to inform the military authorities that they might now act. General Zentz was at once sent to Narbonne.

At three o'clock in the morning a detachment of Turcos reconnoitred the barricades of the Rue du Pont. The Federals, anxious to fraternize, cleared it, and were received with a volley, killing two men and wounding three. On the 31st, at seven o'clock, Zentz in a proclamation announced that the bombardment was about to recommence. Digeon at once wrote to him, "I have the right to reply to such a savage menace in the same style. I warn you that if you bombard the town, I shall have the three prisoners who are in my power shot." Zentz answered by arresting the envoy, and had brandy distributed to the Turcos, the only troops who would march. These brutes arrived at Narbonne eager to loot, and had already pillaged three cafés. The fight was about to begin, when the procureur-general again sent two envoys, offering amnesty to all those who would evacuate the Hotel-de-Ville before the opening of the fire, but the execution of the hostages would be punished by the massacre of all its occupants. Digeon wrote out these conditions under the dictation of one of the envoys, read them to the Federals, and left every one free to withdraw. At this moment the procureur-general presented himself with the Turcos before the terrace of the garden. Digeon rushed thither. The procureur harangued the multitude, and as he spoke of indulgence, Digeon protested that amnesty had just been promised. The procureur drowned the discussion in a roll of drums, read the legal *sommation* in front of the Hôtel-de-Ville, and asked for the hostages, whom the soldiers who had deserted delivered over to him.

All these parleys had profoundly enervated the defence. Besides, the Hôtel-de-Ville could do nothing against a bombardment that would have battered the town. Digeon had the edifice evacuated, and shut himself up alone in the cabinet of the mayor, resolved to sell his life dearly; but the people, in spite of his resistance, carried him off. The Hôtel-de-Ville was empty when the Turcos arrived. They plundered in all its corners, and officers were seen to deck themselves with stolen valuables.

Notwithstanding the formal promises of amnesty, numerous warrants of arrest were issued. Digeon refused to fly, and wrote to the procureur-general that he might arrest him. Such a man at Toulouse would have saved the movement and raised the whole South.

Limoges had one glimpse of hope on the fatal day of the 4th April. That revolutionary capital of the Centre could not look on the efforts of Paris unmoved. On the 23rd March the Société Populaire centralized all the democratic forces and passed a vote of thanks to the army of Paris for its conduct on the 18th. When Versailles called for volunteers, the Society enjoined the municipal council to prevent such an incitement to civil war. The working men's societies despatched a delegate to Paris soon after the proclamation of the Commune, there to inquire into its principles, and to request the sending of a commissar to Limoges. The members of the Commune replied that this was impossible for the present, that they would consider it by and by; and never sent anybody. The Société Populaire was thus obliged to act alone. It urged the municipal council to hold a review of the National Guards , certain that it would result in a demonstration against Versailles. The council, composed, with few exceptions, of timid men, tried to gain time, when the news of the 3rd April became known. On the morning of the 4th, on reading on the walls the triumphant telegram from Versailles, the workmen revolted. A detachment of five hundred soldiers was about to leave for Versailles; the crowd followed them to the station, and the workmen urged them to join the people. The soldiers, surrounded, much excited, fraternized and surrendered their arms, many of which were taken to the Société Populaire, and hidden there.

The call-up was at once beaten. The colonel of cuirassiers, Billet, who, accompanied by orderlies, rode. through the town, was hemmed in by the people, and constrained to cry, "*Vive la République!*" At five o'clock the whole National Guard was in arms on the Place de la *Mairie*. The officers met in the Hôtel-de-Ville, where a councillor proposed to proclaim the Commune. The mayor objected, but the cry resounded on all sides. Captain Coissac took upon himself to go to the station in order to stop the train ready for the departure of the troops. The other officers consulted their companies, which answered with one unanimous cry, "*Vive Paris! À bas Versailles!*" Soon after, the battalions, filing off before the Hôtel-de-Ville, preceded by two municipal councillors in their official costume, went to ask the general for the release of the soldiers arrested during the course of the day. The general gave the order to set them free, and at the same time sent word to Colonel Billet to prepare against the insurrection. From the Place Tourny the Federals repaired to the prefecture, occupying it in spite of the resistance of the Conservative National Guards, and commenced throwing up some barricades. A few soldiers arrived from the Rue des Prisons, and several citizens urged the officers not to commence a civil war. These hesitated, retired, when Colonel Billet, at the head of about fifty cuirassiers, came out on to the Place de l'Eglise St. Michel, and ordered his men to advance and draw swords. They fired their pistols, the Federals answered, and the colonel was mortally wounded. His horse turning about, carried its rider as far as the Place St. Pierre, the other horses following, the Federals thus remained masters of the field. But lacking organization, they disbanded in the night and left the prefecture. The next day the company that occupied the station seeing themselves abandoned withdrew. The arrests began, and many were obliged to hide.

Thus the revolts of the great towns died out one by one like the lateral craters of an exhausted volcano. The revolutionaries of the provinces showed themselves everywhere completely disorganized, without any faculty to wield power. Everywhere victorious at the outset, the workmen had only known how to pronounce for Paris. But at least they showed some vitality, generosity, and pride. Eighty years of bourgeois domination had not been able to transform them into a nation of mercenaries; while the Radicals, who either combated or held aloof from them, once more attested the decrepitude, the egotism of the middle-class, always ready to betray the working men to the "upper" classes.

Chapter 14
The weaknesses of the Council

After an armistice of seventy days, Paris again took up the struggle for France single-handed. It was no longer the territory only which she strove for, but the very ground-work of the nation. Victorious, her victory would not be sterile like those of the battlefield; regenerated, the people would set to the great work of remaking the social edifice; vanquished, all liberty would be quenched, the bourgeoisie turn its whips into scorpions, and a generation glide into the grave.

And Paris, so generous, so fraternal, did not shudder at the impending civil war. She stood up for an idea that exalted her battalions. While the bourgeois refuses to fight, saying, "I have a family," the workman says, "I fight for my children."

For the third time since the 18th March Paris had but one soul. The official despatches, the hireling journalists established at Versailles, pictured her as the pandemonium of all the black-legs of Europe, recounted the thefts, the arrests *en masse*, the endless orgies, detailed sums and names. According to them, honest women no longer dared venture into the streets; 1,500,000 persons oppressed by 20,000 ruffians were offering up ardent prayers for Versailles. But the traveller running the risk of a visit to Paris, found the streets and boulevards tranquil, presenting their usual aspect. The pillagers had only pillaged the guillotine, solemnly burnt before the *mairie* of the eleventh arrondissement. From all quarters the same murmur of execration rose against the assassination of the prisoners and the ignoble scenes at

Versailles. The incoherence of the first acts of the Council was hardly noticed while the ferocity of the Versaillese was the topic of the day.

Persons coming full of indignation against Paris, seeing this calm, this union of hearts, these wounded men crying *"Vive la Commune!"* these enthusiastic battalions — there Mont Valérien vomiting death, here men living as brothers — in a few hours caught the Parisian malady.

It was a fever of faith, of blind devotion, and of hope — of hope above all. What rebellion had been thus armed? It was no longer a handful of desperate men fighting behind a few pavements, reduced to charging their muskets with slugs or stones. The Commune of 1871, much better armed than that of 1793, possessed at least 60,000 men, 200,000 muskets, 1,200 cannon, five forts; a precinct covering Montmartre, Belleville, the Panthéon overtowering the whole city, munitions enough to last for years, and milliards at her bidding. What else is wanted to conquer? Some revolutionary instinct. There was not a man at the Hôtel-de-Ville who did not boast of possessing it.

The sitting of the 3rd April during the battle was stormy. Many loudly opposed this mad sortie. Lefrançais, indignant at having been deceived, withdrew from the Commission, which, called upon to explain, threw all the blame upon the generals. The friends of the latter took up their defence, demanded that news should be waited for. Soon the disastrous tidings were brought, and they could not hesitate any longer. For such a usurpation of authority there was but one atonement possible. Flourens and Duval had made it voluntarily. The others ought to have followed. Thus the dead would have been appeased, similar follies once for all cut short, and the authority of the Commune brought home to the most refractory.

But the men at the Hôtel-de-Ville were not of such inflexibility. Many had fought, plotted together under the Empire, lived in the same prisons, identified the Revolution with their friends. And besides, the generals, were they alone guilty? So many battalions could not have bestirred themselves all the night without the Council being informed thereof. Though blind or deaf, they were none the less responsible. In order to be just they ought to have decimated themselves. They felt this, no doubt, and did not dare strike the generals.

They might at least have dismissed them. They contented themselves with replacing them on the Executive Commission, and notified this measure most respectfully. "The Commune was desirous to leave them all liberty in the conduct of the military operations; it was as far from wishing to disoblige them as from wishing to weaken their authority." And yet their heedlessness, their incapacity, had been mortal. Their ignorance only saved them from the suspicion of having betrayed. This indulgence was big with promises for the future.

This future meant Cluseret. From the first days he had beset the Central Committee, the Ministries, in quest of a generalship, his hands full of war plans against the mayors. The Committee would have nothing to do with him. He then clung to the Executive Commission, which on the 2nd April, at seven o'clock in the evening, appointed him delegate at war, with the order to enter upon his duties immediately. The rappel was being beaten at that moment for the fatal sortie. Cluseret took good care not to take possession of his post, allowed the generals to ruin themselves, and on the 3rd appeared before the Council to denounce their childishness. It was this military pamphlet-monger, with no pledge but the decoration he had won against the Socialists of 1848, who had played the marionette in three insurrections, whom the Socialists of 1871 charged with the defence of their Revolution.

The choice was execrable, the very idea of naming a delegate faulty. The Council had just decided to keep on the defensive. To guard the lines, regularize the services, provision and administer the battalions, the best delegate would have been common sense. A commission, composed of a few active and laborious men, would have offered all guarantees of security.

Moreover, the Council failed to point out what sort of defence they had in view. The defence of the forts, of the redoubts, of the accessory positions, required thousands of men, experienced officers, a war with the mattock as well as the musket. The National Guard was not qualified for such soldiership. Behind the ramparts, on the contrary, it became invincible. It would have sufficed to blow up the forts of the south, to fortify Monmartre, the Panthéon, and the Buttes-Chaumont, to strongly arm the ramparts, to create a second, a third enceinte, to render Paris inaccessible or untenable to the enemy. The Council did not indicate either of these systems, but allowed its delegates to dabble with the two, and finally annulled the one by the other.

If they wished by the appointment of a delegate to concentrate the military power, why not dissolve the Central Committee? The latter acted , spoke more boldly and much better than the Council which had excluded it from the Hôtel-de-Ville. The Committee had installed itself in the Rue de l'Entrepôt, behind the Customs House, near its cradle. Thence on the 5th April it launched a fine proclamation: "Workmen, do not deceive yourselves about the import of the combat. It is the engagement between parasitism and labour, exploitation and production. If you are tired of vegetating in ignorance and wallowing in misery, if you want your children to be men enjoying the benefit of their labour, and not mere animals trained for the workshop and the battlefield, if you do not want your daughters, whom you are unable to educate and care for as you yearn to do, to become instruments of pleasure in the arms of the aristocracy of money, if you at last want the reign of justice, workmen, be intelligent, rise!"

The Committee certainly declared in another proclamation that it did not pretend to any political power, but power in times of revolution of itself belongs to those who define it. For eight days the Council had not known how to interpret the Commune, and its whole baggage consisted in two insignificant decrees. The Central Committee, on the contrary, very distinctly set forth the character of this contest, that had become a social one and, breaking through the political facade, pointed out behind the struggle for municipal liberties the question of the proletariat.

The Council might have profited by the lesson, endorsed if necessary that manifesto, and then, referring to the protestations of the Committee, obliged it to dissolve itself. This was all the more easy in that the Committee, much weakened by the elections, only existed thanks to four or five members and its eloquent mouthpiece, Moreau. But the Council contented itself with mildly protesting at the sitting of the 5th, and as usual letting things get along as best they could.

It was already drifting from weakness to weakness; and yet, if ever it believed in its own energy it was that day. The savagery of the Versaillese, the assassination of the prisoners, of Flourens and Duval, had excited the most calm. They had been there full of life three days ago, these brave colleagues and friends. Their empty places seemed to cry out for vengeance. Well, then, since Versailles waged a war of cannibals, they would answer an eye for an eye, a tooth for a tooth. Besides, if the Council did not act, the people, it was said, would perhaps revenge themselves, and more terribly. They decreed that any one accused of complicity with Versailles would be judged within forty-eight hours, and if guilty, retained as a hostage. The execution by Versailles of a defender of the Commune would be followed by that of a hostage — by three said the decree, in equal or double number said the proclamation.

These different readings betrayed the troubled state of their minds. The Council alone believed it had frightened Versailles. The bourgeois journals certainly shouted "Abomination!" and M. Thiers, who shot without any decrees, denounced the ferocity of the Commune. At bottom they all laughed in their sleeves. The reactionaries of any mark had long since fled; there only remained in Paris the small fry and a few isolated men, whom, if needs be, Versailles was ready to sacrifice. The members of the Council, in their childish impetuosity, had not seen the real hostages staring them in the face — the bank, the civil register, the domains and the suitors" fund. These were the tender points by which to hold the bourgeoisie. Without risking a single man, the Commune had only to stretch out its hand and bid Versailles negotiate or commit suicide.

The timid delegates of the 26th March were not the men to dare this. In allowing the Versaillese army to march off, the Central Committee had committed a heavy fault; that of the Council was incomparably more damaging. All serious rebels have commenced by seizing upon the sinews of the enemy — the treasury. The Council of the Commune was the only revolutionary Government that refused to so so. While abolishing the budget of public worship, which was at Versailles, they bent their knees to the budget of the bourgeoisie, which was at their mercy.

Then followed a scene of high comedy, if one could laugh at negligence that has caused so much bloodshed. Since the 19th March the governors of the bank lived like men condemned to death, every day expecting the execution of the treasure. Of removing it to Versailles they could not dream. It would have required sixty or eighty vans and an army corps. On the 23rd, its governor, Rouland, could no longer stand it, and fled. The deputy governor, De Ploeue, replaced him. From his first interview with the delegates of the Hôtel-de-Ville he had seen through their timidity, given battle, then seemed to soften, yielded little by little, and doled out his money franc by franc. The bank, which Versailles believed almost empty, contained: coin, 77 millions; bank-notes, 166 millions; bills discounted, 899 millions; securities for advances made, 120 millions; bullion, 11 millions; jewels in deposit, 7 millions; public effects and other titles in deposit, 900 millions; that is, 2 milliards 180 million francs: 800 millions in bank-notes only required the signature of the cashier, a signature easily made. The Commune had then three milliards in its hands, of which over a milliard was realized, enough to buy all the generals and functionaries of Versailles; as hostages, 90,000 depositors of titles, and the two milliards in circulation whose guarantee lay in the coffers in the Rue de la Vrillière.

On the 29th March old Beslay presented himself before the tabernacle. De Ploeuc had mustered his 430 clerks, armed with muskets without cartridges. Beslay, led through the lines of these warriors, humbly prayed the governor to be so kind as to supply the pay of the National Guard. De Ploeuc answered superciliously, spoke of defending himself. "But," said Beslay, "if, to prevent the effusion of blood, the Commune appointed a governor. . ." "A governor! Never!" said De Ploeuc, who understood his man; "but a delegate! If you were that delegate we might come to an understanding." And, acting pathetic, "Come, M. Beslay, help me to save this. This is the fortune of your country; this is the fortune of France."

Beslay, deeply moved, hurried off to the Executive Commission, repeated his lesson all the better that he believed it and prided himself on his financial lore. "The bank," he said, "is the fortune of the country: without it, no more industry, no more commerce. If you violate it, all its notes will be so much waste-paper. This trash circulated in the Hôtel-de-Ville, and the Proudhonists of the Council, forgetting that their master put the suppression of the bank at the head of his revolutionary programme, backed old Beslay. At Versailles itself, the capitalist stronghold had no more inveterate defenders than those of the Hôtel-de-Ville. If someone had at least proposed, "Let us at least occupy the bank" — but the Executive Commission had not the nerve to do this, and contented itself with commissioning Beslay. De Ploeuc received the good man with open arms, installed him in the nearest office, even persuading him to sleep at the bank, made him his hostage, and once more breathed freely.

Thus from the first week the Assembly of the Hôtel-de-Ville showed itself weak towards the authors of the sortie, weak towards the Central Committee, weak towards the bank, trifling in its decrees, in the choice of its delegate to the War Office, without a military plan, without a programme, without general views, and indulging in desultory discussions. The Radicals who had remained in the Council saw whither it was drifting, and, not inclined to play the martyrs, they sent in their resignations.

0 Revolution! thou dost not await the well-timed day and hour. Thou comest suddenly, blind and fatal as the avalanche. The true soldier of the people accepts the combat wherever hazard may place him. Blunders, defections, compromising companions do not dishearten him. Though certain of defeat, he struggles still; his victory looms in the future.

Chapter 15
The Commune's first combats

The rout of the 3rd April daunted the timorous but exalted the fervent. Battalions inert until then rose; the armament of the forts no longer lagged. Save Issy and Vanves, rather damaged, the forts were intact. All Paris soon heard these fine cannon of seven, which Trochu had disdained, firing so lustily and with such correct aim, that on the evening of the 4th the Versaillese were obliged to evacuate the plateau of Chatillon. The trenches that protected the forts were manned. Les Moulineaux, Clamart, Le Val-Fleury resounded with the shooting. To the right we reoccupied Courbevoie, and the bridge of Neuilly was barricaded.

Thence we continued to threaten Versailles. Vinoy received the order to take Neuilly. On the morning of the 6th, Mont-Valérien, recently armed with 24-pounders, opened fire on Courbevoie. After six hours of bombardment the Federals evacuated the cross-roads and took up a position behind the large barricade of the bridge of Neuilly. The Versaillese cannonaded it while it was protected by the Porte-Maillot.

This Porte-Maillot, which has become legendary, had only a few cannon exposed to the fire from above of Mont-Valérien. For forty eight days the Commune found men to hold this untenable post. Their courage electrified all. The crowd went to the Arc-de-Triomphe to see them, and the boys hardly waited for the explosion to run after the fragments of shells.

The Parisian intrepidity soon reappeared in the first skirmishes. The bourgeois papers themselves regretted that so much ardour should not have been spent on the Prussians. The panic of the 3rd April had witnessed heroic deeds, and the Council, happily inspired, wanted to give the defenders of the Commune a funeral worthy of them. It appealed to the people. On the 6th, at two o'clock, an innumerable multitude hurried up to the Beaujon Hospital, whither the dead had been transported. Many, shot after the combat, bore on their arms the marks left by cords. There were heart-rending scenes. Morthers and wives bending over these bodies uttered cries of fury and vows of vengeance. Three immense catafalques, each containing thirty-five coffins, covered with black crape, adorned with red flags, drawn by eight horses each, slowly rolled towards the great boulevards, preceded by trumpets and the *Vengeurs de Paris*. Delescluze and five members of the Commune, with their red scarfs on and bare-headed, walked as chief mourners. Behind them followed the relations of the victims, the widows of to-day supported by those of to-morrow. Thousands upon thousands, men, women, and children, immortelles in their button-holes, silent, solemn, marched to the sound of the muffled drums. At intervals subdued strains of music burst forth like the spontaneous mutterings of sorrow too long contained. On the great boulevards we numbered 200,000, and 100,000 pale faces looked down upon us from the windows. The women sobbed, many fainted. This *Via Sacra* of the Revolution, the scene of so many woes and so many joys, has perhaps never witnessed such a communion of hearts. Delescluze exclaimed in ecstasy, "What an admirable people! Will they still say that we are a handful of malcontents?" At the Pere la Chaise he advanced to the common grave. Wrinkled, stooping, sustained only by his indomitable faith, this dying man saluted the dead. "I will make you no long speeches; these have already cost us too dear ... Justice for the families of the victims; justice for the great town which, after five months of siege, betrayed by its Government, still holds in its hands the future of humanity ... Let us not weep for our brothers who have fallen heroically, but let us swear to continue their work, and to save Liberty, the Commune, the Republic!"

The following day the Versaillese shelled the barricade and the Avenue of Neuilly. The inhabitants, whom they had not the humanity to forewarn, were obliged to take refuge in their cellars. Towards half-past four the fire of the Versaillese ceased, and the Federals were snatching a little rest, when the soldiers emerged *en masse* on the bridge. The Federals, surprised, attempted to arrest their progress, wounding one general and killing two, one of whom, Besson, was responsible for the surprise of Beaumont L'Argonne during the march on Sedan. But the soldiers in overwhelming force succeeded in pushing as far as the old park of Neuilly.

The loss of this outlet was all the more serious that Bergeret, in a letter published in the *Officiel*, had answered for Neuilly. The Executive Commission replaced him by the Pole Dombrowski, whom Garibaldi had demanded for his general staff during the war in the Vosges. Bergeret's staff protested, and their bickerings led to the arrest of their chief by the Council, already grown suspicious. The National Guard itself showed some distrust of the new general. The Commission had to present him to Paris, and, misinformed, invented a legend in his favour. Dombrowski was not long in making it good.

The same day the Federals of Neuilly beheld a young man, of small stature, in a modest uniform, slowly inspecting the vanguards in the thick of the fire. It was Dombrowski. Instead of the explosive glowing French bravery, they saw the cool and, as it were, unconscious courage of the Slav. In a few hours the new chief had conquered all his men. The able officer soon revealed himself. On the 9th, during the night, with two battalions from Montmartre, Dombrowski, accompanied by Vermorel, took the Versaillese by surprise at Asnières, drove them off, seized their cannon, and from the ironclad railway carriages cannonaded Courbevoie and the bridge of Neuilly from the flank At the same time his brother stormed the castle of Bécon, that commands the road from Asnières to Courbevoie. Vinoy having tried to retake this post on the night of the 12th-13th, his men were shamefully repulsed, and fled to Courbevoie as fast as their legs would carry them.

Paris was ignorant of this success, so defective was the service of the general staff. This brilliant attack was the deed of one man, just as the defence of the forts was the spontaneous work of the National Guard. There was as yet no direction. Whoever cared to rush into some venture did so; whoever wanted cannon or reinforcements went to ask for them at the Place Vendôme, at the Central Committee, at the Hôtel-de-Ville, of the generalissimo Cluseret.

The latter had made his debut with a blunder, calling out only the unmarried men from seventeen to thirty-five, thus depriving the Commune of its most energetic defenders, the grey-headed men, the first and last under fire in all our insurrections. Three days after, this decree had to be revoked. On the 5th, in his report to the Council, this profound strategist announced that the attack of Versailles masked a movement for occupying the forts of the right bank, at that moment in the hands of the Prussians. Like Trochu, he blamed the cannonades of the last few days, for squandering, as he said, the munitions. And this when Paris abounded in powder and shell; when her young troops should have been amused and sustained by artillery; when the Versaillese of Chatillon, incessantly pursued by our fire, were obliged to remove every night; when an uninterrupted cannonade alone could save Neuilly.

The Council was no wiser in its measures of defence. It decreed compulsory service and the disarmament of the refractory; but the perquisitions, made at random, without the assistance of the police, did not procure a man or a hundred muskets the more. It voted life-pensions to the widows, to the parents of the Federals killed in combat, to their children an annuity till the age of eighteen, and adopted the orphans. Excellent measures these, raising the spirits of the combatants, only they assumed the Commune would be victorious. Was it not better, as in the cases of Duval and Dombrowski, to give at once a few thousand francs to those having a right to them? In fact, these unfortunate pensioners received but fifty francs from the Commune.

These measures, incomplete, ill-managed, implied a want of study and of reflection. The members came to the Council as to a public meeting, without any preparation, there to proceed without any method. The decrees of the day before were forgotten, questions only half solved. The Council created councils of war and court-martials, and allowed the Central Committee to regulate the procedure and the penalties; it organized one-half of the medical service and Cluseret the other; it suppressed the title of general, and the superior officers retained it, the delegate at War conferring it on them. In the middle of a sitting, Félix Pyat bounded from his chair to demand the abolition of the Vendôme column, while Dombrowski was making desperate appeals for reinforcements.

He had hardly 2,500 men to hold Neuilly, Asnières, and the whole peninsula of Gennevilliers, while the Versaillese were accumulating their best troops against him. From the 14th to 17th April they cannonaded the castle of Bécon and on the morning of the 17th attacked it with a brigade. The 250 Federals who occupied it held out for six hours, and the survivors fell back upon Asnières, where panic entered with them. Dombrowski, Okolwitz, and a few sturdy men hastened thither, succeeded in re-establishing a little order and fortified the bridge-head. Dombrowski asking for reinforcements, the War Office sent him only a few companies. The following day our vanguard was surprised by strong detachments, and the cannon of Courbevoie battered Asnières. After a well-contested struggle, towards ten o'clock several battalions, worn out, abandoned the southern part of the village. In the northern part the combat was desperate. Dombrowski, in spite of telegram after telegram, received only 300 men. At five o'clock in the evening the Versaillese made a great effort, and the Federals, exhausted, fearing for their retreat, threw themselves upon the bridge of boats, which they crossed in disorder.

The reactionary journals made much ado about this retreat. Paris was stirred by it. This fierce obstinacy of the combat began to open the eyes of the optimists. Till then many persons believed it all some dreadful misunderstanding and formed groups of conciliation. How many thousands in Paris failed to understand the plan of M. Thiers and the coalition till the day of the final massacre! On the 4th April some manufacturers and tradesmen had created the National Union of the Syndical Chambers, and taken for their programme, maintenance and enfranchisement of the Republic, and acknowledgment of the municipal franchises of Paris. The same day, in the Quartier des Ecoles, professors, doctors, lawyers, engineers, and students posted up a manifesto demanding a democratic, lay Republic, an autonomous Commune and the federation of the communes. An analogous group posted up a letter to M. Thiers: "You believe in a riot, and you find yourself brought face to face with precise and universal convictions. The immense majority of Paris demands the Republic as a right superior to all discussion. Paris has seen in the whole conduct of the Assembly the premeditated design of re-establishing the monarchy." Some dignitaries of the Freemason lodges appealed at once to Versailles and to the Council: 'stop the effusion of such precious blood."

Finally, a certain number of those mayors and adjuncts who had not capitulated till the eleventh hour, like Floquet, Corbon, Bonvalet, etc., pompously got up the Republican Union League for the Rights of Paris. Now they asked for the recognition of the Republic, the right of Paris to govern herself, and the custody of the town exclusively confided to the National Guard; all that the Commune had wanted all that they had contended against from the 19th to the 25th of March.

Other groups were forming. All agreed on two points — the consolidation of the Republic and the recognition of the rights of Paris.

Almost all the Communal journals reproduced this programme, and the Republican journals accepted it. The deputies of Paris were the last to speak, and then only to fall foul of Paris. In that lachrymose and jesuitical tone with which he has travestied history, in those longwinded sentimental periods which serve to mask the aridity of his heart and the pettiness of his mind, that king of gnomes Louis Blanc, wrote in the name of his colleagues: "Not one member of the majority has as yet questioned the Republican principle ... As to those engaged in the insurrection, we tell them that they ought to have shuddered at the thought of aggravating, of prolonging the scourge of the foreign occupation by adding thereto the scourge of civil discords."

It is this that M. Thiers repeated word for word to the first conciliators, the delegates of the *Union Syndicale,* who applied to him on the 8th May: "Let the insurrection disarm; the Assembly cannot disarm. But Paris wants the Republic. The Republic exists; by my honour, so long as I am in power, it will not succumb. But Paris wants municipal franchises. The Chamber is preparing a law for all communes; Paris will get neither more nor less." The delegates read a project of compromise which spoke of a general amnesty and a suspension of arms. M. Thiers let them read on, did not formally contest a single article, and the delegates returned to Paris convinced that they had discovered the basis of an arrangement.

They had hardly left when M. Thiers rushed off to the Assembly, which had just endowed all communes with the right of electing their mayors. M. Thiers ascended the tribune, demanding that this right should be restricted to towns of less than 20,000 souls. They cried to him, "It is already voted." He persisted, declaring that "in a republic the Government must be all the better armed because order is the more difficult to maintain;" threatened to hand in his resignation, and forced the Assembly to annul its vote.

On the 10th, the League of the Rights of Paris sounded the trumpet and had a solemn declaration posted up: "Let the Government give up assailing the facts accomplished on the 18th March. Let the general re-election of the Commune be proceeded with ... If the Government of Versailles remains deaf to these legitimate demands, let it be well understood that all Paris will rise to defend them." The next day the delegates of the League went to Versailles, and M. Thiers took up his old refrain, "Let Paris disarm" and would hear neither of an armistice nor of an amnesty. "Pardon shall be extended' said he, "To those who will disarm, save to the assassins of Clément-Thomas and Lecomte." This was to reserve himself the choice of a few thousands. In short, he wanted to be replaced in his position of the 18th March with victory into the bargain. The same day he said to the delegates of the Masonic lodges, "Address yourselves to the Commune; what is wanted is the submission of the insurgents, and not the resignation of legal power." To facilitate this submission, the next day the *Officiel* of Versailles compared Paris to the plain of Marathon infested by a band of "brigands and assassins." On the 13th, a deputy, Brunet, having asked whether the Government would or would not make peace with Paris, the Assembly adjourned this interpellation for a month.

The League, thus well whipped, went on the 14th to the Hotel-de-Ville. The Council, foreign to all these negotiations, left them entirely free, and had only forbidden a meeting announced at the Bourse by ill-disguised Tirards. It contented itself with opposing to the League its declaration of the 10th: "You have said that if Versailles remained deaf all Paris would rise. Versailles has remained deaf. Arise." And to make Paris the judge, the Council loyally published in *its Officiel* the report of the conciliators.

Chapter 16
The Manifesto and the germs of defeat

For the second time the situation was distinctly marked out. If the Council did not know how to define the Commune, was it not in the most unmistakable manner, and before the eyes of all Paris, declared to mean a camp of rebels by the fighting, the bombardment, the fury of the Versaillese, and the rebuff of the conciliators? The by-elections of the 16th April — death, double election returns, and resignations had given thirty-one vacant seats — revealed the effective forces of the insurrection. The illusion of the 26th March had vanished; the votes were now taken under fire. Also the journals of the Commune and the delegates of the Syndical Chambers in vain summoned the electors to the ballot-box. Out of 146,000 who had mustered in these arrondissements at the election of the 26th March, there came now only 61,000. The arrondissements of the councillors who had deserted their seats gave 16,000 instead of 51,000 votes.

It was now or never the moment to explain their programme to France. The Executive Commission had on the 6th, in an address to the provinces, protested against the calumnies of Versailles, but had confined itself to the statement that Paris fought for all France, and had not set forth any programme. The Republican protestations of M. Thiers, the hostility of the extreme Left, the desultory decrees, had completely led astray the provinces. It was necessary to set them right at once. On the 19th, a commission charged to draw up a programme presented its work, or rather the work of another. Sad and characteristic symbol this; the declaration of the Commune did not emanate from the Council, its twelve publicists notwithstanding. Of the five members charged to draw up the draft, only Delescluze contributed some passages; the technical part was the work of a journalist, Pierre Denis.

In the *Cri du Peuple* he had taken up and formulated as a law the whim of *Paris a free town,* hatched in the first gush of passion of the Vauxhall meetings. According to this legislator, Paris was to become a Hanseatic town, crowning herself with all liberties, and from the height of her proud fortress say to the enchained communes of France, "Imitate me if you can; but mind, I shall do nothing for you but set an example." This charming plan had turned the heads of several members of the Council, and too many traces of it were visible in the declaration.

"What does Paris demand?" it said. "The recognition of the Republic. Absolute autonomy of the Commune extended to all localities of France. The inherent rights of the Commune are: the vote of the communal budget; the settlement and repartition of taxes; the direction of the local services; the organization of its magistracy, of its internal police, and of education; the administration of communal goods; the choice and permanent right of control over the communal magistrates and functionaries; the absolute guarantee of individual liberty, of the liberty of conscience and the liberty of labour; the organization of urban defence and of the National Guard; the Commune alone charged with the surveillance and assurance of the free and just exercise of the right of meeting and of publicity ... Paris wants nothing more .. on condition of finding in the great central administration, the delegation of the federated communes, the realization and practical application of the same principle."

What were to be the powers of that central delegation, the reciprocal obligations of the Communes? The declaration did not state these. According to this text, every locality was to possess the right to shut itself up within its autonomy. But what to expect of autonomy in Lower Brittany, in nine-tenths of the French Communes, more than half of which have not 600 inhabitants, if even the Parisian declaration violated the most elementary rights, charged the Commune with the surveillance of the *just* exercise of the right of meeting and of publicity, forgetting to mention the right of association? It is notorious, it has been proved but too well. The rural autonomous communes would be a monster with a thousand suckers attached to the flank of the Revolution.

No! Thousands of mutes and blind are not fitted to conclude a social pact. Weak, unorganized, bound by a thousand trammels, the people of the country can only be saved by the towns, and the people of the towns guided by Paris. The failure of all the provincial insurrections, even of the large towns, had sufficiently testified this. When the declaration said, "Unity such as has been imposed upon us until to-day by the Empire, the monarchy and parliamentarism is only despotic, unintelligent centralization," it laid bare the cancer that devours France; but when it added, "Political unity, as understood by Paris, is the voluntary association of all local initiative," it showed that it knew nothing whatever of the provinces.

The declaration continued, in the style of an address, sometimes to the point: "Paris works and suffers for all France, whose intellectual, moral, administrative, and economical regeneration she prepares by her combats and her sufferings.... The communal revolution, commenced by the popular initiative of the 18th March, inaugurates a new era." But in all this there was nothing definite. Why not, taking up the formula of the 28th March, "To the commune what is communal, to the nation what is national," define the future commune, sufficiently extended to endow it with political life, sufficiently limited to allow its citizens easily to combine their social action, the commune of 15,000 to 20,000 souls, the canton-commune, and clearly set forth its rights and those of France? They did not even speak of federating the large towns for the conquest of their common enfranchisement. Such as it was, this programme, obscure, incomplete, impossible in many points, could not, in spite of some generous ideas, contribute much to the enlightenment of the provinces.

It was only a draft. No doubt the Council was going to discuss it. It was voted after the first reading. No debate, hardly an observation. This assembly, which gave four days to the discussion on overdue commercial bills, had not one sitting for the study of this declaration, its programme in case of victory, its testament if it succumbed.

To make things worse, a new malady infected the Council, the germs of which, sown for some days, were brought to full maturity by the complementary elections. The Romanticists gave rise to the Casuists, and both came to loggerheads on the verification of the new mandates.

On the 30th March the Council had validated six elections with a relative majority. The reporter on the election of the 16th proposed declaring all those candidates elected who had received an absolute majority. The Casuists grew indignant. "This would be," said they, "the worst blow that any Government had dealt universal suffrage."

But it was impossible to go on continually convoking the electors. Three of the most devoted arrondissements had given no result; one of them, the thirteenth, being deprived of its best men, then fighting at the advanced posts. A new ballot would only set forth in bolder relief the isolation of the Commune; and then, is the moment of the fight, when the battalion is decimated, deprived of its chief, the opportune time for insisting upon a regular promotion.

The discussion was very warm, for in this outlawed Hôtel-de-Ville there sat outrageous legality-mongers. Paris was to be strangled by their saving principles. Already, in the name of holy autonomy, which forbade intervention with the autonomy of one's neighbour, the Executive Commission had refused to arm the communes round Paris that asked to march against Versailles. M. Thiers took no more efficient measure to isolate Paris.

Twenty-six voices against thirteen voted the conclusions of the report. Twenty elections only were declared valid, which was illogical; one with less than 1,100 votes was admitted, another with 2,500 rejected. All the elections should have been declared valid, or none at all. Four of the new delegates were journalists, six only workmen. Eleven sent by the public meetings came to strengthen the Romanticists. Two whose elections had been validated by the Council refused to sit because they had not obtained the eighth part of the votes. The author of the admirable *Propos de Labiénus,*[a book dealing with the abuses of the Second Empire] Rogeard, allowed himself to be deceived by a false scruple of legality — the only weakness of this generous man, who devoted to the Commune his pure and brilliant eloquence. His resignation deprived the Council of a man of common sense, but once more served to unmask the apocalyptic Félix Pyat.

Since the 1st April, scenting the coming storm and professing the same horror for blows as Panurge, Félix Pyat had attempted to leave Paris, sent in his resignation as member of the Executive Commission to the Council, and declared his presence at Versailles indispensable. The Versaillese hussars making the sortie too perilous, he had condescended to stay, but at the same time assuming two masks, one for the Hôtel-de-Ville, the other for the public. In the Council, at the secret sittings, he urged violent measures with the vivacity of a wild cat; in the *Vengeur* he held forth pontifically, shaking his grey hairs, saying, "To the ballot-box, not to Versailles!" In his own paper he had two faces. If he wanted the journals suppressed, he signed "Le Vengeur"; if he wanted to cajole, he signed Félix Pyat. The defeat of Asnières struck him again with fear, and anew he looked out for a loophole. The resignation of Rogeard opened it. Under the shelter of this pure name Félix Pyat slipped in his resignation. "The Commune has violated the law," wrote he. "I do not want to be an accomplice." And, to debar himself from any return to the Council, he involved the dignity of the latter. If, said he, it persisted, he would be forced, to his great regret, to send in his resignation *"before the victory."*

He had counted on stealing away as from the Assembly of Bordeaux; but his roguery disgusted the Council. The *Vengeur* had just condemned the suppression of several reactionary papers demanded many and many a time by Félix Pyat. Vermorel denounced this duplicity. One Member: "It has been said here that resignations would be considered as treason." Another: "A man must not leave his post when that post is one of peril and of honour." A third formally demanded the arrest of Félix Pyat. "I regret," said another, "that it has not been distinctly laid down that resignation can only be tendered to the electors themselves." And Delescluze added, "Nobody has the right to withdraw for personal rancour or because some measure does not chime in with his ideal. Do you then believe that every one approves what is done here? Yes; there are members who have remained, and who will remain till the end, notwithstanding the insults hurled at us. For myself, 1 am decided to remain at my post, and if we do not see victory, we shall not be the last to fall on the ramparts or on the steps of the Hôtel-de-Ville."

These manly words were received with prolonged cheers. No one's devotion was more meritorious. The habits of Delescluze, grave and laborious, his high aspirations, alienated him more than any other from many of his colleagues, light-headed idlers, prone to personal bickerings. One day, weary of this chaos, he wanted to resign. It sufficed to tell him that his withdrawal would be very prejudicial to the cause of the people to persuade him to remain, and await, not victory — as well as Félix Pyat he knew that impossible — but the death that makes the future fruitful.

Félix Pyat, so lashed from all sides, not daring to snap at Delescluze, turned round upon Vermorel, whom for all argument he called 'spy"; and as Vermorel was a member of the Commission of Public Safety, accused him in the *Vengeur* of putting out of the way evidence accumulated against him at the prefecture of police. This member of the hare species called Vermorel a "worm." Such was his mode of discussion. Under the veil of literary refinement lurked the amenities of Billingsgate. In 1848, in the *Constituante,* he called Proudhon *'swine";* and in 1871 in the *Commune,* he called Tridon *"dunghill."* He was the only member of this Assembly, where there were workmen of rude professions, who introduced ribaldry into the discussions.

Vermorel, replying in the *Cri du Peuple,* easily floored him. The electors of Félix Pyat sent him three summations to remain at his post: "You are a soldier; you must stay in the breach. It is we alone who have the right to revoke you." Ferreted out by his mandatories, threatened with arrest by the Council, this Greek chose the lesser danger, and re-entered the Hôtel-de-Ville in mincing attitude.

Versailles was jubilant at these miserable triflings. For the first time the public became acquainted with the interior of the Council, its infinitesimal coteries, made up of purely personal friendships or antipathies. Whoever belonged to such a group got thorough support, whatever his blunders. Far more; in order to be allowed to serve the Commune, it was necessary to belong to such a confraternity. Many sincerely devoted men offered themselves, tried democrats, intelligent employees, deserters from the Government, even Republican officers. They were overweeningly met by some incapable upstarts of yesterday, whose devotion was not to outlast the 20th May. And yet the insufficiency of the personnel and the want of talent each day became more overwhelming. The members of the Council complained that nothing was getting on. The Executive Commission did not know how to command, nor its subordinate how to obey; the Council devolved power and retained it at the same time, interfered every moment with the slightest details of the service; conducted the government, the administration, and the defence like the sortie of the 3rd April.

Chapter 17
Women of the Commune and the opposing armies

The glorious flame of Paris still hid these failings. One must have been enkindled by it to describe it. Beside it the Communard journals, in spite of their romanticism, show pale and dull. It is true the *mise en scène* was unpretending. In the streets, in the silent boulevards, a battalion of a hundred men setting out for the battle or returning from it; a woman who follows, a passer — by who applauds — that is all. But it is the drama of the Revolution, simple and gigantic as a drama of Aeschylus.

The commander in his *vareuse,* dusty, his silver lace singed, his men greyheads or youths, the veterans of June 1848 and the pupils of March, the son often marching by the side of the father.

This woman, who salutes or accompanies them, she is the true Parisienne. The unclean androgyne, born in the mire of the Empire, the madonna of the pornographers, the Dumas fils and the Feydeaux, has followed her patrons to Versailles or works the Prussian mine at St. Denis. She, who is now uppermost, is the Parisienne, strong, devoted, tragic, knowing how to die as she loves. A helpmeet in labour, she will also be an associate in the death-struggle. A formidable equality this to oppose to the bourgeoisie. The proletarian is doubly strong — one heart and four hands. On the 24th of March a Federal addressed these noble words to the bourgeois battalions of the first arrondissement, making them drop their arms: "Believe me, you cannot hold out; your wives are all in tears, and ours do not weep."

She does not keep back her husband. On the contrary, she urges him to battle, carries him his linen and his soup, as she had before done to his workshop. Many would not return, but took up arms. At the plateau de Chatillon they were the last to stand the fire. The *cantinières,* simply dressed as workwomen, not fancy costumes, fell by dozens. On the 3rd April, at Meudon, the Citoyenne Lachaise, *cantinere* of the 66th battalion, remained the whole day in the field of battle, tending the wounded, alone, without a doctor.

If they return, it is to call to arms. Having formed a central committee at the *mairie* of the tenth arrondissement, they issued fiery proclamations: "We must conquer or die. You who say, 'What matters the triumph of our cause if I must lose those I love?' know that the only means of saving those who are dear to you is to throw yourselves into the struggle." Their committees multiplied. They offered themselves to the Commune, demanding arms, posts of danger, and complaining of the cowards who swerved from their duty. Madame André Léo, with her eloquent pen, explained the meaning of the Commune, summoned the delegate at the War Office to avail himself of the "holy fever that burns in the hearts of the women." A young Russian lady, of noble birth, educated, beautiful, rich, called Demitriev, was the Théroigne de Méricourt of this Revolution. The proletarian character of the Commune was embodied in Louise Michel, a teacher in the seventeenth arrondissement. Gentle and patient with the little children, who adored her, in the cause of the people the mother became a lioness. She had organized a corps of ambulance nurses, who tended the wounded even under fire. There they suffered no rivals. They also went to the hospitals to save their beloved comrades from the harsh nuns; and the eyes of the dying brightened at the murmur of those gentle voices that spoke to them of the Republic and of hope.

In this contest of devotion the children fought with men and women. The Versaillese, victorious, took 660 of them, and many perished in the battle of the streets. Thousands served during the siege. They followed the battalions to the trenches, in the forts, especially clinging to the cannon. Some gunners of the Porte-Maillot were boys of from thirteen to fourteen years old. Unsheltered, in the open country, they performed exploits of mad heroism.

This Parisian flame radiated beyond the enceinte. The municipalities of Sceaux and St. Denis united at Vincennes to protest against the bombardment, demand the municipal franchises and the establishment of the Republic. Its heat was even felt in the provinces.

They began to believe Paris was impregnable, and laughed much at the despatches of M. Thiers, saying on the 3rd April, "This day is decisive of the fate of the insurrection; on the 4th, "The insurgents have to-day suffered a decisive defeat;" on the 7th, "This day is decisive;" on the 11th, "Irresistible means are being prepared at Versailles," on the 12th, "We expect the decisive moment." And despite so many decisive successes and irresistible means, the Versaillese army was all the while baffled at our advanced posts. Its only decisive victories were against the houses of the enceinte and the suburbs.

The neighbourhood of the Porte-Maillot, the Avenue de la Grande Armée and the Ternes were continually lighting up with conflagrations. Asnières and Levallois were filling with ruins, the inhabitants of Neuilly starving in their cellars. The Versaillese threw against these points alone 1,500 shells a day; and yet M. Thiers wrote to his prefects, "If a few cannon-shots are heard, it is not the act of the Government, but of a few insurgents trying to make us believe they are fighting. while they hardly dare show themselves."

The Commune assisted the bombarded people of Paris, but could do nothing for those of Neuilly, caught between two fires. A cry of pity went up from the whole press. All the journals demanded an armistice for the evacuation of Neuilly; the Freemasons and the *Ligue des Droits de Paris* interposed. With much trouble, for the generals did not want an armistice, the delegates got a suspension of arms for eight hours. The Council appointed five of its members to receive the bombarded people; the municipalities prepared them an asylum, and some of the women's committees left Paris to assist them.

On the 25th, at nine o'clock in the morning, the cannon from the Porte-Maillot to Asnières were silent. Thousands of Parisians went to visit the ruins of the Avenue and the Porte-Maillot, a mortar of earth, granite, and fragments of shells; stood still, deeply moved, before the artillerists leaning on their famous pieces, and then dispersed all over Neuilly. The little town, once so coquettish, displayed in the bright rays of the sun its shattered houses. At the limits agreed upon were two barriers, one of soldiers of the line, the other of Federals, separated from each other by an interval of about twenty yards. The Versaillese, chosen from amongst their most reliable troops, were watched by officers with hangdog looks. The Parisians, good fellows, approached the soldiers, speaking to them. The officers immediately ran up shouting furiously. When a soldier gave a polite answer to two ladies, an officer threw himself upon him, tore away his musket, and pointing the bayonet at the Parisiennes, cried, "This is how one speaks to them." Some persons having crossed the boundary marked out were taken prisoners. Still five o'clock struck without any massacre having occurred. The Avenue grew empty. Each Parisian on returning home carried his sack of earth to the fortifications of the Porte-Maillot, which found themselves re-established as if by magic.

In the evening the Versaillese again opened fire. It had not ceased against the forts of the south. That same day the enemy unmasked on this side the batteries he had been constructing for a fortnight — the first part of the plan of General Thiers.

He had on the 6th placed all the troops under the command of that MacMahon, his stains of Sedan still upon him. The army at this time was 46,000 strong, for the most part the residuum of depots, incapable of any serious action. To reinforce it and obtain soldiers, M. Thiers had sent Jules Favre whining to Bismarck. The Prussians had set free 60,000 prisoners on harsher conditions of peace, and authorized their ally Thiers to augment to 130,000 men the number of soldiers round Paris, which, according to the preliminaries of peace, were not to have exceeded 40,000 men. On the 25th April the Versaillese army comprised five corps, two of them, those of Douai and Clinchant, composed of the released prisoners from Germany and a reserve commanded by Vinoy, all in all 110,000 men. It increased to 170,000 receiving rations, of whom 130,000 were combatants. M. Thiers displayed real ability in setting it against Paris. The soldiers were well fed, well dressed, severely overlooked; discipline was reestablished. There occurred mysterious disappearances of officers guilty of having given utterance to their horror at this fratricidal war. Still this was not yet the army for an attack, the men always scampering away before a steady resistance. Despite official brag, the generals only counted upon the artillery, to which they owed the successes of Courbevoie and of Asnières. Paris was only to be overcome by fire.

As during the first siege, Paris was literally hemmed in by bayonets, but this time half-foreign, half-French. The German army, forming a semicircle from the Marne to St. Denis, occupying the forts of the east and of the north; the Versaillese army, closing the circle from St. Denis to Villeneuve St. Georges, mistress only of Mont-Valérien. The latter could then only attack the Commune by the west and south. The Federals had then the five forts of Ivry, Bicetre, Montrouge, Vanves, and Issy to defend themselves, with the trenches and the advanced posts that united them to each other, and the principal villages, Neuilly, Asnières, and St. Ouen.

The vulnerable point of the enceinte facing the Versaillese was on the south-west, the salient of the Point du Jour, defended by the fort of Issy. Sufficiently covered on the right by the park, the castle of Issy and a trench uniting it to the Seine, commanded by our gunboats, this fort was overtopped in front and on the left by the heights of Bellevue, Meudon, and Chatillon. M. Thiers armed them with siege pieces which he had sent from Toulon, Cherbourg, Douai, Lyons, and Besancon — 293 ordnance pieces — and their effect was such that from the first days the fort of Issy was shaken. General Cissey, charged with the command of these operations, immediately commenced manoeuvring.

To crush the fort of Issy and that of Vanves, which supported it, then to force the Point du Jour, whence the troops could deploy into Paris, such was

M. Thiers' plan. The only object of the operations from St. Ouen to Neuilly was to prevent our attack by Courbevoie.

What forces and what plan did the Commune oppose?

The returns stated about 96,000 men and 4,000 officers for the active National Guard; for the reserve, 100,000 men and 3,500 officers. Thirty-six free corps claimed to number 3,450 men. All deductions made, 60,000 combatants might have been obtained had they known how to set about it. But the weakness of the Council, the difficulty of supervision and repression, allowed the less brave and those who did not stand in need of pay, to shirk all control. Many contrived to limit their services to the interior of Paris. Thus for want of order the effective forces remained very weak, and the line from St. Ouen to Ivry was never held by more than 15,000 or 16,000 Federals.

The cavalry existed only on paper. There were only 500 horses to drag the guns or the wagons and to mount the officers and despatch-riders. The engineer department remained in a rudimentary state, the finest decrees notwithstanding. Of the 1,200 cannon possessed by Paris, only 200 were utilized. There were never more than 500 artillerymen, while the returns stated 2,500.

Dombrowski occupied the bridge of Asnières, Levallois, and Neuilly with 4,000 or 5,000 men at the utmost. To protect his positions he had at Clichy and Asnières about thirty ordnance pieces and two ironclad railway carriages, which from the 15th April to the 22nd May, even after the entry of the Versaillese, did not cease running along the lines; at Levallois, a dozen pieces. The ramparts of the north assisted him, and the valiant Porte-Maillot covered him at Neuilly.

On the left bank, from Issy to Ivry, in the forts, the villages, and the trenches, there were 10,000 to 11,000 Federals. The fort of Issy contained on an average 600 men and 50 pieces of 7 and 12 centimetres, of which two-thirds were inactive. The bastions 72 and 73 relieved him a little, aided by four ironclad locomotives established on the viaduct of the Point du Jour. Underneath, the gunboats, rearmed, fired on Breteuil, Sevres, Brimborion, even daring to push as far as Chatillon, and, unsheltered, cannonaded Meudon. A few hundred riflemen occupied the park and the castle of Issy, the Moulineaux, Le Val, and the trenches which united the fort of Issy to that of Vanves. This latter, exposed like Issy, valiantly supported its efforts with a garrison of 500 men and about 20 cannon. The bastions of the enceinte supported it very little.

The fort of Montrouge, with 350 men and 10 to 15 ordnance pieces, had only to support the fort of Vanves. That of Bicetre, provided with 500 men and 20 pieces, had to fire at objects hidden from its view. Three considerable redoubts protected it — the Hautes Bruyeres, with 500 men and 20 pieces; the Moulin Saquet, with 700 men and about 14 pieces; and Villejuif, with 300 men and a few howitzers. At the extreme left, the fort of Ivry and its dependencies had 500 men and about 40 pieces. The intermediate villages, Gentilly, Cachan, and Arcueil, were occupied by 2,000 to 2,500 Federals.

The nominal command of the forts of the south, first confided to Eudes, assisted by an ex-officer of Garibaldi, La Cecilia, on the 20th passed into the hands of the Alsatian Wetzel, an officer of the army of the Loire. From his headquarters of Issy he was to superintend the trenches of Issy and of Vanves and the defence of the forts. In reality, their commanders, who often changed, did just as they pleased.

The command, from Issy to Arcueil was, towards the middle of April, entrusted to General Wroblewski, one of the best officers of the Polish insurrection, young, an adept in military science, brave, methodical, and shrewd, turning everybody and everything to account; an excellent chief for young troops.

All these general officers never received but one order: "Defend yourselves." As to a general plan, there never was one. Neither Cluseret nor Rossel held councils of war.

The men were also abandoned to themselves, being neither cared for nor controlled. Scarcely any, if any, relieving of the troops under fire ever took place. The whole strain fell upon the same men. Certain battalions remained twenty, thirty days in the trenches, while others were continually kept in reserve. If some men grew so inured to fire that they refused to return home, others were discouraged, came to show their clothes covered with vermin and asked for rest. The generals were obliged to retain them, having no one to put in their places.

This carelessness soon destroyed all discipline. The brave wanted to rely only upon themselves, and the others slunk from the service. The officers did the same, some leaving their posts to assist the fight at a contiguous place, others returning to the town. The court-martial sentenced a few of them very severely. The Council quashed the sentences, and commuted one condemnation to death to three years' imprisonment.

As they recoiled from rigour, from regular war discipline, they ought to have changed their method and their tactics. But the Council was now even less capable of showing will of its own than on the first day. It always lamented that things were at a stand-still, but did not know how to set them going. On the 26th, the military commission, declaring that decrees and orders remained a dead letter, charged the municipalities, the Central Committee, and the *chefs-de-légions* with the reorganization of the National Guard. Not one of these mechanisms functioned methodically; the Council had not even thought of organizing Paris by sections; the Central Committee intrigued; the *chefs-de-légions* were agitated; certain members of the Council and generals dreamt of a military dictatorship. In the midst of this fatal wrestling, the Council discussed during several sittings whether the pawn tickets to be given back gratuitously to their owners should amount to twenty or thirty francs, and whether the *Officiel* should be sold for five centimes.

Towards the end of April, no observer of any perspicacity could fail to see that the defence had become hopeless. In Paris, active and devoted men exhausted their strength in enervating struggles with the bureaux, the committees, the sub-committees, and the thousand pretentious rival administrations, often losing a whole day in order to obtain possession of a single cannon. At the ramparts, some artillerymen riddled the line of Versailles, and, asking for nothing but bread and iron, stood to their pieces until torn away by shells. The forts, their casemates staved in, their embrasures destroyed, lustily answered the fire from the heights. Brave skirmishers, unprotected, surprised the line-soldiers in their lurking-places. All this devotion and dazzling heroism were spent in vain, like the steam of an engine escaping through hundreds of outlets.

Chapter 18
The Work of the Commune

The insufficiency and the weakness of the Executive Commission became so shocking, that on the 20th the Council decided to replace it by the delegates of the nine commissions, amongst whom it had distributed its different functions. These commissions were renewed the same day. In general they were rather neglected; and how could one man attend to the daily sittings of the Hôtel-de-Ville, to his commission and his *mairie*? For the Council had charged its members with the administration of their respective arrondissements; and the real work of the several commissions weighed on the delegates who had presided over them from their origin, and for the most part were not changed on the 20th April. They continued to act, as heretofore, almost single-handed. Before proceeding with our narrative we will look more closely into their doings.

Two delegations required only good-will — those of the victualling department and of the public or municipal services. The provisioning of the town was carried on through the neutral zone, where M. Thiers, however anxious to starve Paris, could not prevent a regular supply of food. All the foremen having remained at their posts, the municipal services did not suffer. Four delegations — Finance, War, Public Safety, Exterior — required special aptitude. The three others, Education, Justice, Labour and Exchange, had to propound the philosophical principles of this revolution. All the delegates save Frankel, a workman, belonged to the lower middle-class.

The Commission of Finance centred in Jourde, who, with his inexhaustible garrulity, had eclipsed the too modest Varlin. The task imposed was to procure every morning 675,000 francs for the payment of the services, to feed 250,000 persons, and find the sinews of war. Besides the 4,658,000 francs in the coffers of the Treasury, 214 millions in shares and other effects had been found in the Finance Office; but Jourde could not or would not negotiate them, and to fill his exchequer he had to lay hold of the revenues of all the administrations — the telegraph and postal offices, the octrois, direct contributions, custom house offices, markets, tobacco, registration and stamps, municipal funds and the railway duties. The bank, little by little, paid back the 9,400,000 francs due to the town, and even parted with 7,290,000 francs on its own account. From the 20th March to the 30th April, twenty-six millions were thus scraped together. During the same period the War Office alone absorbed over twenty. The Intendance received 1,813,000 francs, all the municipalities together 1,446,000, the Interior 103,000, Marine 29,000, justice 5,500, Commerce 50,000, Education 1,000 only, Exterior 112,000, Firemen 100,000, National Library 80,000, Commission of Barricades 44,500, L'Imprimerie Nationale 100,000, the Association of Tailors and Shoemakers 24,882. These proportions remained almost the same from the 1st May to the fall of the Commune. The expenses of the second period rose to about twenty millions. The sum total of the expenses of the Commune was about 46,300,000 francs, of which 16,696,000 were supplied by the bank, and the rest by the various services, the octrois yielding nearly twelve millions.

Most of these Services were under the superintendence of workmen or former subordinate employees, and were all carried on with a fourth part of their ordinary numerical strength. The director of the postal department, Theisz, a chaser, found the Service quite disorganized, the divisional offices closed, the stamps hidden away or carried off, the material, seals, the carts, etc. taken away, and the coffers empty. Notices posted up in the hall and courts ordered the employees to proceed to Versailles on pain of dismissal, but Theisz acted with promptitude and energy. When the subordinate employees who had not been forewarned came as usual to organize the mail service, he addressed them, discussed with them, and had the doors shut. Little by little they gave way. Some functionaries who were Socialists also lent their help, and the direction of the various services was entrusted to the head-clerks. The divisional offices were opened, and in forty-eight hours the collection and distribution of letters for Paris reorganized. As to the letters destined for the provinces, clever agents threw them into the offices of St. Denis and ten miles round, while for the introduction of letters into Paris every latitude was given to private initiative. A superior council was instituted, which raised the wages of postmen, sorters, porters and office caretakers, shortened the time of service as supernumeraries, and decided that the ability of the employees should be tested for the future by means of tests and examinations.

The Mint, directed by Camélinat, a bronze-mounter, one of the most active members of the International, manufactured the postage stamps. At the Mint, as at the general post-office, the Versaillese director and principal employees had first parleyed, then made off. Camélinat, supported by some friends, bravely took this place, had the works continued, and every one contributing his professional experience, improvements in the machinery as well as new methods were introduced. The bank, which concealed its bullion, was obliged to furnish about 110,000 francs' worth, immediately coined into five-franc pieces. A new coin-plate was engraved, and was about to be put into use, when the Versaillese entered Paris.

The department of Public Assistance also depended on that of the Finances. A man of the greatest merit, Treilhard, an old exile of 1851, reorganized this administration, which he found entirely out of order. Some doctors and agents of the service had abandoned the hospitals; the director and the steward of the Petits-Ménages at Issy had fled, thus reducing many of their pensioners to go out begging. Some employees forced our wounded to wait before the doors of the hospital, while the sisters of mercy tried to make them blush for their glorious wounds; but Treilhard soon put all in order, and, for the second time since 1792, the sick and the infirm found friends in their guardians and blessed the Commune. This kind-hearted, intellectual man, who was assassinated by a Versaillese officer on the 24th May at the Panthéon, has left a very elaborate report on the suppression of bureaux of charity, which chain the poor to the Government and to the clergy. He proposed having them replaced by a bureau of assistance in each arrondissement, under the direction of a communal committee.

The Telegraph Office, Registration, and Domains, cleverly directed by the honest Fontaine; the Service of Contributions, entirely re-established by Faillet and Combault; the National Printing Press, which Debock reorganized and administered with remarkable dexterity, and the other departments connected with that of Finance, ordinarily reserved to the great bourgeoisie, were managed with skill and economy — the maximum salary, 6,000 francs, was never reached — by workmen, subordinate employees; and this is not the least of their crimes in the eyes of the Versaillese bourgeoisie. Compared with the Finance department, that of War was a region of darkness and utter confusion. Officers and guards encumbered the offices of the Ministry, some demanding munitions and victuals, others complaining of not being relieved. They were sent back to the Place Vendôme, maintained in the teeth of common sense, and directed by the rather equivocal colonel, Henri Prudhomme. On the floor below, the Central Committee, installed there by Cluseret, bustled, spent time and breath in endless sittings, found fault with the delegate at war, amused itself with creating new insignia, received the malcontents of the Ministry, asked returns from the general staff, claimed to give advice on military operations. In its turn, the Committee of Artillery, founded on the 18th March, wrangled about the disposal of the cannon with the War Office. The latter had the pieces of the Champ-de-Mars and the Committee those of Montmartre. Attempts at creating a central park of artillery, or even at learning the exact number of the ordnance pieces, were made in vain. Pieces of long range remained to the last moment lying along the ramparts, while the forts had only pieces of seven and twelve centimetres to answer the huge cannon of Marine, and often the munitions sent were not of corresponding calibre. The commissariat, assailed by adventurers of all sorts, took their stores haphazardly. The construction of the barricades, which were to form a second and third enceinte, instituted on the 9th April, had been left to a crotchety fellow, starting jobs everywhere without method and against the plans of his superiors. All the other Services were conducted in the same style, without fixed principles, without limitation of their respective provinces, the wheels of the machine not working within one another. In this concert without a conductor, each instrumentalist played what he liked, confusing his own score with his neighbour's.

A firm and supple hand would soon have restored harmony. The Central Committee, despite its assumption of lecturing the Commune, which it said was "its daughter and must not be allowed to go astray," was now only an assemblage of talkers devoid of all authority. It had, to a great extent, been renewed since the establishment of the Commune, and the much-contested elections to it — for many aspired to the title of member — had given a majority of flighty, heedless men. In its present state this Committee derived its whole importance from the jealousy of the Council. The Committee of Artillery, monopolized by brawlers, would have yielded at once to the slightest pressure. The commissariat and the other services depended entirely upon the action of the delegate at War.

The phantom general, stretched on his sofa, hatched orders, circulars, now melancholy, now commanding, and never stirred a finger to watch over their execution. If some member of the Council came to rouse him, "What are you doing? Such-and-such a place is in peril," he answered loftily, "All my precautions are taken; give my combinations time to be accomplished," and turned over again. One day he bullied the Central Committee, which left the Ministry to go and sulk in the Rue de l'Entrepôt; a week later he went after the same Committee, reinstating it at the War Office. Vain to shamelessness, he showed sham letters from Todleben proposing plans of defence, and spent his time in posing to correspondents of foreign journals. With an affectation of pride, he never put on a uniform, which, however, at that time was the true dress of the proletarian. It took the Council almost a month to recognize that this pithless braggart was only a disappointed officer of the standing army, his airs of an innovator notwithstanding.

Many hopes turned to his chief-of-staff, Rossel, a young Radical, twenty-eight years old, self-restrained, puritanical, who was sowing his revolutionary wild oats. A captain of engineers in the army of Metz, he had attempted to resist Bazaine, and escaped from the Prussians. Gambetta had appointed him colonel of engineers at the camp of Nevers, where he was still lingering on the 18th March. He was dazzled; saw in Paris the future of France, and his own; threw up his commission and hurried thither, where some friends placed him in the 17th Legion. He was haughty, soon became unpopular, and was arrested on the 3rd April. Two members of the Council, Malon and Charles Gérardin, had him set free and presented him to Cluseret, by whom he was accepted as chief of the general staff. Rossel, fancying that the Central Committee was a power, made up to it, appeared to ask it for advice, and sought out the men he thought popular. His coldness, his technical vocabulary, his clearness of speech, his get up as a great man, enchanted the bureaux, but those who studied him more closely noticed his unsteady look, the infallible sign of a perturbed spirit. By degrees the young revolutionary officer became the fashion, and his consular bearing did not displease the public, sickened at the flabbiness of Cluseret.

Nothing, however, justified this infatuation. Chief of the general staff since the 5th April, he allowed all the Services to shift for themselves; the only one in some measure organized, the Control of General Information, was the work of Moreau, who every morning furnished the War Office and the Commune with detailed, and often very picturesque, reports on the military operations and the moral condition of Paris.

This was about all the police the Commune had. The Commission of Public Safety, which should have thrown light upon the most secret recesses, emitted only a fitful glimmering.

The Central Committee had appointed Raoul Rigault, a young man of twenty-four, much mixed up in the revolutionary movement, as civil delegate to the prefecture of police, but under the severe direction of Duval. Rigault well kept in hand might have made a very good subaltern, and so long as Duval lived he did not go wrong. The unpardonable fault of the Council was to place him at the head of a service where the slightest mistake was more dangerous than at the advanced posts. His friends, who, with the exception of a small number, Ferré, Regnard, and two or three others, were as young and as giddy-headed as himself, discharged in a boyish way the most delicate functions. The Commission of Public Safety, which ought to have superintended Rigault, only followed his example. There, above all, did they live as boon companions, apparently unaware of having assumed the guardianship of, and the responsibility for, 100,000 lives.

No wonder the mice were soon seen playing round the prefecture of police. Papers suppressed in the morning were on sale in the evening in the streets; the conspirators wormed themselves into all the services without exciting the suspicion of Rigault or his companions. They never discovered anything; it was always necessary to do it for them. They made arrests like military marches in the daytime, with large reinforcements of National Guards. After the decree on the hostages, they had only managed to lay hands on four or five ecclesiastics of mark: the Gallican Archbishop Darboy, an arrant Bonapartist; his grand-vicar, Lagarde; the curate of the Madeleine; Deguerry, a kind of De Morny in cassock; the Abbé Allard, the Bishop of Surat; and a few Jesuits of nerve. Chance only delivered into their hands the president of the Court of Appeal, Bonjean, and Jecker, the famous inventor of the expedition to Mexico.

This culpable heedlessness, which the people have paid for with their blood, was the salvation of criminals. Some National Guards had brought to light the mysteries of the Picpus convent, discovered three unfortunate women shut up in grated cages, strange instruments, corselets of iron, straps, racks, which smacked strangely of the Inquisition, a treatise on abortion, and two skulls still covered with hair. One of the prisoners, the only one whose reason had not given way, said that she had been in this cage for ten years. The police contented themselves with sending the nuns to St. Lazare. Some inhabitants of the tenth arrondissement had discovered feminine skeletons in the caves of the St. Laurent Church. The prefecture only made a show of inquiry that ended in nothing.

However, in the midst of all these faults, the humanitarian idea revealed itself, so thoroughly sound was this popular revolution. The chief of the Bureau of Public Safety, making an appeal to the public for the victims of the war, said, "The Commune has sent bread to ninety-two wives of those who are killing us. The widows belong to no party. The Republic has bread for every misery and care for all the orphans." Admirable words these, worthy of Chalier and of Chaumette. The prefecture, overrun by denunciations, declared that it would take no account of the anonymous ones. "The man," said the *Officiel*, "who does not dare to sign a denunciation serves a personal rancour and not the public interest." The hostages were allowed to obtain from without food, linen, books, papers, to be visited by their friends, and to receive the reporters of foreign journals. An offer was even made M. Thiers to exchange the hostages of greatest mark, the Archbishop, Deguerry, Bonjean, and Lagarde, for Blanqui alone. To conduct this negotiation the Vicar-General was sent to Versailles, after having sworn to the Archbishop and the delegate to return to his prison in case of non-success. But M. Thiers thought that Blanqui would give a head to the movement, while the Ultramontanes, eagerly covetous of the episcopal seat of Paris, took good care not to save the Gallican Darboy, whose death would be a double profit, leaving them a rich inheritance, and giving them at small expense a martyr. M. Thiers refused, and Lagarde remained at Versailles. The Council did not punish the Archbishop for his want of faith, and a few days after set his sister at liberty. Never even in the days of despair was the privilege of women forgotten. The culpable nuns of Picpus and the other religieuses conducted to St. Lazare were confined in a special part of the building.

The prefecture and the delegation of Justice also evinced their humanity in ameliorating the service of the prisons. The Council in its turn, striving to guarantee individual liberty, decreed that every arrest should be immediately notified to the delegate of justice, and that no perquisition should be made without a regular warrant. National Guards, misinformed, having arrested certain individuals reputed suspicious, the Council declared in the *Officiel* that every arbitrary act would be followed by a dismissal and immediate prosecution. A battalion looking for arms at the gas company's thought itself authorized to seize the cash-box; the Council at once had the sum returned. The commisar of police who arrested Gustave Chaudey, arraigned for having commanded fire on the 22nd January, had also seized the money of the prisoner; the Council dismissed the commissar. To prevent all abuse of power, it ordered an inquiry into the state of the prisoners and the motives of their detention, at the same time authorizing all its members to visit the prisoners. Rigault thereupon sent in his resignation, which was accepted, for he was beginning to weary everybody, and Delescluze had been obliged to rebuke him. His pranks filled the columns of the Versaillese journals, always on the look-out for scandals. They accused this childish policeman of terrorizing Paris, and represented the members of the Council, who refused to endorse the condemnations of the court martial, as assassins. The Figarist historians have kept up this legend. That vile bourgeoisie, which bent its head under the 30,000 arrests of December, the *lettres de cachet* of the Empire, and applauded the 50,000 arrests of May, still howls about the 800 or 900 arrests made under the Commune. They never exceeded this figure in two months of strife, and two-thirds of those arrested were only imprisoned a few days, many only a few hours. But the provinces, only fed with news by the Versaillese press, believed in its inventions, amplified in the circulars of M. Thiers telegraphing to the prefects: "The insurgents are emptying the principal houses of Paris in order to put the furniture to sale."

To enlighten the provinces and provoke their intervention, such was the role of the delegation of the Exterior, which, under an ill-chosen title, was only second in importance to that of War. Since the 4th April — (I shall afterwards recount these movements) — the departments had been stirring. Save that of Marseilles, in part disarmed, the National Guard everywhere had guns. In the centre, east, west and south, powerful diversions might easily have been made, the stations occupied, and thereby the reinforcements and artillery destined for Versailles arrested.

The delegation contented itself with sending some few emissaries, without knowledge of the localities they were sent to, without tact and without authority. It was even exploited by traitors, who pocketed its money and handed over its instructions to Versailles. Well-known Republicans, familiar with the habits of the provinces, offered their services in vain. There. as elsewhere, it was necessary to be a favourite. Finally, for the work of enlightening and rousing France to insurrection, only a sum of 100,000 francs was allowed.

The delegation put forth only a small number of manifestoes, one a true and eloquent résumé of the Parisian revolution, and two addresses to the peasants, one by Madame André Léo, simple, fervent, quite within the reach of the peasantry: "Brother, you are being deceived. Our interests are the same. What I ask for, you wish it too. The affranchisement which I demand is yours.... What Paris after all wants is the land for the peasant, the instrument for the workmen." This good seed was carried away in free balloons, which, by a cleverly-contrived mechanism, from time to time dropped the printed papers. How many were lost, fell among thorns!

This delegation, created only for the exterior, entirely forgot the rest of the world. Throughout all Europe the working-classes eagerly awaited news from Paris, were in their hearts fellow-combatants of the great town, now become their capital, multiplied their meetings, processions, and addresses. Their papers, poor for the most part, courageously struggled against the calumnies of the bourgeois press. The duty of the delegation was to hold out a hand to these priceless auxiliaries: it did nothing. Some of these papers exhausted their last means in defence of the Commune, which allowed its defenders to succumb for want of bread.

The delegation, without experience, without resources, could not fight against the astute cleverness of M. Thiers. It showed great zeal in Protecting foreigners, and sent the rich silver plate of the Ministry to the Mint, but it did almost no real work.

Now we come to the delegations of vital importance. Since, by the force of events, the Commune had become the champion of the Revolution, it ought to have proclaimed the aspirations of the century, and, if it was to die, leave at least their testament on its tomb. It would have sufficed to state lucidly the whole range of institutions demanded for forty years by the revolutionary party.

The delegate of Justice, a lawyer, had only to make a summary of the reforms long since demanded by all Socialists. It was the part of a Proletarian revolution to show the aristocracy of our judicial system the despotic and antiquated doctrines of the Code Napoleon; the sovereign people hardly ever judging themselves, but judged by a caste issued from another authority than their own, the absurd hierarchy of judges and tribunals, the *tabellionat,* the procureurs, 400,000 notaries, solicitors, sheriffs" officers, registrars, bailiffs, advocates and lawyers, draining national wealth to the amount of many hundreds of millions. It was, above all, for a revolution made in the name of the Commune to endow the Commune with a tribunal at which the people, restored to their rights, should judge by jury all cases, civil and commercial, misdemeanours as well as crimes; a final tribunal, without any appeal but for informalities, to state how solicitors, registrars, sheriffs, may be rendered useless, and the notaries replaced by simple registration officers. The delegate mostly limited himself to appointing notaries, sheriffs' officers, and bailiffs, provided with a fixed salary — very useless appointments in a

Louis Bonaparte III. The nephew of Napoleon Bonaparte, he had seized power in a coup and declared himself Emperor. Fearing popular resentment, he hoped to distract the population of France with a quick patriotic war against Prussia. Instead, he brought about the downfall of his own regime.

Bonaparte's forces achieved one spectacular defeat after another in the Franco-Prussian War, before surrendering to the Prussians at Sedan.

(l.) Otto von Bismarck, Prime Minister of Prussia. (r.) General Louis Jules Trochu led the defenses in Paris, and became head of the Government of National Defense after Bonaparte's surrender.

The siege of Paris, depicted in a contemporary painting. Parisian citizens in the militia, known as the National Guard, staunchly defended the city.

(l.) Adolphe Thiers, who was elected President of the National Assembly. (r.) Jules Favre, who negotiated the surrender of Paris to the Prussians.

(l.) Louis Auguste Blanqui. Upon hearing of the surrender negotiations, Blanqui, a socialist revolutionary, took over the City Hall in Paris and formed a Committee of Public Safety to overthrow the French state. He was arrested for treason by the Government of National Defense. (r.) General Claude Martin Lecomte. He was ordered by Thiers into Paris to disarm the National Guard militia. Instead, his own troops joined the insurrection and killed him.

A Proclamation from the Paris Commune. Composed of a variety of socialists, anarchists and other radicals, the Commune was elected by the workers of Paris. Blanqui was elected as its President, even though he was still in jail.

The Communards pulled down and destroyed the Vendome Column – a symbol of Bonapartist power that had been cast from the melted cannons of Napoleon's conquests.

Marshal Patrice MacMahon, the French General who was placed in charge of retaking Paris and crushing the Commune.

Barricades go up next to the destroyed Vendome Column.

A contemporary sketch illustrates National Guard members dragging their cannons to the heights of Montmartre.

A barricade and cannon defense, thrown up by the defending Communards.

Street fighting in Paris. A contemporary illustration.

Captured Commune members being marched past the Prussian lines to prison.

A contemporary composite photo depicting the execution of Commune leaders.

Executed Communards in their coffins. Some 30,000 were summarily shot on MacMahon's orders.

time of war, and which, besides, had the fault of consecrating the principle of the necessity for such officers. Scarcely anything progressive came of it. It was decreed that, in case of arrests, the minutes were to state the motives and the names of the witnesses to be called, while the papers, valuables and effects of the prisoners were to be deposited at the Suitors' Fund. Another decree ordered the directors of lunatic asylums to send the nominal and explanatory statement concerning their patients within four days. If the Council had thrown some light on these institutions, which veil so many crimes, humanity would have been its debtor. However, these decrees were never executed.

Did practical instinct make up for want of science on the part of the delegation? Did it shed light upon the mysteries of the caves of Picpus, the skeletons of St. Laurent? It seemed to take no notice of them, and the reaction made merry at these supposed discoveries. The delegation even missed the opportunity of winning over to the Commune, if only for one day, all Republicans of France. Jecker was in their power. Rich, brave, audacious, he had always lived certain of impunity, since bourgeois legality inflicts no chastisement for crimes like the Mexican expedition. The Revolution alone could smite him. Nothing was more easy than to proceed against him. Jecker, pretending to have been the dupe of the Empire, craved to make revelations. In a public court, before twelve jurors chosen at random, in the face of the world, through him the Mexican expedition might have been sifted, the intrigues of the clergy unveiled, the pockets of the thieves turned out; it might have been shown how the Empress, Miramon, and Morny had set the plot on foot, in what cause and for what men France had lost seas of blood and hundreds of millions. Afterwards the expiation might have been accomplished in the open day, on the Place de la Concorde, in face of the Tuileries. Poets, who rarely get shot, would perhaps have sighed, but the people, the eternal victim, would have applauded, and said, "The Revolution alone does justice." They neglected even to question Jecker.

The delegation at the Education Department was bound to write one of the finest pages of the Commune, for after so many years of study and experiments this question should spring forth ready armed from a truly revolutionary brain. The delegation has not left a memoir, a sketch, an address, a line, to bear witness for it in the future. Yet the delegate was a doctor, a student of the German universities. He contented himself with suppressing the crucifixes in the schoolrooms and making an appeal to all those who had studied the question of teaching. A commission was charged with organizing primary and professional instruction, whose work consisted in announcing the opening of a school on the 6th May. Another commission for the education of women was named on the day the Versaillese entered Paris.

The administrative action of the delegate was confined to impracticable decrees and a few appointments. Two devoted and talented men, Elisée Reclus and B. Gastineau, were charged with the reorganization of the National Library. They forbade the lending of books, thus putting an end to the scandalous practice by which a privileged few carved out a private library from public collections. The federation of artists, presided over by Courbet, elected member of the Council on the 16th April, occupied itself with the reopening and superintendence of the museums.

Nothing would be known of the ideas of this revolution on education were it not for a few circulars of the municipalities. Many had reopened the schools abandoned by the Congregationists and the municipal teachers, or driven away the priests who had remained. The municipality of the twentieth arrondissement clothed and fed the children; that of the fourth said, "To teach children to love and respect their fellow-creatures, to inspire them with a love of justice, to teach them that they must instruct themselves in the interests of all, such are the principles of morality on which the future communal education will be based." "The teachers of the schools and infant asylums," declared the municipality of the seventeenth arrondissement, "will for the future exclusively employ the experimental and scientific method, that which always starts from facts, physical, moral, intellectual." But these vague formulae could not make amends for the want of a complete programme.

Who, then, will speak for the people? The delegation of Labour and Exchange. Exclusively composed of revolutionary socialists, its purpose was, "The study of all the reforms to be introduced into the public services of the Commune or into the relations of the working men and women with their employers; the revision of the commercial code and custom-house duties; the revision of all direct and indirect taxes, the establishment of statistics of labour." It intended collecting from the citizens themselves the materials for the decrees to be submitted to the Commune.

The delegate to this department, Leo Frankel, procured the assistance of a commission of initiative composed of working men. Registers for offers and demands of work were opened in all the arrondissements. At the request of many journey-men bakers night-work was suppressed, a measure of hygiene as much as of morality. The delegation prepared a project for the suppression of pawnshops, a decree concerning stoppages of wages, and supported the decree relative to work-shops abandoned by their runaway masters.

Their plan gratuitously returned the pledged objects to the victims of war and to the necessitous. Those who might refuse to confess this latter title were to receive their pledges in exchange for a promise of repayment in five years. The report terminated with these words: "It is well understood that the suppression of the pawnshops is to be succeeded by a social organization giving serious guarantees of support to the workmen thrown out of employment. The establishment of the Commune necessitates institutions protecting the workmen from the exploitation of capital."

The decree that abolished stoppages from salaries and wages put an end to one of the most crying iniquities of the capitalist regime, these fines often being inflicted on the most futile pretext by the employer himself, who is thus at once judge and plaintiff.

The decree relative to the deserted workshops made restitution to the masses, dispossessed for centuries, of the property of their own labour. A commission of inquiry named by the Trade Union Chambers was to draw up the statistics and the inventory of the deserted workshops to be given back into the hands of the workmen. Thus "the expropriators were in their turn expropriated." The nineteenth century will not pass away without having begun this revolution; every progress in machinery brings it nearer. The more the exploitation of labour concentrates itself in a few hands, the more the working multitude are massed together and disciplined. Soon, conscious and united, the producing class will, like the young France of 1789, have to confront but a handful of privileged appropriators. The most inveterate revolutionary socialist is the monopolist.

No doubt this decree contained voids and stood in need of an elaborate explanation, especially on the subject of the co-operative societies to which the workshops were to be handed over. It was no more than the other applicable in this hour of strife, and required a number of supplementary decrees; but it at least gave some idea of the claims of the working class, and had it nothing else on its credit side, by the mere creation of the Commission for Labour and Exchange, the revolution of the 18th March would have done more for the workmen than all the bourgeois Assemblies of France since the 5th May, 1789.

The delegation for Labour wanted to look carefully into the contracts of the commissariat. It demonstrated that in the case of contracts adjudicated to the lowest bidder, the running down of prices falls upon wages and not on the profit of the contractor. "And the Commune is blind enough to lend itself to such manoeuvres," said the report, "and at this very moment, when the working man dares death rather than submit any longer to this exploitation." The delegate demanded that the estimate of charges should specify the cost of labour, that the orders should be preference be given to the workmen's corporations, and the contracting prices fixed by arbitration between the commissariat, the Trade Union Chamber of the corporation, and the delegate for Labour.

To overlook the financial administration of all the delegations, the Council in the month of May instituted a superior commission charged to audit their accounts. It decreed that functionaries or contractors guilty of peculation or theft should be punished with death.

In short, save for the delegation for Labour, where they did work, the basic delegations were unequal to their task. All committed the same fault.

For two months they had in their hands the archives of the bourgeoisie since 1789. There was the Cour des Comptes (a judicial board of accounts) to disclose the mysteries of official robbery; the Council of State, the dark deliberations of despotism; the Prefecture of Police, the scandalous under-currents of social power; the Ministry of Justice, the servility and crimes of the most oppressive of all classes. In the Hôtel-de-Ville there lay deposited the still unexplored records of the first Revolution, of those of 1815, 1830, 1848, and all diplomatists of Europe dreaded the opening of the portfolios at the Foreign Office. They might have laid bare before the eyes of the people the intimate history of the Revolution, the Directory, the first Empire, the monarchy of July, 1848, and of Napoleon III. They published only two or three instalments. The delegates slept by the side of these treasures, heedless, as it seemed, of their value.

The Radicals, seeing these lawyers, these doctors, these publicists, who allowed Jecker to remain mute and the Cour des Comptes closed, would not believe in such ignorance, and still affect to unriddle the enigma with the word "Bonapartism". A stupid accusation, given the lie by a thousand proofs. For the honour even of the delegates the bitter truth must be told. Their ignorance was not simulated, but only too real. To a great extent it was the offspring of past oppression.

Chapter 19
Formation of the Committee of Public Safety

M. Thiers was fully acquainted with the failings of the Commune, but he also knew the weakness of his army. Besides, he prided himself upon playing the soldier before the Prussians. In order to appease his colleagues, eager for the assault on Paris, he was haughty in receiving the conciliators, who multiplied their advances and their lame combinations.

Everybody intermeddled, from the good and visionary Considérant down to the cynic Girardin, down to Saisset's ex-aide-de-camp Schoelcher, who had replaced his plan of battle of the 24th March by a plan of conciliation. These encounters became the common topics of raillery. Since its pompous declaration, "All Paris will rise," the *Ligue des Droits de Paris* had been altogether sunk out of sight. It was perfectly understood that these Radicals were in search of some decent contrivance to back out of the peril. At the end of April their sham movements served only as a foil to set off the courageous conduct of the Freemasons.

On the 21st April the Freemasons, having gone to Versailles to ask for the armistice, complained of the municipal law recently voted by the Assembly. "What!" M. Thiers replied, "but this is the most liberal one we have had in France for eighty years. "We beg your pardon, and how about the communal institutions of 1791?" "Ah! you want to return to the follies of our fathers?" "But, after all, are you then resolved to sacrifice Paris?" "There will be some houses riddled, some persons killed, but the law will be enforced." The Freemasons had this hideous answer posted up in Paris.

On the 26th they met at the Châtelet, and several proposed that they should go and plant their banners on the ramparts. A thousand cheers answered. M. Floquet, who, with an eye to the future, had sent in his resignation as deputy, together with MM. Lockroy and Clémenceau, protested against this co-operation of the middle class with the people. His shrill voice was drowned in the enthusiastic cries in the hall. On the motion of Ranvier, the Freemasons went up to the Hôtel-de-Ville, preceded by their banner, where they were met by the Council in the Court of Honour. "If at the outset," said their spokesman, Thirifocq, "the Freemasons did not wish to act, it was because they wanted to have certain proof that Versailles would not hear of conciliation. They are ready to-day to plant their banner on the rampart. If one single ball touches it, the Freemasons will march with the same ardour as yourselves against the common enemy." This declaration was loudly applauded. Jules Vallès, in the name of the Commune, tendered his red scarf, which was twisted round the banner, and a delegation of the Council accompanied the brethren to the Masonic temple in the Rue Cadet.

They came three days after to redeem their word. The announcement of this intervention had given great hope to Paris. From early in the morning an immense crowd encumbered the approaches to the Carrousel, the rendezvous of all the lodges; and, despite a few reactionary Freemasons, who had put up posters protesting, at ten o'clock 10,000 brethren, representing fifty-five lodges, had gathered in the Carrousel. Six members of the Council led them to the Hôtel-de-Ville through the midst of the crowd and an avenue of battalions. A band, playing music of solemn and ritual character, preceded the procession; then came superior officers, the grand-masters, the members of the Council, and the brethren, with their wide blue, green, white, red or black ribbon, according to their grade, grouped around sixty-five banners that had never before been displayed in public. The one carried at the head of the procession was the white banner of Vincennes, bearing in red letters the fraternal and revolutionary inscription, "*Love one another.*" A lodge of women was especially cheered.

The banners and a numerous delegation were introduced into the Hôtel-de-Ville, the members of the Council waiting to receive them on the balcony of the staircase of honour. The banners were fixed along the steps. These standards of peace by the side of the red flag, this middle class joining hands with the proletariat under the proud image of the Republic, these cries of fraternity dazzled and brightened up even the most downcast. Félix Pyat indulged in a rhapsody of words and rhetorical antitheses. Old Beslay was much more eloquent in a few words broken by true tears. A brother solicited the honour of being the first to plant on the rampart the banner of his lodge, *La Persévérance*, founded in 1790, in the era of the great federations. A member of the Council presented the red flag: "Let it accompany your banners; let no hand henceforth turn us against each other." And the orator of the delegation, Thirifocq, pointing to the banner of Vincennes: "This will be the first to be presented before the ranks of the enemy. We will say to them, 'Soldiers of the mother country, fraternize with us, come and embrace us'. If we fail, we shall go and join the companies of war."

When the delegates left the Hôtel-de-Ville, a free balloon, marked with the three symbolical points, made an ascent here and there dropping the manifesto of the Freemasons. The immense procession having shown the Bastille and the boulevards its mysterious banners, frantically applauded, arrived about two o'clock at the cross-roads of the Champs-Elysées. The shells of Mont-Valérien obliged them to take the side-streets on their way to the Arc-de-Triomphe. There a delegation of all the venerables went to plant the banners at the most dangerous posts, from the Porte-Maillot to the Porte-Bineau. When the white flag was hoisted on the outpost of the Porte-Maillot the Versaillese ceased firing.

The delegates of the Freemasons and some members of the Council, appointed by their colleagues to accompany them, advanced, headed by their banner, into the Avenue of Neuilly. At the bridge of Courbevoie, before the Versaillese barricade, they found an officer who conducted them to General Montaudon, himself a Freemason. The Parisians explained the object of their demonstration, and asked for a truce. The general proposed that they should send a deputation to Versailles. Three delegates were chosen, and their companions returned to the town. In the evening silence reigned from St. Ouen to Neuilly, Dombrowski having taken upon himself to continue the truce. For the first time for twenty-five days the sleep of Paris was not disturbed by the report of cannon.

The next day the delegates returned. M. Thiers had hardly deigned receive them, had shown himself impatient, irritated, decided to grant nothing and to admit no more deputations. The Freemasons then resolved to march to battle with their insignia.

In the afternoon the *Alliance Républicaine des Départements* made an act of adhesion to the Commune. Millière, who had quite joined the movement without being able to gain the confidence of the Hôtel-de-Ville, exerted himself to group the provincials residing at Paris. Who does not know what the provinces contributed in blood and sinew to the great town? Out of 35,000 prisoners of French origin figuring in the official reports of Versailles, there were, according to their own statement, only 9,000 born Parisians. Each departmental group was to strain itself to enlighten its native place, to send circulars, proclamations, delegates. On the 30th all the groups met in the Court of the Louvre to vote an address to the departments, and all, about 15,000 men, headed by Millière, went to the Hôtel-de-Ville "to renew their adhesion to the patriotic work of the Commune of Paris."

The procession was still passing when a sinister rumour spread: the fort of Issy had been evacuated.

Under cover of their batteries, the Versaillese, pushing forward, had on the night of the 26th to the 27th surprised the Moulineaux, by which the park of Issy may be reached. On the following day sixty pieces of powerful calibre concentrated their shells on the fort, while others occupied Vanves, Montrouge, the gunboats and the enceinte. Issy answered valiantly, but our trenches, to which Wetzel ought to have attended, were in bad condition. On the 29th the bombardment redoubled and the projectiles ploughed the park. At eleven o'clock in the evening the Versaillese ceased firing, and in the nocturnal stillness surprised the Federals and occupied the trenches. On the 30th, at five o'clock in the morning, the fort, which had received no warning of this incident, found itself surrounded by a semi-circle of Versaillese. The commander, Megy, was disconcerted, sent for reinforcements, but received none. The garrison grew alarmed, and these Federals, who had cheerfully withstood a hailstorm of shells, took fright at a few skirmishers. Mégy held a council, and the evacuation was decided upon. The cannon were precipitately spiked — so badly that they were unnailed the same evening — and the bulk of the garrison left. Some men with different notions of duty made it a point of honour to stay at their post. In the course of the day a Versaillese officer summoned them to surrender within a quarter of an hour on pain of being shot. They did not even answer.

At three o'clock Cluseret and La Cécilia arrived at Issy with a few companies picked up in haste. They deployed as skirmishers, drove the Versaillese from the park, and at six o'clock the Federals reoccupied the fort. At the entrance they found a child, Dufour, near a wheelbarrow filled with cartridges and cartouches, ready to blow himself up, and, as he believed, the vault with him. In the evening Vermorel and Trinquet brought other reinforcements, and we reoccupied all our positions.

At the first rumour of the evacuation, National Guards had hurried to the Hôtel-de-Ville to question the Executive Commission. It denied having given any order to evacuate the fort, and promised to punish the traitors if there were any. In the evening it arrested Cluseret on his arrival from the fort of Issy. Strange rumours circulated about him, and he quitted the Ministry without leaving the slightest trace of any useful work whatever. As to the defence of the interior, all he had done was to bury cannon at the Trocadero, which, he said, were to breach Mont-Valérien. At a later period, after the fall of the Commune, he endeavoured to throw his whole incapacity upon his colleagues, treating them in English reviews as vain and ignorant fools, imputing villanies to a man like Delescluze, stating that his arrest had ruined everything, and modestly calling himself the "incarnation of the people."

This panic of Issy was the origin of the Committee of Public Safety. Already on the 28th April, at the end of the sitting, Miot, one of the best-bearded men of 1848, had risen to demand "without phrases" the creation of a Committee of Public Safety, having authority over all the Commissions. Being pressed to give his reasons, he majestically replied that he believed the

Committee necessary. There was only one opinion as to the necessity of strengthening the central control and action, for the second Executive Commission had shown itself as impotent as the first, each delegate going his own way and decreeing on his own account. But what signified this word Committee of Public Safety, this parody of the past and scarecrow of boobies? It jarred with this proletarian revolution, this Hôtel-de-Ville, whence the original Committee of Public Safety had torn away Chaumette, Jacques Roux and the best friends of the people. But the Romanticists of the Council had only a smattering of the history of the Revolution, and this high-sounding title delighted them. They would have there and then voted it but for the energy of some colleagues, who insisted on a discussion. "Yes," said these latter, "we want a vigorous Commission, but give us no revolutionary pasticcio. Let the Commune be reformed; let it cease to be a small talkative parliament, quashing one day, just as it suits its caprices, what it created the day before." And they proposed an Executive Committee. The votes were equally divided.

The affair of Issy turned the scale. On the 1st May 34 *Ayes* against 28 *Noes* carried the title of Committee of Public Safety. On the whole of the project 48 voted for and 23 against. Several had voted for the Committee notwithstanding its title, with the only object of creating a strong power. Many explained their votes. Some alleged they were obeying the *mandat imperatif* of their electors. Some wanted to make the cowards and traitors tremble; others simply declared, like Miot, that "it was an indispensable measure". Félix Pyat, who had egged on Miot, and violently supported the proposition in order to win back the esteem of the ultras, gave this cogent reason. "Yes: considering that the words Public Safety are absolutely of the same epoch as the words French Republic and Commune of Paris." But Tridon: "No: because I dislike useless and ridiculous cast-off old clothes." Vermorel: "No: they are only words, and the people have too long taken up with words." Longuet: "Not believing any more in words of salvation than in talismans and amulets, I vote No." Seventeen collectively declared against the institution of a Committee, which, they said, would create a dictatorship, and others pleaded the same motive, which was puerile enough. The Council remained so sovereign that eight days after it overturned the Committee.

Having protested by this vote, the opponents ought afterwards to have made the best of the situation. Tridon had certainly said, "I see no men to put in such a Committee;" all the more reason not to leave the place to the Romanticists. Instead of coming to an understanding with those of their colleagues who were desirous to concentrate the power and not galvanize a corpse, the opponents folded their arms. "We can," they said, "appoint no one to an institution considered by us as useless and fatal.... We consider abstention as the only dignified, logical, and politic attitude."

The ballot, thus stigmatized beforehand, gave a power without authority; there were only 37 votes. Ranvier, A. Arnaud, Leo Meillet, Charles

Gerardin, Félix Pyat were named. The alarmists might comfort themselves. The only one of real energy, the upright and warm-hearted Ranvier, was at the mercy of his blind kindliness.

The friends of the Commune, the brave soldiers of the trenches and of the forts, then learnt that there was a minority at the Hôtel-de-Ville. It put in its appearance at the very moment when Versailles unmasked its batteries. This minority, which, with the exception of some ten members, comprised the most enlightened and the most laborious members of the Council, was never able to accommodate itself to the situation. These men could never understand that the Commune was a barricade, not a government. This was the general error, the superstitious belief in their governmental longevity; hence, for instance, they delayed for seven months the date for the total return of the pledges at the pawnshops. There were perhaps as many dreamers in the minority as in the majority. Some put forward their principles like the head of a Medusa, and would have made no concessions even for the sake of victory. They strained the reaction against the principle of authority to the verge of suicide. "We," they said, "were for liberty under the Empire; in power we will not deny it." Even in exile they have fancied that the Commune perished through its authoritative tendencies. With a little diplomacy, by yielding to circumstances and the weaknesses of their colleagues, they might have detached from the majority all men of real value. Tridon had come to them uninvited, but his was a superior mind; they ought to have made advances to the others, opposing to the mere braggarts precise ideas, and by true energy reduced the turbulent. They remained unrelenting, dogged, and contented themselves with forcible protests.

Thenceforth divergences degenerated into hostilities. The council-room was small, badly ventilated; the soon over-heated atmosphere ruffled the temper. The discussions grew bitter, and Félix Pyat turned them into attacks. Delescluze never spoke but for union, concord. The other would have preferred the Commune dead rather than saved by one of those he bore a grudge against, and he hated whoever smiled at his craziness. He did not mind discrediting the Council, casting aspersions on its most devoted members, so much did he resent a trespass on his vanity. He could lie with perfect effrontery, carve out some infamous calumny, slaver a colleague, then suddenly, in emotional attitude, open his arms, exclaiming, "Let us embrace." He now accused Vermorel of having sold his journal to the Empire after having offered it to the Orleanists. He glided about in the lobbies, the Commissions, a Barrère of the boards, now insinuating, now foaming, now patriarchal. "The Commune! why it is my child! I have watched over it for twenty years. I have nursed, I have rocked it." To hear him, the 18th March was owing to him. He thus enlisted the naive, the light-headed sent to the Council by the public meetings, and, despite his blank incapacity, shown by the man while a member of the first executive, despite his attempts at flight, he picked up twenty-four votes at the election of the Committee of Public Safety. The aspic profited by it to hiss forth discord.

Disunion within the Council was fatal, the mother of defeat. It ceased — let the people know this as well as their faults — when they thought of the people, when they rose above these miserable personal quarrels. They followed the funeral of Pierre Leroux, who had defended the insurgents of June, 1848; ordered the demolition of the Brea church, built in memory of a justly punished traitor; of the expiatory monument, an affront to the Revolution; were not forgetful of the political prisoners still at the Bagnio, and ennobled the Place d'Italie with the name of Duval. All Socialist decrees passed unanimously; for though they differed they were all Socialists. There was but one vote in the Council to expel two of its members guilty of some former offence, and no one even in the thick of the peril dared to utter the word capitulation.

Prosper Olivier Lissagaray

Chapter 20
Rossel replaces Cluseret

The last act of the second Executive Commission was to name Rossel delegate at War. On the same evening (the 30th April) it sent for him. He came at once, recited the history of famous sieges, and promised to make Paris impregnable. No one asked him for a written plan, and there and then, as on the stage, his nomination was signed. He forthwith wrote to the Council, "I accept these difficult functions, but I want your entire support in order not to succumb under the weight of these circumstances."

Rossel knew these circumstances through and through. For twenty-five days chief of the general staff, he was the best-informed man in Paris as to all her military resources. He was familiar with the members of the Council, of the Central Committee, the officers, the effective forces, the character of the troops he undertook to lead.

At the outset he struck a wrong chord in his answer to the Versaillese officer who had summoned the fort of Issy to surrender. "My dear comrade, the first time you permit yourself to send us such an insolent summons, I shall have your flag of truce shot. Your devoted comrade. "The cynical levity smacked of the condottiere. Certainly he who threatened to shoot an innocent soldier, and bestowed his *dear,* his *devoted comrade* upon a collaborator of Galiffet, was foreign to the great heart of Paris and her civil war.

No man understood Paris, the National Guard, less than Rossel. He imagined that the *Père Duchesne* was the real mouthpiece of the workmen.

Hardly raised to the Ministry, he spoke of putting the National Guard into barracks, of cannonading the runaways; he wanted to dismember the legions and form them into regiments, with colonels named by himself. The Central Committee, to which the *chefs-de-légion* belonged, protested, and the battalions complained to the Council, which sent for Rossel. He set forth his project in a professional way in sober, precise words, so different from the Pyatical declamations, that the Council believed it beheld a man and was charmed. Still his project was the breaking-up of the National Guard, and the Council no more than the Executive Commission got a general plan of defence from him. He certainly demanded that the municipalities should be charged with concentration of arms, the horses, and prosecution of the refractory, but he made no condition *sine qua non.*

He sent in no report on the military situation. He gave orders for the construction of a second enceinte of barricades, and of three citadels at Montmartre, the Trocadero, and the Panthéon, but never personally concerned himself about their execution. He extended the command of General Wroblewski over all troops and forts on the left bank, but three days after restricted it again to bestow it upon La Cécilia, who had none of the qualities necessary in a superior commander. He never gave the generals any instructions for attack or defence. Despite certain fits and starts, he had in reality so little energy that he named Eudes commander of the second active reserve at the very moment when, against formal orders, this latter left the fort of Issy, which he had commanded since the reoccupation.

The Versaillese had recommenced firing with perfect fury. The shells, the bombs, battered the casemates, the grapeshot paved the trenches with iron. In the night of the lst-2nd, the Versaillese, always proceeding by nocturnal surprises, attacked the station of Clamart, which was taken almost without a struggle, and the castle of Issy, which they had to conquer foot by foot. On the morning of the 2nd the fort again found itself in the same situation as three days before. A part of the village of Issy was even in the hands of the soldiers. During the day the francs-tireurs of Paris dislodged them at the point of the bayonet. Eudes, who in vain demanded reinforcements, went to the War Office to declare that he would not remain if Wetzel were not discharged. Wetzel was replaced by La Cécilia, but Eudes did not return to the fort, and left the command to the chief of his staff.

Thus since the 3rd it was evident that everything would go on as under Cluseret, and the Central Committee grew bolder. It had been thrown more and more into the shade, for the Commission of War kept it at a distance. Its sittings, more and more confused and void, were little attended--by about ten members, sometimes even by less.

The enterprise of Rossel against the legions gave it back a little authority and daring. On the 3rd, in accord with the *chefs-de-légion,* they resolved to ask the Council for the direction and administration of the War Office: Rossel got wind of the affair, and had one of its members arrested; the others in great numbers, the *chefs-de-légion* with their sabres at their sides, went up to the Hôtel-de-Ville, where they were received by Félix Pyat, deeply moved by the odd conceit that they came to lay hands on him. "Nothing is getting along at the War Office," said they. "All the services are in disorder. The Central Committee offers itself to direct them. The delegate will conduct the operations, the Committee will see to the administration." Félix Pyat approved of the idea and submitted it to the Council. The minority took umbrage at the pretensions of the Committee, and even spoke of having them arrested. The majority left the matter to the Committee of Public Safety, which issued a decree admitting the co-operation of the Central Committee. Rossel accepted the situation and announced it to the chiefs of corps. The Commission of War continued, in spite of all this, to squabble with the Committee.

Our men paid dearly for these small office revolutions. Tired out, badly commanded, they were negligent of their watches, and thus exposed to every surprise. The most terrible one took place in the night of the 3rd-4th May at the redoubt of the Moulin Saquet, held by 500 men at that moment. They were sleeping in their tents, when the Versaillese, having seized the sentinels, entered the redoubt and butchered about fifty Federals. The soldiers pierced the tents with their bayonets, slashing the corpses, and then made off with five pieces and 200 prisoners. The captain of the 55th was accused of having betrayed the pass word. The truth is not known, as incredible fact! — the Council never inquired into the affair.

M. Thiers announced this "elegant *coup-de-main*" in a bantering despatch to the effect that they had killed two hundred men; that "such was the victory the Commune might announce in its bulletins." The prisoners, taken to Versailles, were received by the elegant rabble who killed time in the cafés of St. Germain, now become the headquarters of high-life prostitution, or who went to the heights to see the shells battering the walls and the Parisians. But what were these insipid amusements by the side of a convoy of prisoners, whom they could beat, spit upon, and revile, a thousand times renewing the agonies of Mathô?

The simply bestial ferocity of the soldiers was much less horrible.

These poor wretches firmly believed that the Federals were thieves or Prussians, and that they tortured their prisoners. There were some who, taken to Paris, for a long time refused all nourishment in dread of poison. The officers propagated these horrible stories; some even believed them. The greater part, arriving from Germany in a state of extreme irritation against Paris, said publicly, "We shall give these scoundrels no quarter," and they set the example of summary executions. On the 25th April, at the Belle-Epine, near Ville-Juif, four National Guards, surprised by mounted chasseurs, called upon to surrender, laid down their arms. The soldiers were leading them when an officer appeared, and, without further ado, discharged his revolver at them. Two were killed; the two others, left for dead, were able to drag themselves as far as the neighbouring trenches, where one of them expired. The fourth was transported to the ambulance. Paris, erstwhile besieged by the Prussians, was now tracked by tigers.

These sinister forebodings of the lot reserved to the vanquished made the Council indignant, but did not enlighten it. The disorder grew greater with the danger. Rossel set nothing going. Pyat, whom he had often silenced with a word, abhorred him, and never ceased undermining his authority. "You see this man," said he to the Romanticists, "well, he is a traitor — a Caesarian! After the Trochu plan, the Rossel plan." On the 8th May he had the direction of the military operations transferred to Dombrowski, leaving only nominal functions to Rossel, who, apprised of this that same evening, hurried to the Committee of Public Safety and forced it to revoke the decree. On the 4th Félix Pyat sent orders to General Wroblewski without informing Rossel. The next day Rossel complained to the Council of the Committee of Public Safety of this mischievous interference, which embroiled everything. "Under these circumstances I cannot be responsible," said he, and demanded the publicity of the sittings, as he had always been received in private audience. Instead of forcing him to communicate his plan, they amused themselves with making him pass a sort of Freemason examination. The antediluvian Miot asked him what were his democratic antecedents. Rossel extricated himself very cleverly. "I will not tell you that I have studied the question of social reforms profoundly, but I abominate this society which has just betrayed France in so dastardly a way. I do not know what will be the new order of Socialism. I like it on trust, and it will anyhow be better than the old one." Everybody put him the questions he chose personally, and not through the medium of the president. He answered them all with sangfroid and precision, disarming all their scruples, and carried away cheers, but nothing more.

Had he possessed the strong head he was credited with, he would long since have fathomed the situation, understood that for this struggle without precedent new tactics were wanted, found a field of battle for these improvised soldiers, organized the internal defence and awaited Versailles from the heights of Montmartre, the Trocadero, and Mont-Valérien. But he dreamt of battles, was at bottom but a bookish soldier, original only in speech and style. While always complaining of want of discipline and of men, he allowed the best blood of Paris to be shed in the sterile struggles without the town, in heroic challenges at Neuilly, Vanves, and Issy.

At Issy above all. It was no longer a fort, hardly a strong position, but a medley of earth and rubble-work battered by shells. The staved-in casemates opened a view upon the country, the powder magazines were laid bare half of Bastion 3 was in the moat, and one could drive up to the breach in a carriage. Ten pieces at most answered the fire of sixty Versaillese ordnance pieces, while the fusillade of the trenches aimed at the embrasures killed almost all our artillerymen. On the 3rd the Versaillese renewed their summons to surrender, they were answered with the word of Cambronne. The chief of the general staff left by Eudes had also made off, but happily the fort remained in the valiant hands of the engineer Rist and of Julien, commander of the 14th battalion of the eleventh arrondissement. It is to them and to the Federals who stood by them that the honour of this prodigious defence belongs. Here are a few notes from their military journal.

4th May. – We are receiving explosive balls that burst with the noise of percussion-caps. The wagons do not come; food is scanty and the shells of seven centimetres, our best pieces, will soon fail us. The reinforcements promised every day do not appear. Two chiefs of battalions have been to Rossel. He received them very badly, and said that he had the right to shoot them for having abandoned their post. They explained our situation. Rossel answered that a fort defends itself with the bayonet and quoted the work of Carnot. Still he has promised reinforcements. The Freemasons have planted their banner on our ramparts. The Versaillese knocked it down in an instant. Our ambulances are full; the prison and corridor that lead to it are crammed with corpses. An ambulance omnibus arrives in the evening. We put in as many of our wounded as possible. During its passage from the fort to Issy the Versaillese pepper it with balls.

5th. – The fire of the enemy does not cease for a moment. Our embrasures no longer exist; the pieces of the front still answer. At two o'clock we receive ten wagons of seven centimetre shells. Rossel has come. He looked at the works of the Versaillese for a long time. The *enfants-perdus* who serve the pieces of Bastion 5 are losing many men; they remain steadfast. There are now in the dungeons corpses two yards deep. All our trenches, riddled by artillery, have been evacuated. The trench of the Versaillese is sixty yards from the counterscarp. They push on more and more. The necessary precautions are taken in case of an attack to-night. All the flank pieces are loaded with grapeshot. We have two machine-guns above the platform to sweep at once the moat and the glacis.

6th. – The battery of Fleury regularly discharges its six rounds on us every five minutes. A cantinière has just been brought to the ambulance, wounded in the left side of the groin. For four days past three women have gone into the thickest of the fire to tend the wounded. This one is dying and bids us remember her two little children. No more food. We eat only horse-flesh. Evening: the rampart is untenable.

7th. – We are receiving as many as ten shells a minute. The ramparts are totally uncovered. All the pieces, save two or three, are dismounted. The Versaillese works almost touch us. There are thirty more dead. We are about to be surrounded.

Chapter 21
Paris bombarded: Rossel flees

The greatest infamy in living memory is now being enacted. Paris is being bombarded. (Proclamation of the Government of National Defence on the Prussian bombardment.) We have crushed a whole district of Paris. (Thiers to the National Assembly, Session of 5th August, 1871.)

We must leave this heroic atmosphere to return to the quarrels of the Council and of the Central Committee. Why did they not hold their sittings at the Muette or under the eyes of the public? The shells of Montretour, which had just unmasked its powerful battery, and the severe attitude of the people, would no doubt have made them unite against the common enemy. He had begun to batter a breach in their ranks.

On the 8th May, in the morning, seventy naval guns began to attack the enceinte from the bastion 60 to the Point du Jour. The shells of Clamart already reached the Quai de Javelle, and the battery of Breteuil covered the Grenelle quarter with projectiles. In a few hours half Passy had become uninhabitable.

M. Thiers accompanied his shells with a proclamation: "Parisians, the Government will not bombard Paris, as the men of the Commune will not fail to tell you. It will discharge its cannon.... It knows, it would have understood, even if you had not said so on all sides, that as soon as the soldiers cross the enceinte you will rally round the national flag." And he invited the Parisians to open the gates to him. What was the action of the Council in reply to this appeal to treason?

On the 8th it entered upon a random discussion on the minutes of its sittings and the publicity of the latter, which one member of the majority wanted to suppress altogether. The minority complained of the Central Committee, which had encroached upon all services in spite of the Commission of War; it had driven away Varlin from the commissariat, entirely reorganized by him. They asked whether the Government called itself Central Committee or Commune. Félix Pyat justified himself by accusing Rossel. "It is not the fault of the Committee of Public Safety if Rossel has neither the strength nor the intelligence to keep the Central Committee within its functions." The friends of Rossel answered, accusing Pyat of continually interfering even in purely military questions. If the Moulin Saquet had been surprised, it was because Wroblewski, who commanded on that side, received a formal order from Félix Pyat to repair to Issy. "It is false," said Pyat; "I have never given such an order." They let him thoroughly enmesh himself, and then produced the order, written entirely in his own hand. He took hold of it, turned it round, feigned astonishment, and was finally obliged to confess. The discussion then reverted to the Central Committee — were they to dissolve it, arrest its members, or surrender to it the administration of the War Office? The Council, as usual, did not dare to decide, and, after a confused debate, confirmed by the resolution of the 3rd May — the Central Committee will be held subordinate to the Military Commission.

At this very moment strange scenes were enacted at the War Office. The *chefs-de-légion*, who were stirring more and more against Rossel, had that day resolved to ask him for the report of all the decisions he was about to take with respect to the National Guard. Rossel knew of their project. In the evening, when they arrived at the Ministry, they found in its court an armed platoon, and beheld Rossel watching them from his window. "You are audacious," said he; "do you know that this platoon is here to shoot you?" They, without appearing to care much: "There is no need of audacity; we simply come to speak to you of the organization of the National Guard." Rossel relaxed, went to the window, gave orders to the platoon to re-enter. This burlesque demonstration did not miss its effect. The *chefs-de-légion* disputed the project on the regiments point by point, demonstrating its impossibility. Tired of arguing, Rossel said to them, "I am fully aware that I have no forces, but I affirm you have not either. You have, say you? Well, give me the proof. To-morrow, at eleven o'clock, bring me 12,000 men to the Place de la Concorde, and I will try to do something." He wanted to make an attack by the Clamart station. The *chefs-de-légion* engaged to find the men, and spent the whole night in search of them.

While these contests went on, the fort of Issy was being evacuated. Since the morning it had been reduced to the last extremity. Any of its defenders who approached the guns was a dead man. In the evening the officers assembled, and came to the conclusion that they could no longer hold out.

Thereupon the men, driven away from all sides by the shells, massed themselves under the entrance vault, when a shell from the Moulin de Pierre fell in their midst, killing sixteen of them. Rist, Julien, and several others, who were stubbornly bent upon holding these ruins, were at last obliged to yield. About seven o'clock the evacuation began. The commander, Lisbonne, one of the members of the first Central Committee, a man of extraordinary courage, covered the retreat amidst a shower of bullets.

A few hours later, the Versaillese, crossing the Seine, established themselves before Boulogne in front of the bastions of the Point du Jour, and opened a trench three hundred yards from the enceinte. All that night and the whole morning of the 9th the War Office and the Committee of Public Safety knew nothing of the evacuation of the fort.

On the 9th, at mid-day, the battalions asked for by Rossel were drawn up along the Place de la Concorde. Rossel arrived on horseback, hardly looked at the front lines, and then addressed the *chefs-de-légion,* "There are not enough men here for me;" and at once turning about, rode off to the War Office, where he was informed of the evacuation of the fort of Issy. He seized his pen, wrote, "The tricolor floats from the fort of Issy, abandoned yesterday evening by the garrison," and, without apprising the Council or the Committee of Public Safety, gave the order to post up ten thousand copies of these two lines, while six thousand was the number usually printed.

He next sent in his resignation: "Citizens, members of the Commune, I feel myself incapable of any longer bearing the responsibility of a command where every one deliberates and no one obeys. The Central Committee of Artillery has deliberated and prescribed nothing. The Commune has deliberated and resolved upon nothing. The Central Committee deliberates and has not yet known how to act. During this delay the enemy has hemmed in the fort of Issy by imprudent attacks, for which I would punish him if I had the smallest military force at my disposal." He then recounted in his own fashion, and very inaccurately, the evacuation of the fort, the review on the Place de la Concorde; said that, instead of the 12,000 men promised, there were only 7,000, and concluded: "Thus the nullity of the Committee of Artillery prevented the organization of the artillery; the hesitation of the Central Committee stopped the administration; the paltry pre-occupations of the *chefs-de-légion* paralysed the mobilization of the troops. My predecessor committed the fault of struggling against this absurd situation. I retire, and have the honour to ask you for a cell at Mazas."

He thus thought to clear his military reputation, but point by point he might have been categorically answered. Why did you accept this "absurd' situation with which you were thoroughly conversant? Why did you make no conditions on entering the Ministry on the 1st April, no condition to the Council on the 2nd and 3rd May? Why did you send away at least 7,000 men this morning, when you pretend not to have "the smallest military force" at your disposal? Why did you know nothing for fifteen hours of the evacuation of a fort whose straits it was your duty to watch from hour to hour? Where is your second line of defence? Why has no work been done at Montmartre and the Panthéon?

Rossel might perhaps have addressed his reproaches to the Council, but he committed an unpardonable fault in sending his letters to the newspapers. Thus in less than two hours he had disheartened 8,000 combatants, spread panic, stigmatized the brave men of Issy, denounced the weakness of the defence to the enemy, and that at the very moment when the Versaillese were rejoicing over the taking of Issy.

There everyone was merry-making. M. Thiers and MacMahon harangued the soldiers, who, singing, brought back the few pieces found in the fort. The Assembly suspended its sittings and came into the marble court to applaud these children of the people who thought themselves victors. M. Thiers a month later said from the tribune, "When I see these sons of our sod, strangers often to an education that elevates, die for you, for us, I am profoundly touched." Touching emotion this of the hunter before his pack. Remember this avowal and the sort of men for whom you die, sons of the sod!

And at the Hôtel-de-Ville they were still disputing! Rigault recriminated. The majority of the Council had named him procureur of the Commune in spite of his culpable levity at the Prefecture. The discussion was growing angry when Delescluze entered hastily and exclaimed, "You discuss when it has been proclaimed that the tricolor floats from the fort of Issy. I make an appeal to you all. I had hoped that France would be saved by Paris and Europe by France. The Commune is pregnant with a power of revolutionary instinct capable of saving the country. Cast aside to-day all your animosities. We must save the country. The Committee of Public Safety has not answered our expectations. It has been an obstacle instead of a stimulus. With what is it occupying itself? With individual appointments instead of general measures. A decree signed Meillet names this citizen himself governor of the fort of Bicetre. We had a man there, a soldier, who was thought too severe. It is desirable that all were as severe as he. Your Committee of Public Safety is undone, crushed beneath the weight of the memories attached to it. I say it must disappear."

The Assembly, thus brought back to a sense of its duty, resolved into a secret committee, thoroughly discussing the Committee of Public Safety. What had it done for a week past? Installed the Central Committee at the War Office, increased the disorder, sustained two disasters. Its members lost themselves in details or else did amateur service. One deserted the Hôtel-de-Ville to go and shut himself up in a fort; if at least it had been that of Issy or of Vanves! Félix Pyat passed the greater part of his time in the office of the *Vengeur,* there venting his spleen in long-winded articles. A member of the Committee of Public Safety endeavoured to defend it by pleading the vagueness of its attributes. He was answered that Article 3 of the decree gave the Committee full powers over all the Commissions. Finally, after many hours, they decided to renew the Committee at once; to appoint a civil delegate to the War Office; to draw up a proclamation; to meet, save in cases of emergency, only three times a week; to establish the new Committee permanently at the Hôtel-de-Ville, while the other members of the Council were to stay regularly in their respective arrondissements. Delescluze was named Delegate at War.

In the evening, at ten o'clock, there was a second meeting for the nomination of the new Committee. The majority voted Félix Pyat, quite exasperated at the attacks of the afternoon, to the chair. He opened the sitting by demanding the arrest of Rossel. Cleverly grouping together appearances which seemed proofs to the suspicious, he made Rossel the scapegoat of the faults of the Committee, turning the anger of the Council against him. For half an hour he disparaged the absent man, whom he would not have dared attack to his face. "I told you, citizens, that he was a traitor. You would not believe me. You are young, you did not, like our paragons of the Convention, know how to mistrust military power." This reminiscence ravished the Romanticists. They had but one dream — to be Conventionnels. So difficult was it for this revolution of proletarians to rid itself of bourgeois tinsel.

The ire of Pyat was not wanted to convince the Assembly. Rossel's act was culpable in the eyes of the least prejudiced. His arrest was decreed unanimously, less two votes, and the Commission of War received the order to carry it out.

They next passed to the nomination of the Committee. The minority, a little reassured by the election of Delescluze and Jourde, which seemed to acknowledge the right of the Council to appoint the delegates, resolved to take part in the vote, and asked for a place in the list of the majority. This was an excellent occasion to efface all differences, to re-establish union against Versailles. But the perfidious promptings of Félix Pyat had induced the Romanticists to look upon their colleagues of the minority as veritable reactionaries. After his speech the sitting was suspended; little by little the members of the minority found themselves alone in the council-hall. They looked for their colleagues and surprised them in a neighbouring room deliberating apart. After a violent altercation they all returned to the Council.

A member of the minority demanded that they should put an end to these shameful divisions. A Romanticist answered by asking for the arrest of the factious minority, and the President, Pyat, was about to empty the vials of his wrath, when Malon cried to him, "Silence! you are the evil genius of this revolution. Do not continue to spread your venomous suspicions, to stir up discords. It is your influence that is ruining the Commune!" And Arnold, one of the founders of the Central Committee, "It is still these fellows of 1848 who will undo the revolution."

But it was too late now to engage in the struggle, and the minority was to expiate its doctrinairism and maladroitness. The whole list of the majority passed; Ranvier, Arnaud, Gamlon, Delescluze and Eudes. The nomination of Delescluze to the War Office having left a vacancy, there was after two days a second vote, and the minority proposed Varlin. The majority, abusing their victory, committed the impropriety of preferring Billioray, a most worthless member.

The Council broke up at one o'clock in the morning. "Did not we do them? and what do you think of the way I managed the business?" said Félix Pyat to his friends on leaving the chair. This honest mandatory, altogether absorbed in the work of "doing" his colleagues, had forgotten to verify the capture of the fort of Issy. And that same evening, twenty-six hours after the evacuation, the Hôtel-de-Ville posted up on the doors of the *mairies*, "It is false that the tricolor floats on the fort of Issy. The Versaillese do not and shall not occupy it." This contradiction was as good as Trochu's apropos of Metz.

During these tempests at the Hôtel-de-Ville the Central Committee had sent for Rossel, reproached him with the poster of the afternoon, and the unusual number of copies printed. He defended himself acrimoniously. "It was my duty. The greater the danger, the greater the duty to make it known to the people." Yet he had done nothing of the kind on the surprise of the Moulin-Saquet. After his departure the Committee deliberated at length. Someone said, "We are lost if we get no dictatorship." For some days this idea was uppermost in the Committee. The latter voted quite seriously that there should be a dictator, and that the dictator was to be Rossel. A deputation of five members gravely went to fetch him; he came down to the Committee, pretended to reflect, and finally said, "It is too late. I am no longer delegate. I have sent in my resignation." Some waxing angry with him, he rebuked them and left. In his office he found the Commission of War, Delescluze, Tridon, Avrial, Johannard, Varlin and Arnold, who had just arrived.

Delescluze explained their mission. Rossel listened very calmly; said that though the decree was unjust, he submitted to it. He then described the military situation, the rivalries of all kinds that had continually clogged him, the weakness of the Council. "It has not known," said he, "how to utilize the Central Committee, nor how to break it at the opportune time. Our resources are quite sufficient, and I am ready, for my own part, to assume all responsibility, but on the condition of being supported by a strong and homogeneous power. I could not in the face of history take upon myself the responsibility for certain necessary repressions without the assent and support of the Commune." He spoke at great length in that clear and nervous style that twice in the Council had won over his most decided adversaries. The Commission, much struck by his arguments, withdrew to another room. Delescluze declared that he could not make up his mind to arrest Rossel till the Council had heard him. His colleagues were of the same opinion, and left the ex-delegate under the guard of Avrial and Johannard, who the next morning conducted him to the Hôtel-de-Ville. Avrial stayed with Rossel in the questor's office, while Johannard went to apprise the Council of their arrival.

Some wanted Rossel to be heard; the greater number, distrustful of themselves, were afraid lest his voice should again bring round the Council, maintained that his hearing was contrary to equity, and cited the example of Cluseret, who had been arrested without being heard, as though one injustice could sanction another. The admission of Rossel was refused.

Charles Gérardin, a member of the Council, repaired to the questor's office. "What has the Commune decided?" said Avrial. "Nothing yet," answered Gérardin, who nevertheless had just left the sitting, and seeing Avrial's revolver on the table, he said to Rossel, "Your guardian fulfils his duty conscientiously." "I do not suppose," answered Rossel hurriedly, "that this precaution concerns me. Besides, Citizen Avrial, I give you my word of honour as a soldier that I shall not seek to escape."

Avrial, very tired of his post as sentry, had already asked the Council to relieve him. Receiving no answer, he thought he might leave his prisoner under the guard of a member of the Committee of Public Safety — for Gérardin had not yet been discharged from his functions — and he proceeded to the Council. When he returned, Rossel and Gérardin were gone. The ambitious young man had slunk like a weasel out of this civil war into which he had heedlessly thrown himself.

One may divine whether Pyat was sparing of adjectives against the fugitive. The new Committee having just been informed of the discovery of two conspiracies, launched a desperate proclamation: "Treason had slipped into our ranks. The abandonment of the fort of Issy announced in an impious poster by the wretch who surrendered it, was only the first act of the drama. A monarchical insurrection in our midst coinciding with the surrender of one of our gates was to follow. All the threads of the dark plot are now in our hands. Most of the culprits are arrested. Let all eyes be open, all arms ready to strike the traitors!"

This was going off into melodrama when cold blood and precision were wanted. And the Committee boasted strangely when it pretended to have arrested "most of the culprits" and that it held "in its hands all the threads of the dark plot."

Chapter 22
Conspiracies against the Commune

The Commune had given rise to the various trades of the plotmonger, the betrayer of gates, the conspiracy-broker. Vulgar sharpers, Jonathan Wilds [character in a novel by Henry Fielding] of the gutter, whom a shadow of police would have scared away, they had no other strength than the weakness of the prefecture and the carelessness of the delegations. The evidence relative to them is to a certain extent still in the keeping of the Versaillese; but they have themselves published a good deal, often borne witness against each other, and what with private information, what with the opportunities offered by our exile, we shall be able to penetrate into this realm of blackguardism.

From the end of March they levied contributions upon all the Ministries of Versailles, offering for a few sous to surrender some of the gates of Paris or to kidnap the members of the Council. By degrees they were more or less classed. The colonel of the staff, Corbin, was charged with the organisation of the faithful National Guards still at Paris. The commander of a reactionary battalion, Charpentier, a former drill officer of St. Cyr, offered him his services, was accepted, and presented a few of his cronies, Durouchoux, Demay, and Gallimard. Their instructions were to recruit clandestine battalions, who were to occupy the strategic points of the town on the day when the general attack would summons all the Federals to the ramparts. A naval officer, Domalain, offered at that moment to surprise Montmartre, the Hôtel-de-Ville, the Place Vendôme, and the commissariat, with a few thousand volunteers, whom he professed to have at hand. He entered into partnership with Charpentier.

They bestirred themselves with might and main, grouped an astonishing number of persons around official posts, and soon gave notice of 6,000 men and 150 artillery men provided with spiking machines. All these brave ones only waited for a signal. In the meanwhile, money was of course wanted to keep up their zeal, and Charpentier and Domalain, through the agency of Durouchoux, indeed drew several hundred thousand francs from the Versaillese.

Towards the end of April they found a redoubtable rival in Le Mere de Beaufond, an ex-naval officer and governor of Cayenne ad interim. Instead of drumming up for bourgeois recruits, an idea he declared ridiculous, Beaufond proposed paralysing the resistance by means of clever agents who should provoke defections and disorganize the services. His plan, quite in accord with M. Thiers' notions, was favourably looked upon at Versailles, which gave him full powers. He took as helpmates two men of resolution, Laroque, a clerk at the bank, and Lasnier, an ex-officer of Schoelcher's legion.

Besides these, the Ministry had still other bloodhounds — the Alsatian Aronshonne, colonel of a free corps during the war, cashiered by his men, who at Tours had accused him of theft; Franzini, later on extradited by England and condemned as a swindler, Barral de Montaut, who boldly presented himself at the War Office, and, thanks to his aplomb, got himself named chief of the seventh legion; the Abbé Cellini, chaplain of one knows not what fleet, patronized by Jules Simon; last, the noble-minded conspirators, the great generals disdained by the revolution, Lullier, Du Bisson, Ganier d'Abin. These honest Republicans could not allow the Commune to ruin the Republic. If they accepted money from Versailles, it was only with a view to saving Paris and the Republican party from the men of the Hôtel-deVille. They wanted to overthrow the Commune, but betray it, oh! no, by no means!

One Briere St.-Lagier framed comprehensive reports on all these knights, and M. Thiers' secretary, Troncin-Dumersan, condemned three years after as swindler, travelled backwards and forwards between Paris and Versailles, brought the money, superintended and held in his hand all the threads of these multifarious conspiracies, the one being often carried on behind the back of the other.

Thence continual collisions. The ragamuffins mutually denounced each other. Briere de St.-Lagier wrote: "I beg M. le Ministre de l'Intérieur to have M. Le Mere de Beaufond watched. I strongly suspect him of being a Bonapartist. The money he has received has been used to a great extent to pay his debts." By way of compensation another report said, "I suspect MM. Domalain, Charpentier, and Briere de St.-Lagier. They often meet at Peter's, and instead of occupying themselves with the great cause of the deliverance, imitate Pantaguruel. [pleasure-loving character in a book by Rabelais] They pass for Orleanists."

The most venturesome of these enterprisers, Beaufond, managed to enter into relations with the general staff of Colonel Henri Prodhomme, with the Ecole Militaire, commanded by Vonot, and with the War Office, where the chief of the artillery, Guyet, contrived to embroil the service of the munitions. His agents, Lasnier and Laroque, worked upon a certain Muley, who, having circumvented the Central Committee, got himself named chief of the seventeenth legion, and to some extent disabled it. An officer of artillery, Captain Piguier, placed at their disposal by the Ministry, traced the plan of the barricades, and one of the band could write on the 8th May, "No torpedoes are laid; the army may enter to the flourish of trumpets." Now they had recourse to direct subornation; now acting the part of fervent Communards, they knew how to draw out information; while the imprudence of the functionaries singularly facilitated their task. Staff officers, service chiefs, fond of assuming consequential airs, discussed the most delicate matters in the cafés of the boulevards, full of spies. Cournet, who had succeeded Rigault at the prefecture of police, despite the gravity of his deportment, did not better the service of general security. Lullier, twice arrested, each time escaping, openly spoke in the cafés of sweeping away the Commune. Troncin-Dumersan, known for twenty years as the police agent of the Ministry of the Interior, freely walked along the boulevards, passing his retainers in full view. The contractors charged with the fortification of Montmartre every day found new pretexts to defer the opening of the works; the Bréa Church remained intact; the undertaker of the demolition of the expiatory monument managed to put it off till the entry of the troops. Chance alone discovered the *brassard* (armlet) plot, and the fidelity of Dombrowski disclosed that of Vaysset.

This commercial agent had gone to Versailles to propose to the Ministry an operation of revictualling. Shown out, he again turned up, but this time with the offer to bribe Dombrowski. Under the patronage of Admiral Saisset — more crazy than ever — he got up his enterprise in the shape of a commercial society, found shareholders, twenty thousand francs for the incidental expenses, and entered into communication with an aide-de-camp of Dombrowski's named Hutzinger, afterwards employed by the Versaillese police as spy amongst the exiles in London. Vaysset told him that Versailles would give Dombrowski a million if the general surrendered the gates under his command. Dombrowski at once apprised the Committee of Public Safety, and proposed to allow one or two Versaillese army corps to enter the town and then to crush them by battalions lying in ambush. The Committee would not risk this venture, but ordered Dombrowski to follow up the negotiation. Hutzinger accompanied Vaysset to Versailles, saw Saisset, who offered to surrender himself as hostage in guarantee of the execution of the promises made to Dombrowski. The admiral was even, on a certain night, to repair secretly to the Place Vendôme, and the Committee of Public Safety, forewarned, was preparing to arrest him, when Barthélemy St. Hilaire dissuaded Saisset from this new blunder.

Then M. Thiers began to abandon the hope of taking the town by surprise. This was his hobby of the first days of May. Upon the faith of a bailiff, who promised to get the Dauphine gate surrendered by his friend Laporte, chief of the sixteenth legion, M. Thiers had built up a whole plan in spite of the repugnance of MacMahon and of the army, eager for a triumphal entry. During the night of the 3rd May the whole active army and part of the reserve were set on foot, and General Thiers went to sleep at Sevres. At midnight the troops were massed in the Bois de Boulogne before the lower lake, their eyes fixed on the closed gates. The latter were to be thrown open by a reactionary company which had formed at Passy under the orders of Wéry, a lieutenant of the thirty-eighth, acting as deputy of his former commander, Lavigne. But the intelligent conspirators had forgotten to warn Lavigne, and the company that was to relieve the Federals having had no order from their superior, suspected an ambush, and refused the service. Thus the trusty watch was not relieved. At dawn, after waiting in vain for several hours, the troops returned to their cantonments. Two days after, Laporte was arrested and set free again, much too soon.

Beaufond, taking up the bailiffs plan, guaranteed the surrender of the gates of Auteuil and Dauphine for the night of the 12th to the 13th May. M. Thiers, again caught, forwarded all the scaling gear, and several detachments were directed towards the Point du Jour, while the army held itself in readiness to follow. But at the last moment the profound combinations of the conspirators were foiled, and, as on the 3rd, the army had to turn tail. This attempt was known to the Committee of Public Safety, who had known nothing of the first one.

Lasnier was arrested the next day. The Committee had just laid hands upon the tricolor armlets which the National Guards of order were to have worn on the entry of the army. The woman Legros, who made them, neglected to pay the girls in her employ. One of them, believing that the work was done on account of the Commune, went to ask for her wages at the Hôtel-de-Ville. Inquiries made at the woman Legros' put them on the traces of Beaufond and his accomplices. Beaufond and Laroque managed to hide; Troncin-Dumersan packed off to Versailles. Charpentier thus remained master of the field. Corbin urged him to organize his men by tens and hundreds, and traced him out a whole plan by which to get possession of the Hôtel-de-Ville immediately after the entry of the troops. Charpentier, always imperturbable, diverted him day by day by news of fresh conquests, spoke of 20,000 recruits, asked for dynamite to blow up the houses, and in true Pantagruelic style gobbled up the considerable sums made over to him by Durouchoux.

After all, the whole gang of conspirators did not succeed in surrendering one single gate, but they lent considerable aid in disorganizing the services. Still great care should be taken in availing oneself of their reports, often inflated with imaginary successes to justify the disbursement of the hundreds of thousands of francs that they pocketed.

Chapter 23
The "Lefts" betray Paris

We took Paris with cannons and politics. (Thiers, Inquiry into the 18th of March.)

Who was the great conspirator against Paris? The Extreme Left.

On the 19th March, what remained to M. Thiers wherewith to govern France? He had neither an army, nor cannon, nor the large towns. These possessed arms, and their workmen were on the alert. If that lower middle-class which makes the provinces endorse the revolutions of the metropolis had followed the movement, imitated their kindred of Paris, M. Thiers could not have opposed to them a single regiment. In order to subsist, retain the provinces, and induce them to provide the soldiers and the cannon that were to reduce Paris, what were the resources of the leader of the bourgeoisie? A word and a handful of men. The word was Republic; the men, the recognized leaders of the Republican party.

Though the dull rurals barked at the mere name of the Republic, and refused to insert it in their proclamations, M. Thiers, more cunning, mouthed it lustily, and distorting the votes of the Assembly, gave it out as the watchword to his underlings. Since the first risings all the provincial officials had the same refrain: "We defend the Republic against the factions."

This was certainly something; but the rural votes, the past of M. Thiers, clashed with these Republican protestations. The former heroes of the National Defence were no longer acceptable as securities even for the provinces. M. Thiers was well aware of it, and invoked the purest of the pure, the experienced men returned from exile. Their prestige was still intact in the eyes of the provincial democrats. M. Thiers met them in the lobbies, told them they held the fate of the Republic in their hands, flattered their senile vanity, and inveigled them so successfully, that, from the 23rd, they served him as bottle-holders. When the middle-class republicans of the provinces beheld the profound Louis Blanc, the intelligent Schoelcher, and the most famous grumblers of the radical vanguard fly to Versailles, and insult the Central Committee, and, on the other hand, received neither programme nor able emissaries from Paris, they turned away, and let the flame enkindled by the workmen die out.

The shelling of the 3rd April roused them a little. On the 5th, the municipal council of Lille, composed of Republican notabilities, spoke of conciliation, and called upon M. Thiers to affirm the Republic. That of Lyons drew up a like address; St. Omer sent delegates to Versailles; Troyes declared that it was "heart and soul with the heroic citizens who fought for their republican convictions." Mâcon summoned the Government and the Assembly to put an end to this struggle by the recognition of republican institutions. The Drôme, the Var, Vaucluse, the Ardeche, the Loire, Savoy, the Hérault, the Gers, and the Eastern Pyrénées, twenty departments, issued similar addresses. The workmen of Rouen declared their adhesion to the Commune; the workmen of Havre, rebuffed by the bourgeois Republicans. constituted an independent group. On the 16th April, at Grenoble, 600 men, women, and children went to the station to prevent the departure of the troops and munitions for Versailles. On the 18th, at Nimes, the people, headed by a red flag, marched through the town to the cry of *"Vive la Commune! Vive Paris!* Down with Versailles!" On the 16th, 17th, 18th, there were disturbances at Bordeaux. Some police agents were imprisoned, some officers ill-treated, the infantry barracks pelted with stones, the people crying, *"Vive Paris!* Death to the traitors!" The movement even spread to the agricultural classes. At Saincoin in the Cher, at the Charité-sur-Loire, at Pouilly in the Nievre, the National Guards in arms carried about the red flag. Cosne followed on the 18th, Fleury-sur-Loire on the 19th. The red flag was permanently hoisted in the Ariege; at Foix they stopped the transport of the cannon; at Varilhes they tried to run the munition trains off the lines. At Périgueux, the workmen of the railway station seized the machine-guns.

On the 15th April five delegates from the municipal council of Lyons presented themselves to M. Thiers. He protested his devotion to the Republic, swore that the Assembly should not turn into a Constituent Assembly. If he chose his functionaries outside the Republicans, it was in order to treat all parties with consideration in the interest of the Republic itself. He defended it against the men of the Hôtel-de-Ville, its worst enemies, said he; the delegates might assure themselves of this even in Paris, and he was quite ready to furnish them with safe-conducts. Besides, if Lyons dared to stir, 30,000 men were ready to quell it. This was his typical speech.

All the deputations received the same answer, given with such an air of bonhommie and such complacent familiarity as quite to overwhelm the provincials.

From the presidency they proceeded to the luminaries of the Extreme Left, Louis Blanc, Schoelcher, Adam, and other eminent democrats, who endorsed M. Thiers' words. These gentlemen, if condescending to admit that the cause of Paris was not altogether wrong, declared it ill-begun and compromised by a criminal combat. When Paris once disarmed they would see what could be done. Opportunism is not of yesterday's growth. It was born into the world on the 19th March, 1871, had Louis Blanc & Co. for godfathers, and was baptized in the blood of 30,000 Parisians. "With whom should they treat in Paris?" asked Louis Blanc. "Without speaking of Bonapartist and Prussian intrigues, the people who were there striving to seize the government were fanatics, fools, or rogues." And all the Radicals bridled up: "Should we not be at Paris if Paris were in the right?" The majority of the delegates, lawyers, doctors, business men, brought up in veneration of these shining lights, hearing besides the young men speaking like the pontiffs, went back to the provinces, and as the Left preached to them, preached in turn that it was necessary to abandon the Commune in order to save the Republic. A few of them had visited Paris; but seeing the divisions of the Hôtel-de-Ville, often received by men unable to formulate their ideas, threatened by Félix Pyat in the *Vengeur,* they came back convinced that nothing could emerge from this disorder. When they again passed through Versailles the deputies of the Left triumphed. "Well, what did we tell you?" Even Martin-Bernard gave his electors the ass's kick.

At Paris there were people who could not believe in such barefaced treachery on the part of the Left, and still adjured them. "What are you about at Versailles when Versailles is bombarding Paris?" said an address of the end of April. "What figure can you cut in the midst of these colleagues who assassinate your electors? If you persist in remaining amongst the enemies of Paris, at least do not make yourselves their accomplices by your silence. What! you allow M. Thiers to write to the departments, "*The insurgents are emptying the principal houses of Paris in order to put the furniture to sale,*" and you do not ascend the tribune to protest! What! the whole Bonapartist and rural press may inundate the departments with infamous articles, in which they affirm that at Paris murder, violation, and theft reign supreme, and you are silent! What! M. Thiers may assert that his gendarmes do not assassinate the prisoners; you cannot be ignorant of these atrocious executions, and you are silent! Ascend the tribune; tell the departments the truth, which the enemies of the Commune conceal from them. But our enemies, are they yours also?"

A useless appeal, which the cowardice of the Left knew how to elude. Louis Blanc, in his Tartuffe style, exclaimed, "O civil war! hideous struggle! The cannon thunder! People are killing each other and dying; and those in the Assembly who would willingly give their life to see this sanguinary problem pacifically resolved are condemned to the torture of not being able to make an act, utter a cry, speak a word." Since the birth of the French Assemblies so ignominious a Left had never been seen. The spectacle of the prisoners smitten, reviled, spat upon, was unable to draw a protest from these wretched Parisian deputies. One only, Tolain, asked for an explanation on the assassination at the Belle-Epine. Louis Blanc, Schoelcher, Greppo, Adam, Langlois, Brisson, etc., the Gérontes and the Scapins, sanctimoniously contemplated their bombarded electors, and, fully aware of the facile forgetfulness of Paris, dreamt of their future re-election.

Their calumnies succeeded in stifling the action but not the anguish of the provinces. With heart and soul the workmen of France were with Paris. The employees at the railway stations harangued the soldiers on their passage, adjuring them to raise the butt-ends of their guns; the official posters were torn down during the night; the large centres sent their addresses by the hundred; all the Republican papers demanded peace, sought for some method of conciliation between Paris and Versailles.

Paris and Versailles! The agitation becoming chronic, M. Thiers launched forth Dufaure, the Chapelier [author of a law of 1791 prohibiting strikes] of the modern bourgeoisie, one of the most odious executors of its dirty work. He enjoined his procureurs to prosecute all the writers countenancing the Commune, "that dictatorship usurped by foreigners and ticket-of-leave men, which signalizes its reign by burglary, breaking open private houses in the dead of night and by force of arms," and to lay hands upon "the conciliators who entreat the Assembly to hold out its noble hand to the blood-stained hand of its enemies." Versailles thus hoped to strike terror at the moment of the municipal elections, which took place on the 30th April.

They were everywhere Republican. These provinces, which had risen against Paris in June, 1848, and in the elections of 1849, did not send a hundred volunteers in 1871, and would only fight the Assembly. At Thiers (Puy-de-Dome) the people occupied the Hôtel-de-Ville, hoisted the red flag, and seized the telegraphs. There occurred disturbances at Souppe, Nemours, Château-Landau, in the arrondissement of Fontainebleau. At Dordives (Loiret) the Communards planted a poplar surmounted by the red flag in front of the *mairie*. At Montargies they raised the red flag, put up posters bearing the appeal of the Commune to the rural districts, and forced a solicitor who had tried to tear down the poster to ask pardon on his knees. At Coulommiers (Seine-et-Marne) a demonstration took place to the cries of *"Vive la République! Vive la Commune!"*

Lyons rose in insurrection. Since the 24th March the tricolor lorded it here, save at the Guillotière, where the people maintained the red one. The Council on its return to the Hôtel-de-Ville had demanded the recognition of the rights of Paris, the election of a Constituent Assembly, and named an officer of francs-tireurs, Bourras, commander of the National Guard. While the Council multiplied its addresses and its applications to M. Thiers, the National Guard was again stirring. It presented a programme to the municipal council, which officially rejected it. The rebuff met by the delegates sent to Versailles increased the irritation. When the communal elections were announced for the 30th April, the revolutionary element maintained that the municipal law voted by the Assembly was null and void, because that Assembly had not the rights of a constituent one. Two delegates from Paris summoned the mayor, Hénon, to postpone the elections; and one of the actors in the affray of the 28th September, Gaspard Blanc, reappeared on the scene. The Radicals, always upon the scent of Bonapartism, have made much ado about the presence of that personage. However, at that time he was as yet but a madcap, and only in exile put on the Imperialist livery. On the 27th, at the Brotteaux, in a large public meeting, abstention from voting was decided upon. All the committees of the Guillotière followed, and in a public sitting of the 29th resolved to oppose the vote.

On the 30th, the day of the elections, from six o'clock in the morning the rappel was beaten at the Guillotière; armed citizens carried off the ballot-boxes, and posted sentinels at the entrance of the hall A proclamation was posted up: "The city of Lyons can no longer"look on while her sister the heroic city of Paris is being strangled. The Lyonnese revolutionaries have with one accord named a Provisional Commission. Its members are above all determined, rather than sustain defeat, to make one heap of ruins of a town cowardly enough to allow the assassination of Paris and the Republic." The Place de la Mairie was thronged with an excited crowd; the mayor, Crestin, and his adjutant, who attempted to interfere, were not listened to, and a Revolutionary Commission installed itself in the *mairie*.

Bourras sent an order to the commanders of the Guillotière to unite their battalions. They drew up towards two o'clock in the Des Brosses court. A great number of guards disapproved the movement, yet no one was willing to be the soldier of Versailles. The crowd surrounded them, and finally broke the ranks; about a hundred, led by their captain, went to the *mairie* to hoist their red field-colours. The mayor was sent for, and the Commission called upon him to join the movement; but he refused, as he had done on the 22nd March. Suddenly the cannon thundered.

Hénon and his council, as they did the month before, would have liked to temporize; while Valentin and Crouzat dreamt of Espivent. At five o'clock the 38th of the line came out by the bridge of the Guillotière; the crowd penetrated into the ranks of the soldiers, conjuring them not to fire, and the officers were constrained to take back their men to the barracks. During this time the Guillotière was fortifying itself. A large barricade, extending from the storehouses of the Nouveau-Monde to the angle of the *mairie*, barred the Grande Rue; another was thrown up at the entrance of the Rue des Trois Rois; a third on a level with the Rue de Chabrol.

At half-past six the 38th came out of their barracks, but this time watched by a battalion of chasseurs. Valentin, Crouzat, and the *procureur de la république* marched at their head. In front of the *mairie* the Riot Act was read; some shots answered it, wounding the prefect. The cavalry swept the Des Brosses court and the Place de la *Mairie*, while two pieces of cannon opened fire on the edifice. Its doors soon gave way and the occupants abandoned it. The troops entered after having killed the sentinel, intent upon mounting guard to the very last. It has been said that five insurgents, taken by surprise in the interior of the building, were killed by a Versaillese officer with shots from his revolver.

The struggle continued during part of the night in the neighbouring streets, and the soldiers, deceived by the darkness, killed about a hundred of their own men. The losses of the Communards were less great. By three o'clock in the morning all was over.

At the Croix-Rousse some citizens had invaded the *mairie* and scattered the voting-papers; the check of the Guillotière cut short their resistance.

The Versaillese took advantage of this victory to disarm the battalions of the Guillotière; but the population refused, rallying round the victors. Some monarchists had been elected during the day, but everybody considering the elections of the 30th null and void, they were obliged to submit to a second ballot, and not one of them was re-elected. The movement in favour of Paris continued.

These newly-elected republican councillors might have effectively counterbalanced the authority of Versailles; the advanced press encouraged them. The *Tribune* of Bordeaux had the honour first to propose a congress of all the towns of France, for the purpose of terminating the civil war, assuring the municipal franchises, and consolidating the Republic. The municipal council of Lyons issued an identical programme, inviting all the municipalities to send delegates to Lyons. On the 4th May the delegates of the councils of the principal towns of the Hérault met at Montpellier. The *Liberté* of the Hérault, in a warm appeal reproduced by fifty newspapers, convoked the departmental press to a congress. A common action was about to take the place of the incoherent agitations of the last few weeks. If the provinces understood their own strength, the time, their wants — if they found a group of men equal to the occasion, Versailles, taken between Paris and the departments, would have been obliged to capitulate to Republican France. M. Thiers, with a vivid presentiment of the danger, affected the attitude of a strong Government, and energetically forbade the congresses. "The Government would betray the Assembly, France, civilization," said the *Officiel* of the 8th May, "if it allowed the assizes of Communism and of the rebellion to constitute themselves by the side of the regular power issued from universal suffrage." Picard, speaking from the tribune on the instigation of the congress, said, "Never was there a more criminal attempt than theirs. Outside the Assembly there exists no right." The *procureurs-*

généraux and the prefects received the order to prevent all meetings. Some members of the *Ligue des Droits de Paris* on their way to Bordeaux were arrested.

More was not needed to frighten the Radicals. The organizers of the congress of Bordeaux held their peace; those of Lyons wrote a piteous address to Versailles, to the effect that they had only intended convoking an assembly of the notables. M. Thiers, having attained his object, disdained to prosecute them, even allowed the delegates of eighteen departments to draw up their grievances, and seriously declare that they "made that one of the two combatants responsible who should refuse their conditions." And yet they might feel proud. Their chief had done less, Gambetta had retired to Spain, to St. Sebastien, and there, mute, without a sign of sympathy for those who sacrificed themselves for the Republic, he in a cynical *far niente* [do-nothing] awaited the issue of the civil war.

Thus the middle class of the provinces missed a rare chance of conquering their liberties, of again taking up their grand role of 1792. It became obvious how much its blood and its intelligence had been impoverished by a long political vassalage and the complete absence of all municipal life. From the 19th March to the 5th April they had forsaken the workmen, when by seconding their efforts they might have saved and continued the Revolution. When at last they wanted to pronounce, they found themselves alone, the toy and laughing-stock of their enemies. Such is their history since Robespierre.

So on the 10th May M. Thiers entirely mastered the situation. Making use of all arms, of corruption as well as of patriotism, lying in his telegrams, making his journals lie, by turns familiar and haughty in his interviews with the deputations, putting forward now his gendarmes, now the deputies of the Left, he had succeeded in baffling all attempts at conciliation. He had just signed the peace of Frankfort, and, free on this side, rid of the provinces, he remained alone face to face with Paris.

It was time. Five weeks of siege had exhausted the patience of the rurals; the suspicions of the first days were reviving; they fancied that the "petty bourgeois" was procrastinating in order to spare Paris. The *Union des Syndicats* had just published a report of a new interview, in which M. Thiers had seemed to relax. A deputy of the Right rushed to the tribune accusing M. Thiers of putting off the entry into Paris. He answered curtly, "The opening by our army of trenches only six hundred yards from Paris does not signify that we do not want to enter there." The following day, 12th May, the Right returned to the charge. Was it true that M. Thiers had said to the mayor of Bordeaux, "If the insurgents will cease hostilities the gates of Paris shall be flung wide open for a week for all except the assassins of the generals?" Could it be that the Government intended withdrawing some Parisians out of the clutches of the Assembly? M. Thiers inveighed, whined. "You select the day when I am exiled, on which my house is being pulled down. It is an indignity. I am obliged to command terrible acts; I command them. I must have a vote of confidence." At last, nettled out of patience, he retorted upon the rural growls with a snarl. "I tell you that there are among you imprudent men, who are in too great a hurry. They must have another eight days. At the end of these eight days there will be no more danger, and the task will be proportionate to their courage and to their capacity."

Eight days! Do you hear, members of the Commune?

Chapter 24
The new Committee at work

At the advent of the new Committee on the 10th May our military situation had not changed within the line from St. Ouen to Neuilly, where both sides faced each other on the same level; but it was becoming serious from La Muette. The powerful battery of Montretout, that of Meudon, of Mont-Valérien, covered Passy with shells and greatly injured the ramparts. The Versaillese trenches extended from Boulogne to the Seine. Their skirmishers were pressing upon the village of Issy, and occupied the trenches between the fort and that of Vanves, which they tried to cut off from Montrouge. The negligence of the defence was still the same. The ramparts from La Muette to the fort of Vanves were hardly armed; our gunboats bore almost alone the fire of Meudon, Clamart, and Val-Fleury.

The first act of the new Committee was to order the demolition of M. Thiers' house. This giddy act helped the bombarder to a palace, which the Assembly voted him the day after. Then the Committee issued its proclamation: "Treason had slipped into ..." etc.

Delescluze issued one on his own account. He dragged himself along, panting for breath, and might well say, "If I consulted only my strength I should have declined this function. The situation is grave; but when I contemplate the sublime future in store for our children, even though it should not be given us to reap what we have sown, I shall still enthusiastically hail the revolution of the 18th March."

On entering the Ministry, he found the Central Committee also elaborating a proclamation. "The Central Committee declares that it is its duty not to allow this revolution of the 18th March, which it had so well begun, to succumb. It will unsparingly break down all resistance. It is determined to make an end of all controversies, put down the malignants, quell rivalry, ignorance and incapacity." This was to speak more authoritatively than the Council, and, above all, to flatter itself strangely.

From the first night it was necessary to repair a disaster. The fort of Vanves, upon which all the fires formerly directed against Issy were now concentrated, had become almost untenable, and its commander had evacuated it. Wroblewski, informed of this, took the command from La Cécilia, who had fallen ill, and in the night of the 10th to the 11th hurried thither at the head of the 187th and the 105th battalions of the celebrated 11th legion, which up to the last day did not cease to supply the defence with men. At four o'clock in the morning Wroblewski appeared before the embankment where the Versaillese were stationed, charged them at the point of the bayonet, put them to flight, took some prisoners, and recovered the fort. Once more our brave Federals showed what they could do when properly commanded.

During the day the Versaillese recommenced the bombardment. They overwhelmed the Des Oiseaux convent and the whole village of Issy, whose principal street was now one heap of ruins, with shells and grenades filled with potassium picrate. On the night of the 12th to the 13th they surprised the Lycée of Vanves, and on the 13th they attacked the seminary of Issy. For five days Brunei exhausted himself in trying to bring a little order into the defence of this village. Rossel had sent for this brave member of the Council, whom the jealousy of coteries kept at a distance, and said to him, "The situation of Issy is almost lost; will you undertake its defence?" Brunei devoted himself, threw up barricades, asked for artillery (there were only four pieces), and new battalions to relieve the 2,000 men who had held out for forty-one days. They only sent him two or three hundred men. He tried to make something of these, and fortified the seminary, which the Federals, under a hailstorm of shells, were unable to hold. Brunei organized a second line of defence in the houses of the village, and in the evening repaired to the War Office, where Delescluze wanted him to attend the Council of War.

It was the first and only Council of War held under the Commune. Dombrowski, Wroblewski and La Cécilia were present. Dombrowski, very enthusiastic, spoke of raising 100,000 men. Wroblewski, more practical, proposed to concentrate all the efforts uselessly spent at Neuilly against the trenches of the south. After a long debate no conclusion was come to. When Brunei arrived the sitting was already raised; so he was obliged to go and look for Delescluze at the Hôtel-de-Ville, and then he retraced his steps to Issy. At the gate of Versailles he perceived his battalions on the other side of the rampart. These, deaf to their chiefs, had evacuated the village and wanted to re-enter the town. Brunel forbade the lowering of the drawbridge, and tried to get out by the gates of Vanves, where they refused to let him pass. He returned to the War Office, explained the situation, asked for men, wandered about the whole night looking for some, and at four o'clock in the morning set out with 150 Federals, but found the village entirely occupied by the Versaillese. The officers of Issy were tried by court-martial. Brunel gave evidence, and complained bitterly of the culpable carelessness which had paralysed the defence. For answer he was arrested.

He spoke but too truly. The disorder of the War Office rendered all resistance chimerical. Delescluze had brought only his devotion. Of a weak character despite his apparent rigidity, he was at the mercy of the general staff, still directed by Prodhomme, who, surviving all his chiefs, had succeeded in making himself thought indispensable. The Central Committee, emboldened by the timidity of the Council, intruded everywhere, published decrees, ordered the payment of expenses without submitting them to the control of the Military Commission. The members of the Commission, men of intelligence, but belonging to the minority, complained to the Committee of Public Safety, which replaced them by Romanticists. The dispute went on all the same, and waxed so violent that rumours of a rupture between the Council and the Central Committee spread amongst the legions.

The Versaillese, on their part, still pushed on. In the night of the 13th to the 14th the fort of Vanves, which now only fired occasional volleys, was quite extinguished, and could no more be rekindled. The garrison, cut off on all sides, retired by the quarries of Montrouge, and the Versaillese occupied what remained of the fort. There was again an ovation at Versailles.

On the 16th May we had not a single man from the left bank to the Petit Vanves, where about 2,000 Federals, under the command of La Cécilia and Lisbonne, were encamped. We attempted to retake the village of Issy, but were repulsed. Henceforth the enemy could continue his approaches and arm the two bastions of the fort of Issy that faced the town. His fire, counteracted for a moment by the ramparts, now showed a marked superiority, and joined the batteries that crushed the sixteenth arrondissement. This unfortunate quarter was now taken, attacked from the front and the flank by nearly a hundred ordnance pieces. It was indeed time to think of the defence of the interior. Delescluze extended the powers of the three generals to the quarters of the town contiguous to their command; he disbanded the battalion of the barricades, which had been of no utility whatever; he confided the works to the military engineers, and made an appeal to the navvies. But all his decrees remained so much waste paper or were crossed by others. When the delegate offered the navvies 3 francs 50 centimes, the Committee of Public Safety, in the same column of the *Officiel*, offered them 3 francs 75 centimes.

The Committee of Public Safety contributed to the defence by a decree obliging all the inhabitants of Paris to provide themselves with an identity card, whose production might be requested by a National Guard — as impracticable and unpractised a decree as that on the refractory recruits. The Hôtel-de-Ville awed nobody; behind its big words impotence made itself felt. On the 12th, some battalions having surrounded the Bank and wanting to make a search, old Beslay prevented them doing so, and the terrible dictators of the Committee of Public Safety disavowed their own agent. The public chaffed — a terrible thing! A last blow, and it was all over with the authority of the Commune; and this blow came from the minority.

The latter was exasperated at seeing its most capable members expelled from the services — Vermorel from the Commission of Public Safety, Longuet from the *Officiel,* Varlin from the Commissariat — and was struck with dismay at the disorder of the War Office. It had the unfortunate idea of denying its own responsibility, prepared a manifesto, and brought it to the sitting of the 15th. The majority, forewarned, with the exception of four or five members, kept away. The minority had their absence verified, and instead of waiting for the next sitting, sent the declaration to the papers. "The Commune," it said, "has abdicated its power into the hands of a dictatorship, to which it has given the name of Committee of Public Safety. The majority has declared itself irresponsible by its vote. The minority, on the contrary, affirms that the Commune owes it to the revolutionary movement to accept all responsibilities. As to ourselves, we claim the right of being alone answerable for our acts without screening ourselves behind a supreme dictatorship. We withdraw to our arrondissements. Convinced that the question of the war takes the lead over all others, we shall spend the time left us by our municipal functions in the midst of our brothers of the National Guard."

A great fault this, and altogether inexcusable. The minority had not the right to cry out about a dictatorship, having voted, without making any express reserve, for the second Committee. It had not the right to say that the elected delegates of the people were encroaching upon its sovereignty, for this concentration of power was quite accidental, necessitated by the battle, and leaving the principle of the people's sovereignty intact under ordinary circumstances. It would have been more dignified to openly disavow the acts of the Committee, and then propose something better themselves. It would have been logical, since "the question of the war took the lead over all others," not to thus morally weaken the defence by deserting the Hotel-de-Ville. It was not with a view to retain them in their arrondissements that the arrondissements had sent delegates to the Council.

Several members of the minority brought the question before public meetings, which called on them to return to their posts. Those of the fourth arrondissement gave an explanation in the Theâtre-Lyrique, in which they said "that their guiding principle was that the Commune was to be only the executive agent of the public will, manifesting itself continually, and indicating day by day what was to be done to secure the triumph of the revolution." No doubt that principle was correct, and the revolution can only be made safe by the direct legislation of the people. But was this a time to legislate when the cannon ruled supreme? And in the midst of the fire, is the "executive agent" to expect that the soldier who does battle for him will also bring him ideas?

The Versaillese journals crowed over this manifesto. Many of those who had signed it understood their mistake, and fifteen of them presented themselves at the sitting of the 17th. The Council had never been so numerous; the roll-call was answered by sixty-six members. The Council was first taken up with a proposition prompted by a traitor. Barral de Montaut, chief of the staff of the 7th legion, had just published that the Versaillese of Vanves had shot an ambulance woman of the Commune. Urbain, urged by Montaut, who had managed to gain his friendship, asked that, as reprisal, five hostages should be shot in the interior of Paris, and five at the advanced posts. The Council passed to the order of the day. Immediately after this incident, a member of the majority challenged those of the minority. He demonstrated without any difficulty the futility of the reasons invoked in their manifesto, and, growing warm, called his adversaries Girondists. "What! Girondists!" answered Frankel, "one can see that you go to bed at night and get up in the morning with the *Moniteur* of 1793, else you would know the difference there is between us Socialist Revolutionaries and the Girondists." The discussion became heated. Vallès, who had signed the manifesto, said, "I have declared that we must come to an understanding with the majority; but they must also respect the minority, which is a force;" and he demanded that all forces should be turned against the enemy. Citizen Miot answered severely from the profound depths of his beard. A member of the majority spoke of conciliation; immediately Félix Pyat, to incense their ire, asked for the reading of the manifesto. In vain Vaillant said, with sense and justice, "When our colleagues come back to us disavowing their programme, we must not put it under their eyes to engage them to persevere in their faults," and a conciliatory order of the day was beaten by that of Miot, drawn up in terms offensive to the minority.

Suddenly a tremendous explosion interrupted the dispute. Billioray rushed into the room with the news that the cartridge factory of the Avenue Rapp had just blown up.

The whole east of Paris was shaken. A pyramid of flame, of molten lead, human remains, burning timber and bullets burst forth from the Champ-de-Mars to an enormous height, and showered down upon the environs. Four houses fell in; more than forty persons were wounded, and the catastrophe would have been still more terrible if the firemen of the Commune had not torn wagons of cartridges and barrels of gunpowder from the midst of the flames. A maddened crowd gathered, and believed in a crime; a few individuals were arrested, and an artilleryman was taken to the Ecole Militaire.

Who was the culprit? Nobody knows. Neither the Council nor the procureur of the Commune examined the affair. Yet the Committee of Public Safety announced in a proclamation that it held four of the culprits, and Delescluze that the case was to be sent before the court-martial. No more was heard about it, although it was as much the duty as the interest of the Council to throw light upon this affair. A serious inquest would probably have revealed a crime. The women, who usually left the factory at seven o'clock, had been on that day dismissed at six o'clock. It has been seen that Charpentier asked Corbin for dynamite; it might have been very useful to the conspirators to spread panic with one stroke at the War Office, the Ecole Militaire, the artillery park and the huts of the Champ-de-Mars, which were always occupied by a few Federals. Paris firmly believed in a plot. The reactionaries said, "This is the revenge for the Vendôme column". [column erected in 1805 in honour of Napoleon's victories. Became a symbol of Bonapartism]

It had been pulled down the evening before with great ceremony. Its demolition, the idea of which had become quite current during the first siege, was decreed on the 12th April. This inspiration, popular, humane, profound, showing that a war of classes was to supersede the war of nations, aimed at the same time a blow at the ephemeral triumph of the Prussian. The rather expensive preparations, costing almost 15,000 francs, had been much protracted, owing to the lukewarmness of the engineer and the continual efforts to suborn the workmen. On the 16th May, at two o'clock, an immense crowd thronged all the neighbouring streets, rather anxious as to the result of the operation. The reactionaries foretold all sorts of catastrophes; the engineer, on the contrary, affirmed that there would be no shock; that the column would break to pieces during its descent. He had sawn it horizontally a little above the pedestal; a slanting groove was to facilitate the fall backwards upon a vast bed of faggots, sand and dung, accumulated in the direction of the Rue de la Paix.

A rope attached to the summit of the column was twisted round a capstan fixed at the entrance of the street. The square was crowded with National Guards; the windows, the roofs were filled with curious spectators. In default of MM. Jules Simon and Ferry, erstwhile warm partisans of the operation, M. Glais-Bizoin congratulated the new prefect of police, Ferre, who had just taken the place of Cournet, and confided to him that for forty years it had been his ardent desire to see the expiatory monument demolished. The bands played the *Marseillaise,* the capstan turned about, the pulley broke, and a man was wounded. Already rumours of treason circulated among the crowd, but a second pulley was soon supplied. At a quarter past five an officer appeared on the balustrade for some time, waved a tricolor flag, then fixed it on the rails. At half-past five the capstan again turned, and a few minutes after the extremity of the column slowly displaced itself, the shaft little by little gave way, then, suddenly reeling to and fro, broke and fell with a low moan. The head of Bonaparte rolled on the ground, and his parricidal arm lay detached from the trunk. An immense acclamation, as that of a people freed from a yoke, burst forth. The ruins were climbed upon and saluted by enthusiastic cries, and the red flag floated from the purified Pedestal, which on that day had become the altar of the human race.

The people wanted to divide among themselves the fragments of the column, but were prevented by the inopportune interference of the Council members present. A week afterwards, the Versaillese picked them up. One of the first acts of the victorious bourgeoisie was to again raise this enormous block, the symbol of their sovereignty. To lift up Caesar on his pedestal they needed a scaffolding of 30,000 corpses. Like the mothers under the First Empire, may those of our days never look upon this bronze without weeping.

Chapter 25
Paris on the eve of death

The Paris of the Commune has but three days more to live; let us engrave upon our memory her luminous physiognomy.

He who has breathed in thy life that fiery fever of modern history, who has panted on thy boulevards and wept in thy faubourgs, who has sung to the morning of thy revolutions and a few weeks after bathed his hands in powder behind thy barricades, he who can hear from beneath thy stones the voices of the martyrs of sublime ideas and read in every one of thy streets a date of human progress, even he does less justice to thy original grandeur than the stranger, though a Philistine, who came to glance at thee during the days of the Commune. The attraction of rebellious Paris was so strong that men hurried thither from America to behold this spectacle unprecedented in the world's history — the greatest town of the European continent in the hands of the proletarians. Even the pusillanimous were drawn towards her.

In the first days of May one of our friends arrived — one of the most timid men of the timid provinces. His kith and kin had escorted him on his departure, tears in their eyes, as though he were descending into the infernal regions. He said to us, "What truth is there in all the rumours spread about?" "Well, come and search all the recesses of the den."

We set out from the Bastille. Street-arabs cry Rochefort's *Mot d'Ordre*, the *Père Duchêne*, Jules Vallès' *Cri du Peuple*, Félix Pyat's *Vengeur*, *La Commune*, *L'Affranchi*, *Le Pilori des Mouchards*. The *Officiel* is little asked for; the journalists of the Council stifle it by their competition. The *Cri du Peuple* has a circulation of 100,000. It is the earliest out; it rises with chanticleer. If we have an article by Vallès this morning, we are in luck; but in his stead, Pierre Denis, with his autonomy a *outrance*, makes himself too often heard. Only buy the *Père Duchêne* once, though its circulation is more than 60,000. Take Félix Pyat's article in the *Vengeur* as a fine example of literary intoxication. The bourgeoisie has no better helpmates than these vain and ignorant claptrap-mongers. Here is the doctrinaire journal *La Commune,* in which Milliere sometimes writes, and in which Georges Duchêne takes the young men and the old of the Hôtel-de-Ville to task with a severity which would better fit another character than his. Do not forget the *Mot d'Ordre*, whatever the romanticists may say. It was one of the first to support the Revolution of the 18th March, and darted terrible arrows at the Versaillese.

In the kiosques are the caricatures. Thiers, Picard, and Jules Favre figure as the Three Graces, clasping each other's paunches. This fine fish, the mackerel, with the blue-green scales, who is making up a bed with an imperial crown, is the Marquis de Gallifet. *L'Avenir,* the mouthpiece of the *Ligue, Le Siècle,* become very hostile since the arrest of Gustave Chaudey; and *La Vérité,* the Yankee Portalis's paper, are piled up, melancholy and intact. Many reactionary papers have been suppressed by the prefecture, but for all that are not dead; for a lad, without any mystery about him, offers them to us.

Read, search, find one appeal to murder, to pillage, a single cruel line in all these Communard journals excited by the battle, and then compare them with the Versaillese papers, demanding fusillades *en Masse* as soon as the troops shall have vanquished Paris.

Let us follow those catafalques that are being taken up the Rue de la Roquette, and enter with them into the Père la Chaise cemetery. All those who die for Paris are entombed with funerals in the great resting-place. The Commune has claimed the honour of paying for their funerals; its red flag blazes from the four corners of the hearse, followed by some comrades of the battalion, while a few passers-by always join the procession. Here is a wife accompanying her dead husband. A member of the Council follows the coffin; at the grave he speaks not of regrets, but of hope, of vengeance. The widow presses her children in her arms, and says to them, "Remember and cry with me, *"Vive la République! Vive la Commune!"* "

On retracing our steps, we pass by the *mairie* of the eleventh arrondissement. It is hung with black, the mourning of the last Imperialist plebiscite, of which the people of Paris was innocent and became the victim. We cross the Place de la Bastille, gay, animated by the ginger-bread fair. Paris will yield nothing to the cannon; she has.

Carriages are rare, for the second siege has cut short the provisions for horses. By the Rue du 4 Septembre we reach the Stock Exchange, surmounted by the red flag, and the Bibliotheque Nationale, where readers are sitting round the long tables. Crossing the Palais-Royal, whose arcades are always noisy, we come to the Museum of the Louvre; the rooms, hung with their pictures, are open to the public. The Versaillese journals none the less say the Commune is selling the national collections to foreigners.

We descend the Rue de Rivoli. On the right, in the Rue Castiglione, a huge barricade obstructs the entrance of the Place Vendôme. The issue of the Place de la Concorde is barred by the St. Florentin redoubt, stretching to the Ministry of Marine on its right, and the garden of the Tuileries on its left, with three rather badly directed embrasures eight yards wide. An enormous ditch, laying bare all the arteries of subterranean life, separates the Place from the redoubt. The workmen are giving it the finishing stroke, and cover the banks with turf. Many people walking by look on inquisitively, and more than one brow lowers. A corridor skilfully constructed conducts us to the Place de la Concorde. The proud profile of the Strasbourg statue stands out against the red flags. The Communards, who are accused of ignoring France, have piously replaced the faded crowns of the first siege by fresh spring flowers.

We now enter the zone of battle. The avenue of the Champs-Elysées unrolls its long-deserted line, cut by the dismal bursting of the shells from Mont-Valérien and Courbevoie. These reach as far as the Palais de l'Industrie, whose treasures the employees of the Commune courageously protect. In the distance rises the mighty bulk of the Arc de Triomphe. The sightseers of the first days have disappeared, for the Place de l"Etoile has become almost as deadly as the rampart. The shells break off the bas-reliefs that M. Jules Simon had caused to be iron-clad against the Prussians. The main arch is walled up to stop the projectiles launched against it. Behind this barricade they are getting ready to mount some pieces on the platform, which is almost as high as Mont-Valérien.

By the Faubourg St. Honoré we pass along the Champs-Elysées. In the right angle comprised between the Avenue de la Grande Armée, that of the Ternes, the ramparts, and the Avenue Wagram there is not a house intact. You see M. Thiers "does not bombard Paris, as the people of the Commune will not fail to say." Some shreds of a poster hang from a half-battered wall; it is M. Thiers' speech against King Bomba, which a group of conciliators have been witty enough to reproduce. "You know, gentlemen," said he to the bourgeois of 1848, "what is happening at Palermo. You all have shaken with horror on hearing that during forty-eight hours a large town has been bombarded. By whom? Was it by a foreign enemy exercising the rights of war? No, gentlemen, it was by its own Government. And why? Because that unfortunate town demanded its rights. Well, then, for the demand of its rights it has got forty-eight hours of bombardment!" Happy Palermo! Paris already has had forty days of bombardment.

We have some chance of getting to the Boulevard Péreire by the left side of the Avenue des Ternes. From there to the Porte-Maillot every spot is beset with danger. Watching for a momentary lull, we reach the gate, or rather the heap of ruins that mark its place. The station no longer exists, the tunnel is filled up, the ramparts are slipping into the moats. And yet there are human salamanders who dare to move about amidst these ruins. Facing the gate there are three pieces commanded by Captain La Marseillaise; on the right, Captain Rouchat with five pieces; on the left, Captain Martin with four. Monteret, who commands this post for the last five weeks, lives with them in this atmosphere of shells. The Mont-Valérien, Courbevoie, and Bécon have thrown more than eight hundred of them. Twelve pieces are served by ten men, naked to the waist, their body and arms blackened with powder, in a stream of perspiration, often a match in each hand. The only survivor of the first set, the sailor Bonaventure, has twenty times seen his comrades dashed to pieces. And yet they hold out, and these pieces, continually dismounted, are continually renewed; their artillery men only complain of the want of ammunition, for the wagons no longer dare approach. The Versaillese have very often attempted, and may attempt, surprise attacks. Monteret watches day and night, and he can without boasting write to the Committee of Public Safety that so long as he is there the Versaillese will not enter by the Porte-Maillot.

Every step towards La Muette is a challenge to death. But our friend must witness all the greatness of Paris. On the ramparts, near the gate of La Muette, an officer is waving his képi toward the Bois de Boulogne; the balls are whistling around him. It is Dombrowski, who amusing himself with inveighing against the Versaillese of the trenches. A member of the Council who is with him succeeds in making him forego this musketeer foolhardiness, and the general takes us to the castle, where he has established one of his headquarters. All the rooms are perforated by shells. Still he remains there, and makes his men remain. It has been calculated that his aides-de-camp on an average lived eight days. At this moment the watch of the Belvedere rushes in with appalled countenance; a shell has traversed his post. "Stay there," says Dombrowski to him; "if you are not destined to die there you have nothing to fear." Such was his courage — all fatalism. He received no reinforcements despite his despatches to the War Office; believed the game lost, and said so but too often.

This is my only reproach, for you do not expect me to apologise for the Commune's having allowed foreigners to die for it. Is not this the revolution of all proletarians? Is it not for the people to at last do justice to that great Polish race which all French governments have betrayed?

Dombrowski accompanies us across Passy as far as the Seine, and shows us the almost abandoned ramparts. The shells crush or mow down all the approaches to the railway; the large viaduct is giving way at a hundred places; the iron-clad locomotives have been overthrown. The Versaillese battery of the Billancourt Isle fires point-blank at our gunboats, and sinks one, *L'Estoc*, under our very eyes. A tug arrives in time, picks up the crew, and ascends the Seine under the fire that follows it up to the Jena Bridge.

A clear sky, a bright sun, peaceful silence envelop this stream, this wreck, these scattered shells. Death appears more cruel amidst the serenity of nature. Let us go and salute our wounded at Passy. A member of the Council, Lefrançais, is visiting the ambulance of Dr. Demarquay, whom he questions as to the state of the wounded. "I do not share your opinions," answers the doctor, "and I cannot desire the triumph of your cause; but I have never seen wounded men preserve more calm and sang-froid during operations. I attribute this courage to the energy of their convictions." We then visit the beds; most of the sick anxiously inquire when they will be able to resume their service. A young fellow of eighteen, whose right hand had just been amputated, holds out the other, exclaiming, "I have still this one for the service of the Commune!" An officer, mortally wounded, is told that the Commune has just handed over his pay to his wife and children. "I had no right to it," answers he. "These, my friend, these are the brutish drunkards who, according to Versailles, form the army of the Commune."

We return by the Champ-de-Mars; its huts are badly manned. Other cadres, a different discipline would be needed to retain the battalions there. Before the Ecole, 1,500 yards from the ramparts, and a few steps from the War Office, a hundred ordnance pieces remain inert, loaded with mud. Leaving on our right the War Office, that centre of discord, let us enter the Corps Législatif, transformed into a work-shop. Fifteen hundred women are there, sewing the sand sacks that are to stop up the breaches. A tall and handsome girl, Marthe, round her waist the red scarf with silver fringe given her by her comrades, distributes the work. The hours of labour are shortened by joyous songs. Every evening the wages are paid, and the women receive the whole sum, eight centimes a sack, while the former contractors hardly gave them two.

We now proceed along the quays, lulled in imperturbable calm. The Academy of Sciences holds its Monday sittings. It is not the workmen who have said, "The Republic wants no savants." M. Delaunay is in the chair. M. Elie de Beaumont looks through the correspondence, and reads a note from his colleague, M. J. Bertrand, who has fled to St. Germain. We shall find the report in the *Officiel* of the Commune.

We must not leave the left bank without visiting the military prison. Ask the soldiers if they have met with a single menace, a single insult in Paris; if they are not treated as comrades, subjected to no exceptional rules, set free when willing to help their Parisian brothers.

Meanwhile evening has set in. The theatres are opening. The Lyrique gives a grand performance for the benefit of the wounded, and the Opéra-Comique is preparing another. The Opéra promises us a special performance for the following Monday, when we shall hear Gossec's revolutionary hymn. The artists of the Gaieté, abandoned by their manager, themselves direct their theatre. The Gymnase, Châtelet, Théatre-Français, Ambigu-Comique,

Délassements, have large audiences every night. Let us pass to more virile spectacles, such as Paris has not witnessed since 1793.

Ten churches open, and the Revolution mounts the pulpits. In the old quarter of the Gravilliers, St. Nicholas des Champs is filling with the powerful murmur of many voices. A few gas-burners hardly light up the swarming crowd; and at the farther end, almost hidden by the shadow of the vaults, hangs the figure of Christ draped in the popular oriflamme. The only luminous centre is the reading-desk, facing the Pulpit, hung with red. The organ and the people chant the *Marseillaise*. The orator, over-excited by these fantastic surroundings, launches forth into ecstatic declamations, which the echo repeats like a menace. The people discuss the events of the day, the means of defence; the members of the Council are severely censured, and vigorous resolutions are voted to be presented to the Hotel-de-Ville the next day. Women sometimes ask to speak; at the Batignolles they have a club of their own. No doubt, few precise ideas come forth from these feverish meetings, but many find there a provision of energy and of courage.

It is only nine o'clock, and we may still be in time for the concert of the Tuileries. At the entrance, citoyennes, accompanied by commissioners, are making a collection for the widows and orphans of the Commune. The immense rooms are animated by a decent and gay throng. For the first time respectably-dressed women are seated on the forms in the court. Three orchestras are playing in the galleries, but the soul of the fete is in the Salle des Maréchaux, where Mademoiselle Agar recites from "Les Châtiments" in that same place, where, ten months before, Bonaparte and his band were enthroned. Mozart, Meyerbeer, Rossini, the great works of art have driven away the musical obscenities of the Empire. From the large central window the harmonious strains vibrate to the garden; joyous lights shine like stars on the green-sward, dance among the trees, and colour the playing fountains. Within the arbours the people are laughing; but the noble Champs-Elysées, dark and desolate, seem to protest against these popular masters, whom they have never acknowledged. Versailles, too, protests by that conflagration of which a wan reflex lights up the Arc de Triomphe, whose sombre mass overtowers the civil war.

At eleven o'clock, as the crowd is retiring, we hear a noise from the side of the chapel. M. Schoelcher has just been arrested. He has been taken to the prefecture, where, a few hours after, the procureur Rigault sets him at liberty.

The boulevards are thronged with the people coming from the theatres. At the Café-Peters there is a scandalous gathering of staff officers and prostitutes. Suddenly a detachment of National Guards appears and leads them off. We follow them to the Hôtel-de-Ville, where Ranvier, who is on duty there, receives them. Short shrift is made: the women to St. Lazare, the officers, with spades and mattocks, to the trenches.

One o'clock in the morning. Paris sleeps tranquilly. Such, my friend, is the Paris of the brigand. You have seen this Paris thinking, weeping, combating, working, enthusiastic, fraternal, severe to vice. Her streets free during the day, are they less safe in the silence of the night? Since Paris has her own police crime has disappeared. Each one is left to his instincts, and where do you see debauchery victorious? These Federals, who might draw milliards, live on ridiculous pay compared with their usual salaries. Do you at last recognize this Paris, seven times shot down since 1789, and always ready to rise for the salvation of France? Where is her programme, say you? Why, seek it before you, and not at the faltering Hôtel-de-Ville. These smoking ramparts, these explosions of heroism, these women, these men of all professions united, all the workmen of the earth applauding our combat, all monarchs, all the bourgeois coalesced against us, do they not speak loudly enough our common thought, and that all of us are fighting for equality, the enfranchisement of labour, the advent of a social society? Woe to France if she does not comprehend! Leave at once; recount what Paris is. If she dies, what life remains to you? Who, save Paris, will have strength enough to continue the Revolution? Who save Paris will stifle the clerical monster? Go, tell the Republican provinces, "These proletarians fight for you too, who perhaps may be the exiles of to-morrow." As to that class, the purveyor of empires, that fancies it can govern by periodical butcheries, go and tell them, in accents loud enough to drown their clamours, "The blood of the people will enrich the revolutionary field. The idea of Paris will arise from her burning entrails and become an inexorable firebrand with the sons of the slaughtered."

Chapter 26
The enemy enters Paris

The St. Cloud gate has just been breached. General Douai has thrown himself at it. (Thiers to the Prefects, 21st May.)

The great attack approached; the Assembly drew up in battlearray. On the 16th May it refused to recognize the Republic as the Government of France, and voted public prayers by 417 out of 420. On the 17th the army established its breach batteries against the gates of La Muette, Auteuil, St. Cloud, Point du Jour, Issy. The batteries in the rear continued to pound the enceinte of the Point du Jour and to confound Passy. The pieces of the Château de Brécon ruined the Montmartre cemetry, and reached as far as the Place St. Pierre. We had five arrondissements under shell.

On the 18th, in the evening, the Versaillese surprised the Federals of Cachan by approaching them with the cry of *"Vive la Commune!"* However, we succeeded in preventing their movement towards the Hautes-Bruyeres. The Dominican monks who from their convent gave signals to the enemy were arrested and taken to the Fort de Bicetre.

May 19th: — Despite the Versaillese approaches, our defence did not become more vigorous. Bastions 72 and 73 threw a few occasional shells upon the village and the fort of Issy. From the Point du Jour to the Porte-Maillot we had only the cannon of the Dauphiné gate to answer the hundred Versaillese pieces and check their works in the Bois de Boulogne. A few barricades at the Bineau and Asnieres gates and the Boulevard d'Italie, two redoubts at the Place de la Concorde and Rue Castiglione, a moat in the Rue Royale and another at the Trocadero; this was all that the Council had done in seven weeks for the defence of the interior. There were no works at the Mont-Parnasse Station, the Panthéon, the Buttes Montmartre, where two or three pieces had been fired off on the 14th, only to kill our own men at Lavallois. At the terrace of the Tuileries about twelve navvies sadly dug away at a useless trench. The Committee of Public Safety could not, they said, find workmen, when they had 1,500 idlers at the Prince-Eugene Barracks, 100,000 sedentary guards, and millions of francs to hand. An iron will and firm direction might still have saved everything; and we were now in the period of coma, of immense lassitude. The competitions, quarrels, and intrigues had absorbed all energy. The Council occupied itself with details, with trifles. The Committee of Public Safety multiplied its romantic proclamations, which moved nobody. The Central Committee thought only of seizing upon a power it was unable to wield, and on the 19th announced itself administrator of the War Office. Its members had made so sure of their sway, that one of them by a decree inserted in the *Officiel* ordered all the inhabitants of Paris to "present themselves at their homes within forty-eight hours," on pain of "having their rent-titles on the grand livre burnt." This was the pendant of the identity card.

Our best battalions, decimated, abandoned to themselves, were but wrecks. Since the beginning of April we had lost 4,000 men, killed or wounded, and 3,500 prisoners. There now remained to us 2,000 men from Ansieres to Neuilly, 4,000 perhaps from La Muette to PetitVanves. The battalions designated for the posts of Passy were not there, or stayed in the houses far from the ramparts; many of their officers had disappeared. At bastions 36 to 70, precisely at the point of attack, there were not twenty artillerymen; the sentinels were absent.

Was it treason? The conspirators boasted a few days after of having dismantled these ramparts; but the terrible bombardment would suffice to explain this dereliction. Still there was a culpable heedlessness. Dombrowski, weary of struggling against the inertness of the War Office, was discouraged, went too often to his quarters at the Place Vendôme, while the Committee of Public Safety, informed of the abandonment of the ramparts, contented itself with warning the War Office instead of hurrying to the rescue and taking the situation in hand.

On Saturday, the 20th May, the breach batteries were unmasked; 300 naval guns and siege-pieces blending together their detonations announced the beginning of the end.

The same day De Beaufond, whom Lasnier's arrest had not discouraged, sent his habitual emissary to warn the chief of the Versaillese general staff that the gates of Montrouge, Vanves, Vaugirard, Point du Jour and Dauphine were entirely deserted. Orders for concentrating the troops were immediately issued. On the 21st the Versaillese found themselves in readiness, as on the 3rd and 12th, but this time success seemed certain; the gate of St. Cloud was dashed to pieces.

For several days some members of the Council had pointed out this breach to the chief of the general staff, Henri Prodhomme. He answered *à la* Cluseret that his measures were taken; that he was even going to throw up a terrible iron-clad barricade before this gate; but he did not stir. On the Sunday morning, Lefrançais, traversing the moat on the ruins of the drawbridge, at about fifteen yards distance, ran up against the Versaillese trenches. Struck by the imminence of the peril, he sent Delescluze a note, which was lost.

At half-past two, under the shade of the Tuileries, a monster concert was being given for the benefit of the widows and orphans of the Commune. Thousands of people had come; the bright spring dresses of the women lit up the green alleys; people eagerly inhaled the fresh air sent forth from the great trees. Two hundred yards off, on the Place de la Concorde, the Versaillese shells burst, uttering their discordant note amidst the joyous sounds of the bands and the invigorating breath of spring.

At the end of the concert a staff officer ascended the platform of the conductor of the orchestra. "Citizens," said he, "M. Thiers promised to enter Paris yesterday. M. Thiers has not entered; he will not enter. I invite you to come here next Sunday, to the same place, to our second concert for the benefit of the widows and orphans."

At that very hour, at that very minute, almost within gunshot, the vanguard of the Versaillese was making its entry into Paris.

The expected signal had at last been given from the St. Cloud gate, but did not come from the licensed conspirators. An amateur spy, Ducatel, was crossing these quarters, when he saw everything, gates and ramparts, quite deserted. He thereupon climbed Bastion 64, waving a white handkerchief, and cried to the soldiers in the trenches, "You can enter; there is no one here." A naval officer came forward, interrogated Ducatel, crossed over the ruins of the drawbridge, and was able to assure himself that the bastions and neighbouring houses were entirely abandoned. Returning immediately to the trenches, the officer telegraphed the news to the nearest generals. The breach batteries ceased firing, and the soldiers of the trenches nearby penetrated by small platoons into the enceinte. M. Thiers, MacMahon, and Admiral Pothuan, who were just then at Mont-Valérien, telegraphed to Versailles to have all the divisions put in motion.

Dombrowski, absent from his headquarters of La Muette for several hours, arrived at four o'clock. A commander met him, and informed him of the entry of the Versaillese. Dombrowski let the officer terminate his report, then, turning to one of his aides-de-camp, with a coolness that he exaggerated in critical circumstances, said, "Send to the Ministry of Marine for a battery of seven cannon; warn such and such battalions. I shall take the command myself." He also addressed a despatch to the Committee of Public

Safety and the War Office, and sent the batallion of volunteers to occupy the gate of Auteuil.

At five o'clock, National Guards, without képis, without arms, uttered a cry of alarm in the streets of Passy; some officers unsheathing their swords tried to stop them; the Federals left their houses, some loading their guns, others maintaining that it was a false alarm. The commander of the volunteers picked up and led off as many men as he could get to follow him.

These volunteers were troops inured to fire. Near the railway station they saw the red-coats, and received them with a volley. A Versaillese officer on horseback, who hurried up trying to urge on his men with drawn sabre, fell beneath our balls, and his soldiers retreated. The Federals established themselves solidly on the viaduct and at the opening of the Murat Boulevard, while, at the same time, the quay abreast of the Jena. Bridge was being barricaded.

Dombrowski's despatch had reached the Committee of Public Safety. Billioray, on duty at this moment, at once proceeded to the Council. The Assembly was just putting Cluseret on trial, and Vermorel was speaking. The ex-delegate, seated on a chair, listened to the orator with that vain nonchalance which the naive took for talent. Billioray, very pale, entered, and for a moment sat down; then, as Vermorel went on, cried to him, "Conclude! conclude! I have to make a communication of the greatest importance to the Assembly; I demand a secret sitting."

Vermorel: "Let citizen Billioray speak."

Billioray rose and read a paper that trembled slightly in his hand.

"Dombrowski to War and Committee of Public Safety. The Versaillese have entered by the Porte de St. Cloud. I am taking measures to drive them back. If you can send me reinforcements, I answer for everything."

There was first a silence of anguish, soon broken by interpellations. "Some battalions have marched off," answered Billioray; "the Committee of Public Safety watches."

The discussion was again taken up, and naturally cut short. The Council acquitted Cluseret; the ridiculous impeachment brought forward by Miot, made up only of gossip, neglected the only incriminating fact — the inactivity of Cluseret during his delegation. They then formed into groups and commented on the despatch. The confidence of Dombrowski, the assurance of Billioray, proved quite sufficient to the romanticists. What with faith in the general, the solidity of the ramparts, the immortality of the cause; what with the responsibility of the Committee of Public Safety, the question at issue was slurred over; let every one go about in search of information, and in case of need betake himself to his own arrondissement.

The time was wasted in small-talk; there were neither motion nor debate; eight o'clock struck , and the president raised the sitting. The last sitting of the Council! And there was no one to demand a permanent committee; no one to call on his colleague to wait here for news, to summon the Committee

---

of Public Safety to the bar of the Council. There was no one to insist that at this critical moment of uncertainty, when perhaps it might be necessary to improvise a plan of defence at a moment's notice or take a great resolution in case of disaster, the post of the guardians of Paris was in the centre, at the Hôtel-de-Ville, and not in their respective arrondissements.

Thus the Council of the Commune disappeared from history and the Hôtel-de-Ville at the moment of supreme danger, when the Versaillese penetrated into Paris.

The same prostration reigned at the War Office, where they had received the news at five o'clock. The Central Committee went to Delescluze, who seemed very calm, and said, what many indeed believed, that the fight in the streets would be favourable to the Commune. The commander of the section of the Point du Jour having just come to report that nothing serious had happened, the delegate accepted his statements without corroboration. The chief of the general staff did not even think it worth while to go and make a personal recognisance, and towards eight o'clock he had this incredible despatch posted up: "The observatory of the Arc de Triomphe denies the entry of the Versaillese; at least, it sees nothing that looks like it. The commander (Renaud) of the section has just left my office, and declares that there has only been a panic, and that the gate of Auteuil has not been forced; that if a few Versaillese have entered, they have been repulsed. I have sent for eleven battalions of reinforcements, by as many officers of the general staff, who are not to leave them till they have led them to the posts which they are to occupy."

At the same hour M. Thiers telegraphed to his prefects, "The gate of St. Cloud has fallen under the fire of our cannon. General Douai has dashed into the town." A twofold lie. The gate of St. Cloud had been wide open for three days without the Versaillese daring to pass it, and General Douai had crept in very modestly, man by man, introduced by treason.

At night the Ministry seemed to wake up a little. Officers flocked thither asking for orders. The general staff would not allow the tocsin to be sounded, on the pretext that the population must not be alarmed. Some members of the Council pored over the plan of Paris at last, studying those strategical points that had been forgotten for six weeks. When it was necessary at once to find an idea, a method, and give precise instructions, the delegate shut himself in his office in order to frame a proclamation.

While in the midst of Paris, confident in her trustees, a few men, without soldiers, without information, prepared the first resistance, the Versaillese continued to slip in through the breaches of the ramparts. Wave on wave their flood grew, silent, veiled by the dusk. By degrees they massed themselves between the railway line and the fortifications. At eight o'clock they were numerous enough to divide into two columns, one of which, turning to the left, crowned Bastions 66 and 67, while the other filed off to the right on the route to Versailles. The first lodged itself in the centre of

Passy, occupying the St. Périne asylum, the church and the place of Auteuil; the other, having swept away the rudimentary barricade constructed on the quay at the top of the Rue Guillon, towards one o'clock in the morning, by the Rue Raynouard, scaled the Trocadero, neither fortified nor manned on this side, and it once took possession of it.

At the Hotel-de-Ville the members of the Committee of Public Safety had at last assembled. Billioray alone had vanished not to appear again. They knew nothing of the number and position of the troops, but knew that under the cover of night the enemy had entered Passy. Staff officers sent to La Muette to reconnoitre came back with the most reassuring news. Thereupon, at eleven o'clock, a member of the Council, Assi, entered the Rue Beethoven, where the lights had been put out. Soon his horse refused to advance; it had slipped down in large pools of blood, and National Guards seemed to lie asleep along the walls. Suddenly men sprang forward. They were the Versaillese waiting in ambush; these sleepers were murdered Federals.

The Versaillese were slaughtering within the walls of Paris and Paris knew it not. The night was clear, starlit, mild, fragrant; the theatres were crowded, the boulevards sparkling with life and gaiety, the bright cafés swarming with visitors, and the cannon were everywhere hushed — a silence unknown for three weeks. If "the finest army that France ever had" were to push straight on by the quays and boulevards, entirely free of barricades, with one bound, without firing a shot, it would crush the Commune of Paris.

The volunteers held out on the railway line till midnight; then, exhausted, left without any reinforcements, they fell back upon La Muette. General Clinchant followed them, occupied the Auteuil gate, passed by that of Passy, and marched on the headquarters of Dombrowski. Fifty volunteers for some time still kept up a skirmish in the Château, but outflanked on the east, about to be closed in from the Trocadero, at half-past one in the morning they beat a retreat on the Champs-Elysées.

On the left bank General Cissey had the whole evening massed his forces at about 200 yards from the enceinte. At midnight his sappers crossed the moat, scaled the ramparts, without even encountering a sentinel, and opened the Sevres and Versailles gates.

At three o'clock in the morning the Versaillese inundated Paris through the five gaping wounds of the gates of Passy, Auteuil, St. Cloud, Sevres, and Versailles. The greater part of the fifteenth arrondissement was occupied, the Muette taken; all Passy and the heights of the Trocadero were taken, and the powder-magazine of the Rue Beethoven, immense catacombs running underneath the sixteenth arrondissement, crammed with 3,000 barrels of powder, millions of cartridges, thousands of shells. At five o'clock the first Versaillese shell fell upon the Légion d'Honneur. As on the morning of the 2nd December, Paris was asleep.

Chapter 27
The invasion continues

"The generals who commanded the entry into Paris are great military men." (Thiers to the National Assembly 22 May 1871)

At two o'clock Dombrowski arrived at the Hôtel-de-Ville, pale, dejected, his chest bruised with stones ploughed up by shot. He told the Committee of Public Safety of the entry of the Versaillese, the surprise of Passy, his useless efforts to rally the men. As he was pressed for news, as they appeared astonished at such a rapid invasion, so little did the Committee know of the military situation, Dombrowski, who misunderstood them, exclaimed, "What! the Committee of Public Safety takes me for a traitor! My life belongs to the Commune." His gesture, his voice, testified to his bitter despair.

The morning was warm and bright as the day before. The call to arms, the tocsin, set three or four thousand men on foot, who hurried towards the Tuileries, the Hotel-de-Ville, and the War Office; but hundreds of others at that moment had abandoned their posts, left Passy, and emptied the fifteenth arrondissement. The Federals of Petit-Vanves came back to Paris at five o'clock, and seeing the Trocadero occupied by the Versaillese, refused to hold out. On the left bank, at the St. Clothilde Square, some officers attempted to stop them, but were repulsed by the guards. "It is now a war of barricades," said they; "everyone to his quarter." At the Légion d'Honneur they forced their way; the proclamation of Delescluze had released them.

Thus began that fatal proclamation posted up on all the walls:

"Enough of militarism! No more staff-officers with their gold-embroidered uniforms! Make way for the people, for the combatants bare-armed! The hour of the revolutionary war has struck! The people know nothing of learned manoeuvres. But when they have a gun in their hands, a pavement under their feet, they fear not all the strategists of the monarchical school!

"When the Minister of War thus stigmatizes all discipline, who will henceforth obey? When he repudiates all method, who will listen to reason? Thus we shall see hundreds of men refusing to quit the pavement of their street, paying no heed to the neighbouring quarter in agonies, remaining motionless up to the last hour waiting for the army to come and overwhelm them."

At five o'clock in the morning the official retreat began. The chief of the general staff, Henri Prodhomme, had the War Office precipitately evacuated, without carrying off or destroying the papers. The next day they fell into the hands of the Versaillese, and furnished the courts-martial with thousands of victims.

On leaving the Ministry, Delescluze met Brunel, who, set at liberty only the evening before, had at once rallied his legion, and now came to offer his services, for he was one of those men of convictions too strong to be shaken by the most cruel injustice. Delescluze gave him the order to defend the Place de la Concorde. Brunel repaired thither, and disposed 150 tirailleurs, three pieces of 4 cm., one of 12 and two of 7 on the terrace of the Tuileries and by the bank of the river. He provided the St. Florentin redoubt with a machine-gun and a piece of 4; that of the Rue Royale, at the entrance of the Place de la Concorde, with two pieces of 12.

In front of Brunel, at the Place Beauvan, some men of the 8th legion made vain efforts to stop the fugitives from Passy and Auteuil, and then betook themselves to put the quarter in a fit state of defence. Barricades were thrown up in the Faubourg St. Honoré as far as the English Embassy, in the Rue de Suresne and Ville-Leveque; obstacles were heaped up at the Place St. Augustin, the opening of the Boulevard Haussmann, and in front of the Boulevard Malesherbes, when the Versaillese presented themselves.

Early in the morning they had begun their onward march. At half-past five Douai, Clinchant, and Ladmirault, passing along the ramparts, set foot on the Avenue de la Grande Armée. The artillery, men of the Porte-Maillot, turning round, beheld in their rear the Versaillese, their neighbours for some ten hours. Not a sentinel had denounced them. Monteret marched off his men by the Ternes; then, alone with a child, charged one of the cannon of the Porte-Maillot, fired his last round at the enemy, and succeeded in escaping by the Batignolles.

The Douai column remounted the Avenue as far as the barricade in front of the Arc de Triomphe, which they took without a struggle, the Federals hardly having time to carry off the cannon that were to have surmounted the

Arc de Triomphe. The soldiers marched up the quay, and ventured onto the silent Place de la Concorde; suddenly the terrace of the Tuileries lit up; the Versaillese, received with a pointblank volley, fled as far as the Palais de L'Industrie, leaving many dead.

On the left the soldiers occupied the abandoned Elysée, and by the Rues Morny and Abbatucci emerged on the Place St. Augustin, where the barricades, hardly begun, could not resist, and towards half-past seven the Versaillese installed themselves at the Pepiniere Barracks. The Federals formed a second line in the rear, closing the Boulevard Malesherbes at the top of the Rue Boissy d'Anglas.

On the left of Douai, Clinchant and Ladmirault continued their movement along the ramparts. The important works at the gates of Bineau, Courcelles, Asnieres and Clichy, directed against the fortifications. became useless, and the Ternes were occupied without striking a blow. At the same time one of the Clinchant divisions passed by the outer ramparts. The Federal battalions on duty at Neuilly, Levallois-Perret, and St. Ouen were assailed with balls from the rear − (this was the first intimation they got of the entry of the Versaillese) − and many Federals were taken prisoners. Others succeeded in returning to Paris by the gates of Bineau, Asnieres, and Clichy, spreading panic and rumours of treason in the seventeenth arrondissement.

The rappel had been beaten all night in the Batignolles, and had called out the sedentary guards and the youths. A battalion of engineers rushed forward to encounter Clinchant's skirmishers, and began firing in front of the Parc Monceaux and the Place Wagram, when the National Guards, deceived by their red trousers, opened a deadly fire upon them. They retreated and laid bare the Parc, which the Versaillese occupied, and then pushed on to the Batignolles.

There they were stopped by barricades rising on all sides; on the left, from the Place Clichy to the Rue Lévis; in the centre, in the Rues Lebouteux, La Condamine, and Des Dames; on the right, La Fourche, the rival position of the Place Clichy, had been fortified, and soon the Batignolles formed a serious outwork for Montmartre, our principal fortress.

The latter, for seventeen hours, had looked silently on the entry of the troops of Versailles. In the morning the columns of Douai and Ladmirault, their artillery and their waggons, had met each other, and become entangled on the Place du Trocadero. A few shells from Montmartre would have changed this confusion into a rout, and the least check met with by the troops on their entry would have been for Paris a second 18th March; but the cannon of the Buttes remained mute.

Monstrous negligence, which alone would suffice to condemn the Council, the War Office, and the delegates of Montmartre. Eighty-five cannon and about twenty machine-guns were lying there, dirty, pell-mell, and no one during these eight weeks had even thought of cleaning them.

Projectiles of 7 cm. abounded, but there were no cartridges. At the Moulin de la Galette three pieces of 24 cm. alone were supplied with carriages, but there were neither parapets, blindages, nor even platforms. At nine o'clock in the morning they had not yet fired; after the first discharge the recoil overthrew the carriages, and much time was required to set them up again. These three pieces themselves had very little ammunition. Of fortifications or earthworks there were none; merely a few barricades at the foot of the external boulevards had been begun. At nine o'clock La Cécilia sent to Montmartre, and found the defence in this disgraceful state. He immediately addressed despatches to the Hôtel-de-Ville, conjuring the members of the Council to come themselves, or at least to send reinforcements of men and munitions.

A similar thing occurred at the same time on the left bank at the Ecole Militaire. Face to face with its park of artillery, the Versaillese since one o'clock in the morning were manoeuvring on the Trocadero without a single cannon shot being fired at them. What, then, was the governor of the Ecole about?

At daybreak the Langourian brigade attacked the huts of the Champ-de-Mars. The Federals defended themselves several hours, and were only dislodged by the shells of the Trocadero, which enkindled a conflagration. They then fell back upon the Ecole, and for a long time checking the effort of the troops, gave the seventeenth arrondissment time to rise. The quay as far as the Légion d'Honneur, the Rues de Lille, De l'Université, and the Boulevard St. Germain up to the Rue Solferino were being barricaded. Half-a-dozen of the armlet conspirators, led by Durouchoux and Vrignault, were coming down the Rue du Bac at great speed, when a member of the Council, Siscard, arrested them before the Petit St. Thomas. A bullet struck Durouchoux, his acolytes carried him away, and took advantage of the occasion not to appear again. The Rue de Beaune, Verneuil, and St. Pères were put in a state of defence, and a barricade was thrown up in the Rue de Sevres at the Abbaye-au-Bois.

On the right Cissey's soldiers descended the Rue de Vaugirard without hindrance as far as the Avenue du Maine; another column filed off along the railway, and at half-past six reached the Montparnasse station. This position, of supreme importance, had been utterly neglected; about twenty men defended it, and they were soon short of cartridges, and obliged to retreat to the Rue de Rennes, where, under the fire of the troops, they constructed a barricade at the top of the Rue du Vieux Colombier. On his extreme right Cissey occupied the Vanves gate and lined the whole railway of the west.

Paris rose to the roar of the cannon and read the proclamation of Delescluze. The shops were at once shut up again, the boulevards remained empty, and Paris, the old insurgent, resumed her combative physiognomy. Despatch riders dashed through the streets, and remainders of battalions came to the Hôtel-de-Ville, where the Central Committee, the Committee of Artillery, and all the military services were concentrated.

At nine o'clock twenty members of the Council had assembled. A miracle! There was Félix Pyat, who had cried "To arms!" in his paper that very morning. He had put on his patriarchal air. "Well, my friends, our last hour has come. Oh, for myself what matters it! My hair is grey, my career run out. What more glorious end could I hope for than that of the barricade. But when I see around me so many in the prime of youth, I tremble for the future of the Revolution!" Then he demanded that the names of the members present should be entered, in order to mark out distinctly those true to their duty. He signed his name, and, with tears in his eyes, the old comedian trotted off to a hiding-place, surpassing by his last cowardice all his former villainies.

A sterile meeting this, spent in discussing the news of the day; no impulsion given, no system of defence propounded. The Federals were left to their own inspirations — left to look after themselves. During the whole past night neither Dombrowski, nor the War Office, nor the Hotel-de-Ville had thought of the battalions outside the town. Henceforth each corps had nothing to expect but from its own initiative, from the resources it might be able to create and the intelligence of its leaders.

In default of direction proclamations abounded. "Let good citizens rise! To the barricades! The enemy is within our walls. No hesitation. Forward, for the Commune and for liberty. To arms!"

"Let Paris bristle up with barricades, and from behind these improvised ramparts still hurl at her enemies her cry of war, of pride, of defiance, but also of victory; for Paris with her barricades cannot be wiped out."

Great words; nothing but words.

Mid-day — General Cissey had turned on the Ecole Militaire, and thereby forced its last defenders. The soldiers invaded the Esplanade des Invalides and entered the Rue Grenelle St. Germain, when the Ecole d'Etat-major exploded and put them to flight. Two of our cannon flanked the Rue de l'Université; four gunboats, anchored under the Pont-Royal, opened fire on the Trocadero. In the centre, in the eighth arrondissement, the Versaillese skirmished. At the Batignolles they did not advance, but their shells harassed the Rue Lévis. We also lost many men in the Rue Cardinet, where children were fighting furiously.

Malon and Jaclard, who directed this part of the defence, had since morning in vain applied to Montmartre for reinforcements; so towards one o'clock they themselves went in search of them. Not one of the staff-officers could give them the slightest information. The Federals were wandering about the streets or chatting in small groups. Malon wanted to take them back with him, but they refused, reserving themselves, they said, for the defence of their own quarter. The cannon of the Buttes were mute, being short of cartridges; the Hotel-de-Ville had sent only words.

Still there were two generals on the heights, Cluseret and La Cécilia, the ex-delegate melancholily airing his somnolent incapacity, while La Cécilia, unknown in this quarter, at once found himself powerless.

Two o'clock — The Hôtel-de-Ville had again assumed its grand aspect of March. On the right the Committee of Public Safety and on the left the War Office were overrun. The Central Committee was multiplying its orders and exclaiming against the incapacity of the members of the Council, though itself incapable of setting forth a single precise idea. The Committee of Artillery, more beset than ever, could not yet make out its cannon, did no know to whom to give them, and often refused pieces for the most important positions.

The delegates of the Congress of Lyons, conducted by Jules Amigues and Larroque, came to offer their intervention, but they had no mandate, and id not even know whether M. Thiers would admit them. They were received rather coldly. Besides, many at the Hotel-de-Ville believed in victory, and almost rejoiced at the entry of the Versaillese; for indeed Paris seemed to be rising.

The barricades increased quickly. That of the Rue de Rivoli, which was to protect the Hotel-de-Ville, was erected at the entrance of the St. Jacques Square, at the corner of the Rue St. Denis. Fifty workmen did the mason-work, while swarms of children brought wheelbarrows full of earth from the square. This work, several yards deep, six yards high, with trenches, embrasures and an outwork, as solid as the Florentin redoubt, which had taken weeks to raise, was finished in a few hours — an example this of what an intelligent effort at the right time might have done for the defence of Paris. In the ninth arrondissement, the Rues Auber, De la Chaussée d'Antin, De Châteaudun, the cross-roads of the Faubourg Montmartre, Notre Dame de Lorette, De la Trinité, and the Rue des Martyrs were being unpaved. The broad approaches, La Chapelle, Buttes Chaumont, Belleville, Méndmontant, the Rue de la Roquette, the Bastile, the Boulevards Voltaire and Richard Lenoir, the Place du Chateau d'Eau, the broad boulevards especially from the Porte St. Denis; and on the left bank the whole length of the Boulevard St. Michel, the Panthéon, the Rue St. Jacques, the Gobelins, and the principal avenues of the thirteenth arrondissement, were being barricaded. A great many of these works of defence were never finished.

While Paris was preparing for the last struggle, Versailles was wild with joy. The Assembly had met at an early hour, and M. Thiers would not leave to any of his Ministers the glory of announcing the first butcheries in Paris. His appearance on the tribune was hailed by ferocious cheers. "The cause of justice, order, humanity, and civilization has triumphed," screamed the little man. "The generals who have conducted the entry into Paris are great men of war. The expiation be complete. It will take place in the name of the law, by the law, with the law." The Chamber, understanding this promise of carnage, to a man, and by a unanimous vote, Right, Left, Centre, Clericals,

Republicans, Monarchists, swore that "the Versailles army and chief of the executive power had merited well of the country." sitting was at once raised, the deputies rushing off to the Lanterne Diogène, Châtillon, and Mont-Valérien, to all the heights whence they could, as from an immense Colosseum, observe the butchery of Paris without incurring the least danger. The population of idlers accompanied them, and on this Versailles road deputies, courtesans, women of the world, journalists, functionaries stung by the same craving, sometimes crammed into the same carriage, displayed before the Prussians and France the spectacle of a saturnalia of the bourgeoisie.

After eight o'clock the army ceased to advance, save in the eighth arrondissement, where the barricade before the English Embassy was turned by the gardens. Our line of the Faubourg St. Germain resisted from the Seine to the Mont-Parnasse station, which we were cannonading.

With nightfall the shooting slackened, but the shelling still went on. A red light glared in the Tuileries; the Ministry of Finance was burning. It had during the whole day received part of the Versaillese shells, destined for the terrace of the Tuileries, and the papers piled up in its upper storeys had taken fire. The firemen of the Commune had at first extinguished this conflagration, interfering with the defence of the St. Florentin redoubt, but it had soon lit up again, and become unquenchable.

Then began those nights of horror, where, amidst the roaring of the cannon, by the glimmer of burning houses, men sought each other in pools of blood. The Paris of the revolt had at length been roused. Her battalions descended towards the Hotel-de-Ville headed by bands and the red flag. Small in number, a battalion perhaps two hundred strong, but resolute, these Federals marched on in silence; there were seen also, muskets on their shoulders, those men, devoted to the Social Revolution, whom personal jealousy had kept at a distance. But in this hour none thought of such recriminations. Because of the incapacity of the chiefs ought the soldiers to desert their flag? The Paris of 1871 represented against Versailles the Social Revolution and the new destinies of the nation; one must be against or for her despite the faults committed. Cowards only abstained. All the true revolutionaries rose, even those who had no illusions as to the issue of the struggle, eager to defy death in the service of their immortal cause .

Ten o'clock — We proceeded to the Hotel-de-Ville. An irritated group of Federals had just arrested Dombrowski. The general, without any command since morning, had repaired with his officers to the outposts of St. Ouen, and believing his role terminated, wanted in the night to ride through the Prussian ranks and gain the frontier. A commander, who was afterwards shot as a traitor, had incited his men against the general under the pretext that he was betraying them. Led before the Committee of Public Safety, Dombrowski indignantly exclaimed, "They say I have betrayed!" The members of the Committee welcomed him affectionately, and the incident had no further consequences.

Messengers arrived at the War Office from all the points of the battle. A great number of guards and officers issued orders and despatches in the midst of a continual bustle. The inner courts were full of waggons and carriages, the horses all ready harnessed; munitions were being taken out or brought in, and not the least sign of discouragement, or even of anxiety, was visible, but everywhere an almost gay activity.

The streets and boulevards, with the exception of the invaded quarters, had been lighted as usual. At the entrance of the Faubourg Montmartre the light ceased abruptly, giving it the appearance of an enormous black hole. This obscurity was guarded by Federal sentinels, uttering every now and then their cry, "Passez au large!" Beyond this only a menacing silence. These shadows moving about in the night seemed to assume gigantic forms; one fancied oneself haunted by a sinister dream; the bravest were appalled.

There were nights more noisy, more glaring, more grandiose, when the conflagrations and the cannonade enveloped Paris, but none made a more lugubrious impression. A night of meditation this, the vigil of battle. We sought each other in the gloom, spoke softly, giving and taking comfort. At the cross-roads we consulted each other in order to examine our positions, and then to work! Now for the spade and the paving-stones! Let the earth be heaped up where the shells may flatten themselves against it; let the mattresses thrown from the windows shelter the combatants. Henceforth there is to be no more rest; let the stones cemented with hate press against each other like the shoulders of men arrayed for the battlefield. The enemy has taken us by surprise, defenceless. May he tomorrow encounter a Saragossa or a Moscow!

Every passer-by was requisitioned. "Come, citizen, lend a hand for the Republic!" At the Bastille and in the interior boulevards one met crowds of workers, some digging the earth, others carrying the paving-stones; children using spades and mattocks as big as themselves. The women encouraged the men; the delicate hand of the young girl raised the heavy pickaxe that fell with a sharp sound, emitting fiery sparks. It took an hour to seriously break through the soil. What matter! they will spend their night at it. On the Tuesday evening, at the intersection of the Square St. Jacques and the Boulevard Sebastopol, many *dames de la halle* [market women] worked for a long time, filling earth sacks and wicker baskets.

And these were no longer the traditional redoubts two storeys high. Save four or five in the Rue St. Honoré and the Rue de Rivoli, the barricades of May consisted of a few paving-stones hardly a man's height; behind these sometimes a cannon or a machine-gun; and in the midst, wedged in by two paving-stones, the red flag, the colour of vengeance. Behind these shreds of ramparts thirty men held regiments in check.

If this general effort had been directed by the least thought of combination, if Montmartre and the Panthéon had crossed their fires, the Versaillese army would have melted away in Paris; but the Federals, without directions, without military knowledge, saw no further than just their own quarter, or even their own streets; so that instead of 200 strategical, solid barricades, easy to defend with 7,000 or 8,000 men, hundreds were scattered about which it was impossible to arm sufficiently. The general mistake was a belief that they would be attacked from the front; while the Versaillese, thanks to their numbers, everywhere executed flank movements.

In the evening the Versaillese line extended from the station of the Batignolles to the extremity of the Railway of the West on the left bank, passing by the St. Lazare Station, the Pépiniere Barracks, the British Embassy, the Palais de L'Industrie, the Corps Législatif, the Rue de Bourgogne, the Boulevard des Invalides, and the Montparnasse Station. To face the invader there were but embryo barricades. If with one effort he were to break through this line still so weak, he would surprise the centre quite disarmed. But these 130,000 men did not dare to. Soldiers and chiefs were afraid of Paris. They fancied the streets would open, the houses fall upon them; as witness the fable of the torpedoes, of the mines under the sewers, invented later on to justify their indecision. On the Monday evening, masters of several arrondissements, they still trembled, fearful of some terrible surprise. They needed all the tranquillity of the night to recover from their conquest, and convince themselves that the Committee of Defence, despite their boasting, had neither foreseen nor prepared anything.

Chapter 28
The street battles continue

The defenders of the barricades slept on their paving-stones. The hostile outposts were on the watch. At the Batignolles the Versaillese reconnaissance carried off a sentinel. The Federal cried out with all his might, *"Vive la Commune!"* and his comrades, thus warned, were able to put themselves on their guard. He was shot there and then. In like manner fell D'Assas and Barra.

At two o'clock La Cécilia, accompanied by the members of the Council, Lefrançais, Vermorel and Johannard, and the journalists Alphonse Humbert and G. Maroteau, brought up a reinforcement of 100 men to the Batignolles. To Malon's reproaches for having left the quarter without succour the whole day, the General answered, "I am not obeyed."

Three o'clock — To the barricades! The Commune is not dead! The fresh morning air bathes the fatigued faces and revives hope. The enemy's cannonade along the whole line salutes the break of day. The artillery men of the Commune, from Mont-Parnasse to the Buttes Montmartre, which seem awaking, answered as well as they could.

Ladmirault, almost motionless the day before, now launched his men along the fortifications, taking all the gates from Neuilly to St. Ouen in the rear. On his right, Clinchant attacked by the same movement all the barricades of the Batignolles. The Rue Cardinet yielded first, then the Rues Noblet, Truffaut, La Condamine, and the lower Avenue of Clichy. Suddenly the gate of St. Ouen opened, and the Versaillese poured into Paris; it was the

Montaudon division, which since evening had been operating in the exterior. The Prussians had surrendered the neutral zone, and so, with the help of Bismarck, Clinchant and Ladmirault were able to take the Buttes by the two flanks.

Nearly surrounded in the *mairie* of the seventeenth arrondissement, Malon ordered the retreat on Montmartre, whither a detachment *of* twenty-five women, come to offer their services under the conduct *of* the citoyennes Dimitriev and Louise Michel, were also sent.

Clinchant, pursuing his route, was arrested by the barricade *of* the Place Clichy. To reduce these badly disposed paving-stones, behind which hardly fifty men were fighting, required the combined effort of the Versaillese of the Rue de St. Pétersbourg and the tirailleurs of the College Chaptal. The Federals, having no more shells, charged with stones and bitumen; their powder exhausted, they fell back upon the Rue des Carrières, and Ladmirault, master of the St. Ouen Avenue, turned on their barricade by the Montmartre Cemetery. About twenty guards refused to surrender, and were at once shot by the Versaillese.

In the rear, the Des Epinettes district still held out for a time; at last all resistance ceased, and about nine o'clock the entire Batignolles belonged to the army.

The Hôtel-de-Ville knew nothing yet of the progress of the troops when Vermorel rushed thither in search of munitions for Montmartre. As he was setting out at the head of the wagons he met Ferré, and, with the smile familiar to him, said, "Well, Ferré, the members of the minority fight." "The members of the majority will do their duty," answered Ferré. Generous emulation of these men, who were both devoted to the people, and who were to die so nobly.

Vermorel could not take his wagons as far as Montmartre, the Versaillese already surrounding the heights. Masters of the Batignolles, they had but to stretch out their hand to seize upon Montmartre. The Buttes seemed dead; during the night panic had hurried on its underhand work; the battalions, one after the other, had grown smaller, vanished. Individuals seen later on in the ranks of the army had stirred defections, spread false news, and every moment arrested civil and military chiefs, under the pretext that they were betraying. Only about a hundred men lined the north side of the hill; a few barricades had been commenced in the night, but without spirit; the women alone had shown any ardour.

Cluseret had, according to his usual habit, gone off in a huff. Despite his despatches and the promises of the Hôtel-de-Ville, La Cécilia had received neither reinforcements nor munitions. At nine o'clock, no longer hearing the cannon of the Buttes, he hurried up, and found the gunners gone. The runaways from the Batignolles arriving at ten o'clock only brought in panic. The Versaillese might have presented themselves; there were not 200 combatants there to receive them.

MacMahon, however, only dared attempt the assault with his best troops, so redoubtable was this position, so great the renown of Montmartre. Two entire army corps assailed it by the Rues Lepic, Mercadet, and the Chaussée Clignancourt. From time to time some shots were fired from a few houses; forthwith frightened columns came to a standstill and began regular sieges. These 20,000 men, who completely surrounded Montmartre, helped by the artillery established on the platform of the enceinte, took three hours to climb these positions, defended without method by a few dozen tirailleurs.

At eleven o'clock the cemetery was taken, and shortly afterwards the troops reached the Château-Rouge. In the environs there were some shootings, but the few obstinate men who still fought were soon killed, or withdrew discouraged at their isolation. The Versailles, scrambling up to the Buttes by all the slopes that lead to them, at midday installed themselves at the Moulin de la Galette, descended by the Place St. Pierre to the *mairie,* and occupied the whole of the eighteenth arrondissement without any resistance.

Thus without a battle, without an assault, without even a protestation of despair, was this impregnable fortress abandoned, from which a few hundred resolute men might have kept the whole Versaillese army in check, and constrained the Assembly to come to terms.

Hardly arrived at Montmartre, the Versaillese staff offered a holocaust to the fighters of Lecomte and Clément-Thomas. Forty-two men, three women, and four children were conducted to No. 6 in the Rue des Rosiers and forced to kneel bare-headed before the wall, at the foot of which the generals had been executed on the 18th March; then they were killed. A woman, who held her child in her arms, refused to kneel down, and cried to her companions, "Show these wretches that you know how to die upright."

On the following day these massacres continued. Each batch of prisoners halted some time before this wall, marked with bullets, and were then despatched on the slope of the Buttes that overlooks the St. Denis route.

The Batignolles and Montmartre witnessed the first wholesale massacres. Every individual wearing a uniform or regulation boots was shot, as a matter of course, without questions put, without explanations given. Thus the Versaillese had been assassinating since the morning in the Place des Batignolles, Place de L'Hôtel-de-Ville, and at the gate of Clichy. The Parc Monceaux was their principal slaughter-house in the seventeenth arrondissement. At Montmartre the centres of massacre were the Buttes, the Elysée, of which every step was strewn with corpses, and the exterior boulevards.

A few steps from Montmartre the catastrophe was not known. At the Place Blanche the women's barricade held out for several hours against Clinchant's soldiers; they then retreated towards the Pigalle barricade, which fell at about two o'clock. Its leader was led before a Versaillese chief of battalion. "Who are you?" asked the officer. "Léveque, mason, member of the Central Committee." The Versaillese discharged his revolver in his face; the soldiers finished him.

On the other bank of the Seine our resistance was more successful. The Versaillese had been able since morning to occupy the Babylone Barracks and L'Abbaye-au-Bois, but Varlin stopped them at the cross-roads of the Croix-Rouge. This cross-road will remain celebrated in the defence of Paris. All the streets that open into it had been powerfully barricaded, and this stronghold was only abandoned when fire and shells had reduced it to a heap of ruins. On the banks of the river, the Rues de l'Université, St. Dominique, St. Germain, and de Grenelle, the 67th, 135th, 138th, and 147th battalions, supported by the *enfants perdus* and *les tirailleurs,* resisted obstinately. In the Rue de Rennes and on the adjoining boulevards the Versaillese exhausted their strength. In the Rue Vavin, where Lisbonne conducted the defence, the resistance was prodigious; for two days this advanced sentinel kept back the invasion from the Luxembourg.

We were less secure on our extreme left. The Versaillese had early in the day surrounded the Mont-Parnasse Cemetery, which we held with a handful of men. Near the restaurant Richefeu, the Federals, allowing the enemy to approach, unmasked their machine-guns; but in vain, for the Versaillese were numerous enough to surround the few defenders of the cemetery on all sides, and soon stormed it. From there, passing by the ramparts of the fourteenth arrondissement, they arrived at the Place St. Pierre. The fortifications of the Avenue d'Italie and of the Route de Châtillon, long since carefully prepared, but still against the ramparts, were taken in the rear by the Chausée du Maine, and the whole defence of the cross-roads of the Quatre-Chemins was concentrated round the church. From the top of the steeple about a dozen Federals of Montrouge supported the barricade that barred two-thirds of the Chaussée du Maine, held by thirty men for several hours. At last, their cartridges exhausted, the tricolor flag was hoisted at the *mairie,* at the same hour that it floated above the Buttes Montmartre. Henceforth the route to the Place d'Enfer was open, and the Versaillese arrived there after having undergone the fire from the Observatoire, where some Federals had made a stand.

Behind these lines thus forced other defences were thrown up, thanks to the care of Wroblewski. The day before, the general, receiving the order to evacuate the forts, had answered, "Is it treachery or a misunderstanding? I will not evacuate." Montmartre taken, the general went to Delescluze, urging him to transfer the defence to the left bank. The Seine, the forts, the Panthéon, the Bievre, formed, in his opinion, a safe citadel, with the open fields for a retreat; a very just conception this with regular troops, but one cannot at will displace the heart of an insurrection, and the Federals were more and more bent on remaining in their own quarters.

Wroblewski returned to his headquarters, assembled the commanders of the forts, prescribed all the dispositions to be taken for their defence, and came back to resume the command of the left bank, given him by earlier decrees. But on sending orders to the Panthéon, he was answered that Lisbonne commanded there. Wroblewski, undeterred, placed the section left to him in a state of defence. He installed a battery of eight pieces and two batteries of four on the Butte-aux-Cailles, a dominant position between the Panthéon and the forts; he fortified the Boulevards d'Italie, de l'Hôpital, and de la Gare. His headquarters were established at the Mairie des Gobelins, and his reserve at the Place d'Italie, Place Jeanne d'Arc, and at Bercy.

At the other extremities of Paris the fourteenth and twentieth arrondissements also prepared their defence. The brave Passedouet had replaced Du Bisson, who still dared to present himself as *chef-de-legion* of La Villette. They barricaded the Grande Rue de la Chapelle behind the Strasbourg Railway, the Rues d'Aubervilliers, de Flandre, and the canal, so as to form five lines of defence, protected on the flank by the boulevards and the fortifications. Cannon were placed in the Rue Riquet at the gasworks, while rampart pieces were carried by the men on to the Buttes Chaumont and others to the Rue de Puebla. A battery of six was mounted on the height of the Père la Chaise, covering Paris with its rumbling reports.

A mute and desolate Paris. As on the day before, the shops remained closed, and the streets, bleached by the sun, looked empty and menacing. Despatch riders riding at full speed, pieces of artillery shifted from their places, combatants on the march, alone broke this solitude. Cries of "Open the shutters!" "Draw up the blinds!" alone interrupted this silence. Two journals, *Le Tribun du Peuple* and *Le Salut Public*, were published, notwithstanding the Versaillese shells that were falling into the printing-office of the Rue Aboukir.

A few men at the Hôtel-de-Ville did their best to attend to details. One decree authorized the chiefs of barricades to requisition the necessary implements and victuals; another condemned every house from which Federals were shot at to be burned. In the afternoon the Committee of Public Safety issued an appeal to the soldiers:

"The people of Paris will never believe that you could raise your arms against them. When they face you your hands will recoil from an act that would be a veritable fratricide. Like us, you too are proletarians. That which you did not the 18th March you will do again. Come to us, brothers, come to us; ours are open to receive you."

The Central Committee at the same time posted up a similar appeal — a puerile but generous illusion — and on this point the people of Paris entirely agreed with their representatives. In spite of the frenzy of the Assembly, the fusillade of the wounded, the treatment inflicted upon the prisoners for six weeks, the working men did not admit that children of the people could rend the entrails of that Paris who combated for them.

At three o'clock M. Bonvalet and other members of the *Ligue des Droits de Paris* presented themselves at the Hôtel-de-Ville, where some members of the

Council and of the Committee of Public Safety received them. They bewailed this struggle, proposed to interfere, as they had so successfully done during the siege, and to carry to M. Thiers the expression of their sorrow; further, they placed themselves at the disposition of the Hôtel-de-Ville. "Well, then," they were answered, "shoulder a gun and go to the barricades!" Before this direct appeal the League fell back upon the Central Committee, which had the weakness to listen to them.

There was no question of negotiating in the midst of the battle. The Versaillese, following up their success at Montmartre, were at this moment pushing towards the Boulevard Ornano and the Northern Railway station. At two o'clock the barricades of the Chaussée Clignancourt were abandoned, and in the Rue Myrrha, by the side of Vermorel, Dombrowski fell mortally wounded. In the morning Delescluze had told him to try his best in the neighbourhood of Montmartre; and, without hope, without soldiers, suspected since the entry of the Versaillese, all Dombrowski could do was to die. He expired two hours afterwards at the Lariboisière Hospital. His body was taken to the Hôtel-de-Ville, the men of the barricades presenting arms as he was carried by. His glorious death had disarmed suspicion.

Clinchant, thenceforth free on his left, proceeded to the ninth arrondissement. A column marched down the Rues Fontaine, St. Georges, and Notre Dame de Lorette, and made a halt at the crossroads; while another cannonaded the Rollin College before penetrating into the Rue Trudaine, where it was held in check until the evening.

More in the centre, at the Boulevard Haussmann, Douai pressed close upon the barricade of the Printemps shop, and with gunshots dislodged the Federals who occupied the Trinité Church. Five pieces established under the porch of the church were then directed at the very important barricade that barred the Chaussée d'Antin at the entrance of the boulevard. A detachment penetrated into the Rues Châteaudun and Lafayette, but at the cross-roads of the Faubourg Montmartre a barricade, a yard high at the utmost, defended by twenty-five men, held them up until night.

Douai's right was still powerless against the Rue Royale. There for two days Brunel sustained a struggle only equalled by that of the Butte-aux-Cailles, of the Bastille, and the Château d'Eau. His main barricade, transversely crossing the street, was overlooked by the neighbouring houses, from which the Versaillese decimated the Federals; and Brunel, impressed with the importance of the post confided to him, ordered these murderous houses to be burned down. A Federal obeying him was struck by a ball in the eye, and came back dying to Brunel's side, saying, "I am paying with my life for the order you have given me. *Vive la Commune!*" All the houses between 13 and the Faubourg St. Honoré were caught in the flames, and the Versaillese, appalled, ran away, some passing over to the Federals. One of them put on the Parisian uniform and became Brunel's orderly.

On the right the Boulevard Malesherbes, on the left the terrace of the Tuileries, which Bergeret occupied since the day before, seconded Brunel's efforts. The Boulevard Malesherbes, furrowed by shells, was like a field ploughed up by gigantic shares. The fire of eighty pieces of artillery at the Quai d'Orsay, Passy, the Champ-de-Mars, the Barrière de l'Etoile converged on the terrace of the Tuileries and the barricade St. Florentin. About a dozen Federal pieces bore up against this shower. The Place de la Concorde, taken between these crossfires, was strewn with fragments of fountains and lamp-posts. The statue of Lille was beheaded, that of Strasbourg pitted by the grapeshot.

On the left bank the Versaillese made their way from house to house. The inhabitants of the quarter lent their assistance, and from behind their closed blinds fired on the Federals, who, indignant, forced and set fire to the treacherous houses. The Versaillese shells had already begun the conflagration, and the rest of the quarter was soon in flames. The troops continued to gain ground, occupied the Ministry of War, the telegraph office, and reached the Bellechasse Barracks and the Rue de l'Université. The barricades of the quay and the Rue du Bac were battered down by the shells; the Federal battalions, which for two days had held out at the Légion d'Honneur, had no longer any retreat but the quays. At five o'clock they evacuated this unclean place after having set it on fire.

At six o'clock the barricade of the Chaussée d'Antin was lost to us; the enemy advancing by the side streets had occupied the Nouvel Opéra, entirely dismantled, and from the top of the roofs the marines commanded the barricade. Instead of imitating them, of also occupying the houses, the Federals, there as everywhere else, obstinately kept behind the barricade.

At eight o'clock the barricade of the Rue Neuve des Capucines, at the entrance of the Boulevard, gave way under the fire of the pieces of 4 cm. established in the Rue Caumartin. The Versaillese approached the Place Vendôme.

At all points the army had made decided progress. The Versaillese line, starting from the Northern Railway station, following the Rues Rochechouart, Cadet, Drouot, whose *mairie* was taken, the Boulevard des Italiens, stretched to the Place Vendôme and the Place de la Concorde, passed along the Rue du Bac, the Abbaye-au-Bois, and the Boulevard d'Enfer, ending at Bastion 8 1. The Place de la Concorde and the Rue Royale, surrounded on their flanks, stood out like a promontory in the midst of a tempest. Ladmirault faced La Villette; on his right Clinchant occupied the ninth arrondissement; Douai presented himself at the Place Vendôme; Vinoy supported Cissy operating on the left bank. At this hour hardly one-half of Paris was still held by the Federals.

The rest was given over to massacre. They were still fighting at one end of a street when the conquered part was already being sacked. Woe to him who possessed arms or a uniform! Woe to him who betrayed dismay! Woe to him who was denounced by a political or personal enemy! He was dragged away. Each corps had its regular executioner, the provost; but to speed the business there were supplementary provosts in the streets. The victims were led there — shot. The blind fury of the soldiers encouraged by the men of order served their hatred and liquidated their debts. Theft followed massacre. The shops of the tradesmen who had supplied the Commune, or whom their rival shopkeepers accused, were given over to pillage; the soldiers smashed their furniture and carried off the objects of value; jewels, wine, liqueurs, provisions, linen, perfumery, disappeared into their knapsacks.

When M. Thiers was apprised of the fall of Montmartre, he believed the battle over, and telegraphed to the prefects. For six weeks he had not ceased to announce that, the ramparts taken, the insurgents would flee; but Paris, contrary to the habits of the men of Sedan and Metz and of the National Defence, contested street by street, house by house, and rather than surrender, burned them.

A blinding glare arose at nightfall. The Tuileries were burning, so also the Légion d'Honneur, the Conseil d'Etat, and the Cour des Comptes. Formidable detonations were heard from the palace of the kings, whose walls were failing, its vast cupolas giving way. Flames, now slow, now rapid as darts, flashed from a hundred windows; the red tide of the Seine reflected the monuments, thus redoubling the conflagration. Fanned by an eastern wind, the blazing flames rose up against Versailles, and cried to the conqueror of Paris that he will no longer find his place there, and that these monarchical monuments will not again shelter a monarchy. The Rue du Bac, the Rue du Lille, the Croix-Rouge, dashed luminous columns into the air; the Rue Royale to St. Sulpice seemed a wall of fire divided by the Seine. Eddies of smoke clouded all the west of Paris, and the spiral flames shooting forth from these furnaces emitted showers of sparks that fell upon the neighbouring quarters.

Eleven o'clock — We go to the Hôtel-de-Ville. Sentinels on far advanced posts made it secure against any surprise; at long intervals a gaslight flickered in the obscurity; at several barricades there were torches, and even bivouac fires. That of the St. Jacques Square, opposite the Boulevard Sebastopol, made of large trees, whose branches swung to and fro in the wind, muttered and fluttered in the redoubtable gloom.

The façade of the Hôtel-de-Ville was reddened by distant flames; the statues, which the reflection seemed to move, stirred in their niches. The interior courts were filled with crowds and tumult. Artillery ammunition wagons, carts, omnibuses crammed with munitions, rolled off with a great noise under the vaults. The fetes of Baron Haussmann awoke no such sonorous echoes. Life and death, agony and laughter, jostled each other on these staircases, on every storey illumined by the same dazzling light of the gas.

The lower lobbies were encumbered by National Guards rolled up in their blankets. The wounded lay groaning on their reddened mattresses; blood was trickling from the litters placed along the walls. A commander was brought in who no longer presented a human aspect; a ball had passed through his cheek, carried away the lips, broken the teeth. Incapable of articulating a sound, this brave fellow still waved a red flag, and summoned those who were resting to replace him in the combat.

In the notorious chamber of Valentine Haussmann the corpse of Dombrowski was laid out upon a bed of blue satin. A single taper threw its lurid light on the heroic soldier. His face, white as snow, was calm, the nose fine, the mouth delicate, the small fair beard standing out pointed. Two aides-de-camp seated in the darkened corners watched silently, another hurriedly sketched the last traits of his general.

The double marble staircase was filled with people coming and going, whom the sentinels could hardly keep away from the delegate's office. Delescluze signed orders, mute and wan as a spectre. The anguish of those later days had absorbed his last vital powers; his voice was only a death-rattle; the eye and the heart alone lived still in this moribund athlete.

Two or three officers calmly prepared the orders, stamped and sent the despatches; many officers and guards surrounded the table. No speeches, a little conversation, among the various groups. If hope had waned, resolution had not grown less.

Who are these officers who have laid aside their uniforms, these members of the Council, these functionaries who have shaved their beards? What are they doing here amongst these brave men? Ranvier, meeting two of his colleagues thus disguised, who during the siege had been among the most beplumed, harangued them, threatening to shoot them if they did not at once return to their arrondissements.

A great example would not have been useless. From hour to hour all discipline foundered. At that same moment the Central Committee, which believed itself invested with power by the abdication of the Council, launched a manifesto, in which it made conditions: "Dissolution of the Assembly and of the Commune; the army to leave Paris; the Government to be provisionally confided to the delegates of the large towns, who will have a Constituent Assembly elected; mutual amnesty." The ultimatum of a conqueror. This dream was posted up on a few walls, and threw new disorder into the resistance.

From time to time some greater clamour arose from the square. A spy was shot against the barricade of the Victoria Avenue. Some were audacious enough to penetrate into the most intimate councils. That evening, at the Hôtel-de-Ville, Bergeret had received the verbal authorization to fire the Tuileries, when an individual pretending to be sent by him asked for this order in writing. He was still speaking when Bergeret returned. "Who sent you?" said he to the personage. "Bergeret." "When did you see him?" "Just here, a moment ago."

During this evening, Raoul Rigault, taking orders from himself only, and without consulting any of his colleagues, repaired to the prison of Sainte Pélagie, and signified to Chaudey that he was to die. Chaudey protested, said he was a Republican, and swore that he had not given the order to fire on the 22nd January. However, he had been at that time the only authority in the Hôtel-de-Ville. His protestations were of no avail against Rigault's resolution. Led into the exercise ground of Sainte Pélagie, Chaudey was shot, as were also three gendarmes taken prisoner on the 18th March. During the first seige he had said to some partisans of the Commune, "The strongest will shoot the others." He died perhaps for those words.

Chapter 29
On the barricades

Our valiant soldiers conduct themselves in such a manner as to inspire foreign countries with the highest esteem and admiration. (Thiers' speech to the National Assembly, 24th May, 1871.)

The defenders of the barricades, already without reinforcements and munitions, were now left even without food, and altogether thrown on the resources of the neighbourhood. Many, quite worn out, went in search of some nourishment; their comrades, not seeing them return, grew desperate, while the leaders of the barricades strained themselves to keep them back.

At nine o'clock Brunel received the order to evacuate the Rue Royale. He went to the Tuileries to tell Bergeret that he could still hold out, but at midnight the Committee of Public Safety again sent him a formal order to retreat. Forced to abandon the post he had so well defended for two days, the brave commander first removed his wounded and then his cannon by the Rue St. Florentin. The Federals followed; when at the top of the Rue Castiglione, they were assailed by shots.

It was the Versaillese, who, masters of the Rue de la Paix and the Rue Neuve des Capucines, had invaded the Place Vendôme, entirely deserted, and by the Hôtel-du-Rhin turned the barricade of the Rue Castiglione. Brunel's Federals, abandoning the Rue de Rivoli, forced the rails of the garden, went up the quays, and regained the Hôtel-de-Ville. The enemy did not dare to pursue them, and only at daybreak occupied the Ministry of Marine, long since abandoned.

The rest of the night the cannon were silent. The Hôtel-de-Ville had lost its animation. The Federals slept in the square; in the offices the members of the committees and the officers snatched a few moments of repose. At three o'clock a staff officer arrived from Notre Dame, occupied by a detachment of Federals. He came to tell the Committee of Public Safety that the Hôtel-Dieu harboured eight hundred sick, who might suffer from the proximity of the struggle, and the Committee commanded the evacuation of the cathedral in order to save these unfortunate people.

And now the sun rose, eclipsing the glare of the conflagrations; the day dawned radiant, but with no ray of hope for the Commune. Paris had no longer a right wing; her centre was broken; to assume the offensive was impossible. The prolongation of her resistance could now only serve to bear witness to her faith.

Early in the morning the Versaillese moved on all points. They pushed towards the Louvre, the Palais-Royal, the Bank, the Comptoir d'Escompte, the Montholon Square, the Boulevard Ornano, and the line of the Northern Railway. From four o'clock they cannonaded the Palais-Royal, round which desperate battles were being fought. By seven o'clock they were at the Bank and at the Bourse; thence they descended to St. Eustache, where they met an obstinate resistance. Many children fought with the men; and when the Federals were outflanked and massacred, these children had the honour not to be excepted.

On the left bank the troops with difficulty marched up the quays and all that part of the sixth arrondissement bordering upon the Seine. In the centre, the barricade of the Croix-Rouge had been evacuated during the night, like that of the Rue de Rennes, which thirty men had held for two days. The Versaillese were then able to enter the Rues d'Assas and Notre-dame-des-Champs. On the extreme right they reached the Val de Grace, and advanced against the Panthéon.

At eight o'clock about fifteen members of the Council assembled at the Hôtel-de-Ville and decided to evacuate it. Two only protested. The third arrondissement, intersected by narrow and well-barricaded streets, sheltered the flank of the Hôtel-de-Ville, which defied every attack from the front and by the quays. Under such conditions of defence to fall back was to fly, to strip the Commune of the little prestige still remaining to it; but no more than the days before were they able to collect two sound ideas. They feared everything, because ignorant of everything. Already the commander of the Palais Royal had received the order to evacuate that edifice, after having set it on fire. He had protested, and declared he could still hold out, but the order was repeated. Such was the state of bewilderment, that a member proposed a retreat on Belleville. They might as well abandon the Château d'Eau and the Bastille at once. As usual, the time was spent in small-talk. The governor of the Hôtel-de-Ville went backwards and forwards impatient.

Suddenly the flames burst forth from the summit of the belfry; an hour after the Hôtel-de-Ville was but one glow. The old edifice, witness of so many perjuries, where the people have so often installed powers that have afterwards shot them down, now cracked and fell with its true master. With the noise of the crumbling pavilions, of the toppling vaults and chimneys, of the dull detonations and the loud explosions, mingled the sharp reports of the cannon from the large St. Jacques barricade, that swept the Rue de Rivoli.

The War Office and all the services moved off to the *mairie* of the eleventh arrondissement. Delescluze had protested against the desertion of the Hôtel-de-Ville, and predicted that this retreat would discourage many combatants.

The next day they left the Imprimerie Nationale, where the *Officiel* of the Commune appeared on the 24th for the last time. Like an *Officiel* that respects itself, it was a day behind time; it contained the proclamations of the day before and a few details of the battle, but not beyond the Tuesday morning.

This flight from the Hôtel-de-Ville, cutting the defence in two, increased the difficulty of the communications. The staff officers who had not disappeared reached the new headquarters with great trouble; they were stopped at every barricade and constrained to carry paving-stones. On producing their despatches pleading urgency, they were answered, "Today there are no more epaulettes." The anger they had inspired for a long time broke out this very morning. In the Rue Sedaine, near the Place Voltaire, a young officer of the general staff, the Count de Beaufort, was recognized by the guards of the 166th battalion, whom he had threatened some days before at the War Office. Arrested for having tried to violate the orders of the post, Beaufort, losing his temper, had flung out a menace to purge the battalion. Now, the day before, near the Madeleine, the battalion had lost sixty men, and believed in a revenge on the part of Beaufort. This officer was arrested and conducted before a court-martial, which installed itself in a shop of the Boulevard Voltaire. Beaufort produced such certificates that the accusation was abandoned. Nevertheless, the judges decided that he was to serve in the battalion as a simple guard. Some of those present objected and named him captain. He came out triumphant. The crowd, ignorant of his explanation, grumbled on seeing him free. A guard rushed at him, and Beaufort was imprudent enough to draw out his revolver. He was immediately seized and thrown back into the shop. The chief of the general staff did not dare to come to the rescue of his officer. Delescluze hurried up, asked for a respite, said that Beaufort should be judged; but the crowd would not hear of it, and it was necessary to yield in order to prevent a terrible affray. Beaufort was conducted to the open space situated behind the *mairie* and shot.

Close by this outburst of fury at the Père la Chaise, Dombrowski was receiving the last honours. His corpse had been transported thither in the night, and during the passage to the Bastille a touching scene had taken place. The Federals of these barricades had stopped the cortege and placed the corpse at the foot of the July column; some men, torches in their hands, formed into a circle, and all the Federals, one after the other, came to place a last kiss on the brow of the general, while the drums beat a salute. The body, enveloped in a red flag, was then put into the coffin. Vermorel, the general's brother, his aides-de-camp, and about 200 guards were standing up bareheaded. "There is he," cried Vermorel, "who was accused of treachery! One of the first, he has given his life for the Commune. And we, what are we doing here instead of imitating him?" He went on stigmatizing cowardice and panics. His speech, usually intricate, now flowed from him, heated by passion, like molten metal. "Let us swear to leave here only to seek death!" This was his last word; he was to keep it. The cannon a few steps off had at intervals covered his voice; few of the men present but shed tears.

Happy those who may have such funerals! Happy those buried during the battle saluted by their cannon, wept over by their friends.

At that same moment the Versaillese agent who had flattered himself he could corrupt Dombrowski was being shot. Towards mid-day the Versaillese, vigorously pushing their attack on the left bank had stormed the Ecole des Beaux-Arts, the Institute, the Mint, which its director, Camélinat, left only at the last minute. On the point of being shut up in the Ile Notre Dame, Ferré had given the order to evacuate the Prefecture of Police and to destroy it. The 450 prisoners arrested for slight offences were, however, first set at liberty; one only, Vaysset, was retained and shot on the Pont-Neuf before the statue of Henry IV. Just before his death he uttered these strange words, "You will answer for my death to the Comte de Fabrice."

The Versaillese, neglecting the Prefecture, entered the Rue Tarranes and the contiguous streets. They were held in check for two hours at the barricade of the Place de l'Abbaye, which the inhabitants of the quarter helped to outflank. Eighteen Federals were shot. More to the right the troops penetrated into the Place St. Sulpice, where they occupied the *mairie* of the sixth arrondissement; thence they entered the Rue St. Sulpice on one side, and on the other penetrated by the Rue de Vaugirard into the garden of the Luxembourg. After two days of struggle the brave Federals of the Rue Vavin fell back, and on their retreat blew up the powder-magazine of the Luxembourg garden. The commotion for a moment suspended the combat. The Palace of Luxembourg was not defended. Some soldiers crossed the garden, broke down the rails facing the Rue Soufflot, traversed the boulevard, and surprised the first barricade in that street.

Three barricades were raised before the Panthéon; the first at the entrance of the Rue Soufflot — it had just been taken; the second in the centre; the third extending from the *mairie* of the fifth arrondissement to the Ecole de Droit. Varlin and Lisbonne, hardly escaped from the Croix-Rouge, had hastened up again to face the enemy. Unfortunately the Federals would listen to no chief, remained on the defensive, and, instead of attacking the handful of soldiers exposed at the entrance of the Rue Soufflot, gave the reinforcements time to arrive.

The bulk of the Versaillese reached the Boulevard St. Michel by the Rues Racine and De l'Ecole de Médecine, which women had defended. The St. Michel Bridge ceased firing for want of ammunition, so that the soldiers were able to pass over the boulevard in a body, and got as far as the Place Maubert, while at the same time on the right they remounted the Rue Mouffetard. At four o'clock the height of Sainte Genevieve, well-nigh abandoned, was invaded by all its slopes and its few defenders dispersed. Thus the Panthéon, like Montmartre, fell almost without a struggle. As at Montmartre, too, the massacres commenced immediately. Forty prisoners were shot one after the other in the Rue St. Jacques, under the eyes of and by the orders of a colonel.

Rigault was killed in this neighbourhood. The soldiers, seeing a Federal officer knocking at the door of a house in the Rue Gay-Lussac, fired without hitting him. The door opened and Rigault went in. The soldiers followed at full speed, rushed into the house, seized the landlord, who proved his identity, and hastened to deliver up Rigault. The soldiers were dragging him to the Luxembourg, when, in the Rue Royal-Collard, a Versaillese staff colonel met the escort, and asked the name of the prisoner. Rigault bravely answered, "*Vive la Commune!* Down with assassins!" He was immediately thrown against a wall and shot. May this courageous end be counted to him!

When the fall of the Panthéon, so valiantly defended in June, 1848, became known in the *mairie* of the eleventh arrondissement, they at once cried out against traitors; but what then had the Council and the Committee of Public Safety done for the defence of this capital post? At the *mairie,* as at the Hôtel-de-Ville, they were deliberating.

At two o'clock the members of the Council, of the Central Committee, superior officers, and the chiefs of the services were assembled in the library. Delescluze spoke first, amidst a profound silence, for the least whisper would have covered his dying voice. He said all was not lost; that they must make a great effort, and hold out to the last. Cheers interrupted him. He called upon each one to state his opinion. "I propose," said he, "that the members of the Commune, engirded with their scarfs, shall make a review of all the battalions that can be assembled on the Boulevard Voltaire. We shall then at their head proceed to the points to be conquered."

The idea appeared grand, and transported those present. Never since the sitting when he had said that certain delegates of the people would know how to die at their post, had Delescluze so profoundly moved all hearts. The distant firing, the cannon of the Père la Chaise, the confused clamours of the battalions surrounding the *mairie,* blended with, and at times drowned his voice. Behold, in the midst of this defeat, this old man upright, his eyes luminous, his right hand raised defying despair, these armed men fresh from the battle suspending their breath to listen to this voice which seemed to ascend from the tomb. There was no scene more solemn in the thousand tragedies of that day.

There was a superabundance of most vigorous resolutions. Open on the table lay a large case of dynamite; an imprudent gesture might explode the *mairie*. They spoke of cutting off the bridges, of upheaving the sewers. What was the use of this tall talking? Very different munitions were needed now. Where is the engineer-in-chief who had said that at his bidding an abyss would open and swallow up the enemy? He is gone. Gone too the chief of the general staff. Since the execution of Beaufort, he has felt an ill wind blowing for his epaulettes. More motions were made, and motions will still be made to the end. The Central Committee condescended to declare that it would subordinate itself to the Committee of Public Safety. It seemed settled at last that the chief of the 11th legion was to group all the Federals who had taken refuge in the eleventh arrondissement; perhaps he might succeed in forming the columns of which Delescluze had spoken.

The Delegate for War then visited the defences. Solid preparations were being made at the Bastille. In the Rue St. Antoine, at the entrance of the square, a barricade provided with three pieces of artillery was being finished; another at the entrance of the faubourg covered the Rues de Charenton and de la Rouquette; but here, as everywhere else, the flanks were not guarded. Cartridges and shells were piled up along the houses, exposed to all projectiles. The approaches to the eleventh arrondissement were hastily armed, and at the intersection of the Boulevards Voltaire and Richard-Lenoir a barricade was being thrown up with casks, paving stones, and large bales of paper. This work, inaccessible from the front, was also to be turned. Before it, at the entrance of the Boulevards Voltaire, Place du Château d'Eau, a wall of paving-stones two yards high was raised. Behind this mortal rampart, assisted by two pieces of cannon, the Federals for twenty-four hours stopped all the Versaillese columns setting foot on the Place du Château d'Eau. On the right, the bottom of the Rues Oberkampf, d'Angouleme and du Faubourg du Temple, the Rue Fontaine-au-Roi, and the Avenue des Amandiers were already on the defensive. Higher up, in the tenth arrondissement, Brunel, arrived that same morning from the Rue Royale, was again to the fore, like Lisbonne, like Varlin, eager for new perils. A large barricade cut off the intersection of the Boulevards Magenta and Strasbourg; the Rue du Château d'Eau was barred, and the works of the Porte St. Martin and St. Denis, at which they had worked day and night, were filling with combatants.

Towards ten o'clock the Versaillese had been able to gain possession of the Northern Railway station by turning the Rue Stephenson and the barricades of the Rue de Dunkerque; but the Strasbourg Railway, the second line of defence of La Villette, withstood their shock, and our artillery harassed them greatly. On the Buttes Chaumont, Ranvier, who directed the defence of these quarters, had established three howitzers of 12cm., two pieces of 7 near the Temple de la Sybille, and two pieces of 7 on the lower hill, while five cannon flanked the Rue Puebla and protected the Rotonde. At the Carrières d'Amérique there were two batteries of three pieces; the pieces of the Père la Chaise fired incessantly at the invaded quarters, seconded by cannon of large calibre at bastion 24.

The ninth arrondissement filled with the sound of firing. We lost much ground in the Faubourg Poissinnière. Despite their success in the Halles, the Versaillese were not able to get into the third arrondissement, sheltered by the long arm of the Boulevard Sebastopol, and we commanded the Rue Turbigo by the Prince Eugène Barracks. The second arrondissement, almost totally occupied, still held out on the banks of the Seine; from the Pont-Neuf the barricades of the Avenue Victoria and Quai de Gevres resisted till night. Our gunboats having been abandoned, the enemy seized and re-armed them.

The only success of our defence was at the Butte aux Cailles, where, under the impulsion of Wroblewski, it changed into the offensive. During the night the Versaillese had examined our positions, and at daybreak they mounted to the assault. The Federals did not wait for them, and rushed forward to meet them. Four times the Versaillese were repulsed, four times they returned; four times they retreated, and the soldiers, discouraged, no longer obeyed their officers.

Thus La Villette and the Butte aux Cailles, the two extremities of our defence, kept their ground; but what gaps all along the line! Of Paris, all theirs on Sunday, the Federals now only possessed the eleventh, twelfth, nineteenth, and twentieth arrondissements, and a part only of the third, fifth, and thirteenth.

On that day the massacres took that furious flight which in a few hours left St. Bartholomew's Day far behind. Till then only the Federals or the people denounced had been killed; now the soldiers knew neither friend nor foe. When the Versaillese fixed his eye upon you, you must die; when he searched a house, nothing escaped him. "These are no longer soldiers accomplishing a duty," said a conservative journal, *La France*. And indeed these were hyenas, thirsting for blood and pillage. In some places it sufficed to have a watch to be shot. The corpses were searched, and the correspondents of foreign newspapers called those thefts the last perquisition. And the same day M. Thiers had the effrontery to tell the Assembly: "Our valiant soldiers conduct themselves in such a manner as to inspire foreign countries with the highest esteem and admiration."

Then, too, was invented that legend of the petroleuses, which, born of fear and propagated by the press, cost hundreds of unfortunate women their lives. The rumour was spread that furies were throwing burning petroleum into the cellars. Every woman who was badly dressed, or carrying a milk-can, a pail, an empty bottle, was pointed out as a petroleuse, her clothes torn to tatters, she was pushed against the nearest wall, and killed with revolver-shots. The monstrously idiotic side of the legend is that the petroleuses were supposed to operate in the quarters occupied by the army.

The fugitives from the invaded quarters brought the news of these massacres to the *mairie* of the eleventh arrondissement. There, within smaller compass and more menacing, reigned the same confusion as at the Hôtel-de-Ville. The narrow courts were full of wagons, cartridges, and powder; every step of the principal staircase was occupied by women sewing sacks for the barricades. In the Salle des Mariages, whither Ferré had removed the office of Public Safety, the delegate, assisted by two secretaries, gave orders, signed free passes, questioned the people brought to him with the greatest calm, and pronounced his decisions in a polite, soft, and low voice. Farther on, in the rooms occupied by the War Office, some officers and chiefs of services received and expedited despatches; some of them, as at the Hôtel-de-Ville, doing their duty with perfect sangfroid. At this hour certain men revealed extraordinary strength of character, especially among the secondary actors of the movement. They felt that all was lost, that they were about to die, perhaps even at the hands of their own people, for the fever of suspicion had reached its utmost degree of paroxysm; yet they remained in the furnace, their hearts calm, their minds lucid. Never had a Government, with the exception of that of the National Defence, more resources, more intelligence, more heroism at its disposal than the Council of the Commune; never was there one so inferior to its electors.

At half-past seven a great noise was heard before the prison of La Roquette, where the day before the three hundred hostages, detained until then at Mazas, had been transported. Amidst a crowd of guards, exasperated at the massacres, stood a delegate of the Public Safety Commission, who said, "Since they shoot our men, six hostages shall be executed. Who will form the platoon?" "I! I!" was cried from all sides. One advanced and said, "I avenge my father," another, "I avenge my brother." "As for me," said a guard, "they have shot my wife." Each one brought forward his right to vengeance. Thirty men were chosen and entered the prison.

The delegate looked over the jail register, pointed out the Archbishop Darboy, the President Bonjean, the banker Jecker, the Jesuits Allard, Clerc, and Ducoudray; at the last moment Jecker was replaced by the Curé Deguerry.

They were taken to the exercise-ground. Darboy stammered out, "I am not the enemy of the Commune. I have done all I could. I have written twice to Versailles." He recovered a little when he saw death was inevitable. Bonjean could not keep on his legs. "Who condemns us?" said he. "The justice of the people." "Oh, this is not the right one," replied the president. One of the priests threw himself against the sentry-box and uncovered his breast. They were led further on, and, turning a corner, met the firing-party. Some men harangued them; the delegate at once ordered silence. The hostages placed themselves against the wall, and the officer of the platoon said to them, "It is not we whom you must accuse of your death, but the Versaillese, who are shooting the prisoners." He then gave the signal and the guns were fired. The hostages fell back in one line, at an equal distance from each other. Darboy alone remained standing, wounded in the head, one hand raised. A second volley laid him by the side of the others.

The blind justice of revolutions punishes in the first-comers the accumulated crimes of their caste.

At eight o'clock the Versaillese closed in upon the barricade of the Porte St. Martin. Their shells had long since set the theatre on fire, and the Federals, pressed by this conflagration, were obliged to fall back.

That night the Versaillese bivouacked in front of the Strasbourg Railway, the Rue St. Denis, the Hôtel-de-Ville (occupied towards nine o'clock by Vinoy's troops), the Ecole Polytechnique, the Madelonnettes, and the Monsouris Park. They presented a kind of fan, of which the fixed point was formed by the Pont-au-Change, the right side by the thirteenth arrondissement, the left by the streets of the Fauborg St. Martin and the Rue de Flandre, the arc by the fortifications. The fan was about to close at Belleville, which formed the centre.

Paris continued to burn furiously. The Porte St. Martin, the St. Eustache Church, the Rue Royale, the Rue de Rivoli, the Tuileries, the Palais-Royale, the Hôtel-de-Ville, the Theatre-Lyrique, the left bank from the Légion d'Honneur up to the Palais de Justice and the Prefecture de Police, stood out bright red in the darkness of night. The caprices of the fire displayed a blazing architecture of arches, cupolas, spectral edifices. Great volumes of smoke, clouds of sparks flying into the air, attested formidable explosions; every minute stars lit up and died out again in the horizon. These were the cannon of the fort of Bicêtre, of the Père la Chaise, and the Buttes Chaumont, which fired on the invaded quarters. The Versaillese batteries answered from the Panthéon, the Trocadéro, and Montmartre. Now the reports followed each other at regular intervals; now there was a continuous thunder along the whole line. They aimed at random, blindly, madly. The shells often exploded in the midst of their career; the whole town was enveloped in a whirl of flame and smoke.

What men this handful of combatants, who, without leaders, without hope, without retreat, disputed their last pavements as though they implied victory! The hypocritical reaction has charged them with the crime of incendiarism, as if in war fire were not a legitimate arm; as if the Versaillese shells had not set fire to at least as many edifices as those of the Federals; as if the private speculation of certain men of order had not its share in the ruins. And that same bourgeois who spoke of "burning everything before the Prussians, calls this people scoundrels because they preferred to bury themselves in the ruins rather than abandon their faith, their property, their families, to a coalition of despots a thousand times more cruel and more lasting than the foreigner.

At eleven o'clock two officers entered Delescluze's room and informed him of the execution of the hostages. He listened to the recital without ceasing to write, and then only asked, "How did they die?" When the officers were gone, Delescluze turned to the friend who was working with him, and, hiding his face in his hands, "What a war!" cried he, "what a war!" But he knew revolutions too well to lose himself in bootless reflections, and, mastering his emotion, he claimed, "We shall know how to die!"

During the whole night despatches succeeded each other without intermission, all demanding cannon and men under the threat of abandoning such or such a position.

But where to find cannon? And men began to be as rare as the bronze.

Chapter 30
The Left bank falls

A few thousand men could not indefinitely hold a line of battle several miles long. When night had set in, many Federals abandoned their barricades in order to snatch a little rest. The Versaillese, who were on the look-out, took possession of their defences, and the glimmering of dawn saw the tricolor where on the eve had floated the red flag.

In the darkness the Federals evacuated the greater part of the tenth arrondissement, whose artillery pieces were transported to the Château d'Eau. Brunel and the brave *pupilles de la Commune* still stood their ground in the Rue Magnan and on the Quai Jemappes, the troops holding the top of the Boulevard Magenta.

On the left bank, the Versaillese erected batteries at the Place d'Enfer, the Luxembourg, and Bastion 81. More than fifty cannon and machine-guns were levelled at the Butte aux Cailles; for, despairing of taking it by assault, Cissey wished to crush it with his artillery. Wroblewski, on his side, did not remain inactive. Besides the 175th and 176th battalions, he had under his command the legendary 101st, which was to the troops of the Commune what the 32nd brigade had been to the army of Italy. Since the 3rd April the 101st had not rested. Day and night, their guns hot, they had roamed about the trenches, the villages, the fields; the Versaillese of Neuilly, of Asnières, ten times fled before them. They had taken three cannon from them, which, like faithful mastiffs, followed them everywhere. All citizens of the thirteenth arrondissement and the Mouffetard quarter, undisciplined, undisciplinable, wild, rough, their clothes and flag torn, obeying only one order, that to march forward, mutineering when inactive, when hardly out of fire rendering it necessary to plunge them into it again. Sérizier commanded, or rather accompanied them; for indeed their rage was their only commander. While at the front they attempted surprises, seized outposts, kept the soldiers in alarm, Wroblewski, uncovered on his right since the taking of the Panthéon, secured his communications with the Seine by a barricade on the Bridge of Austerlitz, and furnished the Place Jeanne d'Arc with cannon, in order to check the troops who might venture along the railway station.

That day M. Thiers dared to telegraph to the provinces that Marshal MacMahon had just, for the last time, summoned the Federals to surrender. This was an odious lie added to so many others. Like Cavaignac in 1848, M. Thiers, on the contrary, wanted to prolong the battle. He knew that his shells were setting Paris on fire, that the massacre of the prisoners, of the wounded, would fatally entail that of the hostages. But what cared he for the fate of a few priests and a few gendarmes? What cared the bourgeoisie if it triumphed amidst ruins — if on these ruins it could write, "Paris waged war with the privileged; Paris is no more!"

The Hôtel-de-Ville and the Panthéon in the power of the troops, their whole efforts concentrated upon the Château d'Eau, the Bastille, and the Butte aux Cailles. At four o'clock Clinchant resumed his march towards the Château d'Eau. One column, setting out from the Rue Paradis, went up the Rues du Château d'Eau and De Bondy; another advanced against the barricade of the Boulevards Magenta and Strasbourg; while a third from the Rue des Jeuneurs pushed on between the boulevards and the Rue Turbigo. The Douay corps on the right supported this movement, and endeavoured to remount the third arrondissement by the Rues Charlot and de Saintonge. Vinoy advanced towards the Bastille by the small streets that abut upon the Rue St. Antoine, the quays of the right and of the left banks. Cissey, with more modest strategy, shelled the Butte aux Cailles, before which his men had so often turned tail.

Painful scenes were enacted in the forts. Wroblewski, whose left wing was covered by them, relied for their preservation upon the energy of the member of the Council who had assumed the functions of delegate. The evening before the commander of Montrouge had abandoned that fort and had retreated to Bicêtre with his garrison. The fort of Bicêtre did not hold out much longer. The battalions declared that they wanted to return to the town in order to defend their districts, and the delegate, in spite of his threats, was unable to retain them; so, after having spiked their guns, the whole garrison returned to Paris. The Versaillese occupied the two evacuated forts, and there at once erected batteries against the fort of Ivry and the Butte aux Cailles.

The general attack on the Butte did not begin till midday. The Versaillese followed the ramparts as far as the Avenue d'Italie and the Route de Choisy, with the view of making sure of the Place d'Italie, which they attacked from the side of the Gobelins. The Avenues d'Italie and de Choisy were defended by powerful barricades which they could not dream of forcing; but that of the Boulevard St. Marcel, protected on one side by the conflagration of the Gobelins, could be taken by the numerous gardens intersecting this quarter, and the Versaillese succeeded in doing this. They first took possession of the Rue des Cordillières St. Marcel, where twenty Federals who refused to surrender were massacred, and then entered the gardens. For three hours a prolonged and obstinate firing enveloped the Butte aux Cailles, battered down by the Versaillese cannon, six times as numerous as Wroblewski's.

The garrison of Ivry arrived towards one o'clock. On leaving the fort they had let off a mine which sprung two bastions. Soon after the Versaillese penetrated into the abandoned fort, and then there was no struggle, as M. Thiers tried to make it appear in one of those bulletins in which he very cleverly intermingled truth and falsehood.

Towards ten o'clock on the right bank the Versaillese reached the barricade of the Faubourg St. Denis, near the St. Lazare prison, outflanked and shot seventeen Federals. Thence they went to occupy the St. Laurent barricade at the junction of the Boulevard Sebastopol, erected batteries against the Château d'Eau, and by the Rue des Récollets gained the Quai Valmy. On the night, their advance on to the Boulevard St. Martin was retarded by the Rue de Lanery, against which they fired from the Ambigu-Comique Théâtre. In the third arrondissement they were stopped in the Rue Meslay, Rue Nazareth, Rue du Vert-Bois, Rue Charlot, Rue de Saintonge.

The second arrondissement, invaded from all sides, was still disputing its Rue Montorgueuil. Nearer the Seine, Vinoy succeeded in entering the Grenier d'Abondance by circuitous streets, and in order to dislodge him the Federals set fire to this building, which overlooks the Bastille.

Three o'clock – The Versaillese invaded the thirteenth arrondissement more and more. Their shells falling upon the prison of the Avenue d'Italie, the Federals evacuated it, at the same time taking out the prisoners, amongst whom were the Dominicans of Arcueil, who had been brought back to Paris with the garrison of Bicêtre. The sight of these men, doubly odious, exasperated the combatants, whose guns, so to say, spontaneously went off, and a dozen of the apostles of the Inquisition fell under the bullets at the moment they were running away by the Avenue. All the other prisoners were respected.

Since the morning Wroblewski had received the order to fall back upon the eleventh arrondissement. He persisted in holding out, and had shifted the centre of his resistance a little further to the rear, to the Place Jeanne d'Arc. But the Versaillese, masters of the Avenue des Gobelins, made their junction with the columns of the Avenues d'Italie and Choisy in the thirteenth arrondissement. One of their detachments, continuing to file along the rampart, reached the embankment of the Orleans Railway, and the red-coats were already showing themselves on the Boulevard St. Marcel. Wroblewski, almost hemmed in on all sides, was at last forced to consent to a retreat. Moreover, the subaltern chiefs had, like their general, received the order to fall back; and so, protected by the fire of the Austerlitz Bridge, the able defender of the Butte aux Cailles passed the Seine in good order with his cannon and a thousand men. A certain number of Federals, who obstinately remained behind in the thirteenth arrondissement, were surrounded and taken prisoners.

The Versaillese did not dare to disturb Wroblewski's retreat, although they held part of the Boulevard St. Marcel, the Orleans Station, and their gunboats were ascending the Seine. The latter were delayed for a moment at the entrance of the St. Martin's Canal, but putting on full steam, they overcame the obstacle, and in the evening lent assistance in the attack on the eleventh arrondissement.

The whole left bank now belonged to the enemy; the Bastille and the Château d'Eau became the centre of the combat.

In the Boulevard Voltaire might now be seen all the true-hearted men who had not perished, or whose presence was not indispensable in their quarters. One of the most active was Vermorel, who during the whole struggle showed a courage composed at once of fire and coolness. On horseback, his red scarf tied round him, he rode from barricade to barricade, encouraging the men, fetching and bringing reinforcements. At the *mairie* another meeting was held towards twelve o'clock. Twenty-two members of the Council were present; about ten more were defending their arrondissements, the others had disappeared. Arnold explained that the evening before, the secretary of Mr. Washburne, the ambassador of the United States, had come to offer the mediation of the Germans. The Commune, he said, had now only to send commissaries to Vincennes in order to regulate the conditions of an armistice. The secretary, introduced to the meeting, renewed this declaration, and the discussion began. Delescluze showed great reluctance to accept this plan. What motive induced the foreigner to intervene? To put an end to the conflagration and preserve their guarantee, he was answered. But their guarantee was the Versaillese Government, whose triumph was no longer doubtful at this moment. Others gravely asserted that the inveterate defence of Paris had inspired the Prussian with admiration. No one asked whether this insensate proposition did not hide some snare; if the pretended secretary were not a simple spy. They clung like drowning men to this last chance of salvation. Arnold even set forth the basis of an armistice similar to that of the Central Committee. Four of the members present, and amongst them Delescluze, were charged to accompany the American secretary to Vincennes.

At three o'clock they reached the gate of Vincennes, but the commisar of police refused to let them pass. They showed their scarfs, their cards of members of the Council. The commissar insisted upon a safe-conduct from the Commission of Public Safety. While the discussion was going on some Federals came up. "Where are you going?" said they. "To Vincennes." "Why?" "On a mission." A painful controversy ensued. The Federals thought the members of the Council wanted to abscond, and they were even about to ill-use them, when someone recognized Delescluze. His name saved the others; but the commissar still insisted upon a safe-conduct.

One of the delegates ran off to the *mairie* of the eleventh arrondissement to procure it, but, even on Ferré's order, the guards refused to lower the drawbridge. Delescluze addressed them and said that the common weal of all was at stake; but prayers and threats proved alike unable to overcome the idea of a defection. Delescluze came back shivering all over. For one moment he had been suspected of cowardice; this was to him a death-blow.

Before the *mairie* he found a crowd shouting at some flags, surmounted by eagles, which had just, they said, been taken from the Versaillese. Wounded were being brought from the Bastille. Mademoiselle Dimitriev, wounded herself, supported Frankel, wounded at the barricade of the Faubourg St. Antoine. Wroblewski just arriving from the Butte aux Cailles, Delescluze offered him the command-in-chief. "Have you a few thousand resolute men?" asked Wroblewski. "A few hundred at most," answered the delegate. Wroblewski could not accept any responsibility of command under such unequal conditions, and continued to fight as a simple soldier. He was the only general of the Commune who had showed the qualities of a chef-de-corps. He always asked to have those battalions sent him which everybody else declined, undertaking to utilize them.

The attack was coming nearer and nearer the Château d'Eau. This square, constructed with the object of checking the faubourgs, and opening into eight large avenues, had not been really fortified. The Versaillese, masters of the Folies-Dramatiques Théatre and of the Rue du Château d'Eau, attacked it by skirting the Prince Eugène Barracks. House by house they tore the Rue Magnan from the *pupilles de la Commune*. Brunel, after facing the enemy for four days, fell wounded in the thigh. The *pupilles* carried him away on a litter across the Place du Château d'Eau amidst a shower of bullets.

From the Rue Magnan the Versaillese soon reached the barracks, and the Federals, too few in number to defend this vast monument, had to evacuate it.

The fall of this position uncovered the Rue Turbigo, thus enabling the Versaillese to occupy the whole upper part of the third arrondissement, and to surround the Conservatoire des Arts et Métiers. After a rather long struggle the Federals abandoned the barricade of the Conservatoire, leaving behind them a loaded machine-gun. A woman also remained. As soon as the soldiers were within range she discharged the machine-gun at them.

The barricades of the Boulevards Voltaire and Dejazet's Theatre had henceforth to sustain the whole fire of the Prince Eugène Barracks, the

Boulevard Magenta, the Boulevard St. Martin, the Rue du Temple, and the Rue Turbigo. Behind their fragile shelter the Federals gallantly received this avalanche. How many men have been called heroes who never showed a hundredth part of this simple courage, without any stage effects, without a history, which shone forth during these days in a thousand places in Paris! At the Château d'Eau a young girl of nineteen, rosy and charming, with black, curling hair, dressed as a marine fusilier, fought desperately a whole day. At the same place a lieutenant was killed in front of the barricade; a child of fifteen, Dauteuille, went to pick up the képi of the dead man in the thick of the bullets, and brought it back amidst the cheers of his companions.

For in the battle of the streets, as in the open field, the children proved themselves as brave as the men. At a barricade of the Faubourg du Temple the most indefatigable gunner was a child. The barricade taken, all its defenders were shot, and the child's turn also came. He asked for three minutes' respite; "so that he could take his mother, who lived opposite, his silver watch, *In order that she might at least not lose everything.*" The officer, involuntarily moved, let him go, not thinking to see him again; but three minutes after the child cried, "Here I am!" jumped on to the pavement, and nimbly leant against the wall near the corpses of his comrades. Paris will never die as long as she brings forth such people.

The Place du Château d'Eau was ravaged as by a cyclone. The walls crumbled beneath the shells and bombs; enormous blocks were thrown up; the lions of the fountains perforated or overthrown, the basin surmounting it shattered. Fire burst out from twenty houses. The trees were leafless, and their broken branches hung like limbs all but parted from the main body. The gardens, turned up, sent forth clouds of dust. The invisible hand of death alighted upon each stone.

At a quarter to seven, near the *mairie* of the eleventh arrondissement, we saw Delescluze, Jourde, and about a hundred Federals marching in the direction of the Château d'Eau. Delescluze wore his ordinary dress, black hat, coat, and trousers, his red scarf, inconspicuous was was his wont, tied round his waist. Without arms, he leant on a cane. Apprehensive of some panic at the Château d'Eau, we followed the delegate. Some of us stopped at the St. Ambrose Church to get arms. We then met a merchant from Alsace, who, exasperated at those who had betrayed his country, had been fighting for five days, and had just been severely wounded; farther on, Lisbonne, who, like Brunel, having too often defied death, had at last fallen at the Château d'Eau; he was being brought back almost dead; and finally, Vermorel, wounded by the side of Lisbonne, whom Theisz and Jaclard were carrying off on a litter, leaving behind him large drops of blood. We thus remained a little behind Delescluze. At about eighty yards from the barricade the guards who accompanied him kept back, for the projectiles obscured the entrance of the boulevard.

Delescluze still walked forward. Behold the scene; we have witnessed it; let it be engraved in the annals of history. The sun was setting. The old exile, unmindful whether he was followed, still advanced at the same pace, the only living being on the road. Arrived at the barricade, he bent off to the left and mounted upon the paving-stones.

For the last time his austere face, framed in his white beard, appeared to us turned towards death. Suddenly Delescluze disappeared. He had fallen as if thunderstricken on the Place du Château d'Eau.

Some men tried to raise him. Three out of four fell dead. The only thing to be thought of now was the barricade, the rallying of its few defenders. A member of the Council, Johannard, almost in the middle of the boulevard, raising his gun, and weeping with rage, cried to those who hesitated, "No! you are not worthy of defending the Commune!" Night set in. We returned heart-broken, leaving, abandoned to the outrages of an adversary without respect for death, the body of our friend.

He had forewarned no one, not even his most intimate friends. Silent, having for confidant only his severe conscience, Delescluze walked to the barricade as the old Montagnards went to the scaffold. An eventful life had exhausted his strength; he had but a breath left, and he gave it. The Versaillese have stolen his body, but his memory will remain enshrined in the heart of the people as long as France shall be the mother-country of the Revolution. He lived only for justice. That was his talent, his science, the pole-star of his life. He proclaimed her, confessed her, through thirty years of exile, prisons, insult, disdaining the persecutions that crushed him. A Jacobin, he fell with the men of the people to defend her. It was his recompense to die for her, his hands free, in the open daylight, at his own time, not afflicted by the sight of the executioner.

Compare the conduct of the Minister of War of the Commune with the cowardice of the Bonapartist Minister and generals escaping death by surrendering their swords.

The whole evening the Versaillese attacked the entrance of the Boulevard Voltaire, protected by the conflagration of the two corner houses. On the side of the Bastille they did not get beyond the Place Royale, but they were breaking into the twelfth arrondissement. Under the shelter of the wall of the quay, they had in the course of the day penetrated beneath the Austerlitz Bridge; in the evening, protected by their gunboats and the batteries of the Jardin des Plantes, they pushed as far as Mazas.

Our right wing held out better. The Versaillese had not been able to proceed further than the Eastern Railway line. From afar they attacked the Rue d'Aubervilliers, aided by the fire of the Rotonde. Ranvier vigorously shelled Montmartre, when a despatch from the Committee of Public Safety informed him that the red flag was floating from the Moulin de la Galette. Ranvier, unable to believe this, refused to cease firing.

In the evening the Versaillese formed in front of the Federals a broken line, commencing from the Eastern Railway, passing the Château d'Eau and the Bastille, and ending at the Lyons Railway. There remained to the Commune but two arrondissements intact, the nineteenth and twentieth, and about half of the eleventh and twelfth.

The Paris of Versailles no longer presented a civilized aspect. Fear, hate, and fiendish brutishness smothered all feelings of humanity. It was a universal "furious madness," said the *Siècle* of the 26th. "One no longer distinguishes the just from the unjust, the innocent from the guilty. The life of citizens weighs no more than a hair. For a cry, for a word, one is arrested, shot." The ventilators of the cellars were blocked up by order of the army, which wanted to give credit to the legend of the petroleuses. The National Guards of order crept out from their lurking-places, proud of their armlets, offering their services to the officers, ransacking the houses, requesting the honour of presiding at the shootings. In the tenth arrondissement the former mayor, Dubail, assisted by the commander of the 109th battalion, led the soldiers to hunt those who had formerly been under his administration. Thanks to the *brassardiers,* the tide of prisoners swelled so that it became necessary to centralize the carnage. The victims were pushed into the *mairies,* the barracks, the public edifices, where prevotal courts were organized, and shot in troops. When the firing squad proved insufficient the machine-gun mowed them down. All did not die at once, and in the night there arose from these bleeding heaps ghastly cries of agony.

The shades of night brought back the spectacle of the conflagrations. Where the rays of the sun had only shown sombre clouds, Pyramids of fire now appeared. The Grenier d'Abondance illuminated the Seine far beyond the fortifications. The column of the Bastille, entirely perforated by the shells, which had set its covering of crowns and flags on fire, blazed like a gigantic torch. The Boulevard Voltaire was burning on the side of the Château d'Eau.

The death of Delescluze had been so simple and so rapid, that even at the *mairie* of the eleventh arrondissement it was doubted. Towards midnight some members of the Council agreed to evacuate the *mairie.*

What! always fly before powder and shot! Is the Bastille taken? Does not the Boulevard Voltaire still hold out? The whole strategy of the Committee of Public Safety, its whole plan of battle, was to retreat. At two o'clock in the morning, when a member of the Commune was wanted to support the barricade of the Château d'Eau, only Gambon was found, asleep in a corner. An officer awoke him and begged his pardon. The worthy Republican answered, "It is as well it should be I as another; I have lived," and he departed. But the balls already swept the Boulevard Voltaire up to the St. Ambrose Church. The barricade was deserted.

Chapter 31
The Commune's last stand

Major Ségoyer was captured by the scoundrels who were defending the Bastille, and, without respect for the laws of war, was immediately shot. (Thiers to the Prefects, 27th May.)

The soldiers continuing their nocturnal surprises, got hold of the deserted barricades of the Rue d'Aubervilliers and the Boulevard de la Chapelle. On the side of the Bastille they occupied the barricade of the Rue St. Antoine at the corner of the Rue Castex, the Gare de Lyons, and the Mazas prison; in the third, all the abandoned defences of the market and of the Square du Temple. They reached the first houses of the Boulevard Voltaire, and established themselves at the Magasins Réunis.

In the darkness of the night a Versaillese officer was surprised by our outposts of the Bastille and shot; "without respecting the laws of war, 'said M. Thiers the next day. As though during the four days that he had been mercilessly shooting thousands of prisoners, old men, women, and children, M. Thiers obeyed any other law than that of the savages.

The attack recommenced at daybreak. At La Villete the Versaillese, crossing the Rue d'Aubervilliers; turned and occupied the abandoned gasworks; in the centre, they got as far as the Cirque Napoléon; on the right, in the twelfth arrondissement, they invaded the bastions nearest the river without a struggle: One detachment went up the embankment of the Vincennes Railway and occupied the station, while another took possession of the Boulevard Mazas, the Avenue Lacuée, and penetrated into the

Faubourg St. Antoine. The Bastille was thus close pressed on its right flank, while the troops of the Place Royale attacked it on the left by the Boulevard Beaumarchais.

The sun did not shine forth. This five days' cannonade had drawn on the rainfall that usually accompanies great battles. The firing had lost its sharp, quick voice, but rolled on in muffled tones. The men, harassed, wet to the skin, hardly distinguished through the misty veil the point whence the attack came. The shells of a Versaillese battery established at the Gare d'Orléans disturbed the entrance of the Faubourg St. Antoine. At seven o'clock the presence of soldiers at the top of the faubourg was announced. The Federals hurried thither with their cannon. If they do not hold out, the Bastille will be taken.

They did hold out. The Rue d'Aligre and the Avenue Lacuée vied with each other in devotion. Entrenched in the houses, the Federals fell, but neither yielded nor retreated; and, thanks to their self-sacrifice, the Bastille for six hours still disputed its shattered barricades and ruined houses. Each stone had its legend in this estuary of the Revolution. Here encased in the wall is a bullet launched in 1789 against the fortress. Leaning against the same wall the sons of the combatants of June fought for the same pavement as their fathers. Here the conservatives of 1848 gave vent to their rage; but what was their fury compared with that of 1871? The house at the corner of the Rue de la Roquette, the angle of the Rue de Charenton, disappeared like the scenery of a theatre, and amidst these ruins, under these burning beams, some men fired their cannon, and twenty times raised up the red flag, as often overthrown by the Versaillese balls. Powerless as it well knew to triumph over an entire army, the old glorious place will at least succumb honourably.

How many were there at mid-day? Hundreds, since at night hundreds of corpses lay around the chief barricade. In the Rue Crozatier they were dead; they were dead too in the Rue d'Aligre, killed in the struggle or after the combat. And how they died! In the Rue Crozatier an artilleryman of the army, gone over to the people on the 18th March, was surrounded. "We are going to shoot you," cried the soldiers. He, shrugging his shoulders, answered, "We can only die once!" Farther on an old man was struggling; the officer by a refinement of cruelty wanted to shoot him upon a heap of filth. "I fought bravely," said the old man; "I have the right not to die in the mire."

Indeed they died well everywhere. That same day Millière, arrested on the left bank of the Seine, was taken to Cissey's staff. This Imperialist general, ruined by the vilest debauchery, and who terminated his Ministerial career, by treachery, had made of his headquarters at the Luxembourg one of the slaughter-houses of the left bank. Millière's role during the Commune had been one of mere conciliation, and his polemic in the journals entirely one of doctrine, and of a most elevated character; but the hatred of the officers for every Socialist, the hatred of Jules Favre, lay in wait for him. The assassin, the staff-captain Garcin, has recounted his crime, head erect. Before history we must let him speak.

"Millière was brought in when we were breakfasting with the general at the restaurant De Tournon, near the Luxembourg. We heard a great noise, and went out. I was told, 'It is Milière.' I took care that the crowd did not take justice into its own hands. He did not come into the Luxembourg; he was stopped at the gate. I addressed myself to him, and said, 'You are Millière?' 'Yes, but you know that I am a deputy.' 'That may be, but I think you have lost your character of deputy. Besides, there is a deputy amongst us, M. de Quinsonnas, who will recognize you.'

"I then said to Millière that the general's orders were that he was to be shot. He said to me, 'Why?'

"I answered him, 'I only know your name. I have read articles by you that have revolted me [probably the articles on Jules Favre]. You are a viper, to be crushed underfoot. You detest society.' He stopped, saying, with a significant air, 'Oh, yes! I indeed hate this society.' 'Well, it will remove you from its bosom; you are going to be shot.' 'This is summary justice, barbarity, cruelty.' 'And all the cruelty you have committed, do you take that for nothing? At any rate, since you say you are Millière, there is nothing else to be done.'

"The general had ordered that he was to be shot at the Panthéon, on his knees, to ask pardon of society for all the ill he had done. He refused to be shot kneeling. I said to him, 'It is the order; you will be shot on your knees, and not otherwise.' He played a little comedy, opening his coat, and baring his breast before the firing party. I said to him, 'You are acting; you want them to say how you died; die quietly, that will be the best.' 'I am free in my own interest and for the sake of my Cause to do as I like.' 'So be it; kneel down.' Then he said to me, 'I will only do so if you force me down by two men.' I had him forced on his knees, and then his execution was proceeded with. He cried, '*Vive l'Humanité!*' He was about to cry something else when he fell dead."

An officer ascended the steps, approached the corpse, and discharged his chassepôt into the left temple. Millière's head rebounded, and, falling back, burst open, black with powder, seemed to look at the frontispiece of the monument.

"*Vive l'Humanité!*" The word implies two causes. "I care as much for the liberty of other people as for that of France," said a Federal to a reactionary. In 1871, as in 1793, Paris combats for all the oppressed.

The Bastille succumbed about two o'clock. La Villette still struggled on. In the morning the barricade at the corner of the boulevard and of the Rue de Flandre had been surrendered by its commander. The Federals concentrated in the rear along the line of the canal, and barricaded the Rue de Crimée. The Rotonde, destined to support the principal shock, was reinforced by a barricade on the quay of the Loire. The 269th, which for two days had withstood the enemy, recommenced the struggle behind the new positions. This line from La Villette being of great extent, Ranvier and Passedouet went to fetch reinforcements in the twentieth arrondissement, where the remnants of all the battalions took refuge.

They crowded round the *mairie*, that distributed lodgings and orders for food. Near the church the wagons and horses were noisily put up. The headquarters and different services were established in the Rue Haxo at the Cité Vincennes, a series of constructions intersected by gardens.

The very numerous barricades in the inextricable streets of Ménilmontant were almost all turned against the boulevard. The strategical route, which on this point overlooks the Père la Chaise, the Buttes Chaumont, and the exterior boulevard, was not even guarded.

From the heights of the ramparts the Prussians were discernible in arms. According to the terms of a convention previously concluded between Versailles and the Prince of Saxony, the German army since Monday surrounded Paris on the north and east. It had cut off the Railway of the North, manned the canal line from St. Denis, posted sentinels from St. Denis to Charenton, erected barricades on all the routes. From five o'clock in the evening of Thursday 5,000 Bavarians marched down from Fontenay, Nogent, and Charenton, forming an impenetrable cordon from the Marne to Montreuil; and during the evening another corps of 5,000 men occupied Vincennes, with eighty artillery pieces. At nine o'clock they surrounded the fort and disarmed the Federals, who wanted to return to Paris. They did still better-trapped the game for Versailles. Already during the siege the Prussians had given an indirect support to the Versaillese army; their cynical collusion with the French conservatives showed itself undisguised during the eight days of May. Of all M. Thiers' crimes, one of the most odious will certainly be his introducing the conquerors of France into our civil discords, and begging their help in order to crush Paris.

Towards mid-day fire broke out in the west part of the docks of La Villette, an immense warehouse of petroleum, oil and combustible matters, set alight by the shells from both sides. This conflagration forced us to leave the barricades of the Rues de Flandre and Riquet. The Versaillese, attempting to traverse the canal in boats, were stopped by the barricades of the Rue de Crimée and the Rotonde.

Vinoy continued to ascend the twelfth arrondissement after having left the few thousand men necessary for the perquisitions and executions at the Bastille. The barricade of the Rue de Reuilly, at the corner of the Faubourg St. Antoine, held out a few hours against the soldiers who shelled it from the Boulevard Mazas. At the same time the Versaillese, marching along the Boulevard Mazas and the Rue Picpus, moved towards the Place du Trône, which they tried to outflank by the ramparts. The artillery prepared and covered their slightest movement. Generally they charged the pieces at the corner of the roads they wanted to reduce, advanced them, fired, and drew them back again under shelter. The Federals could only reach this invisible enemy from the heights; but it was impossible to centralize the artillery of the Commune, for each barricade wanted to possess its gun without caring where it carried.

There was no longer authority of any kind. At the headquarters there was a pell-mell of bewildered officers. The march of the enemy was only known by the arrival of the survivors of the battalions. Such was the confusion, that in this place, mortal to traitors, there might be seen, in a general's uniform, Du Bisson, turned out of La Villette. The few members of the Council to be met with in the twentieth arrondissement wandered about at random, absolutely ignored; but they had not foregone deliberating. On the Friday there were twelve of them in the Rue Haxo, when the Central Committee arrived and claimed the dictatorship. It was given them, in spite of some who protested, Varlin being added to their number. The Committee of Public Safety was no longer heard of.

The only one of its members who played any part was Ranvier, splendidly energetic in the combats. During these days he was the soul of La Villette and Belleville, urging on the men, watching over everything. On the 26th he issued a proclamation: "Citizens of the twentieth arrondissement! if we succumb you know what fate is in store for you. To arms! Be vigilant, above all in the night. I ask you to execute our orders faithfully. Lend your support to the nineteenth arrondissement; help it to repulse the enemy. There lies your safety. Do not wait for Belleville itself to be attacked. Forward then. *Vive la République!*"

But very few read or obeyed. The shells from Montmartre, which from the day before crushed Bellville and Ménilmontant, the cries, the sight of the wounded, dragging themselves from house to house in search of succour, the too evident signs of the approaching end, precipitated the ordinary phenomena of defeat. The people became fierce and suspicious. Any individual without a uniform ran the risk of being shot if he had not a well-known name to recommend him. The news that came from all points of Paris augmented the anguish and despair. It was known that the soldiers gave no quarter; that they despatched the wounded, killing even doctors; that every individual taken in a National Guard's uniform, shod with regulation boots, or whose clothes showed traces of stripes recently unstitched, was shot in the street or in the yard of his house; that the combatants who surrendered, under the promise of having their lives spared, were massacred; that thousands of men, women, children, and aged people were taken to Versailles bareheaded, and often killed on the way; that it sufficed to be related to a combatant, or to offer him a refuge in order to share his fate; the numberless executions of so-called petroleuses were recounted.

About six o'clock forty-eight gendarmes, ecclesiastics, and civilians marched up the Rue Haxo between a detachment of Federals. At first they were supposed to be prisoners recently taken, and marched on in the midst of perfect silence. But the rumour spread that they were the hostages of La Roquette, and that they were being led to death. The crowd grew larger, followed, harangued, but did not strike them. At half-past six the cortege reached the Cité Vincennes; the gates closed upon them, and the crowd dispersed in the neighbouring grounds.

The escort tumultuously pushed the hostages against a kind of trench at the foot of a wall. The chassepôts were being levelled, when a member of the Council said, "What are you doing? There is a powder-magazine here; you will blow us up." He thus hoped to delay the execution. Others, quite distracted, went from group to group, attempting to discuss, to appease the wrath. They were repulsed, menaced, and their notoriety hardly sufficed to save them from death.

The chassepôts went off on all sides; by degrees the hostages fell. outside the crowd applauded. And yet for two days the soldiers taken prisoners passed through Belleville without exciting a murmur; but these gendarmes, these spies, these priests, who for fully twenty years had trampled upon Paris, represented the Empire, the bourgeoisie, the massacres under their most hateful forms.

The same morning Jecker, the accomplice of Morny, had been shot. The Council had not known how to punish him; the justice of the people alighted upon him. A platoon of four Federals went to fetch him at La Roquette. He appeared to resign himself quietly, and even chatted on the way. "You are mistaken," said he, "if you think I did a good piece of business. Those people cheated me." He was executed in the open grounds adjoining the Père la Chaise from the side of Charonne.

During this day the troops did not execute any great movements. The corps Douay and Clinchant were stationed on the Boulevard Richard-Lenoir. The double barricade in the rear of Bataclan stopped the invasion of the Boulevard Voltaire; a Versaillese general was killed in the Rue St. Sébastian; the Place du Trone still held out by means of the Philippe-Auguste barricade. The Rotonde and docks of La Villette also prolonged their resistance. Towards the close of the day the conflagration spread to the part of the docks nearest the *mairie.*

In the evening, the army hedged in the defence between the fortifications and a curved line which from the slaughter-houses of La Villette extended to the gate of Vincennes, passing by the St. Martin Canal, the Boulevard Richard-Lenoir, and the Rue du Faubourg St. Antoine-Ladmirault and Vinoy occupying the two extremities, Douay and Clinchant the centre.

The night of the Friday to Saturday was sombre and feverish in Ménilmontant and Belleville, ravaged by the shells. At the turning of each street the sentinels demanded the watchword (Bouchotte-Belleville), and often even that did not suffice, and one had to prove being sent upon an errand. Every leader of a barricade claimed the right to stop your passage.

The remainder of the battalions continued arriving in disorder, and encumbered all the houses. The majority, finding no shelter, rested in the open air amidst the shells, always saluted with cries of "*Vive la Commune!*"

In the Grande Rue de Belleville some National Guards carried coffins on their crossed muskets, men preceding them with torches, the drums beating. These combatants, who amidst the shells silently interred their comrades, appeared in touching grandeur. They were themselves at the gates of death.

In the night the barricades of the Rue d'Allemagne were abandoned. A thousand men at the utmost had for two days kept in check Ladmirault's 25,000 soldiers. Almost all these brave men were sedentary guards and children.

The humid glimmer of the Saturday morning discovered a sinister prospect. The fog was dense and penetrating, the soil steeped in moisture. Clouds of white smoke rose slowly above the rain, it was the firing. The Federals shivered under their drenched cloaks.

Since daybreak barricades of the strategic route, the gates of Montreuil and Bagnolet, were occupied by the troops, who without resistance invaded Charonne. At seven o'clock they established themselves in the Place du Trône, whose defences had been abandoned. At the entrance of the Boulevard Voltaire the Versaillese erected a battery of six pieces against the *mairie* of the eleventh arrondissement. Henceforth certain of victory, the officers wanted to triumph noisily. This barricade against which they fired during the whole day of the 27th, had but two pieces of the most irregular projection. Many a Versaillese shell strayed to the legs of the statue of Voltaire, who, with his sardonic smile, seemed to remind his bourgeois descendants of the *beau tapage* he had promised them.

At La Villette the soldiers deviated from the line on all sides, passed by the fortifications and attacked the Rues Puebla and De Crimée. Their left, still engaged in the upper part of the tenth arrondissement, endeavoured to gain possession of all its streets leading to the Boulevard de la Villette. Their batteries of the Rue de Flandre, of the ramparts and the Rotonde united their fire to that of Montmartre, and overwhelmed the Buttes Chaumont with shells. The barricade of the Rue Puebla yielded towards ten o'clock. A sailor who had remained alone, hidden behind the paving-stones, awaited the Versaillese, discharged his revolver at them, and then, hatchet in hand, dashed into the midst of their ranks. The enemy deployed in all the adjacent streets up to the Rue Ménadier, steadily held by our tirailleurs. At the Place des Fêtes two of our pieces covered the Rue de Crimée and protected our right flank.

At eleven o'clock nine or ten members of the Council met in the Rue Haxo. One of them, Jules Allix, whom his colleagues had been obliged to shut up as mad during the Commune, came up radiant. According to him, all was for the best; the quarters of the centre were dismantled; they had only to descend thither. Others thought that by surrendering themselves to the

Prussians, who would deliver them up to Versailles, they might put an end to the massacres. One or two members demonstrated the absurdity of this hope, and that besides the Federals would allow no one to leave Paris. They were not listened to. A solemn note was being drawn up, when Ranvier, who wandered about in all corners picking up men one by one for the defence of the Buttes Chaumont, broke in upon their deliberations, exclaiming, "Why do you not go and fight instead of discussing!" They dispersed in different directions, and this was the last meeting of these men of everlasting deliberations.

At this moment the Versaillese occupied Bastion 16. At mid-day the rumour spread that the troops were issuing by the Rue de Paris and the ramparts. A crowd of men and women, driven from their houses by the shells, beset the gate of Romainville, asking with loud cries to be allowed to flee into the neighbouring fields. At one o'clock the drawbridge was lowered in order to give passage to the fugitives. The crowd dashed out and dispersed in the houses of the Village des Lilas. As some women and children attempted to push on further and to cross the barricade thrown up in the middle of the road, the sergeant of gendarmerie of Romainville threw himself upon them, crying to the Prussians, "Fire! come, fire on this *canaille!*" A Prussian soldier fired, wounding a woman.

Meanwhile the drawbridge had been raised. About four o'clock Colonel Parent, on horseback, and preceded by a trumpet, dared on his own authority to go and ask the Prussian troops for permission to pass. Useless degradation. The officer answered that he had no orders, and that he would refer to St. Denis.

The same day the member of the Council, Arnold, who still believed in an American intervention, went to take a letter for Mr. Washburne to the German outposts. He was conducted from one officer to another, received rather rudely, and sent back with the promise that his letter would be forwarded to the ambassador.

Near two o'clock several Versaillese battalions, having swept the strategic route, reached the Rue de Crimée by the Rue des Lilas and the open grounds of the fortifications, but were stopped in the Rue de Bellevue. From the Place du Marché three cannon joined their fire to that of the Place des Fêtes in order to protect the Buttes Chaumont. These pieces were the whole day served by only five artillerymen, their arms bare, without witnesses, needing neither a leader nor orders. At five o'clock the cannon of the Buttes were silent, having no more ammunition, and their gunners rejoined the skirmishers of the Rues Méandier, Fessart, and Des Annelets.

At five o'clock Ferré brought up to the Rue Haxo the line soldiers of the Prince Eugène Barracks, removed since Wednesday to the prison of La Petite Roquette, which had just been evacuated, as also the Grande Roquette. The crowd looked at them, not uttering a single threat, for they felt no hatred for the soldiers, who belonged, like themselves, to the people. They were quartered in Belleville church. Their arrival caused a fatal diversion. The people ran up to see them pass, and the Place des Fêtes was dismantled. The Versaillese came up, occupied it, and the last defenders of the Buttes fell back on the Faubourg du Temple and the Rue de Paris.

While our front was yielding we were attacked from the rear. Since four o'clock in the afternoon the Versaillese had been laying siege to the Père la Chaise, which enclosed no more than 200 Federals, resolute, but without discipline or foresight. The officers had been unable to make them embattle the walls. Five thousand Versaillese approached the enceinte from all sides, while the artillery of the bastion furrowed the interior. The pieces of the Commune had scarcely any ammunition since the afternoon. At six o'clock the Versailese, not daring, in spite of their numbers, to scale the enceinte, cannonaded the large gate of the cemetery, which soon gave way, notwithstanding the barricade propping it up. Then began a desperate struggle. Sheltered behind the tombs, the Federals disputed their refuge foot by foot; they closed in with the enemy in frightful hand-to-hand scuffles; in the vaults they fought with side-arms. Foes rolled and died in the same grave. The darkness that set in early did not end the despair.

On the Saturday evening there only remained to the Federals part of the eleventh and twentieth arrondissements. The Versaillese camped in the Place des Fêtes, Rue Fessart, Rue Pradier up to Rue Rebeval, where, as on the boulevard, they were detained. The quadrilateral comprised between the Rue de Faubourg du Temple, the Rue Folie Méricourt, the Rue de la Roquette and the exterior boulevard was in part occupied by the Federals. Douay and Clinchant awaited on the Boulevard Richard-Lenoir the moment when Vinoy and Ladmirault would have carried the heights, and thus forced the Federals against the guns.

What a night for the few combatants of the last hours! It rained in torrents. The conflagration of La Villette lit up this gloom with its blinding glare. The shells continued to pound Belleville; they even reached as far as Bagnolet and wounded some Prussian soldiers.

The wounded arrived in large numbers at the *mairie* of the twentieth arrondissement. There were neither doctors, nor medicines, nor mattresses, nor blankets, and the unhappy people expired without succour. Some spies, surprised in the dress of National Guards, were there and then shot in the court. The *Vengeurs de Flourens* arrived, headed by their captain, a fine, handsome young fellow, reeling in his saddle. The cantinière, delirious, a handkerchief tied round her bleeding brow, swore, called the men together with the cry of a wounded lioness. From between the convulsive hands the guns went off at random. The noise of the wagons, the threats, the lamentations, the fusillades, the whizzing of the shells, mingled in a maddening tumult, and who in those frightful hours did not feel his reason giving way? Every moment brought with it a new disaster. One guard rushed up and said, "The Pradier barricade is abandoned!" another, "We want men in the Rue Rebeval," a third, "They are fleeing in the Rue des Près." To hear these deathknells there were but a few members of the Council present, among whom were Trinquet, Ferré, Varlin and Ranvier. Desperate of their powerlessness, broken down by these eight days, without sleep and without hope, the strongest were lost in grief.

From four o'clock Vinoy and Ladmirault launched their troops along the ramparts on the defenceless strategic route, and soon effected a junction at the Romainville gate. Towards five o'clock the troops occupied the barricade of the Rue Rebeval in the Boulevard de la Villette, and by the Rue Vincent and the Passage du Renard attacked the barricades of the Rue de Paris from behind. The *mairie* of the twentieth arrondissement was not taken till eight o'clock. The barricade of the Rue de Paris at the corner of the boulevard was defended by the commander of the 191st and five or six guards, who held out till their ammunition was exhausted.

A column set out from the Boulevard Philippe-Auguste, penetrated into the Roquette towards nine o'clock, and released the hostages who were there. Masters of the Père la Chaise from the day before, the Versaillese might at least from nine o'clock in the evening have penetrated into the abandoned prison. This delay of twelve hours sufficiently shows their contempt for the lives of the hostages. Four of the latter — among whom was the Bishop Surat — who had made their escape in the afternoon of Saturday, had been retaken at the neighbouring barricades and shot before the Petite Roquette.

At nine o'clock the resistance was reduced to the small square formed by the Rues du Faubourg du Temple, Des Trois Bornes, Des Trois Couronnes, and the Boulevard de Belleville. Two or three streets of the twentieth arrondissement still struggled on, among others the Rue Ramponeau. A small phalanx of fifty men, led by Varlin, Ferré, and Gambon, their red scarfs round their waists, their chassepôts slung across their shoulders, marched down the Rue des Champs, and from the twentieth arrondissement came out on the boulevard. A gigantic Garibaldian carried an immense red flag in front of them. They entered the eleventh arrondissement. Varlin and his colleagues were going to defend the barricade of the Rue du Faubourg du Temple and of the Rue Fontaine au Roi. From the front it was inaccessible; the Versaillese, masters of the St. Louis Hospital, succeeded in turning it by the Rues St. Maur and Bichat.

At ten o'clock the Federals had almost no cannon left, and twothirds of the army hemmed them in. What mattered it? In the Rue du Faubourg du Temple, Rue Oberkampf, Rue St. Maur, Rue Parmentier, they still wanted to fight. There were barricades not to be overturned and houses without exits. The Versaillese artillery shelled them till the Federals had used up their ammunition. Their last cartridge spent, overwhelmed by shells, they threw themselves upon the muskets bristling around them.

By degrees the firing was lulled, all was silent. About ten o'clock the last Federal cannon was discharged in the Rue du Paris, which the Versaillese had taken. The piece, charged with double shot, with a terrible crash exhaled the last sigh of the Paris Commune.

The last barricade of the May days was in the Rue Ramponeau. For a quarter of an hour a single Federal defended it. Thrice he broke the staff of the Versaillese flag hoisted on the barricade of the Rue de Paris. As a reward for his courage, this last soldier of the Commune succeeded in escaping.

At eleven o'clock all was over. The Place de la Concorde had held out two days, the Butte aux Cailles two, La Villette three, the Boulevard Voltaire two days and a half. Of the seventy-nine members of the Council filling functions on the 21st of May, one, Delescluze, had died on the barricades; two, J. Durand and R. Rigault, had been shot; two, Brunel and Vermorel (who died some days after at Versailles), were severely wounded; three, Oudet, Protot, Frankel, slightly. The Versaillese had lost few men. We had 3,000 killed or wounded. The losses of the army in June, 1848, and the resistance of the insurgents had been relatively more serious. But the insurgents of June had only to face 30,000 men; those of May combated against 130,000 soldiers. The struggle of June lasted only three days; that of the Federals eight weeks. On the eve of June the revolutionary army was intact; on the 21st May it was decimated. The most valiant defenders had fallen at the advance posts. What might not these 15,000 men, uselessly sacrificed outside the town, have done within Paris? What might not the brave men of Neuilly, Asnières, Issy, Vanves, Cachan, have done at the Panthéon and Montmartre?

The occupation of the fort of Vincennes took place on Monday the 29th. This fort, disarmed in conformity with the stipulations of the treaty of peace, had been unable to take any part in the strife. Its garrison consisted of 350 men and twenty-four officers, commanded by the *chef-de-légion* Faltot, a veteran of the wars of Poland and of Garibaldi, one of the most active men on the 18th March. He was offered a perfectly secure asylum, but answered that honour forbade his deserting his companions in arms.

On the Saturday a Versaillese staff colonel came to negotiate a capitulation. Faltot demanded free passes, not for himself, but for some of his officers of foreign nationality, and on the refusal of the Versaillese, Faltot committed the fault of applying to the Germans. But MacMahon, foreseeing a siege, had solicited the assistance of the Prince of Saxony, and the German was on the lookout on behalf of his brother officer . During the negotiations General Vinoy had managed to hold communication with the place, where a few disreputable individuals offered to reduce the intractable Federals. Among the latter was Merlet, *garde-général* of engineering and artillery, ex-noncommissioned officer, able, energetic, and quite resolved to blow up the place rather than surrender it. The powder-magazine contained 1,000 kilogrammes of powder and 400,000 cartridges.

On Sunday, at eight o'clock in the morning, a shot sounded in Merlet's chamber. His room was entered, and he was found lying on the ground, his head pierced by the ball of a revolver. The disorder of the room attested a struggle; and a captain of the 99th, released later on by the Versaillese, B — , admitted that he had dispersed the elements of the electric battery by means of which Merlet intended to spring the fort.

On Monday towards mid-day the Versaillese colonel renewed the proposal for a surrender. For twenty-four hours the struggle had been over in Paris. The officers deliberated; it was agreed that the gates should be opened, and at three o'clock the Versaillese entered. The garrison, having laid down their arms, had drawn up at the end of the court. Nine officers were incarcerated apart.

In the night, in the ditches, a hundred yards from the spot where the Duke of Enghien had fallen, these nine officers formed a line before a firing party. One of them, Colonel Delorme, turned to the Versaillese in command with the words, "Feel my pulse; see if I am afraid."

Chapter 32
The Versaillese fury

We are honest men: justice will be done in accordance with the ordinary laws. (Thiers to the National Assembly, 22nd May 1871.

Honest, honest Iago! (Shakespeare.)

Order reigned in Paris. Everywhere ruins, death, sinister crepitations. The officers walked provokingly about clashing their sabres; the non-commissioned officers imitated their arrogance. The soldiers bivouacked in all the large roads. Some, stupefied by fatigue and carnage, slept on the pavement; others prepared their soup by the side of the corpses, singing the songs of their native homes.

The tricolor flag hung from all the windows in order to prevent house-searches. Guns, cartridge-boxes, uniforms, were piled up in the gutters of the popular quarters. Before the doors sat women leaning their heads upon their hands, looking fixedly before them, waiting for a son or a husband who was never to return.

In the rich quarters the joy knew no bounds. The runaways of the two sieges, the demonstrators of the Place Vendôme, many emigrants of Versailles, had again taken possession of the boulevards. Since the Thursday this kid-glove populace followed the prisoners, acclaiming the gendarmes who conducted the convoys applauding at the sight of the blood-covered vans. The civilians strove to outdo the military in levity. Such a one, who had ventured no further than the Café du Helder, recounted the taking of the

Château d'Eau, bragged of having shot his dozen prisoners. Elegant and joyous women, as in a pleasure trip, betook themselves to the corpses, and, to enjoy the sight of the valorous dead, with the ends of sunshades raised their last coverings.

"Inhabitants of Paris," said MacMahon on the 28th at mid-day, "Paris is delivered! Today the struggle is over. Order, labour, security are about to revive."

"Paris delivered' was parcelled into four commands under the orders of General Vinoy, Ladmirault, Cissey, Douay, and once more placed under the regime of the state of siege raised by the Commune. There was no longer any government at Paris than the army which massacred Paris. The passers-by were constrained to demolish the barricades, and any sign of impatience brought with it an arrest, any imprecation death. It was posted up that any one in the possession of arms would immediately be sent before a court-martial; that any house from which shots were fired would be given over to summary execution. All public places were closed at eleven o'clock. Henceforth officers in uniform alone could circulate freely. Mounted patrols thronged the streets. Entrance into the town became difficult, to leave it impossible. The tradespeople not being allowed to go backwards and forwards, victuals were on the point of failing.

"The struggle over," the army transformed itself into a vast platoon of executioners. On the Sunday more than 5,000 prisoners taken in the neighbourhood of the Père la Chaise were led to the prison of La Roquette. A chief of Battalion standing at the entrance surveyed the prisoners and said, "To the right," or "To the left." Those to the left were to be shot. Their pockets emptied, they were drawn up along a wall and then slaughtered. Opposite the wall two or three priests bending over their breviaries mumbled the prayers for the dying.

From the Sunday to the Monday morning in La Roquette alone more than 1,900 persons were thus murdered. Blood flowed in large pools in the gutters of the prison. The same slaughter took place at the Ecole Militaire and the Parc Monceaux.

It was butchery, nothing more, nothing less. At other places the prisoners were conducted before the prevotal courts, with which Paris swarmed since the Monday. These had not sprung up at random, and, as has been believed, in the midst of the fury of the struggle. It was proved before the courts-martial that the number and seats of these prevotal courts, with their respective jurisdictions, had been appointed at Versailles before the entry of the troops. One of the most celebrated was that of the Châtelet Theatre, where Colonel Vabre officiated. Thousands of prisoners who were led there were first of all penned in upon the stage and in the auditorium, under the guns of the soldiers placed in the boxes; then, little by little, like sheep driven to the door of the slaughter-house, from wing to wing they were pushed to the saloon, where, round a large table, officers of the army and the honest National Guard were seated, their sabres between their legs, cigars in their mouths. The examination lasted a quarter of a minute. "Did you take arms? Did you serve the Commune? Show your hands." If the resolute attitude of a prisoner betrayed a combatant, if his face was unpleasant, without asking for his name, his profession, without entering any note upon any register, he was *classed*. "You?" was said to the next one, and so on to the end of the file, without excepting the women, children, and old men. When by a caprice a prisoner was spared, he was said to be *ordinary*, and reserved for Versailles. No one was liberated.

The *classed* ones were at once delivered to the executioners, who led them into the nearest garden or court. From the Châtelet, for instance, they were taken to the Lebau Barracks. There the doors were no sooner closed than the gendarmes fired, without even grouping their victims before a platoon. Some, only wounded, ran along by the walls, the gendarmes chasing and shooting at them till they fell dead. Moreau of the Central Committee perished in one of these gangs. Surprised on the Thursday evening in the Rue de Rivoli, he was conducted into the garden and placed against a terrace. There were so many victims, that the soldiers, tired out, were obliged to rest their guns actually against the sufferers. The wall of the terrace was covered with brains; the executioners waded through pools of blood.

The massacre was thus carried on, methodically organized, at the Caserne Dupleix, the Lycée Bonaparte, the Northern and Eastern Railway Stations, the Jardin des Plantes, in many *mairies* and barracks, at the same time as in the abattoirs. Large open vans came to fetch the corpses, and went to empty them in the square or any open space in the neighbourhood.

The victims died simply, without fanfaronade. Many crossed their arms before the muskets, and themselves commanded the fire. Women and children followed their husbands and their fathers, crying to the soldiers, "Shoot us with them!" And they were shot. Women, till then strangers to the struggle, were seen to come down into the streets, enraged by these butcheries, strike the officers and then throw themselves against a wall waiting for death.

In June, 1848, Cavaignac had promised pardon, and he massacred. M. Thiers had sworn by the law, and he gave the army carte-blanche. The officers returned from Germany might now glut to their hearts" content their wrath against that Paris which had insulted them by not capitulating; the Bonapartists revenge on the Republicans the old hatreds of the Empire; the boys just fresh from St. Cyr serve their apprenticeship of insolence upon the *pékins*. A general (Cissey most probably) gave the order to shoot M. Cernuschi, whose crime consisted in having offered 100,000 francs for the anti-plebiscitary campaign of 1870. Any individual of some popular notoriety was sure to die. Dr. Tony Moilin, who had played no part during the Commune, but had been implicated in several political trials during the

Empire, was in a few moments judged and condemned to death; "not", his judges condescended to tell him, "that he had committed any act that merited death, but because he was a chief of the Socialist party, one of those men of whom a prudent and wise Government must rid itself when it finds a legitimate occasion". The Radicals of the Chamber, whose hatred of the Commune had been most clearly demonstrated, did not dare to set foot in Paris for fear of being included in the massacres.

The army, having neither police nor precise information, killed at random. Any passer-by calling a man by a revolutionary name caused him to be shot by soldiers eager to get the premium. At Grenelle they shot a pseudo-Billioray, notwithstanding his despairing protests; at the Place Vendôme they shot a pseudo-Brunel in the apartments of Madame Fould. The Gaulois published the recital by a military surgeon who *knew* Vallès, and was present at his execution. An eye-witness declared he had seen Lefrançais shot on the Thursday in the Rue de la Banque. The real Billioray was tried in the month of August; Brunel, Vallès, and Lefrançais succeeded in escaping from France. Members and functionaries of the Commune were thus shot, and often several times over, in the persons of individuals who resembled them more or less.

Varlin, alas! was not to escape. On Sunday, the 28th May, he was recognized in the Rue Lafayette, and led, or rather dragged, to the foot of the Buttes Montmartre before the commanding general. The Versaillese sent him to be shot in the Rue des Rosiers. For an hour, a mortal hour, Varlin was dragged through the streets of Montmartre, his hands tied behind his back, under a shower of blows and insults. His young, thoughtful head, that had never harboured other thoughts than of fraternity, slashed open by the sabres, was soon but one mass of blood, of mangled flesh, the eye protruding from the orbit. On reaching the Rue des Rosiers, he no longer walked; he was carried.

They set him down to shoot him. The wretches dismembered his corpse with blows of the butt-ends of their muskets.

The Mount of Martyrs has no more glorious one than Varlin. May he too be enshrined in the great heart of the working-class! Varlin's whole life was an example. He had quite alone, by the mere force of his will, educated himself, giving to study the rare hours left him in the evening after the workshop; learning not with the view to push into the bourgeoisie, as many others did, but to instruct and enfranchise the people. He was the heart and soul of the working men's associations at the end of the Empire. Indefatigable, modest, speaking little, always at the right moment, and then enlightening a confused discussion with a word, he had preserved that revolutionary instinct which is often blunted in educated workmen. One of the first on the 18th March, labouring during the whole Commune, he was at the barricades to the last. His death is all to the honour of the workmen. It is to Varlin and to Delescluze that this history should be dedicated, if there were room in the frontispiece for any other name than that of Paris.

The Versaillese journalists spat on his corpse; said that some hundreds of thousands of francs had been found on him. Returned to Paris behind the army, they followed it like jackals. Those of the demi-monde, above all, were mad with a sanguinary hysteria. The coalition of the 21st March was re-made. All uttered one howl against the vanquished workmen. Far from moderating the massacre, they encouraged it, published the names, the hiding-places of those who were to be killed, unflagging in inventions calculated to keep up the furious terror of the bourgeoisie. After every shooting they cried encore.

I quote at random, and could quote pages: "We must make a Communard hunt" (*Bien Public*). "Not one of the malefactors in whose hands Paris has been for two months will be considered as a political man. They will be treated like the brigands they are, like the most frightful monsters ever seen in the history of humanity. Many journals speak of re-erecting the scaffold "destroyed by them, in order not even to do them the honour of shooting them" (*Moniteur Universal*). "Come, honest people, an effort to make an end of this international democratic vermin" (*Figaro*). "These men, who have killed for the sake of killing and stealing, are taken, and we should answer, Mercy! These hideous women, who stabbed the breast of dying officers, are taken, and we should cry, Mercy!" (*Patrie*).

To encourage the hangmen, if that were necessary, the press threw them crowns.

"What an admirable attitude is that of our officers and soldiers!" said the Figaro. "It is only to the French soldier that it is given to recover so quickly and so well." "What an honour!" cried the *Journal des Débats*. "Our army has avenged its disasters by an inestimable victory."

Thus the army wreaked on Paris revenge for its defeats. Paris was an enemy like Prussia, and all the less to be spared that the army had its prestige to reconquer. To complete the similitude, after the victory there was a triumph. The Romans never adjudged it after the civil struggles. M. Thiers was not ashamed, under the eye of the foreigner, before still smoking Paris, to parade his troops in a grand review. Who then will dare to blame the Federals for having resisted the army of Versailles as they would have the Prussians?

And when did foreigners show such fury? Death even seemed to whet their rancour. On Sunday, the 28th, near the *mairie* of the eleventh arrondissment, about fifty prisoners had just been shot. Urged not by an unworthy curiosity, but by the earnest desire to know the truth, we went, at the risk of being recognized, as far as the corpses lying on the pavement. A woman lay there, her skirts turned up; from her ripped-up body protruded the entrails, which a marine-fusilier amused himself by dividing with the end of his bayonet. The officers, a few steps off, let him do this. The victors, in order to dishonour these corpses, had placed inscriptions on their breasts, "assassin", "thief", "drunkard', and stuck the necks of bottles into the mouths of some of them.

How to justify this savagery? The official reports only mention very few deaths among the Versaillese — 877 during the whole time of the operations, from the 3rd April up to the 28th May. The Versaillese fury had then no excuse for these reprisals. When a handful of exasperated men, to avenge thousands of their brothers, shoot sixtythree of their most inveterate enemies out of nearly 300 whom they had in their hands, the hypocritical reaction veils its face and protests in the name of justice. What, then, will this justice say when those shall be judged who methodically, without any anxiety as to the issue of the combat, and, above all, the battle over, shot 20,000 persons, of whom three-fourths had not taken part in the fight? Still some flashes of humanity were shown by the soldiers, and some were seen coming back from the executions their heads bowed down; but the officers never slackened for one second in their ferocity. Even after the Sunday they still slaughtered the prisoners, shouted "Bravo!" at the executions. The courage of the victims they called insolence. Let them be responsible before Paris, France, the new generation, for these deeds of infamy.

At last the smell of the carnage began to choke even the most frantic. The plague was coming, if pity did not. Myriads of flesh-flies flew up from the putrefied corpses. The streets were full of dead birds. The *Avenir Libéral* singing the praises of MacMahon's proclamations, applied the words of Flechier; "He hides himself, but his glory finds him out." The glory of the Turenne of 1871 betrayed him even up to the Seine. In certain streets the corpses encumbered the pathway, looking at the passers-by from out of their dead eyes. In the Faubourg St. Antoine they were to be seen everywhere in heaps, half white with chloride of lime. At the Polytechnic School they occupied a space of 100 yards long and three deep. At Passy, which was not one of the great centres of execution, there were 1,100 near the Trocadero. These, covered over by a thin shroud of earth, also showed their ghastly profiles. "Who does not recollect," said the *Temps*, "even though he had seen it but one moment, the square, no, the charnel of the Tour St. Jacques? From the midst of this moist soil, recently turned up by the spade, here and there look out heads, arms, feet, and hands. The profiles of corpses, dressed in the uniform of National Guards, were seen impressed against the ground. It was hideous. A decayed, sickening odour arose from this garden, and occasionally at some places it became fetid." The rain and heat having precipitated the putrefaction, the swollen bodies reappeared. The glory of MacMahon displayed itself too well. The journals were taking fright. "These wretches," said one of them, "who have done us so much harm during their lives, must not be allowed to do so still after their death." And those that had instigated the massacre cried "Enough!"

"Let us not kill any more," said the *Paris Journal* of the 2nd June, "even the assassins, even the incendiaries. Let us not kill any more. It is not their pardon we ask for, but a respite." "Enough executions, enough blood, enough victims," said the *Nationale* of the 1st June. And the *Opinion Nationale* of the same day: "A serious examination of the accused is imperative. One would like to see only the really guilty die."

The executions abated, and the sweeping off began. Carriages of all kinds, vans, omnibuses, came to pick up the corpses and traversed the town. Since the great plagues of London and Marseilles, such cart-loads of human flesh had not been seen. These exhumations proved that a great number of people had been buried alive. Imperfectly shot, and thrown with the heaps of dead into the common grave, they had eaten earth, and showed the contortions of their violent agony. Certain corpses were taken up in pieces. It was necessary to shut them as soon as possible into closed wagons, and to take them with the utmost speed to the cemeteries, where immense graves of lime swallowed up these putrid masses.

The cemetries of Paris absorbed all they could. The victims, placed side by side, without any other covering than their clothes, filled enormous ditches at the Père la Chaise, Montmartre, Mont-Parnasse, where the people in pious rememberance will annually come as pilgrims. Others, more unfortunate, were carried out of the town. At Charonne, Bagnolet, Bicêtre, etc. the trenches dug during the first siege were utilized. "There nothing is to be feared of the cadaverous emanations," said *La Liberté* "an impure blood will water the soil of the labourer, fecundating it. The deceased delegate at war will be able to pass a review of his faithful followers at the hour of midnight; the watchword will be *Incendiarism and assassination.*" Women by the side of the lugubrious trench endeavoured to recognize these remains. The police waited that their grief should betray them, in order to arrest those "females of insurgents."

The burying of such a large number of corpses soon became too difficult, and they were burnt in the casemates of the fortifications; but for want of draught the combustion was incomplete, and the bodies were reduced to a pulp. At the Buttes Chaumont the corpses, piled up in enormous heaps, inundated with petroleum, were burnt in the open air.

The wholesale massacres lasted up to the first days of June, and the summary executions up to the middle of that month. For a long time mysterious dramas were enacted in the Bois de Boulogne. Never will the exact number of the victims of the Bloody Week be known. The chief of military justice admitted 17,000 shot, the municipal council of Paris paid the expenses of burial of 17,000 corpses; but a great number were killed out of Paris or burnt. There is no exaggeration in saying 20,000 at least.

Many battlefields have numbered more dead, but these at least had fallen in the fury of the combat. The century has not witnessed such a slaughtering after the battle; there is nothing to equal it in the history of our civil struggles. St. Bartholomew's Day, June 1848, the 2nd December, would form but an episode of the massacres of May. Even the great executioners of Rome and modern times pale before the Duke of Magenta. The hecatombs of the Asiatic victors, the fetes of Dahomey alone could give some idea of this butchery of proletarians.

Such was the repression "by the laws, with the laws." And during these atrocities of incomparably worse than Bulgarian type, the bourgeoisie, raising to heaven its bloody hands, undertook to incite the whole world against this people, who, after two months of domination and the massacre of thousands of their own, had shed the blood of sixty-three prisoners.

All social powers covered the death-rattle of the victims by their applause. The priests, those great consecrators of assassination, celebrated the victory in a solemn service, at which the entire Assembly assisted. The reign of the *Gesu* was about to commence.

Chapter 33
The fate of the prisoners

The cause of justice, order, humanity and civilization has triumphed. (Thiers to the National Assembly.)

Happy the dead! They had not to mount the Calvary of the prisoners.

From the wholesale shootings one may guess the number of arrests. It was a furious razzia; men, women, children, Parisians, provincials, foreigners, a crowd of people of all sexes and all ages, of all parties and all conditions. All the lodgers of a house, all the inhabitants of a street, were carried off in a body. A suspicion, a word, a doubtful attitude were sufficient to cause one to be seized by the soldiers. From the 21st to the 30th May they thus picked up 40,000 persons.

These prisoners were formed into long chains, sometimes free, sometimes, as in June, 1848, bound by cords so as to form only one body. Whoever refused to walk on was pricked with the bayonet, and, if he resisted, shot on the spot, sometimes attached to a horse's tail. In front of the churches of the rich quarters the captives were forced to kneel down, bareheaded, amidst an infamous mob of lackeys, fashionable folk, and prostitutes, crying, "Death! death! Do not go any further; shoot them here!" At the Champs-Elysées they wanted to break lines to taste blood.

The prisoners were sent on to Versailles. Gallifet awaited them at La Muette. In the town he escorted the chains, halting under the windows of the aristocratic clubs in order to earn plaudits and hurrahs. At the gates of Paris he levied his tithe, walked past the ranks, and, with his look of a famished wolf, "You seem intelligent," said he to some one; "step out of the ranks." "You have a watch," said he to another; "you must have been a functionary of the Commune," and he placed him apart. On the 26th, in one single convoy, he chose eighty-three men and three women, made them draw up along the talus of the fortifications and had them shot. Then he said to their comrades, "My name is Gallifet. Your journals in Paris had sullied me enough. I take my revenge." On Sunday, the 28th, he said, "Let those who have white hairs step out from the ranks." One hundred and eleven captives advanced. "You," continued Gallifet, "you have seen June, 1848; you are more culpable than the others," and he had their corpses thrown over into the fortifications.

This purgation over, the convoys entered upon the route to Versailles, pressed between two lines of cavalry. It looked like the population of a city dragged away by fierce hordes. Lads, grey-bearded men, soldiers, dandies, all and every condition; the most delicate and the most rude confounded in the same vortex. There were many women, some with manacles on their hands; one with her baby, pressing its mother's neck with its frightened little hands; another, her arm broken, her blouse stained with blood; another depressed, clinging to the arm of her more vigorous neighbour; another in a statuesque attitude, defying pain and insults; always that woman of the people, who, after having carried the bread to the trenches and given consolation to the dying, hopeless — "weary of giving birth to unhappy souls" — longed for liberating death.

Their attitude, which inspired foreign journals with admiration, exasperated the Versaillese ferocity. "In seeing the convoys of insurgent women," said the *Figaro* "one feels in spite of oneself a kind of pity; but one is reassured by thinking that all the brothels of the capital have been thrown open by the National Guards, who patronized them, and that the majority of these ladies were inhabitants of these establishments."

Panting, covered with filth, idiotic with fatigue, hunger, and thirst, burnt by the sun, the convoys dragged themselves along for hours in the over-heated dust of the roads, harassed by the cries, the blows from the mounted chasseurs. The Prussians had not thus cruelly treated these soldiers when, prisoners themselves some months before, they had been led away from Sedan or Metz. The captives who fell were sometimes shot, sometimes they were only thrown into the carts that followed.

At the entry into Versailles the crowd awaited them, always the *élite* of French society, deputies, functionaries, priests, officers, women of all sorts. The fury of the 4th April and the preceding convoys were as much surpassed as the sea swells at the equinoctial tide. The Avenues de Paris and de St. Cloud were lined by savages, who followed the convoys with vociferations, blows, covered them with filth and broken pieces of bottle. "One sees," said the Liberal-Conservative newspaper, the *Siècle*, of the 30th May, "women, not prostitutes, but elegant ladies, insult the prisoners on their passage, and even strike them with their sunshades." Woe to whoever did not insult the vanquished! Woe to him who allowed a movement of commiseration to escape him! He was at once seized, led to the post, or else simply forced into the convoy. Frightful retrogression of human nature, all the more hideous in that it contrasted with the elegance of the costume! Prussian officers came from St. Denis once more to see what governing classes they had had to oppose them.

The first convoys were promenaded about as a spectacle in the streets of Versailles; others were stationed for hours at the torrid Place d'Armes, a few steps from the large trees, whose shade was refused them. The prisoners were then distributed in four depots, the cellars of the Grandes-Ecuries, the Orangerie of the castle, the docks of Satory, and the riding-school of the Ecole de St. Cyr. Into these damp, nauseous cellars, where light and air only penetrated by some narrow openings, men, children, of whom some were not more than ten years old, were crowded without straw during the first days. When they did get some, it was soon reduced to mere dung. No water to wash with; no means of changing their rags, as the relations who brought linen were brutally sent back. Twice a day, in a trough, they got a yellowish liquid, a porridge. The gendarmes sold tobacco at exorbitant prices, and confiscated it in order to sell it over again. There were no doctors. Gangrene attacked the wounded; opthalmia broke out; deliriousness became chronic. In the night were heard the shrieks of the feverstricken and the mad. Opposite, the gendarmes remained impassive, their guns loaded.

Even these horrors were outdone by the Fosse-aux-Lions, a vault without air, absolutely dark, the antechamber of the tomb, under the large red marble staircase of the terrace. Whoever was noted as dangerous, or whoever had simply displeased the corporal, was thrown into it. The most robust could only bear up against it a few days. On leaving it, giddy, the mind a blank, dazzled by the broad daylight, they swooned. Happy he who met the look of his wife. The wives of the captives pressed against the outer rails of the Orangerie, striving to distinguish some one amidst the dimly seen herd. They tore their hair, implored the gendarmes, who thrust them back, struck them, called them infamous names.

The open-air hell was the docks of the plateau of Satory, a vast parallelogram enclosed by walls. The soil is clayey, and the least rain soaks it. The first arrivals were placed within the buildings, which could contain about thirteen hundred persons, the others remained outside, bareheaded, for their hats had been knocked off at Paris or at Versailles. The gendarmes were on duty, being more reliable, more hardened than the soldiers.

On the Thursday evening at eight o'clock a convoy, composed chiefly of women, arrived at the dock. "Many of us," one of them has reported to me, the wife of a *chef-de-légion,* "had died on the way; we had had nothing since morning.

"It was still daylight. We saw a great multitude of prisoners. The women were apart in a hut at the entrance. We joined them.

"We were told that there was a pond, and, dying of thirst, we rushed thither. The first who drank uttered a loud cry, vomited. 'Oh, the wretches! they make us drink the blood of our own people.' For since evening the wounded went there to bathe their wounds; but thirst tormented us so cruelly, that some had the courage to rinse out their mouths with this bloody water.

"The hut was already full, and we were made to lie on the earth in groups of about 200. An officer came and said to us, 'Vile creatures! listen to the order I give. Gendarmes, the first who moves, fire on these — !'

"At ten o'clock we heard reports quite near. We jumped up. 'Lie down, wretches!' cried the gendarmes, taking aim at us. It was some prisoners being shot a few steps from us. We thought the balls would pass through our heads. The gendarmes who had just been shooting came to relieve our guardians. We remained the whole night watched by men heated with carriage. They grumbled at those who writhed with terror and cold. 'Do not be impatient; your turn is coming.' At daybreak we saw the dead. The gendarmes said to each other, 'Oh! Isn't this a jolly vintage?'

"In the evening the prisoners heard a sound of spades and hammers in the wall of the south. The shootings, the menaces had maddened them. They awaited death from all sides and in every shape; they thought that this time they were going to be blown up. Holes opened and machine-guns appeared, some of which were discharged."

On Friday evening a storm of several hours broke out above the camp. The prisoners were forced, on pain of being shot, to lie down all night in the mud. About twenty died of cold.

The camp of Satory soon became the Longchamp of Versailles high life. Captain Aubrey did the honours with the ladies, the deputies, the literary men, showing them his subjects grovelling in the mud, devouring a few biscuits, taking tumblers of water from the pond into which the gendarmes stood on no ceremony in relieving themselves. Some, going mad, dashed their heads against the walls; others howled, tearing their beards and hair. A fetid cloud arose from this living mass of rags and horrors. "There are," said the *Indépendence Française,* "several thousands of people poisoned with dirt and vermin spreading infection of a kilometre around. Cannon are levelled at these wretches penned up like wild beasts. The inhabitants of Paris are afraid of the epidemic resulting from the burying of the insurgents killed in the town. Those whom the *Officiel* of Paris called the rurals are much more afraid of the epidemic resulting from the presence of the live insurgents at Satory."

Those are the honest people of Versailles, who had just caused the triumph of "the cause of justice, order, humanity, and civilisation." How good and humane, despite the bombardment and the sufferings of the siege, those *brigands* of Paris had been, above all by the side of these *honest people!* Who ever ill-treated a prisoner in the Paris of the Commune? What woman perished or was insulted? What obscure corner of the Parisian prisons had hidden a single one of the thousand tortures which displayed themselves in broad daylight at Versailles?

From the 24th May to the first days of June the convoys did not cease flowing into this abyss. The arrests went on in large hauls by day and night. The sergents-de-ville accompanied the soldiers, and, under the pretext of perquisitions, forced the locks, appropriating objects of value. Several officers, were in the sequel condemned for the embezzlement of objects seized. They arrested not only the persons compromised in the late affairs, those who were denounced by their uniforms, or documents found in the *mairies* and at the War Office, but whoever was known for his republican opinions. They arrested, too, the purveyors of the Commune, and even the musicians, who had never crossed the ramparts. The ambulance attendants shared the same fate. And yet during the siege a delegate of the Commune, having inspected the ambulances of the press, had said to the personnel, "I am aware that most of you are the friends of the Government of Versailles, but I hope you may live long enough to recognize your mistake. I do not trouble myself to know whether the lancets at the service of the wounded are royalist or republican. I see that you do your task worthily. I thank you for it. I shall report it to the Commune."

Some poor wretches had taken refuge in the Catacombs. They were hunted by torchlight. The police agents, assisted by dogs, fired at every suspicious shadow. Hunts were organized in the forests near Paris. The police watched all the stations, all the ports Of France. Passports had to be renewed and checked at Versailles. The masters of boats were under supervision. On the 26th Jules Favre had solemnly asked the foreign powers for the extradition of the fugitives, under the pretext that the battle of the streets was not a political act.

Extradition flourished at Paris. Fear closed all doors. No shelter was there for the fugitives. Few friends were left — no comrades. Everywhere pitiless refusals or denunciations. Doctors renewed the infamies of 1834, and delivered up the wounded. Every cowardly instinct rose to the surface, and Paris disclosed sloughs of infamy whose existence she had not suspected even under the Empire. The honest people, masters of the streets, had their rivals, their creditors, arrested as Communards, and formed committees of inquiry in their arrondissements. The Commune had rejected denunciators; the police of order received them with open arms. The denunciations rose to the fabulous height of 399,823, of which a twentieth at most were signed.

A very considerable part of these denunciations issued from the press. For several weeks it did not cease stirring the rage and panic of the bourgeoisie. M. Thiers, reviving one of the absurdities of June, 1848, in a bulletin spoke of "poisonous liquids collected in order to poison the soldiers." All the inventions of that time were again taken up, appropriated to the hour, and horribly amplified; chambers in the sewers with wires all prepared, 8,000 petroleuses enrolled, houses marked with a stamp for burning, pumps, injectors, eggs filled with petroleum, poisoned balls, roasted gendarmes, hanged sailors, violated women, prostitutes requisitioned, endless thefts — all was printed, and the gulls believed all. Some journals had the speciality of false orders for arson; false signatures, of which the originals could never be produced, but which were to be admitted as positive evidence by the courts-martial and honest historians. When it fancied the of the bourgeoisie was flagging, the press fanned it again, each journal outbidding the other in villainy. "Paris, we know," said the *Bien Public,* "asks for nothing better than to go to sleep again; though we should trouble her, we will awaken her." And on the 8th June the *Figaro* still drew up plans of carnage. The revolutionary writer who will take the pains to collect in a volume extracts from the reactionary press of May and June, 1871, from the Parliamentary inquiries, the bourgeois pamphlets, and histories of the Commune — a mixture as monstrous as that of the witches" cauldron — will do more for the edification and the future justice of the people than a whole band of mouthing agitators.

There were, to French honour, some traits of generosity, and even heroism, amidst this epidemic of cowardice. Vermorel, wounded, was taken in by the wife of a concierge, who succeeded for a few hours in passing him off for her son. The mother of a Versaillese soldier gave several members of the Council of the Commune an asylum. A great number of insurgents were saved by unknown people; and yet it was during the first days a matter of death, afterwards of transportation, to shelter the vanquished. The women once again showed their great heart.

The average of arrests kept up in June and July to a hundred a day. At Belleville, Ménilmontant, in the thirteenth arrondissement, in certain streets, there were only old women left. The Versaillese, in their lying returns, have admitted 38,568 prisoners, amongst whom were 1,058 women and 651 children, of whom forty-seven were thirteen years of age, twenty-one twelve, four ten, and one seven, as though they had by some secret method counted the herds whom they fed at the troughs. The number of those arrested very probably reached 50,000 men.

The errors were numberless. Some women of that *beau monde* who went with dilated nostrils to contemplate the corpses of the Federals were included in the razzias, and led off to Satory, where, their clothes in rags, devoured by vermin, they figured very well as the imaginary petroleuses of their journals.

Thousands of individuals were obliged to hide; thousands gained the frontier. An idea of the general losses may be gathered from the fact that at the by-elections of July there were 100,000 less electors than in February. Parisian industry was crushed by it. Most of the workmen who gave this branch of manufacture its artistic *cachet* perished, were arrested, or emigrated in masses. In the month of October the municipal council proved in an official report that certain industries were obliged to refuse orders for want of hands.

The savageness of the searches, the number of the arrests, joined to the despair of the defeat, tore from this town — bled to the last drop of blood — some supreme convulsions. At Belleville, at Montmartre, in the thirteenth arrondissement, shots were fired from houses. At the Café du Helder, in the Rue de Rennes, the Rue de la Paix, Place de la Madeleine, soldiers and officers fell, struck by invisible hands; near the Pépinière Barracks a general was shot at. The Versaillese journals wondered, with naive impudence, that popular fury was not calmed, and could not understand "what reason, even the most futile, of hatred one could have for soldiers who had the most inoffensive look in the world' (*La Cloche*).

The Left followed to the very end the line it had traced out for itself on the 19th March. Having prevented the provinces from coming to the rescue of Paris and voted its thanks to the army, it also joined its maledictions to those of the provincials. Louis Blanc, who in 1877 was to defend the red flag, wrote to the *Figaro* to stigmatize the vanquished, to bow down before their judges, and declare "the public indignation legitimate". This Extreme Left, which five years later grew enthusiastic for the amnesty, would not hear the death-groans of the 20,000 shot, nor even, though but a hundred yards from them, the shrieks from the Orangerie. In June, 1848, the sombre imprecation of Lammennais fell upon the massacres, and Pierre Leroux defended the insurgents. The great philosophers of the Rural Assembly, Catholic or Positivist, were all one against the working men. Gambetta, delighted at being rid of the Socialists, hurried back from St. Sebastien, and in a solemn speech at Bordeaux declared that the Government which had been able to crush Paris "had even by that proved itself legitimate."

There were some men of courage in the provinces. The *Droits de l'Homme* of Montpelier, the *Emancipation* of Toulouse, the *National du Loiret*, and several advanced journals recounted the assassinations of the conquerors. Most of these journals were prosecuted and suppressed. Some movements took plate; a commencement of riots at Pamiers (Ariège) and at Voiron (Isère). At Lyons the army was confined in its barracks, and the prefect, Valentin, had the town closed in order to arrest the fugitives of Paris. There were arrests at Bordeaux.

At Brussels Victor Hugo protested against the declaration of the Belgian government, which promised to deliver up the fugitives. Louis Blanc and Schoelcher wrote him a letter full of blame, and his house was stoned by a fashionable mob. Bebel in the German Parliament and Whalley in the House of Commons denounced the Versaillese fury. Garcia Lopez said from the tribune of the Cortes, "We admire this great revolution, which no one can appreciate justly today."

The working men of foreign countries solemnized the obsequies of their brothers of Paris. At London, Brussels, Zurich, Geneva, Leipzig, and Berlin, monster meetings proclaimed themselves in accord with the Commune, devoted the slaughterers to universal execration, and declared accomplices of these crimes the Governments which had not made any remonstrances. All the Socialist journals glorified the struggle of the vanquished. The great voice of the International recounted their effort in an eloquent address and confided their memory to the workmen of the whole world.

On the triumphal entry of Moltke at the head of the victorious Prussian army into Berlin, the workmen received them with hurrahs for the Commune, and at several places the people were charged by the cavalry.

Chapter 34
The trials of the Communards

Conciliation is the angel descending after the storm. (Dufaure to the National Assembly, 26th April, 1871.)

The human lakes of Versailles and Satory were soon overflowing. From the first days of June the prisoners were filed off to the seaports and crowded into cattle-wagons, the awnings of which, hermetically closed, let in no breath of air. In a corner was a heap of biscuits; but themselves thrown upon this heap, the prisoners had soon reduced it to mere crumbs. For twenty-four hours, and sometimes thirty-two hours, they remained without anything to drink. They fought in this throng for a little air, a little room. Some, maddened, flung themselves upon their comrades. One day at La Ferté-Bemard cries were uttered in a wagon. The chief of the escort stopped the convoy; the sergeants-de-ville discharged their revolvers through the awning. Silence ensued, and the rolling coffins set out again at full speed.

From the month of June to the month of September 28,000 prisoners were thus thrown into the harbours, the forts and the oceanic isles, from Cherbourg to the Gironde. Twenty-five pontoons took in 20,000, the forts and isles 8,087.

On the pontoons tortures were inflicted by regulation. The traditions of June and of December were religiously observed with the victims of 1871. The prisoners, penned in cages made of wooden planks and iron bars, received only a dim light through the nailed down port-holes. Ventilation there was none. From the first hours the exhalations were unbearable. The sentinels walked up and down in this menagerie with the order to fire at the slightest alarm. Cannon charged with grapeshot overlooked the batteries. There were neither hammocks nor blankets, and for all food some biscuits, bread, and beans, but no wine or tobacco. The inhabitants of Brest and Cherbourg having sent some provisions and little luxuries, the officers sent them back.

This cruelty relaxed somewhat after a time. The prisoners received a hammock for every two, some shirts, some blouses, and now and then some wine. They were allowed to wash, to come on to the deck to snatch a little fresh air. The sailors showed some humanity, but the marines were still the same bandits as in the days of May, and the crew was often obliged to tear the prisoners from them.

The regime of the pontoons varied according to the officers. At Brest the second officer, commander of the *Ville de Lyon,* forbade the insulting of the prisoners; while the master-at-arms of the *Breslau* treated them like convicts. At Cherbourg one of the lieutenants of the *Tage,* Clémenceau, was ferocious. The commander of the *Bayard* turned his vessel into a diminutive Orangerie. This ship had witnessed the most abominable acts perhaps that have sullied the history of the French navy. Absolute silence was the rule on board. As soon as anyone spoke in the cages the sentry menaced and several times shot. For a complaint, or mere forgetfulness of a rule, the prisoners were tied to the bars of their cages by the ankles and wrists.

The dungeons on shore were as terrible as the pontoons. At Quélern as many as forty prisoners were shut up in the same casemate. The lower ones were deadly. The cesspools emptied into them, and in the morning the faecal matter covered the floor some two inches deep. By the side of these was salubrious unoccupied accommodation, but they would not remove the prisoners thither. One day M. Jules Simon came, thought that his former electors were looking but poorly, and decided that recourse must be taken to severity. Elisée Reclus had opened a school, and tried to raise out of their ignorance a hundred and fifty-one prisoners who could neither read nor write. The Minister of Public Education had the classes stopped, and had the small library, which the prisoners had got together by making the greatest sacrifices, closed.

The prisoners of the forts, like those of the pontoons, were fed on biscuits and bacon; later on, soup and broth were added on Sundays; knives and forks were forbidden; it cost several days' struggle to get spoons. The profit of the sutler, which, according to the list of charges, ought to be limited to a tenth, reached as much as five hundred per cent.

At the Fort Boyard men and women were packed into the same enclosure, separated only by a screen. The women were forced to perform their ablutions under the eyes of the sentinels. Sometimes their husbands were in the neighbouring compartment. "We noticed," wrote a prisoner, "a young and beautiful woman, twenty years old, who fainted every time she was forced to undress."

According to much evidence which we have received, the most cruel prison was that of St. Marcouf. The prisoners remained there for over six months, deprived of air, light, and tobacco, forbidden to speak, having for their only nourishment the crumbs of brown biscuits and rancid fat. All were attacked with scurvy.

This continual severity got the better of the most robust constitutions; there were in consequence 2,000 sick in the hospitals. The official reports admit 1,179 dead out of 33,665 civil prisoners. This figure is evidently below the truth. During the first days at Versailles a certain number of individuals were killed, and others died without being counted. There were no statistics before the transfer to the pontoons. There is no exaggeration in saying that 2,000 prisoners died while in the hands of the Versaillese. A great number perished afterwards of anaemia, and of maladies contracted during their captivity.

Some idea of the tortures of the pontoons and the forts, far from the surveillance of public opinion, may be gathered from those that were openly displayed at Versailles, under the eyes of the Government, the Chamber, and the Radicals. Colonel Gaillard, chief of military justice, had said to the soldiers who guarded the prisoners of the Chantiers, "As soon as you see any one move, raising their arms, fire; it is I who give you the order."

At the Grenier d'Abondance of the Western Railway there were eight hundred women. For weeks and weeks they slept on straw, were unable to change their linen. At the slightest noise, a quarrel, the guards threw themselves upon them, struck them, more especially on the breasts. Charles Mercereau, a former Cent-Garde, the governor of this sink, had those that displeased him tied down and then beat them with his cane. He led about over his dominions the ladies of Versailles, covetous of petroleuses, and before them said to his victims, "Come, hussies, cast down your eyes." And indeed that was the least our Federal women could do before these worthy persons.

Prostitutes, carried off in the razzias, and carefully kept there in order to spy upon the other prisoners, publicly abandoned themselves to the guardians. The protests of the women of the Commune were punished by blows with cords. With a refinement of infamy, the Versaillese wished to bow down these valiant women to the level of the others. All the prisoners were subjected to inspection.

Dignity and outraged nature revenged themselves by terrible cries. "Where is my father? Where my husband? and my son? What! alone, quite alone, and all these cowards against me! I, the mother, the laborious wife, subjected to the whip, insult, and sullied by these unclean hands for having defended liberty!" Many went mad. All passed through their hours of madness. Those who were pregnant miscarried or brought forth still-born children.

The priests were no more wanting in the prisons than at the shootings. The chaplain of Richemont said to the prisoners, "I know that I am here in a forest of Bondy but my duty," etc. On the day of St. Magdalene the Bishop of Algiers, making a delicate allusion to the saint of the day, said to them, "That they were all Magdalenes, but not repentant; that Magdalene had neither burned nor assassinated;" and uttering other evangelical amenities.

The children were shut up in a part of the women's prison, and were just as brutally treated. A corporal, the secretary of Mercereau, kicked open the stomach of a boy; another received the bastinado, and lingered for a long time at the infirmary. The son of Ranvier, twelve years old, was cruelly beaten for refusing to betray the hiding-place of his father.

All these unfortunate prisoners of the pontoons, the forts, and the houses of correction were for several months devoured by vermin before their cases were inquired into. The Versaillese Moloch held more victims than he could digest. After the first days of June he disgorged 1,090 persons reclaimed by the reactionaries. But how to draw up indictments against 36,000 prisoners? It was all very well for Dufaure to let loose all the police agents of the Empire into the prisons; in the month of August only 4,000 prisoners had been interrogated.

Still it was necessary to satiate the rage of the bourgeoisie, which wanted a sensational trial. A few celebrities who had escaped the massacre had been taken, some members of the Council of the Commune, of the Central Committee, Rossel, Rochefort, etc. M. Thiers and Dufaure got up a grand performance.

The trial was to be the model to serve as a type for the jurisprudence of the courts-martial, for the prisoners were to be judged by the same soldiers who had conquered them. The old procureur and his president applied all their pettifogging cunning to lowering the debate.

They refused the character of political men to the accused, and reduced the insurrection to an ordinary crime, thus securing to themselves the right of cutting short effective defences, and the advantage of condemnations to the penal colony and to death, which the hypocritical bourgeoisie pretends to have abolished in political cases. The third court-martial was carefully selected. The commissar chosen was Gaveau, a base fanatic, who had shown signs of mental derangement and had struck the prisoners in the streets of Versailles; the president, Merlin, a colonel of engineers, one of the capitulationists of Bazaine's army; the rest an assortment of trusty Bonapartists. Sedan and Metz were going to judge Paris.

The ceremony commenced on the 7th August, in a large hall containing two thousand seats. Personages of rank reclined in the red velvet arm-chairs; deputies occupied three hundred seats; the remainder belonged to the bourgeois of note, to "worthy" families, to the aristocracy of prostitution, and to the howling press. The talking journalists, the brilliant dresses, the smiling faces, the toyings with fans, the gay bouquets, the opera-glasses pointed in all directions, reminded one of the most elegant first-night performances. The staff officers, in full uniform, smartly conducted the ladies to their seats, not forgetting to make the indispensable bow.

All this scum boiled over when the prisoners appeared. There were seventeen: Ferré, Assi, Jourde, Paschal Grousset, Régere, Billioray, Courbet, Urbain, Victor Clément, Trinquet, Champy, Rastoul, Verdure, Decamps, Parent, members of the Council of the Commune; Ferrat and Lullier, members of the Central Committee.

Gaveau read the accusation act. This revolution was born of two plots, that of the revolutionary party and that of the International; Paris had risen on the 18th March, in answer to the appeal of a few scoundrels; the Central Committee had ordered the execution of Lecomte and Clément-Thomas; the demonstration of the Place Vendôme was an unarmed demonstration; the head-surgeon of the army had been assassinated while making a supreme appeal to conciliation; the Commune had committed thefts of all kinds; the implements of the nuns of Picpus were transformed into instruments of orthopaedy; the explosion of the Rapp magazines was the work of the Commune; desirous of kindling violent hatred of the enemy in the hearts of the Federals, Ferré had presided at the execution of the hostages of La Roquette, set fire to the Ministry of Finance, as was proved by the facsimile of an order written in his hand, *"Burn Finances!"* Each one of the members of the Council of the Commune had to answer for facts relating to his particular functions and collectively for all the decrees issued. This indictment, worthy of a low police agent, communicated beforehand to M. Thiers, indeed made of the cause a simple affair of robbery and arson.

It took up a whole sitting. The next day, Ferré, interrogated the first, refused to answer, and laid his conclusions upon the table. "The conclusions of the incendiary Ferré are of no moment!" cried Gaveau, and the witnesses against him were called. Fourteen out of twentyfour belonged to the police; the others were priests or Government employees. An expert in handwriting, celebrated at the lawcourts for his blunders, affirmed that the order *"Burn Finances"* was certainly in Ferré's hand. In vain the accused demanded that the signature of this order should be compared with his, which figured very often in the jail register; that at least the original should be produced, and not the facsimile. Gaveau exclaimed indignantly, "Why, this is want of confidence!"

Thus set to rights from the outset as to the plot and the character of their judges, the accused might have declined every debate; they committed the fault of accepting it. If even they had proudly proclaimed their political character! But it was not so; some even denied it. Almost all, confining themselves to their personal defence, abandoned the Revolution of the 18th March, whose mandate they had solicited or accepted. Their preoccupation for their own safety betrayed itself by sad defections. But from the very dock of the accused the voice of the people thus denied arose avengingly. A workman of that brave Parisian race, the first in labour, study, and combat, a member of the Council of the Commune, intelligent and convinced, modest in the Council, one of the foremost in the struggle, the shoemaker Trinquet, proclaimed the honour of having fulfilled his mandate to the end. "I was," said he, 'sent to the Commune by my co-citizens; I have paid with my person; I have been to the barricades, and I regret not having died there; I should not today assist at this sad spectacle of colleagues who, after having taken their share in the action, will no longer bear their part of the responsibility. I am an insurgent; I do not deny it."

The examinations were drawn out with fastidious slowness during seventeen sittings. Always the same public of soldiers, bourgeois, courtesans, hissing the accused; the same witnesses, priests, police agents, and functionaries; the same fury in the accusation, the same cynicism in the tribunal, the same howling of the press. The massacres had not glutted this. It yelled at the accused, demanded their death, and every day dragged them through the mire of its reports. Foreign correspondents were revolted. *The Standard*, a great reviler of the Commune, said, "Anything more scandalous than the tone of the demi-monde press during this trial it is impossible to imagine." Some of the accused having asked for the protection of the president, Merlin took up the defence of the newspapers.

Then came the prosecutor's address to the court. Gaveau to remain true to his instructions, was to demonstrate that Paris had fought for six weeks in order to enable a few individuals to steal the remainder of the public chests, to bum some houses, and to shoot a few gendarmes. This epauletted limb of the law overthrew as a soldier all the arguments he built up as a magistrate. "The Commune, "he said, "had acted as a Government," and five minutes after he refused the members of the Council of the Commune the character of political men. Passing in review the different accused, he said of Ferré, "I should be wasting my time and yours by discussing the numerous charges weighing upon him," of Jourde, "The figures he has given you are quite imaginary. I shall not trespass upon your time by discussing them." During the battle in the streets Jourde had received the order of the Committee of Public Safety to remit a thousand francs to every member of the Council. About thirty only had received this sum. Gaveau said, "They divided millions amongst each other;" and a man of his sort must have believed this. What sovereign has ever abandoned power without carrying off millions? He lengthily accused Grousset of having stolen paper in order to print his newspaper; another of having lived with a mistress. A coarse *lansquenet*, incapable of understanding that the more he lowered the men the greater he made this Revolution, so vital despite all defections and incapacities.

The audience emphasised this accusation with frantic applause. At the conclusion there were calls as in a theatre. Merlin gave Ferré's advocate permission to speak, but Ferré declared he wished to defend himself, and commenced reading:

Ferré: "After the conclusion of the treaty of peace consequent upon the shameful capitulation of Paris, the Republic was in danger, the men who had succeeded the Empire fallen in the midst of mire and blood' —

Merlin: Fallen in the midst of mire and blood! Here I must stop you. Was not your Government in the same situation?

Ferré: "Clung to power, and, though overwhelmed by public contempt, they prepared in the dark a coup-d'état; they persisted in refusing Paris the election of her municipal council" —

Gaveau: This is not true.

Merlin: What you are saying, Ferré, is false. Continue, but at the third time I shall stop you.

Ferré: "The honest and sincere journals were suppressed, the best patriots condemned to death" —

Gaveau: The prisoner cannot go on reading this. I shall ask for the application of the law.

Ferré: "The Royalists were preparing for the partition of France. At last, in the night of the 18th March, they believed themselves ready, and attempted to disarm the National Guard, and the wholesale arrest of Republicans" —

Merlin: Come, sit down. I allow your advocate to speak.

(The advocate of Ferré demanded that his client might be allowed to read the last sentences of his declaration, and Merlin gave way.)

Ferré: "A member of the Commune, I am in the hands of its victors. They want my head; they may take it. I will never save my life by cowardice. Free I have lived, so I will die. I add but one word. Fortune is capricious; I confide to the future the care of my memory and my revenge."

Merlin: The memory of an assassin!

Gaveau: Such manifestoes should be sent to the penal colony.

Merlin: All this does not answer to the acts for which you are here.

Ferré: This means that I accept the fate that is in store for me.

During this duel between Merlin and Ferré the hall had remained silent. Ferocious hisses burst forth when Ferré concluded. The president was obliged to raise the sitting, and the judges were going out when a barrister demanded that notice should be taken for the defence that the president had called Ferré "assassin".

The hisses of the audience answered. The advocate indignantly turned to the tribunal, to the seats of the press, to the public. Cries of rage arose from all corners of the hall, drowning his voice for several minutes. Merlin, who was radiant, at last obtained silence, and answered cavalierly, "I acknowledge that I made use of the expression of which the advocate spoke. The court takes notice of your conclusions."

The day before, as a barrister remarked to him, "We are all answerable, not to the public opinion of today, but to history, which will judge us;" Merlin had cynically answered, "History! At that epoch we shall no longer be here!" The French bourgeoisie had found its Jeffries.

Early the next day the hall was crowded. The curiosity of the public, the anxiety of the judges, were extreme. Gaveau, in order to accuse his adversaries of all crimes at once, had for two days talked politics, history, socialism. It would have sufficed to answer each one of his arguments, in order to give the cause that political character which he denied it, if one of the prisoners were at last to rouse up, and, less careful of his person than of the Commune, follow up the accusation step by step, oppose to the grotesque theories of conspiracy the eternal provocation of the privileged classes; describe Paris offering herself to the Government of National Defence, betrayed by it, then attacked by Versailles, abandoned; the proletarians reorganizing all the services of this great city, and in a state of war, surrounded by treason, governing for two months without police spies and without executions, remaining poor in sight of the milliards of the bank; if he were to confront the sixty-three hostages with the 20,000 assassinated, unveil the pontoons, the jails, swarming with 40,000 unfortunate beings; take the world to witness in the name of truth, of justice, of the future, and make of the accused Commune the accuser.

The president might have interrupted him, the cries of the public drowned his appeal, the court after the first words declared him outlawed. Such a man, reduced to silence, would, like Danton gagged, find a gesture, a cry, which should pierce the walls and hurl his anathema at the head of the tribunal.

The vanquished missed this revenge. Instead of presenting a collective defence or of maintaining a silence which would have saved their dignity, the accused entrusted themselves to the barristers. Each one of these gentlemen stretched a point to save his client even at the expense of his brother lawyers. One barrister was also the *Figaro's* and the confidant of the Empress; another, one of the demonstrators of the Place Vendôme, begged the court not to confound his cause with that of the scoundrel's near him. There were scandalous pleadings. This debasement disarmed neither the tribunal nor the public. Every moment Gaveau bounded out of his arm-chair. "You are an insolent fellow," said he to a lawyer. "If there is anything absurd here, it is you." The audience applauded, ever ready to pounce upon the prisoners. On the 31st August its fury rose to such a pitch that Merlin threatened to have the court cleared.

On the 2nd September the court feigned to deliberate the whole day. At nine o'clock in the evening it returned to the sitting, and Merlin read the judgment. Ferré and Lullier were condemned to death; Trinquet and Urbain to hard labour for life; Assi, Billioray, Champy, Regere, Grousset, Verdure, Ferrat to transportation in a fortress; Courbet to six months' and Victor

Clément to three months' imprisonment. Decamps and Parent were acquitted. The audience retired much disappointed at having got only two condemnations to death.

As a fact, this judicial performance had proved nothing. Could the Revolution of the 18th March be appreciated from the conduct of secondary actors, and Delescluze, Varlin, Vermorel, Tridon, Moreau, and many others, by the attitude of Lullier, Decamps, Victor Clément, or Billioray? And even if the hearing of Ferré and Trinquet had not proved that there had been men in the Council of the Commune, what then did the defection of the majority show if not that this movement was the work of all, not of a few great minds; that in this crisis the people only had been great, they only revolutionary; that the Revolution was to be found in the people, not in the Government of the Commune?

The bourgeoisie, on the contrary, had displayed all its hideousness. The audience, the tribunal, had been on the same level. Some witnesses had manifestly perjured themselves. During the debates, in the lobbies, in the cafés, all the ragamuffins who had endeavoured to dupe the Commune impudently ascribed to themselves the success of the army. The *Figaro*, having opened a subscription for Ducatel, had picked up 100,000 francs and an order of the Légion d'Honneur for him. Allured by this success, all the conspirators demanded their aims and their order. The partisans of Beaufond-Lasnier, those of Charpentier-Domalain, fell out, recounted their prowess, each and all swearing that he had betrayed better than his rivals.

While society was being avenged at Versailles, the Court of Assizes of Paris avenged the honour of Jules Favre. Immediately after the Commune, the Minister for Foreign Affairs had had M. Laluyé arrested, who was guilty of having communicated to Millière the documents published in the *Vengeur*. The honest Minister, not having succeeded in getting his enemy shot as a Communard, summoned him before the assizes for libel. Here the former member of the Government of National Defence, the former Minister of Foreign Affairs, the deputy of Paris, publicly confessed that he had committed forgeries, but he pleaded having done so to secure his children a fortune. This touching avowal melted the *patres familias* of the jury, and Laluyé was condemned to imprisonment for one year. Some months later he died at Sainte Pélagie. Jules Favre was terribly lucky. In less than six months the firing squad and the dungeon had delivered him of two redoubtable enemies.

While the third court-martial was quarrelling with the lawyers, the fourth hurried through its business without more ado. On the 16th August, almost immediately after its opening, it had already pronounced two sentences of death. If the one court had its Jeffries, the other had its Trestaillon in Colonel Boisdenemetz, a kind of wild boar, a drunkard, seeing all red, a wit at times, and correspondent of the *Figaro*. On the 4th September some women were brought before him, accused of setting fire to the Légion d'Honneur. This was the trial of the petroleuses. The eight thousand enrolled furies who had been announced by the newspapers of order were reduced to the number of five. The cross-examination proved that the so-called petroleuses were only admirably kind-hearted ambulance nurses. One of them, Rétiffe, said, "I should have looked after a soldier of Versailles as wen as a National Guard." "Why," another was asked, "did you remain when all the battalion ran away?" "There were wounded and dying," answered she simply. The witnesses for the prosecution themselves declared that they had not seen any of them kindle fire; but their fate was decided beforehand. Between two sittings Boisdenemetz cried in a café, "Death to all these trulls!"

Three barristers out of five had deserted the bar. "Where are they?" said the president. "They have asked to be allowed to absent themselves to go to the country," answered the commissar. The court charged soldiers with the defence of these poor women. One of them, the Quatermaster Bordelais, made this fine speech: "I defer to the wisdom of the tribunal."

His client, Suétens, was condemned to death, as were also Rétiffe and Marchais, "for having attempted to change the form of the Government;" the two others to transportation and confinement. One of the condemned, turning to the officer who read the sentence, cried to him in a heartrending voice, "And who will feed my child?"

"Thy child! See, he is here!"

Some days after, before this same Boisdenemetz, fifteen children of Paris appeared; the eldest was sixteen years old, the youngest, so small that he could hardly be seen in the dock of prisoners, was eleven. They wore blue blouses and military képis.

"Druet," said the soldier, "what did your father do?"

"He was a mechanic."

"Why did you not work like him?"

"Because there was no work for me."

"Bouverat, why did you join the *Pupilles de la Commune?*"

"To get something to eat."

"You have been arrested for vagrancy?"

"Yes, twice; the second time for stealing a pair of stockings."

"Cagnoncle, you were *Enfant de la Commune?*"

"Yes, sir."

"Why did you leave your family?"

"Because they had no bread."

"Did you discharge many shots?"

"About fifty."

"Lescot, why did you leave your mother?"

"Because she could not keep me."

"How many children were there of you?"

"Three."

"You have been wounded?"

"Yes, by a ball in the head."

"Leberg, you have been with a master, and you were surprised taking the cash-box. How much did you take?"

"Ten sous."

"Did not that money burn your hands?"

And you, red-handed man! these words, do they not burn your lips? Sinister fools! who do not understand that before these children, thrown into the streets without education, without hope, through the necessity you have made for them, the culprit is you, lace-bedecked soldier, you, the public minister of a society in which children twelve years old, capable and willing to work, are forced to steal in order to get a pair of stockings, and have no other alternative than to fall beneath bullets or die of hunger!

Chapter 35
The executions

At Versailles, every means was used to ensure that the cases were heard with the utmost attention and seriousness ... I think therefore that the verdicts given are not only unquestionably right, according to all our laws, but that for the most scrupulous consciences, they are verdicts which speak the truth. ("Hear, hear!") (Dufaure's speech against the amnesty, session of 18th May, 1876.)

The verdict of the military tribunals was, I must admit, for the best. (Allain-Targé, pro-Gambetta deputy, session of 19th May, 1876.)

Twenty-six courts-martial, twenty-six judicial machine-guns, were at work at Versailles, Mont-Valérien, Paris, Vincennes, St. Cloud, Sevres, St. Germain, Rambouillet, as far as Chartres. In the composition of these tribunals not only all semblance of justice, but even all military rules had been despised. The Assembly had not even troubled itself to define their prerogatives. And these officers, hot from the struggle, and for whom every resistance, even the most legitimate, is a crime, had been let loose upon their overwhelmed enemies without any other jurisprudence than their fancy, without any other rein than their humanity, without any other instruction than their cornmission. With such janissaries and a penal code comprising everything in its elastic obscurity, there was no need for emergency laws in order to attaint all Paris. Soon one saw the most extravagant theories invented and propagated in these judicial dens. Thus, being at the place of the crime constituted legal complicity; with these magistrates this was a dogma.

Instead of removing the courts-martial into the ports, the prisoners were forced to again undergo the painful journey from the sea to Versailles. Some, like Elisée Reclus, had thus to pass through fourteen prisons. From the pontoons they were conducted to the railway station on foot, their hands manacled; but at Brest, when they passed through the streets showing their chains, the passers-by uncovered their heads before them.

With the exception of a few prisoners of note, whose trials I shall briefly recount, the bulk of the prisoners were thrust before the tribunals after an examination which did not even always make sure of their identity. Too poor to get a defender, these unfortunate people, without guides, without witnesses for the defence — those whom they called did not dare to come for fear of being arrested — only appeared and disappeared before the tribunal. The accusation, the examination, the sentence were shuffled through in a few minutes. "You fought at Issy, at Neuilly? Sentenced to transportation." "What! for life? And my wife, my children?" To another: "You served in the battalions of the Commune?" "And who would have fed my family when the workshop and factory were closed?" Again sentenced to transportation. "And you? Guilty of an illegal arrest. To the penal colony." On the 14th October, in less than two months, the first and second courts had pronounced more than six hundred sentences.

Would that I could recount the martyrdom of the thousands who marched past thus in sombre lines, National Guards, women, children, old men, ambulance attendants, doctors, functionaries, of this decimated town! It is you whom I should honour, you above all, you, the nameless, to whom I should give the first place, as you took it in the work at the barricades, where you did your duty in obscurity. The true drama of the courts-martial was not in those solemn sittings in which the accused, the tribunal, the barristers prepared for public performance, but in those halls which only saw the unhappy ones, ignored by the whole world, face to face with a tribunal as inexorable as the chassepôt. How many of these humble defenders of the Commune held up their heads more proudly than the chiefs, and whose heroism no one will tell! When the insolence, the insults, the grotesque arguments of the conspicuous judges are known, it may be guessed with what ignominy the unknown accused were overwhelmed in the shade of these new prevotal courts. Who will avenge these hecatombs of the Père la Chaise in the darkness of the night?

The newspapers have left no trace of their trials; but, in default of the names of the victims, I can scatter those of some judges to the four winds of history.

Formerly, in the days of honour of the French army, in 1795, after Quiberon, it was necessary to threaten the officers of the Republic with death in order to form the courts-martial that were to judge the Vendéens. And yet those vanquished had, under the cannon, with English arms, attacked their country in the rear, while the coalesced Powers struck her in front. In 1871 the accomplices of Bazaine solicited the honour of judging the vanquished of that Paris which had been the bulwark of national honour. Through long months 1,509 officers of this degraded army, that has not an hour too much for its rehabilitation and for study, 14 generals, 266 colonels and lieutenant-colonels, and 284 commanders, were dubbed judges and commisars. How select amongst this pick of bestiality? When I mention a few presidents at random — Merlin, Boisdenernetz, Jobey, Delaporte, Dulac, Barthel, Donnat, Aubert — I shall be wronging a hundred others.

Merlin and Boisdenemetz are known. Colonel Delaporte was of the Gallifet species. Old, used up, valetudinarian, he only revived after a sentence of death. It is he who pronounced the greatest number, aided by the clerk of the court, Duplan, who prepared the sentences beforehand, and afterwards committed the most impudent forgeries in the minutes. Jobey had, it was said, lost a son in the struggle with the Commune, and now he avenged himself. His small wrinkled eye watched for the anguish in the face of the unfortunate he condemned. Every appeal to good sense was to him an insult. "He would have been happy," said he, "to stew the lawyers together with the culprits."

And yet how few lawyers did their duty! Many had declared that one could not decently assist such prisoners. Others wanted to be requisitioned. With four or five exceptions these unworthy defenders banqueted with the officers. Barristers and commissars communicated to each other their means of attack or defence; the officers announced the verdicts beforehand. The advocate Riché boasted of having drawn up the accusation act against Rossel. The advocates officially designated did not answer the call.

These ignorant judges, making a parade of violence, insulting the prisoners, witnesses, and lawyers, were worthily seconded by the commissar. One of them, Grimal, sold to the demi-monde journals the papers of the celebrated prisoners. Gaveau, a savage simpleton, without a shadow of talent, died some months after in a madhouse. Bourboulon, eager for display, aimed at oratorical effects. Barthelemy, a beer-drinker, fair and fat, made puns while asking for the heads of the accused. Charrière, at fifty years of age still captain, a kind of wild-cat, an imbecile, and a pretentious liar, said that he had made a vow of cruelty to Caesar. Jouesne, notorious in the army for his stupidity, made up for it by his stubborn animosity. Not much was needed in such courts. The most implacable, on the whole, were the third, fourth, and sixth courts, and the thirteenth at St. Cloud, which publicly boasted of acquitting nobody.

So much for the judges and the justice which the bourgeoisie gave those proletarians they had not shot down. I should like to be able to follow up step by step their swash-buckling jurisprudence, take the trials one by one, show the laws violated, the most elementary rules of procedure despised, the documents falsified, the evidence distorted, the prisoners condemned to hard labour and to death without what would have been the ghost of a proof with a serious jury; the cynicism of the prevotal courts of the Restoration and of the Mixed Commissions of December ingrafted on the brutality of the soldier who revenges his caste. Such a work would require long technical labour. I shall only indicate the principal lines. Besides, are not these judgments already judged?

In 1871 the Versailles Government demanded of Switzerland the extradition of the governor of the Ecole Militaire, in 1876 that of the delegate Frankel from Hungary, both condemned to death for assassination and incendiarism. They were at once arrested. Liberal Switzerland and rural Hungary, considering the acts of the Commune as common crimes, were ready to deliver up the prisoners if Versailles furnished the legal proof required by treaties of extradition that they had committed the acts for which they had been condemned. The Versaillese Government only produced the sentences of the courtsmartial, and could not add the least "trace of proof or any precise evidence establishing culpability. The prisoners had to be released.

On the 8th September Rossel appeared before the third court. His defence consisted in saying that he had served the Commune in the hope that the insurrection would recommence the war against the Prussians. Merlin treated the prisoner with the greatest consideration, who in turn testified the most profound respect for the army. But an example was needed for romantic soldiers, and Rossel was condemned to death.

On the 21st Rochefort was sentenced to transportation in a fortress. The Bonapartists of the court especially had their eye on the author of the *Lanterne*. Merlin had defended Pierre Bonaparte. Gaveau, accused the prisoner of having outraged the person of the Emperor. Trochu, whom Rochefort had called as a witness for the defence, answered the man who during the siege had for him sacrificed his popularity, by an insulting letter!

Revolutionary journalism had the honour of counting some victims in its ranks. Young Maroteau, for two articles — two only — in the *Salut Public* was condemned to death; Alphonse Humbert, for three or four articles in the *Père Duchesne*, to hard labour for life.

Other journalists were condemned to transportation. What was their crime? Having defended the Commune. Yet the Commune had contented itself with suppressing the papers that defended Versailles. In point of fact, the courts-martial were charged to exterminate the revolutionary party.

Fear of the future rendered them implacable. After the numberless assassinations in the Rue des Rosiers, they too wanted to offer a holocaust to the manes of Lecomte and Clément-Thomas. The real executioners were not to be found. The explosion of fury which cost the two generals their lives had been spontaneous, sudden as that which in 1789 killed Flesselles, Foulon and Berthier. The actors of the drama were legion, and with it all traces of them were lost. The military judges selected the accused at random, as their colleagues had on the Buttes Montmartre shot the first-comers.

'simon Mayer," said the report, "tried to the last moment to defend the prisoners, and Kazdansky did his best to oppose the carrying out of the threats of death. The crowd insulted him and tore off his gold lace." HerpinLacroix had made desperate efforts; Lagrange, who had refused to form the firing-party, felt so secure in his innocence that he had come to give himself up to the judges of his own free will. The report made the principal accused of him, along with Simon Mayer, Kazdansky, Herpin-Lacroix, and a sergeant of the line, Verdagnier, who on the 18th March had raised the butt-end of his gun.

The trial was conducted by Colonel Aubert, a sneering melodramatic bigot. Despite his efforts and those of the commissar, not the slightest proof could be brought forward against the prisoners. Even the officers of the army, companions of General Lecomte, gave evidence in their favour. "Simon Mayer did all that was possible to save us," said the Commander Poussargue. This officer had heard a voice cry, "Do not kill even traitors without judgment; form a courtmartial", literally the words of Herpin-Lacroix. Of all the accused, he only recognized Mayer. Another officer gave similar evidence. Verdagnier proved that at the time of the executions he had been at the huts of Courcelles. The prosecution denied all, but without being able to produce a single witness. Ribemont proved that he had withstood the assailants in the room of the Rue des Rosiers. Masselot had against him nothing but the evidence of some hostile women, pretending that he had boasted of having shot at the generals. Captain Beugnot, aide-de-camp of the Minister, and present at the execution, affirmed, on the contrary, that the generals had been surrounded by the soldiers; M. de Maillefu, that the front of the platoon was composed of nine soldiers, whose regiments he named.

There were not even false official witnesses, as in the trial of the members of the Commune; and yet the prosecution, far from letting them escape its clutches, was most implacable with regard to these very men who had risked their lives to save the generals. The commissar threatened to arrest a witness who warmly gave evidence in favour of a prisoner. After several sittings they discovered that they were judging one individual for another. The president ordered the press to hush up the incident. Each sitting, each new evidence, cleared the prisoners and made a condemnation more impossible. Yet on the 18th November Verdagnier, Mayer, Herpin-Lacroix, Masselot, Leblond, and Aldenhoff were condemned to death; the others to penalties varying from hard labour to imprisonment. One of those condemned to death, Leblond, was only fifteen and a half years old.

This satisfaction given the army, the courts, as good courtiers, avenged the offences against M. Thiers. The functionary Fontaine, charged by the Commune with the demolition of the house of him who had demolished hundreds of houses, appeared before the fifth court-martial, which did its utmost to make him appear a thief. Every one knew that M. Thiers' furniture and silver plate had been sent to the Garde-Meuble, the objects of art to the museums, the books to the public libraries, the linen to the ambulances, and that after the entry of the troops the little man had regained possession of most of these objects. Some having perished in the conflagration of the Tuileries, the report accused Fontaine of having abstracted them, although only two valueless medals had been found in his house. To this accusation, from which he believed himself secured by a long life of probity and honour, Fontaine could only reply with tears. The Figarists laughed at it a good deal, and he was condemned to twenty years' hard labour.

On the 28th November the Assembly recommenced its shootings. M. Thiers, cleverly throwing upon the representatives the right of commuting the penalties, had a Commission of Pardons named by the Chamber. It was composed of fifteen members, purveyors of the Mixed Commission of 1852, great proprietors, inveterate Royalists. One of them, the Marquis de Quinsonnas, had during the battle in the streets superintended the executions at the Luxembourg. The president, Martel, was an old satyr, who sold his pardons to pretty solicitresses.

The first cases which they took up were those of Rossel and Ferré. The Liberal press pleaded warmly for the young officer. In his restless mind, without unsound political opinions, who had so cavalierly turned his back upon the Commune, the bourgeoisie soon recognized one of her prodigal children. He had besides made an *amende honorable*. The press published his memoirs, in which he reviled the Commune and the Federals. Day by day they recounted the life of the prisoner, his sublime colloquies with a Protestant clergyman, his heart-rending interviews with his family. Of Ferré not a word, except to say he was "hideous". His mother had died mad; his brother was shut up as mad in the dungeons of Versailles; his father was a prisoner in the citadel of Fouras; his sister, a young girl of nineteen, silent, resigned, stoical, spent her days and nights earning the twenty francs that she every week sent her brother. She had refused the aid of her friends, unwilling to share with any one the honour of accomplishing her pious duty. Indeed, one can imagine nothing more "hideous!"

For twelve weeks death remained suspended above the heads of the condemned. At last, on the 28th November, at six o'clock in the morning, they were told that they must die. Ferré jumped out of bed without showing the slightest emotion, declined the visit of the chaplain, wrote to ask the military tribunals for the release of his father, and to his sister that she should have him buried so that his friends would be able to find him again. Rossel, rather surprised at first, afterwards conversed with his clergyman. He wrote a letter demanding that his death should not be avenged — a very useless precaution — and addressed a few thanks to Jesus Christ. For comrade in death they had a sergeant of the 45th line, Bourgeois, who had gone over to the Commune, and who showed the same calm as Ferré. Rossel was indignant when they put on the handcuffs; Ferré and Bourgeois disdained to protest.

The day was hardly dawning; it was bitterly cold. Before the Butte of Satory 5,000 men under arms surrounded three white stakes, each one guarded by twelve executioners. Colonel Merlin commanded, thus uniting the three functions of conqueror, judge, and hangman.

Some curious lookers-on, officers and journalists, composed the whole public.

At seven o'clock the carts of the condemned appeared; the drums beat a salute, the trumpets sounded. The prisoners descended, escorted by gendarmes. Rossel, on passing before a group of officers, saluted them. The brave Bourgeois, looking on at the whole drama with an indifferent air, leant against the middle stake. Ferré came last, dressed in black and smoking a cigar, not a muscle of his face moving. With a firm and even step he walked up and leant against the third stake.

Rossel, attended by his lawyer and his clergyman, asked to be allowed to command the fire. Merlin refused. Rossel wished to shake hands with him, in order to do homage to his sentence. This was refused. During these negotiations Ferré and Bourgeois remained motionless, silent. In order to put a stop to Rossel's effusions an officer was obliged to tell him that he was prolonging the torture of the two others. At last they blindfolded him. Ferré pushed back the bandage, and, fixing his eyeglass, looked the soldiers straight in the face.

The sentence read, the adjutants lowered their sabres, the guns were discharged. Rossel and Bourgeois fell back. Ferré remained standing; he was only hit in the side. He was again fired at and fell. A soldier placing his chassepôt at his ear blew out his brains.

On a gesture of Merlin a flourish of trumpets burst forth, and, emulating the customs of the cannibals, the troops marched past in triumph before the corpses. What cries of horror the bourgeoisie would have uttered if before the executed hostages the Federals had paraded to the sound of music!

The bodies of Rossel and Ferré were claimed by their families; that of Bourgeois disappeared in the common grave of the St. Louis Cemetery. The people will not disassociate his memory from that of Ferré, for they both died with the same courage for the cause they had served with the same devotion.

The Liberal press reserved its tears for Rossel. Some courageous provincial papers did honour to all the victims, and devoted to the hatred of France the Commission of Pardons — "the Commission of Assassins," as a deputy, Ordinaire junior, said in the Assembly. Prosecuted before juries, all these journals were acquitted.

Two days after the execution of Satory, the Commission of Pardons ordered Gaston Crémieux to be killed. Six months had elapsed since his condemnation, and this long delay seemed to make the murder impossible.

But the rural Commission wanted to avenge his famous speech of Bordeaux. On the 30th November, at seven o'clock in the morning, Gaston Crémieux was led to the Prado, a large plain bordering the sea. He said to his guardians, "I will show how a Republican should die." He was placed against the same stake where a month before the soldier Paquis had been shot for going over to the insurrection.

Gaston Crémieux wished to have his eyes unbandaged and to command the fire. They consented. Then addressing himself to the soldiers, "Aim at the chest; do not touch my head. Fire! *Vive la République!*" The last word was cut short by death. As at Satory, the dance of the soldiers round the corpse followed.

The death of this young enthusiast made a deep impression in the town. Registers placed at the door of his house filled in a few hours with thousands of signatures. The revolutionaries of Marseilles will not forget his children.

The same day the sixth court avenged the death of Chaudey. This had been ordered and superintended by Raoul Rigault alone. The men who formed the platoon were abroad. Préau de Védel, the principal accused, then imprisoned in Sainte Pélagie for a common offence, had only held the lantern. But the jurisprudence of the officers attributed to simple agents the same responsibility as to the chiefs. Préau de Védel was condemned to death.

On the 4th December, in the hall of the third court, a kind of phantom, pale-faced and sympathetic, appeared. It was Lisbonne, who for six months had dragged about his wounds of the Chateau d'Eau. The same before the court-martial as during the Commune and at Buzenval, this bravest of the brave gloried in having fought, and only denied the accusations of pillage. Other judges would have been proud to spare such an enemy; the Versaillese condemned him to death.

Some days after, this same court-martial heard a woman's voice. "I will not defend myself; I will not be defended," cried Louise Michel. "I belong entirely to the social revolution, and I declare that I accept the responsibility of all my acts. I accept it entirely and without reserve. You accuse me of having participated in the execution of the generals. To this I answer, yes. If I had been at Montmartre, when they wished to fire on the people, I should not have hesitated to order fire myself on those who gave such commands. As to the conflagrations of Paris, yes, I did participate in them. I wanted to oppose a barrier of flames to the invaders of Versailles. I have no accomplices; I acted on my own account."

Commissar Dailly demanded the penalty of death.

Louise Michel: What I ask of you, you who style yourselves a court-martial, who proclaim yourselves my judges, who do not hide yourselves like the Commission of Pardons, is the field of Satory, where our brothers have already fallen. I must be cut off from society; you have been told to do so. Well, the Commissar of the Republic is right. Since it seems that every heart which beats for liberty has only right to a little lead, I too demand my part. If you let me live, I shall not cease to cry vengeance, and I shall denounce to the vengeance of my brothers the assassins of the Commission of Pardons.

The President: I cannot allow you to go on.

Louise Michel: I have done. If you are not cowards, kill me.

They had not courage to kill her at one blow. She was condemned to transportation to a fortress.

Louise Michel did not stand alone in her courageous attitude. Many others, amongst whom must be mentioned Lemel and Augustine Chiffon, showed the Versaillese what terrible women these Parisians are, even vanquished, even in chains.

The affair of the executions of La Roquette came on at the beginning of 1872. There, as in the Clément-Thomas and Chaudey trials, they had none of the real actors except Genton, who had carried the order. Almost all the witnesses, former hostages, gave evidence with the rage natural to people who have trembled. The prosecution, refusing to believe in an outburst of fury, had built up a ridiculous scaffolding of a court-martial discussing and ordering the death of the prisoners. It asserted that one of the accused had commanded the fire, and he was about to be condemned, in spite of the solemn protests of Genton, when the real chief of the firing-party, who had just been discovered dying in a prison, was brought in. Genton was condemned to death. His advocate had odiously slandered him, then fled, and the court refused to allow him a second defender.

The most important affair which followed was that of the Dominicans of Arcueil. No execution had been less premeditated. These monks had fallen in crossing the Avenue d'Italie, shot down by the men of the 101st. The report accused Sérizier, who at that moment was not even in the Avenue. The only witness called against him said, "I do not affirm anything myself; I have heard it said." But we know what close bonds unite army and clergy. Sérizier was condemned to death, as was also one of his lieutenants, Bouin, against whom not a single witness could be brought forward. The court took advantage of the occasion to pronounce sentences of death against Wroblewski, who at that time had been at the Butte-aux-Cailles, and against Frankel, who had been fighting at the Bastille.

On the 12th March the affair of the Rue Haxo came on before the sixth court, still presided over by Delaporte. The executioners of the hostages had been no more discoverable than those of the Rue des Rosiers. The indictment fell back upon the director of the prison, Francois, who for a long time had disputed the surrender of his prisoners, and upon twenty-two persons denounced by gossip contradicted at the trial. Not one of the witnesses recognized the accused. Delaporte multiplied his menaces with such a cynicism that the Commissar Rustaud, who had, however, given proofs of his animosity in the preceding trials, could not refrain from exclaiming, "But do you want to condemn them all?" He was the next day replaced by the idiot Charrière. In spite of all this, the indictment frittered away from hour to hour before the disavowals of the witnesses. Still not one of the prisoners escaped. Seven were condemned to death, nine to hard labour, and the others to transportation.

The Commission of Pardons awaited, chassepôt in hand, the prey given up to them by the courts-martial. On the 22nd of February, 1872, it shot three of the so-called murderers of Clément-Thomas and Lecomte, even those whose innocence had most clearly come out in the trial — Herpin-Lacroix, Lagrange, and Verdagner. Upright at the stake of the 28th November, they cried *"Vive la Commune!"* and died, their faces radiant. On the 19th March Préau de Védel was executed. On the 30th April it was Genton's turn. The wounds which he had received in May had reopened, and he dragged himself to the Butte on his crutches. Arrived at the stake, he threw them from him, cried *"Vive la Commune!"* and fell under the fire. On the 25th May the three stakes were again occupied by Sérizier, Bouin, and Boudin, the latter condemned as chief of the platoon which in front of the Tuileries had executed a Versaillese who attempted to prevent the erection of the barricades of the Rue Richelieu. They said to the soldiers of the platoon, "We are children of the people, and you are too. We shall show you that the children of Paris know how to die!" And they, also, fell, crying *"Vive la Commune!"*

These men who went to the grave so courageously, who with a gesture defied the musket, who, dying, cried that their cause died not, these ringing voices, these steadfast looks, disconcerted the soldiers profoundly. The muskets trembled, and almost within point-blank range they rarely killed at the first discharge. So at the next execution, the 6th July, the Commander Colin, who presided at these shootings, ordered the eyes of the victims bandaged. There were two of them Baudoin, accused of setting fire to the St. Eloi Church, and of killing an individual who had fired at the Federals; and Rouilhac, an insurgent who had shot at a bourgeois who was potting Federals. Both pushed back the sergeants who came to blindfold them. Colin gave the order to tie them to the stake. Three times Baudoin tore assunder the cords; Rouilhac struggled desperately. The priest who came to assist the soldiers received some blows in the chest. At last, overwhelmed, they cried, "We die for the good cause." They were mangled by the balls. After the march past, an officer of a psychological turn of mind, moving with the tip of his boot the brains that trickled down, remarked to a colleague, "It is with this that they thought."

In June, 1872, all the celebrated cases being disposed of, military justice avenged the death of a Federal, Captain Beaufort. There is but one explanation for this strange fact, which is that Beaufort belonged to the Versailles. We have received important evidence on this head. At all events, if Delescluze or Varlin had been shot by the Federals, Versailles would not have avenged their death.

Three of those accused out of four were present, Deschamps, Denivelle, and Madame Lachaise, the celebrated cantinière of the 66th. She had followed Beaufort before the council held at the Boulevard Voltaire, and, having heard explanations, had done her best to protect him. The indictment none the less made of her the principal instigator of his death. On the written evidence of a witness who was not to be found, and who had never been confronted with her, the commissar accused Madame Lachaise of having profaned Beaufort's corpse. At this abominable accusation this noble woman burst into tears. She, as well as Denivelle and Deschamps, were condemned to death.

The obscene imagination of soldiers with Algerian habits taxed itself to pollute the accused. Colonel Dulac, judging an intimate friend of Rigault's, pretended that their friendship had been of an infamous character. Despite the indignant protests of the prisoner, the wretched officer persisted.

The bourgeois press, far from stigmatizing, applauded. Without truce, without lassitude, since the opening of the courts-martial it accompanied all the trials with the same chorus of imprecations and the same slanders. Some persons having protested against these executions so long after the battle, Francisque Sarcey wrote, "The axe ought to be riveted to the hand of the executioner."

Till then the Commission of Pardons had only killed three at a time. On the 24th of July it slaughtered four — Francois, the director of La Roquette, Aubry, Dalivoust, and De St. Omer, condemned for the affair of the Rue Haxo. De St. Omer was more than suspected, and in the prison his comrades kept aloof from him. Before the muskets they cried *"Vive la Commune!"* He answered, "Down with it!"

On the 18th September, Lolive (accused of having participated in the execution of the Archbishop), Denivelle, and Deschamps were executed. These last cried, "Long live the Universal and Social Republic! Down with the cowards!" On the 22nd January, 1873, nineteen months after the battle in the streets, the Commission of Pardons tied three more victims to its stakes — Philippe, member of the Council of the Commune, guilty of having energetically defended Bercy; Benot, who set fire to the Tuileries; and Decamps, condemned for the conflagration of the Rue de Lille, although they had not been able to bring forward any evidence whatever against him. "I die innocent," cried he. "Down with Thiers!" Philippe and Benot: "Long live the Social Republic! *Vive la Commune!*" They fell, not having belied the courage of the soldiers of the Revolution of the 18th March.

This was the last execution at Satory. The blood of twenty-five victims had reddened the stakes of the Commission of Pardons. In 1875 it had a young soldier shot at Vincennes, accused of the death of the detective Vizentini, thrown into the Seine by hundreds of hands at the demonstration of the Bastille.

The movements of the provinces were judged by courts-martial or assize courts, according to the department being or not being in a state of siege. Everywhere the issue of the Parisian struggle had been waited for. Immediately after the defeat of Paris the reaction ran riot. Espivent's court-martial initiated these trials. He had his Gaveau in Commander Villeneuve, one of the bombarders of the 4th April, his Merlin, and his Boisdenemetz in the colonels Thomassin and Douat. On the 12th June Gaston Crémieux, Etienne, Pélissier, Roux, Bouchet, and all those who could be connected with the movement of the 23rd March appeared before the soldiers. The pretentious block-headedness of Villeneuve served as type of the military prosecutor's addresses with which France was inundated. Crémieux, Etienne, Pélissier, and Roux were condemned to death. This was not enough for the jesuitical bourgeois reaction. Espivent had declared through the Court of Cassation that the department of the Bouches-du-Rhône was in a state of siege since the 9th August, 1870, in virtue of a decree by the Empress, which had neither been published in the bulletin of laws, nor been sanctioned by the Senate, nor even promulgated. Provided with this arm, he persecuted all marked out by the hand of the Congregation. The municipal councillor, David Bosc, ex-delegate to the Commission, a millionaire shipowner, accused of having stolen a silver watch from a police agent, was only acquitted by a small majority of votes. The next day the colonel-president was replaced by the lieutenant-colonel of the 4th Chasseurs, Donnat, half-mad with absinthe-drinking. A working man, aged seventy-five, was condemned to ten years' hard labour and twenty years' deprivation of civil and political rights for having on the 4th September arrested for half an hour a police agent who had sent him to Cayenne in 1852. A crazy old woman, purveyor of the Jesuits, arrested for a few moments on the 4th September, accused the former commander of the Civil Guard of her arrest. Her accusation was contradicted by herself and quite overthrown by alibis and numberless proofs. The ex-commander was condemned to five years' of prison and ten years' privation of civil rights. One of the soldier-judges, coming out after committing this crime, said, "One must have very profound political convictions to condemn in similar affairs." With these cynical collaborators Espivent could satisfy all his hatred. He asked the courts of Versailles to deliver up to him the member of the Council of the Commune, Amouroux, delegate for a time at Marseilles. "I am prosecuting him for tampering with soldiers," wrote Espivent, "a crime punished by death; and I am persuaded that this punishment will be applied to him."

The court-martial of Lyons was not very inferior. Forty-four persons were prosecuted for the movement of the 22nd March, and thirty-two condemned to penalties varying from transportation to imprisonment. The insurrection of the 30th April furnished seventy prisoners, taken at random at Lyons, as was the custom at Versailles. The mayor of the Guillotière, Crestin, called as witness, did not recognize amongst them any of those he had seen on that day in his *mairie*. Presidents of the courts, the Colonels Marion and Rébillot.

At Limoges, Dubois and Roubeyrol, democrats esteemed by the whole town, were condemned in default to death, as the principal actors in the movement of the 4th April; two were condemned to twenty years" imprisonment for having boasted of knowing who had shot at Colonel Billet. Another got ten years for having distributed ammunition.

The verdicts of the jury varied. That of the Basses-Pyrénées on the 8th August acquitted Duportal, and the four or five persons accused of the movement of Toulouse. The same aquittal took place at Rhodez, where Digeon and the accused of Narbonne appeared after a preliminary imprisonment of eight months. A sympathetic public filled the hall and the approaches of the tribunal and cheered the accused at their departure. The energetic attitude of Digeon once more showed the strong cast of his character.

The jury of Riom condemned for the affairs of St. Etienne twentyone prisoners, among whom was Amouroux, who had only sent two delegates. A young working man, Caton, distinguished himself by his intelligence and firmness.

The jury of Orléans was severe upon the accused of Montargis, all of whom they condemned to prison, and atrocious to those of Cosnes and Neury-sur-Loire, where there had been no resistance. There were twenty-three altogether, of whom three were women. Their whole crime had been carrying about a red flag and crying *"Vive Paris!* Down with Versailles!"* Malardier, a former representative of the people, who only arrived on the eve of the demonstration, and who had taken no part in it, was condemned to fifteen years' imprisonment. None of the accused was spared. The proprietors of the Loiret avenged the fright of their fellow-proprietors of the Nievre.

The movements of Coulommiers, Nimes, Dordives, and Voiron gave rise to some convictions.

In the month of June, 1872, the greater part of the work of repression was done. Of the 36,309 prisoners, men, women, and children, without counting the 5,000 military prisoners, to whom the Versailles have confessed, 1,179, said they, had died in their prisons; 22,326 had been liberated after long winter months in the pontoons, the forts, and the prisons; 10,488 brought before the courts-martial, who had condemned 8,525 of them. The persecutions did not cease. On the advent of MacMahon, the 24th May, 1873, there set in a recrudescence. On the 1st January, 1875, the general résumé of Versaillese justice gave 10,137 condemnations pronounced in presence of the accused, and 3,313 in default. The sentences passed were distributed thus:

	Total	Women	Children
Condemnations to death	270	8	
Hard labour	10	29	
Transportation in a fortress	3989		
Simple transportation	3507	16	1
Detention	1269	8	
Confinement	64	10	
Hard labour at public works	29		
Imprisonment from three months or less	432		
Imprisonment from three months to one year	1622	50	1
Imprisonment for more than one year	1344	15	4
Banishment	322		
Surveillance of the police	117	1	
Fines	9		
Children under 16 sent to houses of correction			56
Total	13,440	157	62

This résumé contained neither the sentences pronounced by the courts-martial beyond the jurisdiction of Versailles nor those of the courts of assizes. We must therefore add 15 condemnations to death, 22 to hard labour, 28 to transportation in a fortress, 29 to simple transportation, 74 to detention, 13 to confinement, and a certain number to imprisonment. The total figure of the condemned of Paris and the provinces exceeds 13,700, among whom were 170 women and 62 children.

Three-fourths of the 10,000 condemned while present — 7,418 out of 10,137 — were simple guards or non-commissioned officers, 1,942 subaltern officers. There were only 225 superior officers, 29 members of the Council of the Commune, 49 of the Central Committee. Despite their savage jurisprudence, the inquiries, and the false witnesses, the courts-martial had been unable to bring forward against nine-tenths of the condemned — 9,285 — any other crime than the bearing of arms or the exercise of public functions. Of the 766 condemned for so-called common crimes, 276 were for simple arrests, 171 for the battle in the streets, 132 for crimes classed as "others" by the report, all evidently for acts of war. Notwithstanding the great number of ticket-of-leave men designedly included in these prosecutions, nearly three-fourths of the condemned — 7,119 — had no judiciary antecedents; 524 had incurred condemnation for misdemeanour against public order (political or simple police cases); 2,381 for crimes or misdemeanours, which the report took care not to specify. Finally, this insurrection, provoked and conducted by the foreigner according to the bourgeois press, furnished in all but 396 prisoners of foreign origin.

This is the balance-sheet of 1874. The following years added new condemnations. The number of the courts was reduced, but their institution was maintained and the prosecutions are going on. Even now, six years after the defeat, the arrests and convictions have not ceased.

Chapter 36
The balance-sheet of bourgeois vengeance

The deported men are happier than our soldiers, for our soldiers have fighting to do, while the deportee lives in the midst of the flowers in his garden. (Speech against amnesty by Admiral Fourichon, Navy Minister, session of 17th May, 1876.)

It is above all the Republicans who must be adverse to the amnesty. (Victor Lefranc, session of 18th May, 1876.)

Two days' journey from France there is a colony eager for hands, rich enough to enrich thousands of families. After every victory over Parisian workmen the bourgeoisie has always preferred throwing its victims to the antipodes to fecundating Algeria with them. The Republic of 1848 had Nouka-Hiva; the Versaillese Assembly, New Caledonia. It was to this rock, six thousand leagues from their native land, that it decided to transport those condemned for life. "The Council of the Government," said the reporter on the law, "gives the transported a family and a home." The machine-gun was more honest.

Those condemned to transportation were huddled together into four depots, Fort Boyard, St. Martin de Ré, Oléron, and Quélern, where for long months they languished between despair and hope, which never abandon political victims. One day, when they believed themselves almost forgotten, a brutal call resounded. To the surgery! A doctor looked at them, questioned them, did not listen to their answers, and said, "Fit for departure !" And then farewell family, country, society, human life, *en route* for the sepulchre of the antipodes. And happy he who was condemned to transportation only. He could for a last time press a friendly hand, see tears in kindly eyes, give a last kiss. But the galley-slave of the Commune will only see the taskmaster. At the call of the whistle he must undress, be searched, then have the livery of the voyage thrown him, and, without a farewell, ascend the floating prison.

The transport ship was a moving pontoon. Large cages built on the gun-deck shut in the prisoners. In the night these became centres of infection. In the daytime, the uncaged people had but one-half hour to come up on the deck and breathe a little fresh air. Around the cages the jailers stood grumbling, punishing with the black hole the slightest infringement of the rules. Some unhappy beings made the whole voyage at the bottom of the hold, sometimes almost naked, for having refused to comply with a caprice. The women, like the men, were sent to the black hole; the nuns who watched them were worse than the jailers. For five months they had to live in this promiscuous fashion in the cage, in the filth of their neighbours, fed upon biscuits often musty, on bacon, on almost salt water; now burnt by the tropics, now frozen by the cold of the South, or by the spray dashing over the gun-deck. And what spectres arrived! When the *Orne* dropped anchor off Melbourne there were 360 sick of scurvy out of 588 prisoners. They inspired even the rough colonials of Australia with pity. The inhabitants of Melbourne came to succour them, collecting in a few hours 40,000 francs. The commander of the *Orne* refused to transmit the sum to the prisoners, even in the shape of clothes, tools, and simple necessities.

The *Danaé* was the first ship that set sail, on the 3rd May, 1872; the *Guerrière, Garonne, Var, Sibylle, Orne, Calvados, Virginie,* etc., followed. By the 1st July, 1875, 3,859 prisoners had landed in New Caledonia.

This Caledonian sepulchre has three circles: the peninsula Ducos, not far from Noumea, the capital of New Caledonia, for those condemned to transportation in a fortress — 805 men and 6 women; the Ile des Pins, thirty miles south-east of the principal island, for those condemned to simple transportation — 2,795 men and 13 women; and, quite in the background, worse than death, the penal settlement of the Ile Nou, for 240 galley-slaves.

The peninsula Ducos, a narrow neck of land commanded by cannon, with its mouth guarded by soldiers, without a watercourse, without verdure, is traversed by and hills and swampy valleys. For all shelter the condemned found a few dilapidated hovels; for all furniture, a saucepan and a hammock. The Ile des Pins, a tableland, its centre perfectly desolate, is bounded by fertile plains, but in the hands of the Marist monks, who exploit the labour of the natives. Nothing was prepared for the reception of the condemned. The first who arrived wandered about in the woods; only very long after did they receive poor tents and hammocks. The natives, incited by the missionaries, fled from them, or sold them provisions at enormous prices.

The administration was to have provided the indispensable clothing. None of the prescribed rules was observed. The képis and boots were soon worn out, and the immense majority of the condemned having no means whatever, had to bear the sun and the rainy season bare-headed and bare-footed. They had neither tobacco nor soap; there was no brandy to mix with the brackish water.

The prisoners did not lose heart at this beginning. Laborious, active, with that universal aptitude of the Parisian workman, they felt themselves equal to overcoming the first difficulties. The reporter on the law had extolled the thousand revenues of New Caledonia fisheries, cattle-breeding, the working of mines — and represented this compulsory emigration as the founding of a new French Empire in the Pacific. The condemned hoped to make themselves a home in this far-off land. These proletarians were free of the false dignity affected by the proscribed bourgeois; far from refusing work, they sought for it. In the Ile des Pins there were a hospital, an aqueduct, administrative warehouses to be finished, a large road to be constructed; 2,000 condemned presented themselves; 800 only were employed, and their wages never exceeded 85 centimes a day. Some of those rebuffed by the Administration then demanded concessions of territory; they were granted a few yards of land, and at exorbitant prices some seeds and tools. With the greatest efforts they could hardly make the soil yield a few vegetables. The others, who possessed nothing, applied to private industry, offering their services to the trades-people of Noumea. But the colony, stifled by the military regime, hampered by bureaucratic officials, and of very limited resources besides, could only furnish work to about 500 at the most. Moreover, many of them who had undertaken farming were obliged to give it up very soon and return to the Ile des Pins.

This was the golden age of the transportation. Towards the middle of 1873 a despatch of the Minister of Marine reached Noumea. Ile Versaillese Government suspended all administrative credits in support of the state works. "If one admitted," said he, "the right to labour of the convict, one would soon see the renewal of the scandalous example of the national workshops of 1848." Perfectly logical this. Versailles owes no means of labour to those it has deprived of their liberty to labour. So the workshops were closed. The woods of the Ile des Pins offered valuable supplies to the cabinet-makers, and some of the condemned manufactured furniture much in request at Noumea. They were ordered to discontinue. And on the 13th December the Minister of Marine dared to pronounce from the tribune that the majority of the condemned refused every kind of work .

At the very moment that the Administration thus curtailed the life of the transported, it summoned their wives to the Ministry of Marine, where the most charming picture of New Caledonia was exhibited to them. They were to find there, on their arrival, a house, a piece of land, seeds, and tools. Most of them, suspecting some snare, refused to set out unless invited by their husbands. Sixty-nine, however, were inveigled, and embarked on board the *Fénélon* with women sent forth by the Public Assistance Office as helpmates for the colonials. These unfortunate wives of the convicts, on landing, found only the despair and misery of their husbands. The Government refused to send them back again.

Thus there are thousands of men accustomed to work, to activity of mind, penned up, idle and miserable, some in the narrow peninsula, others in the Ile des Pins, without clothes, ill-fed, under orders executed by brutes revolver in hand, hardly in connection with the world, save for a few rare letters, and these are even delayed for three weeks at Noumea. In the beginning endless reveries, then discouragement and sombre despair; cases of madness occurred, at last death. The first one set free was the teacher Verdure, member of the Council of the Commune. The commissar of the court-martial had accused him of but one crime: "He was a philanthropic Utopian." He wanted to open a school in the peninsula; permission was refused him. Useless, far from his wife and daughter, he languished and died. One morning in 1873 the jailers and the priests saw in the winding pathway that leads to the cemetery a coffin covered with flowers carried by some of the condemned. Behind them walked 800 friends in a deep silence. "The coffin," one of them has told us, "was lowered into the grave. A friend spoke a few words of farewell; each one threw in his little red flower, cried, '*Vive la République! Vive la Commune!*' and all was over." In November, in the Ile des Pins, Albert Grandier, one of the staff of the *Rappel,* died. His heart had remained in France, with a sister whom he adored. Every day he went to the sea-shore to wait for her; so he became mad. The Administration refused to admit him into an asylum. He escaped from the friends who guarded him, and one morning was found dead of cold in the swamps, not far from the road that leads to the sea.

These at least have the consolation of suffering with their equals. But the convicts chained in the sink of the scoundrels! "I know but one penal colony," replied the Republican Minister, Victor Lefranc, to a mother begging for her son. And there is indeed but one penal colony, where heroes like Trinquet and Lisbonne, men all compact of devotion and probity like Fontaine, Roques, the mayor of Puteaux (so many names press forward that I am ashamed to mention a few), journalists of high character like Brissac and Humbert, some whose sole crime was to have carried out a warrant of arrest, have been chained for five years to assassins and thieves, enduring their insults. and bound at night to the same camp-bed. The Versaillese want more than the body; they must attaint the rebellious mind, surround it with an atmosphere of stench and vice, in order to make it fail and founder. The "felons" of the Commune, assimilated to criminals, subjected to the same labour, to the same rule of the stick and whip, are beset by the special hatred of the jailers, who incite the convicts against them. From time to time a letter escapes, and even reaches us. Thus writes a member of the Council of the Commune, a man of thirty-three, at one time in robust health:

"St. Louis.

... The work of the camp is considered the most severe. It includes the digging up of stones, earthworks, etc. It is only interrupted on the Sunday morning for the religious service. For nourishment we have coffee without sugar at five o'clock in the morning, 700 grammes of bread, and 100 grammes of beans; in the evening a small piece of beef; and, finally, 69 centilitres of wine a week. When I am able to buy a quarter of a pound of bread, my health leaves less to be desired. Already several of ours are no more. Many are attacked with anaemia. Fifteen out of sixty in St. Louis are at the hospital. All this would be nothing if there were not that commingling with men of infamous passions. There are fifty of us in one compartment. As to the employments, shops, and offices, the Communards are excluded from these."

Another writes:

"Ile Nou, 15th February.

I isolate myself as much as I can, but there are hours when I must be in the compound on pain of death. There are hours when I must defend my rations from the voracity of my companions, when I must submit to the familiarity of a Mano or of a Lathauer. This is horrible, and I blush with shame when I think that I have become almost insensible to all this infamy. These wretches are cowards, and are not the least of our tormentors. It is enough to drive one mad, and I believe that many amongst us will become so. Berezowski, this unfortunate man, who has suffered so much for eight years, is almost demented, and it is painful to look upon him. it is terrible and I dare not think of this. How many months, years, are we still to pass in this penal colony? I tremble at the thought. Despite all, believe that I shall not allow myself to be crushed; my conscience is tranquil, and I am strong. My health alone could betray me and be vanquished, but of myself I am sure, and shall never swerve."

A third:

"I have suffered much; the penal settlement of Toulon, the chains, the convicts' dress, and, what is still worse, the ignoble contact of the criminals — all this I have had to bear with. I have, it is true, one consolation for so much suffering — my tranquil conscience, the love of my old parents, and the esteem of men such as you .... How many times have I been discouraged! What despair, what doubts have seized me! I believed in mankind, and all my illusions have been lost one by one; a great change has come over me, and I have almost failed to resist so many disillusions."

Yet another:

"I do not deceive myself; these years are entirely lost for me; not only is my health undermined, but I feel myself getting lower every day. This life is really too hard to bear, without books (save those of the Marne library), in this filthy penal settlement, exposed to all insults, to all blows; shut up in caves; in the workshops treated as beasts; insulted by our jailers and our comrades of the chain, we must submit to it all without a murmur, the slightest infringement entailing terrible punishment — the cell, quarter ration of bread, irons, thumbscrews, the lash. It is ignominious, and I shudder at the thought of it. Many of our comrades are in double chains in the correction platoon, subjected to the hardest labour, dying of hunger, driven on with blows of a cane, often with revolver-shots, unable to communicate with us, who cannot even pass them a mouthful of bread. It is terrible, and I am afraid all this will not end very soon. But protestations will be made; we shall not be abandoned; it would be horrible if we were left here. I am unable to work, so I am right in saying that these years are completely lost, and this drives me to despair; yet I was willing to learn; but what is to be done without books and without a guide? We are almost without news. Still we know that the Republic is affirming itself from day to day; our hope is there, but I dare not believe it; we have had so many deceptions."

How many live today? It is not known. Maroteau left in March, 1875. The Commission of Pardons had increased his sentence; commuted Satory to the Ile Nou. At twenty-five years of age he died in the penal colony for two articles, when the jackals of the Versaillese press, whose every line has demanded and obtained carnage, sway our Paris. To the last moment his courage did not forsake him. "It is not a great affair to die," said he to the friends who surrounded his deathbed; "but I should have preferred the stake of Satory to this filthy pallet. My friends, think of me! What will become of my mother?"

Hear this knell tolled by one of the convicts:

"Ile Nou (Limekiln Works), 18th April.

I cannot help saying that many friends are dying, and that this month five have succumbed."

"15th May.

Old Audant, one of the transported of the 2nd December, has been for ever released from his chain. He was sickly, old (fifty-nine), and our labour had overcome him. One day, tired out, attacked by acute bronchitis, he was unable to get up; still he was obliged to recommence his work. Two days after he asked for the visit of the doctor. He got the dungeon. Five days after he died in the hospital; and a few days later on, another, Gobert, followed him to the tomb."

"Canala, 25th December.

... Add to that the death of old and good friends. After Maroteau, Morten, Mars, Lecolle, whom we buried a month ago."

They die, but none have faltered. The political convicts are men; they succeed in remaining in the pitch without being debased. It is the general inspector Raboul who has allowed this avowal to escape him. What is the

Christian martyr's vaunted heroism of an hour in comparison with these men, who each day, in the indefatigable, merciless clutches of the jailers, maintain unbent their revolutionary faith and their dignity?

And do we even know all their sufferings? Chance alone has raised a corner of the veil. On the 19th March, 1874, Rochefort, Jourde, Paschal Grousset, and three others, condemned to transportation, succeeded in escaping on board an Australian ship. They landed safely in Australia, and the information they brought with them has thrown a little light upon the den. It was then we learnt that the convicts of the Commune had suffered additional tortures; that the torture of the thumbscrews, which mutilated the hands, is still in use at the penal colony; that four convicts had been shot at the Ile des Pins for a simple assault, which would have been punished by a few months' imprisonment by ordinary tribunals; that the severity and insults of the jailers seemed intended to cause a rising which would permit of all those condemned to transportation being sent to the penal colony. The convicts had to pay dearly for these revelations. The Versaillese Government immediately sent out the Rear-Admiral Ribourt, and the torture-screw was turned more tightly than ever.

Those who had obtained permission to sojourn in the principal island were again shut up in the peninsula Ducos or the Ile des Pins; fishing was prohibited; every sealed letter confiscated; the right to fetch wood in the forest for cooking food suppressed. The jailers redoubled their brutality, fired at the convicts who went beyond bounds, or who had not returned to their huts at the regulation hour. Some merchants of Noumea, accused of having facilitated the escape of Rochefort and his friends, were expelled from the isle.

Ribourt had brought the dismissal of the governor, La Richerie, former governor of Cayenne, who by dint of rapine had made a great fortune in New Caledonia. Of course it was not for his dishonesty, but for the escape of the 19th March that he was punished. The provisional government was confided to Colonel Alleyron, who had become famous by the massacres of May. Alleyron decreed that every prisoner was to give the State half-a-day's labour, on pain of receiving only the strictly indispensable food, 700 grammes of bread, I centiletre of oil, and 60 grammes of dried vegetables. As the prisoners protested, he began by applying the decree to fifty-seven persons, of whom four were women.

For the women were subjected to the same rigorous treatment as the men, and they had courageously demanded the right of sharing the common lot of all. Louise Michel and Lemel, whom they had wanted to separate from their comrades, declared that they would kill themselves if the law were violated. Insulted by the jailers, abused sometimes in the order of the day of the commander of the peninsula, scarcely provided with dresses, more than once they had been obliged to put on men's clothes.

The arrival at the beginning of 1876 of the new governor, De Pritzbuer, terminated the short but brilliant career of Alleyron. Pritzbuer, a renegade of Protestantism turned arrant Jesuit, and sent to New Caldeonia through the Jesuitical tendencies of the Ministry, found ways and means with his mawkish airs to even aggravate the misery of the convicts. He was guided in this task by Colonel Charrière, general director of the New Caledonian Penitentiary, who declared the criminals of the penal settlement much more honourable than the political convicts. Pritzbuer renewed the order of his predecessor, adding that those of the convicts who in one year should not have been able to create for themselves sufficient resources would no longer receive full rations; and, finally, that the Administration intended exonerating itself at the end of a certain time of all expenses with regard to the convicts. An agent was appointed to act as intermediary between them and the traders of Noumea. But all the decrees in the world cannot extend the commerce or industry of a country without natural resources. It has been said, been proved a hundred times, that New Caledonia has no employment for these thousands of men, who would prosper in a vital and flourishing colony. Those few who could be employed have proved their intelligence, and have carried off several medals or been honourably mentioned at the exhibition of Noumea. The less favoured — hundreds of them — suffer under the blow of the decree of 1875. In reality, the immense majority of those condemned to transportation are now subjected to hard labour. The regulations put into force since the escape of Rochefort have never been mitigated. The wives, the mothers of the convicts, are only allowed to communicate with them at rare intervals, and under the eye of the jailers. More than one has been expelled from the colony.

Despite so many efforts to break them, the honour of the majority of the prisoners has not yielded; far more, it is an example to others. Although the courts-martial have mixed up with the condemned of the Commune a bad element, totally foreign to this revolution, common misdemeanours are very rare. Their condemnation for political misdemeanour, the contact with the best workmen, has even re-made the conscience of many men with but sorry antecedents. The majority of the condemned are punished only for infringements of the rules or for attempts to escape; attempts almost always condemned to failure beforehand. How fly without money and without confederates? There have been but fifteen successful escapes. Towards the middle of March, 1875, twenty prisoners of the Ile des Pins, amongst whom were the member of the Council of the Commune, Rastoul, fled in a bark which they had secretly constructed. Their fate has never been known, but a few days after their flight the wreck of a craft was found amongst the reefs. In November, 1876, Trinquet and some of his comrades managed to abscond in a steamboat. They were pursued, overtaken. Two threw themselves into the sea to escape their pursuers. One died; the other, Trinquet, was restored to life and the penal settlement.

Before such abysses of misery the exiles must not speak of their sufferings, but they may say in a word that they have not sullied the honour of the Cause. Thousands of workmen, with their families, thrown helpless, without resources, into a strange country, speaking a foreign language, employees, professors, still more forlorn, have succeeded by dint of energy in gaining a livelihood. The workmen of the Commune of Paris have won an honourable place in the workshops of foreign countries. They have even, especially in Belgium, rendered prosperous industries till then languishing; they have imparted to certain manufactures the secret of Parisian taste. The proscription of the Communards, like that of the Protestants formerly, has thrown across the frontiers a part of the national wealth. The exiles of the so-called liberal professions, often more unfortunate than the workmen, have not shown less courage. Some fill posts of confidence; one perhaps condemned to death as an incendiary or to hard labour for pillage, is a teacher in a large college or examines the candidates for Government schools. Despite the difficulty at the commencement, sickness, slackness of work, not one exile has given way, and not a single condemnation before the police court has occurred. Not a single woman has fallen. Yet it is the women who bear the greater share of the common misery. Amongst these thousands of exiles there have been discovered but two or three spies; and there was only one, Landeck, to get up a journal of denunciations more vile than the *Figaro*. Justice was soon done, for no proscription has been more careful of its dignity. One ex-member of the Council of the Commune had to defend himself before the refugees for having received money from the deputies of the Extreme Left. Never was the commemorative meeting of the 18th March better attended than that of 1876 during the debate on the amnesty, for one and all would have blushed to hide their colours at such a moment. No doubt, like any other proscription, that of 1871 has its groups and its animosities, but all these opinions disappear behind the red flag escorting the coffin of a comrade. No doubt there have been virulent manifestoes, which, however, only affect their authors. Finally, these exiles have not forgotten their brothers of New Caledonia, and they have opened a permanent subscription for them, which has its centre in London. Poor help, no doubt; but this mite from the exiles goes and says to the unfortunate convict of the Commune, "Courage, brother! thy comrades do not forget thee; they honour thee." It is the hand of the wounded held out to the dying.

Twenty-five thousand men, women, and children killed during the battle or after; three thousand at least dead in the prisons, the pontoons, the forts, or in consequence of maladies contracted during their captivity; thirteen thousand seven hundred condemned, most of them for life; seventy thousand women, children, and old men deprived of their natural supporters or thrown out of France; one hundred and eleven thousand victims at least — that is the balance-sheet of bourgeois vengeance for the solitary insurrection of the 18th March.

What a lesson of revolutionary vigour given to the working men! The governing classes shoot *en masse* without taking the trouble to select the hostages. Their vengeance lasts not an hour; neither years nor victims appease it, they make of it an administrative function, methodical and continuous.

For four years the Rural Assembly allowed the courts-martial to work, and the Liberal element, which so many elections had sent up in great force, at once followed the track of the Rurals. One or two motions for amnesty were burked by the previous question. In the month of January, 1876, when the Rural Assembly broke up, it had removed a few convicts from one part of New Caledonia to another, shortened a few terms of imprisonment, and given full pardon to six hundred persons, condemned to the lightest penalties. The Caledonian reservoir remained intact.

But at the general elections the people did not forget the vanquished. In all the large towns *Amnesty* was the watchword, it was inscribed at the head of all the democratic programmes; at all the public meetings the question was put to the candidates. The Radicals, tears in their eyes and their hands on their fraternal hearts, pledged themselves to ask for a free and complete amnesty; even the Liberals promised "to wipe out the last traces of our civil discords," as the bourgeoisie is wont to say when it condescends to have the pavingstones cleaned which itself has reddened with blood.

The elections of February, 1876, were Republican. The famous Gambettist layers had come to the surface. A crowd of lawyers, Liberal landlords, had carried away the provinces in the name of liberty, reforms, appeasement. The Minister of the reaction, Buffet, was beaten along the whole line, even in Rural corners. The Radical papers declared the democratic Republic once for all founded; and one of these in its enthusiasm cried, "May we be cursed if we do not close the era of revolutions!"

The hopes for amnesty became now a certainty. No doubt this was the boon by which the reparative Chamber would signalise its joyous advent. A convoy of convicts was about to set sail for New Caledonia. Victor Hugo summoned the President, MacMahon, to adjourn the departure until the discussion and the certainly favourable decision of the two Chambers. A petition, hurriedly organized, in a few days had over a hundred thousand signatures. Soon the question of the amnesty effaced all others, and the Ministry insisted upon an immediate discussion.

Five propositions had been laid on the table. One only demanded the full and complete amnesty. The others excepted the crimes qualified as common crimes, and amongst which were classed newspaper articles. The Chamber appointed a commission to draw up a report. Seven commissioners out of ten declared against all the propositions.

The new layers were manifesting themselves. It was always this same middle-class, bare of ideas and courage, hard to the people, timid before Caesar, pettifogging and jesuitical. The workmen already shot down in June,

1848, by an Assembly of Republicans were to see in 1876 a Republican Assembly rivet the chain forged by the Rurals.

The motion for a full and complete amnesty was supported by those same Radicals who had combated the Commune or abetted M. Thiers. They were now the democratic lions of a Paris without a Socialist press, without popular tribunes, without a history of the Commune, watched by the courts-martial, always on the look-out for more victims, bereft of all revolutionary electors. In this town which he had helped to bleed, there were arrondissements which disputed the honour of electing Louis Blanc. The deputy of Montmartre was the same man who, on the 18th March, had congratulated Lecomte on the capture of the cannon, M. Clémenceau.

He made a jejune, garbled, timid exposé of the immediate causes of the 18th March, but took good care not to touch upon the veritable causes. Other Radicals, in order to make the vanquished more interesting, strove to lower them. "You are absolutely mistaken as to the character of this revolution," said M. Lockroy very grandly. "You see m it a social revolution, where there has really been only a fit of hysterics and an attack of fever." M. Floquet, nominated in the most revolutionary arrondissement, the one in which Delescluze had fallen, called the movement "detestable." M. Marcou wisely declared that the Commune was "an anachronism."

No one even in the Extreme Left dared courageously to tell the country the truth. "Yes; they were right to cling to their arms, these Parisians, who remembered June and December; yes, they were right to maintain that the monarchists were plotting for a revolution; yes, they were right to struggle to the death against the advent of the priest." No one dared to speak of the massacres, to call the Government to account for the bloodshed. They were even less outspoken than the *Enquete Parlementaire.* It is evident from this weak and superficial discussion that they only wanted to redeem their word given to their electors.

To advocates who stooped so low the answer was easy enough. As M. Thiers and Jules Favre had done on the 21st March, 1871, the Minister Dufaure pertinently set forth the true question at issue. "No, gentlemen," said he, "this was not a communal movement; this was in its ideas, its thoughts, and even in its acts, the most radical revolution which has ever been undertaken in the world." And the reporter of the Commission: "There have been hours in our contemporary history when amnesty may have been a necessity, but the insurrection of the 18th March cannot from any point of view be compared with our civil wars. I see a formidable insurrection, a criminal insurrection, an insurrection against all society. No, nothing obliges us to give back to the condemned of the Commune the rights of citizens." The immense majority applauded Dufaure, singing the praises of the courtsmartial, and not a Radical had the courage to protest, to defy the Minister to produce a single document, a single regular judgment. It would be easy to retort to this Extreme Left: "Silence, pharisees, who allow the people to be massacred and then come supplicating for them; mute or hostile during the battle, grandiloquent after their defeat." Admiral Fourichon denied that the convicts of the Commune are put on the same footing as the others; denied their ill-treatment; said the convicts lived in a very garden of flowers. Some intransigents having stated that, "The torture has been re-established," this delicious answer was vouchsafed them, "It is we whom you put to the torture."

On the 18th May, 1876, 396 noes against 50 ayes rejected the full and complete amnesty. Gambetta did not vote. The next day they discussed one proposition of amnesty, which excluded those condemned for acts qualified as common crimes by the courts-martial.

The Commission again rejected this motion, saying that it must be left to the mercy of the Government, which had promised a considerable number of pardons. The Radicals discussed a little to save appearances. M. Floquet said, "It is not on a question of generosity and mercy that we should ever doubt of the intentions of the Government," and the proposition was thrown over.

Two days after, in the Senate, Victor Hugo asked for the amnesty in a speech in which he drew a comparison between the defenders of the Commune and the men of the 2nd December. His proposition was not even discussed.

Two months after, MacMahon completed this hypocritical comedy by writing to the Minister-at-War, "Henceforth no more prosecutions are to take place unless commanded by the unanimous sentiment of honest people." The honest officers understood. The condemnations continued. Some persons condemned by default, who had ventured to return to France on the strength of the hopes of the first days, had been captured; the sentences against them were confirmed. The organizers of working men's groups were mercilessly struck when their connection with the Commune could be established. In November, 1876, the courts-martial pronounced sentences of death.

This merciless tenacity alarmed public opinion to such an extent that the Radicals were again obliged to bestir themselves a little. Towards the end of 1876 they demanded that the Chamber should put a stop to the prosecutions, or at least limit them. An illusory law was voted; the Senate threw it out; our Liberals reckoned upon that.

The mercy of MacMahon was on a par with the rest. The day after the rejection of the motion for an amnesty, Dufaure had installed a consulting Commission of Pardons, composed of functionaries and reactionaries carefully culled by himself. The penitentiary establishments in France then contained 1,600 persons condemned for participation in the Commune, and the number of the transports rose to about 4,400. The new commission continued the system of the former one, commuted some penalties, granted pardons of a few weeks or a few months, even liberated two or three condemned who were dead. A year after its institution it had recalled from

New Caledonia a hundred at the utmost of the least interesting of the prisoners.

Thus the Liberal Chamber continued the vengeance of the Rural Assembly; thus the bourgeois Republic appeared to the working men as hostile to their rights, more implacable perhaps than the Monarchists, justifying the remark of one of M. Thiers' Ministers, "It is above all the Republicans who must be adverse to the amnesty." Once again there was justified the instinct of the people on the 18th March, when they perceived in the conservative republic held out to them by M. Thiers an anonymous oppression worse than the Imperialist yoke.

At the present time, six years after the massacres, near fifteen thousand men, women, and children are maintained in New Caledonia or in exile.

What hope remains? None. The bourgeoisie has been too much frightened. The cries for amnesty, the blazoned-forth elections, will not disquiet the conservative republicans or monarchists. All the apparent concessions will only be so many snares. The most valiant, the most devoted, will die in the penal colony, in the Peninsula Ducos, in the Ile des Pins.

It belongs to the workmen to do their duty so far as it is possible today.

The Irish, after the Fenian insurrection, opened hundreds of public subscriptions for the benefit of the victims. Near £1,200 were devoted to their defence before the tribunals. The three men hanged at Manchester received on the morning of their death the formal promise that their families should want for nothing. This promise was kept. The parents of the one, the wife of the other, were provided for, the children were educated, dowered. In Ireland alone the donations for the families exceeded £5,000. When the partial amnesty was granted, all Irish people rushed forward to help the amnestied. A single paper, the *Irishman,* in a few weeks received £1,000, for the most part in penny and sixpenny subscriptions. In one single donation the Irish of America sent them £4,000, and the poorest of the poor Irish, the emigrants of New Zealand, over £240. And this was not the outburst of one day. In 1874 the Political Prisoners" Family Fund still received £425. The total of the subscriptions exceed £10,000. Finally, in 1876, a few Fenians chartered a vessel and carried off some of their comrades still retained in Australia.

In France all the subscriptions for the families of the condemned of the Commune have not exceeded £8,000. The Irish victims numbered only a few hundreds; those of Versailles must be counted by thousands.

Nothing has been done for the transported "convicts". The Greppos, Louis Blancs and Co., who, without mandate, without any surveillance, have arrogated to themselves the right of centralizing the subscriptions, of distributing them at Pleasure, have thus formed themselves a retinue out of the families of those whom they had betrayed. They have refused to transmit anything to the convicts, that is to say, to the most necessitous, who, six thousand leagues from France, pine away without resources and with no possibility of work.

Do you understand, working men, you who are free? You now know what the whole situation is and what the men are. Remember the vanquished not for a day, but at all hours. Women, you whose devotion sustains and elevates their courage, let the agony of the prisoners haunt you like an everlasting nightmare. Let all workshops every week put something aside from their wages. Let the subscriptions no longer be sent to the Versaillese committee, but made over to loyal hands. Let the Socialist party attest its principles of international solidarity and its power by saving those who have fallen for it.

Glossary

Arrondissements — The 20 administrative districts, each with a mayor, into which Paris was divided.

Brassardiers — Arm-band wearers.

Cantiniere — Canteen woman attached to each battalion.

Catafalques — Decorated coffins used in funeral processions.

Chassepots — An early type of rifle.

Code Napoleon — The French legal code upholding bourgeois property and rights drawn up under Napoleon I but still the basis of the French legal system.

Corps Legislatif — Legislative Assembly.

Enceinte — The wall around the old city of Paris.

Faubourgs — Suburbs.

Feuilles-de-route — Travel document issued to a soldier giving the route to be followed and destination, and used for passing from one army unit to another.

Franc-tireurs — Irregular soldiers.

Gallicans — The Church faction which wanted the independence of the Church in France and questioned the appointment of bishops. (Cf. Ultramontanes below.)

Girondists — The right wing of the Revolution in 1793, opposed by the Jacobins.

Hôtel-de-Ville — The central town hall of Paris.

Lettres de cachet — The famous order by which the monarchs of the old regime could have people imprisoned indefinitely in the Bastille or other prisons.

Levée en masse — The general mobilisation of the populace for battle.

Mairie — Town hall of each arrondissement.

Montagnards — A name for the Jacobins — the left wing of the bourgeois revolution — deriving from the high benches they occupied in the revolutionary assembly of 1791-2.

Octrois — Local taxes levied at the city limits.

Pekin — Term for civilian used by the military.

Procureur de la République — Public Prosecutor.

Pupilles de la Commune — Orphans — largely of men who had died in the fighting — who were taken care of by the Commune.

Rappel — The call to arms.

Rurales — Provincials.

Sbirri — Police thugs.

Sergents-de-ville — Municipal police.

Tabellionat — Scriveners (a category of members of the legal profession).

Tirailleurs — Riflemen.

Turcos — Algerian units of the French army, so called by the Russians in the Crimean War who took them for Turks.

Ultra-montanes — Church faction which looked to Rome.

Vareuse — Cross-fastening jacket.

Lightning Source UK Ltd.
Milton Keynes UK
UKHW011841090119
335290UK00023B/626/P